Theatre Cultures within Globalising Empires

Theatre Cultures within Globalising Empires

―

Looking at Early Modern England and Spain

Edited by
Joachim Küpper and Leonie Pawlita

DE GRUYTER

This book is published in cooperation with the project DramaNet, funded by the European Research Council

Early Modern European Drama
and the Cultural Net

European Research Council
Established by the European Commission

ISBN 978-3-11-053687-4
e-ISBN (PDF) 978-3-11-053688-1
e-ISBN (EPUB) 978-3-11-061203-5

This work is licensed under a Creative Commons Attribution-NonCommercial-No-Derivatives 4.0 License. For details go to https://creativecommons.org/licenses/by-nc-nd/4.0/.

Library of Congress Control Number: 2018945984

Bibliographic information published by the Deutsche Nationalbibliothek
The Deutsche Nationalbibliothek lists this publication in the Deutsche Nationalbibliografie; detailed bibliographic data are available from the Internet at http://dnb.dnb.de.

© 2018 Joachim Küpper and Leonie Pawlita, published by Walter de Gruyter GmbH, Berlin/Boston
Typesetting: Integra Software Services Pvt. Ltd.
Printing and binding: CPI books GmbH, Leck
Cover image: photodeedooo/iStock/Thinkstock

MIX
Papier aus verantwortungsvollen Quellen
FSC® C083411

www.degruyter.com

Preface

The present volume comprises the revised proceedings of the international conference "Theatre Cultures within Globalising Empires: Looking at Early Modern England and Spain" which was organised in November 2012 within the framework of the European Research Council Advanced Grant Project "Early Modern European Drama and the Cultural Net (DramaNet)" at the Freie Universität Berlin.[1]

The DramaNet project investigates early modern European drama and its global dissemination through the theoretical conceptualisation of the "cultural net." Understood as a non-hierarchical structure created deliberately by human agency for given purposes, the cultural net enables the multidirectional circulation of conceptual and material forms, while facilitating the withdrawal of floating material from the net, irrespective of its spatial or temporal origin. Taken as an analytical tool, the concept of the cultural net frees literary texts from the boundaries of national cultures and enables reflection upon common traits shared by spatially or temporally separated dramatic works, as well as regarding the reception of a particular work in a given time or place remote from its origin. Moreover, the project explores the role of theatre as a mass cultural phenomenon in social integration and, furthermore, examines the relationship of theatre to other phenomena of early modern culture, while considering the extent to which early modern theatre can be regarded as organically modern. In the first chapter of this collection, Joachim Küpper, Principal Investigator of the DramaNet research project, elaborates on his concept of culture as a net and describes the scope of the overarching research project's aim.[2]

The conference hosted scholars from the US, the UK, Germany and India to explore the particular cases of drama and theatre in early modern England and Spain. These two European powers represented the only two competing "imperial" systems of the period, the former on the ascendant and the latter in decline, and they were also the two great theatre cultures of the time. By the late

---

[1] This was the first of several international conferences organised by the DramaNet research group whose proceedings already have been or will be published as well: Katja Gvozdeva, Tatiana Korneeva, and Kirill Ospovat, edd., *Dramatic Experience: The Poetics of Drama and the Early Modern Public Sphere(s)* (Leiden/Boston, MA: Brill, 2016; Open Access); Sven T. Kilian, Toni Bernhart, Jaša Drnovšek, and Jan Mosch, edd., *Poetics and Politics: Net Structures and Agencies in Early Modern Drama* (Berlin/Boston, MA: De Gruyter, forthcoming 2018; Open Access); DS Mayfield, ed., *Rhetoric and Drama* (Berlin/Boston, MA: De Gruyter, 2017; Open Access); Jan Mosch, ed., *History and Drama* (Berlin/Boston, MA: De Gruyter, forthcoming 2018; Open Access).
[2] For an extended presentation of this new approach to conceptualizing culture see Joachim Küpper, *The Cultural Net: Early Modern Drama as a Paradigm* (Berlin/Boston, MA: De Gruyter, 2018).

sixteenth and early seventeenth centuries, in both countries dramatic culture had been taken to the masses and, through public staging in stationary theatres for affordable prices, reached a broad, socially diversified audience. England and Spain were, moreover, globalising empires with wide-ranging cultural influence and growing multidimensional contacts with geographical spaces transcending Europe.

The articles gathered in the first section of this volume address phenomena of transnational transfer and travel in early modern European drama and theatre, considering questions of how and to what extent early modern Spanish and English theatre cultures interrelated with other European cultures (here mainly the Italian and German contexts are taken into account). M. A. Katritzky's "Stefanelo Botarga and Pickelhering: Fishy Italian and English Stage Clowns in Spain and Germany" investigates the important topic of Italian and English travelling actors; focusing on the shaping and diffusion of fish-related stage names, it shows, by means of transnational perspectives, that in this process literary, religious and cultural relations came into play that were relevant to the actor's home and host nations. Tatiana Korneeva's "The Art of Adaptation and Self-Promotion: Carlo Gozzi's *La Principessa filosofa* [The Princess Philosopher, 1772]" addresses the complex of Spanish Golden Age theatre culture's impact on late eighteenth-century Italian theatre. Taking the Venetian playwright's adaptation of Agustín Moreto's *El desdén con el desdén* [Disdain Meets with Disdain, 1654] as a case study, Korneeva investigates what is transferred and what is transformed in the transculturation process; and, furthermore, by raising the issue of the development of understandings of intellectual property and including the history of performance of Gozzi's play, the paper provides insight on the role of authorial agency concerning the circulation of artefacts in the cultural net and the specificity of theatrical works in this regard. Robert Henke's "From Augsburg to Edgar: Continental Beggar Books and *King Lear*" explores how the idea of the beggar that originated in late medieval/early modern southern German catalogues of beggars and vagabonds travelled to the early modern English stage, namely informing Edgar's performance as Poor Tom in Shakespeare's play. Henke shows that religious and social aspects, concepts of poverty and charity connected to and, in particular, theatrical notions and techniques thematised in the continental beggar catalogues meet in the figure of Poor Tom.

In the second section, aspects of "Intercultural Connections between English and Spanish Drama" are discussed. Leonie Pawlita's article "Dream and Doubt: Skepticism in Shakespeare's *Hamlet* and Calderón's *La vida es sueño*" considers the circulation of philosophical material put into dramatic form, considering these two dramas. It investigates the questions of why and how both plays dramatise the fundamental epistemological question of skepticism in early modern

Europe, the unreliability of sensory perception, and, taking into account the respective cultural-ideological context, discusses the different answers the two dramas give in the face of the challenges posed by this extra-literary discourse. Madeline Rüegg's "The Patient Griselda Myth and Marriage Anxieties on Early Modern English and Spanish Stages" focuses on a concrete narrative (linked to moral philosophical questions) available in the cultural net of early modern Europe and explores its use in Lope de Vega's *El ejemplo de casadas o prueba de la paciencia* [The Example for Married Women or the Test of Patience] (c. 1599–1603) and Dekker, Chettle and Haughton's *Comedy of Patient and Meek Grissil* (c. 1599). In her comparative analysis, Rüegg shows the changes that the Patient Griselda figure and her story, originally from Boccaccio's *Decameron* and made popular through Petrarch's Latin translation, underwent in its early modern English and Spanish dramatic adaptations. The similarities between these dramatisations (in purpose or rhetorical devices, for example) and the differences, as Rüegg argues, are connected with the plays' national-cultural contexts, i.e. the notions of marriage and virginity according to either Catholic or Protestant principles.

Ralf Haekel's and Saugata Bhaduri's studies address aspects concerning the "Images of Spain on the English Stage" in the light of the historico-political situation from the 1580s to the beginning of the seventeenth century. In 1580 Portugal became part of the Spanish Empire (until 1640); tensions between England and Spain increased and ended in open military conflict, the Anglo-Spanish War (1585–1604), with the defeat of the Spanish Armada in 1588 as its peak — to mention just some of the most important events. Haekel's "'Now Shall I See the Fall of Babylon': The Image of Spain in the Early Modern English Revenge Tragedy" focuses on Thomas Kyd's *The Spanish Tragedy*, probably written between 1582 and 1587 and first published in 1592, and raises the question of why the image of Spain as it appears in Kyd's play, the model of a revenge tragedy and a most successful and influential drama throughout Europe, is one of the few aspects that did not have an influence on later Elizabethan and Jacobean revenge tragedies. As Haekel shows, *The Spanish Tragedy* (in its 1592 print version) is detached from the immediate political circumstances, lacks anti-Spanish propaganda and is rather centred on the political situation on the Iberian Peninsula itself (the play's setting thematises the annexation of Portugal and the unification of the Iberian Peninsula). He argues that the Spain of Kyd's play is more a general concept of an aspiring nation and empire, reflecting the tensions in England itself, and, moreover, pointing toward the insecurity of a society in transition. Saugata Bhaduri's "Polycolonial Angst: Representations of Spain in Early Modern English Drama" discusses representative English plays from the twenty-year period of the Anglo-Spanish War that mention Spain. These references to Spain in English theatre are not, however, as one might expect (given the actual conflicts and the emergence of a discourse that came to be called "The Black Legend"), large in number nor marked exclusively by Hispanophobia, but rather by ambivalence and often even Hispanophilia. Bhaduri explains this characteristic with what he defines as "polycolonial angst," the mutual anxiety of multiple European powers, primarily England and Spain, in the process of concurrently colonising parts of the world (Asia, the Americas) or also with regard to "proximal colonies" on the European continent. He recalls that when England entered the "colonial game" the Spanish(-Portuguese) empire was already a global power, a rival that the English may at the same time have admired. A similar admiration, as Bhaduri argues, may have been caused by Spain's annexation of Portugal; England's annexation of Ireland and unification with Scotland would be realised only in 1603.

Considering the over-arching transmissive impact of England and Spain upon the spaces they conquered, a closing section examines the cultural connections in terms of theatre "Between Europe and the Colonies" and the problematics such a cultural "export" entails. The first article, Barbara Ventarola's "Multi-Didaxis in the Drama of Lope de Vega and Sor Juana Inés de la Cruz," is dedicated to the Spanish and Hispano-American contexts, comparing Lope de Vega's *Fuenteovejuna* (1619) and the *auto sacramental El divino Narciso* [The Divine Narcissus] by the Mexican nun Juana Inés de la Cruz, composed around 1688 and first published in 1690. The concept of "multi-didaxis" that Ventarola proposes as a theoretical framework for her comparative analysis is part of her "poly-contextural literary theory" (drawing on Gotthard Günther's theory of poly-contexturality). It refers to the multidirectional potential of performed dramatic texts, being able to refer to a plurality of cultural contexts, to address a diversified audience and to evoke simultaneously imagined universal contexts, thus allowing a variety of combinations of pragmatic aims, ranging from propaganda to critical transgression. Lope's critique aims at aspects of social hierarchy, while Sor Juana's targets the hierarchy of cultures (Iberian and colonial). With regard to the relationship between the metropolitan and the colonial theatre cultures, Ventarola interprets Sor Juana's dramatic writing as "independent and constructive *aemulatio*." Jonathan Gil Harris' "Tamburlaine in Hindustan" focuses on intercultural connections, travels, and transformations—linguistic, geographical, historical, imaginative and theatrical—concerning the English empire's drama, shedding light on different forms of Western understandings of transcultural encounter. Harris considers in a first step of his analysis the historical figure on which the theatrical figure in Christopher Marlowe's *Tamburlaine the Great* (1587) is based, the medieval Turkic king Temür who at the end of the fourteenth century supposedly conquered Hindustan, setting up the Mughal dynasty, of which Temür/Timūr-e-Lang was later made the legendary founding figure, present in Mughal literature and art. Narratives of Timur migrated westward (from Persia to Arabia, through Spain to England), as Harris shows, referring to Marlowe's *Tamburlaine* as an example. The volume's concluding article, Gautam Chakrabarti's "'Eating the Yaban's Rice': Socio-Cultural Transactions on the Mid-Colonial Bengali Stage," broadens the perspective, as it considers a later period of the effects that had begun in the early modern age by focusing on nineteenth-century Indian drama. Chakrabarti investigates the 1860 Bengali play *Nil Darpan; or, The Indigo Planting Mirror* written by Dinabandhu Mitra, which, structured as a Shakespearean tragedy, dramatises exploitative and oppressive mechanisms, drawing on the Indigo Revolt of Spring 1859 in Bengal, when indigo farmers refused to sow indigo in their fields to protest against a system of enforced cultivation. Chakrabarti's study is about the circulation of cultural-ideological material, the material extracted from the net being the (European) ideological narrative based on Marxist and socialist ideas. Chakrabarti shows that, set in an Indian framework, the story presented in *The Indigo Planting Mirror* refers to Marx' *Communist Manifesto*. The play thus problematises the firm social hierarchy present in its contemporary context.

Finally, we would like to express our gratitude to the institutions and individuals who made conference and volume possible. We are grateful to the European Research Council for its generous financial support and to the Freie Universität Berlin for hosting the conference. Our gratitude goes to the publisher DeGruyter who helped make the papers available to an international readership. And we would like to thank our contributors as well as all the participants in the conference for the inspiring academic exchange.

Leonie Pawlita
Joachim Küpper

Contents

Preface —— V

Joachim Küpper
The Early Modern European Drama and the Cultural Net: Some Basic Hypotheses —— 1

Part I: Transnational Aspects of European Drama

M. A. Katritzky
Stefanelo Botarga and Pickelhering: Fishy Italian and English Stage Clowns in Spain and Germany —— 15

Tatiana Korneeva
The Art of Adaptation and Self-Promotion: Carlo Gozzi's *La Principessa filosofa* —— 40

Robert Henke
From Augsburg to Edgar: Continental Beggar Books and *King Lear* —— 59

Part II: Intercultural Connections between English and Spanish Drama

Leonie Pawlita
Dream and Doubt: Skepticism in Shakespeare's *Hamlet* and Calderón's *La vida es sueño* —— 79

Madeline Rüegg
The Patient Griselda Myth and Marriage Anxieties on Early Modern English and Spanish Stages —— 107

Part III: Images of Spain on the English Stage

Ralf Haekel
"Now Shall I See the Fall of Babylon": The Image of Spain in the Early Modern English Revenge Tragedy —— 135

Saugata Bhaduri
Polycolonial Angst: Representations of Spain in Early Modern English Drama —— 150

Part IV: **Between Europe and the Colonies**

Barbara Ventarola
Multi-Didaxis in the Drama of Lope de Vega and Sor Juana Inés de la Cruz —— 163

Jonathan Gil Harris
Tamburlaine in Hindustan —— 188

Gautam Chakrabarti
"Eating the Yaban's Rice": Socio-Cultural Transactions on the Mid-Colonial Bengali Stage —— 205

Notes on Contributors —— 230

Joachim Küpper
The Early Modern European Drama and the Cultural Net: Some Basic Hypotheses

The research project within which the conference whose proceedings are published in this volume took place[1] has two main objectives, one historical, the other theoretical. In terms of literary and cultural history, it aims to undertake an analysis of (Western) European early modern drama as the first phenomenon of mass culture in human history. In terms of theory, it explores the metaphor of culture as a (virtual) network, with regard to the specific cultural field just mentioned and beyond.

The early modern age bears its name because the basis of modernity proper was cast in that period. This applies to science (think of the theoretical foundation of empiricism and of rationalism), religion (the establishment of [intra-Christian] religious pluralism as the main result of the Thirty Years War), political organisation (I am referring to the "invention" of the centralised and bureaucratic state), political theory (I am thinking here of the theory of absolutism, and of international law), the development of a pervasively allegorical understanding of Scripture (within certain Protestant denominations, but partly within Catholicism as well), and the conception of the world at large (the discoveries and the subsequent adoption of an experience-based model of world and cosmos), to name only the most important points. In all these respects, European societies crossed a threshold of global historical importance: the abandonment of cyclical conceptualisations of time and the establishment of the concept of (possibly never-ending) "progress."[2] It was this conceptual distancing from the cyclical model that laid the foundations for the effective, material transformation of the world beginning in the eighteenth century, that is, massive industrialisation.

According to the dominant view, the changes in the cultural sphere in general and in the literary sphere in particular were much less radical. The overcoming

---
[1] This volume is part of a larger collaborative research project funded by an Advanced Grant from the European Research Council (ERC). Within the project there are six doctoral thesis sub-projects and another six post-doctoral ("second book") sub-projects focusing on specific aspects of the question addressed by the larger research project; in addition, there are five volumes presenting the proceedings of the conferences organized by the DramaNet reaearch project. I elaborate on the concepts outlined in this essay in my book *The Cultural Net: Early Modern Drama as a Paradigm* (Berlin/Boston: De Gruyter, 2018; Open Access)
[2] On this point see my essay "The Traditional Cosmos and the New World," *Modern Language Notes* 118 (2003), pp. 363–392.

of medieval cultural patterns is supposed to have largely taken the path of re-activating an already existing paradigm, the culture of classical antiquity ("Renaissance"), blending it with a limited set of "new" ideas. Early modern culture would thus have to be subsumed under an age that begins already at the end of the fourteenth century. Cultural modernity proper—understood as the emancipation from culture as cyclical recurrence—would thus begin only during the age of Enlightenment or rather with the age of Romanticism and its anti-classical, anti-normative turn as well as its positing, for the first time in human history, of art as autonomous. Early modern literary culture would be, as it were, belated with regard to contemporary scientific progress, philosophical achievements, or even religious "pluralisation."

Early modern drama, however, is an apt example for showing that these current views neglect important, even crucial traits of the cultural dynamics of that period. Sixteenth- and seventeenth-century European drama was, indeed, inspired by classical models (mainly Terence and Seneca) and by classical poetology (neo-Aristotelianism). Nevertheless, it differs fundamentally from its classical "sources." In that period, drama as performance established the basis of what has become the main element of present-day culture, occidental and non-occidental: visual culture as mass media. This most significant "leap" in terms of cultural practices may be observed in all major European countries with slight differences regarding periodisation: first in England, then in Spain, some decades later in France and Germany. The pre-history of the corresponding development is to be found in early sixteenth-century Italy, where one can rightly speak of a "Renaissance," as we are dealing mainly with a revival of classical models. The new cultural pattern spread rapidly to other western and central European countries (the Low Countries and Scandinavia, Portugal, Poland and the non-German-speaking parts of the Habsburg Empire), where it came in contact with a partially still existing "local" theatre tradition, which goes back to the shared European tradition of medieval Christian drama (moralities and mysteries).[3]

The main common characteristic of works of early modern drama is that they are written with the aspiration of being performed on stage, thus differing from Renaissance drama, which was written mainly to be read (as, e.g., the most

---

[3] The nomenclature for the sub-genres of medieval didactic drama differs from one vernacular to another, but in all the relevant "national" theatre cultures there is the bi-partition designated by the English terms used above, namely, dramas that are mainly moralising and make use of the device of allegory (mostly in the sense of personifications of vices and virtues) and, secondly, dramas that present the miracles and mysteries from Biblical history and the saints' and martyrs' lives.

famous drama text of that period, the *Celestina*⁴). This entails a radical change of audiences. Early modern drama addressed highly diverse audiences, from the illiterate class to the intellectuals and the nobility. As such, its themes and objectives underwent a fundamental transformation: the highly refined and elitist Renaissance culture was replaced by a mass culture, a phenomenon that will affect the other genres, mainly narrative, only in an age when literacy became ubiquitous, i.e. in the nineteenth century.

Court theatre, which emerged at the end of the fifteenth and the beginning of the sixteenth centuries, continues to exist, but becomes a more and more recessive phenomenon. "Regular" early modern drama is either performed in institutionalised play-houses and on play-grounds, depending on climate conditions, or on carts, by itinerant companies. Performances are public in the sense that everyone who is ready to pay an (affordable) fee is admitted. The comparison with religious drama in the strict sense, which still exists in certain countries—mainly Spain—allows the most important difference to be determined between early modern drama and the medieval drama performances, which were commonly accessible as well but became restricted because they were bound to the festivals of the Christian calendar, primarily Christmas and Easter. The theatre created in the sixteenth century establishes for the first time in human history the cultural practice of a public visual culture that is not bound to ritual patterns (religious or political, as was the case in classical Athens) and the ensuing constraints.

The research conducted on European early modern drama has been confined to the companion-style type of monograph so far. Existing monographs on the European drama of that age largely lack a discussion of extra-literary discourses that ought to be considered. They follow traditional patterns of literary history in the narrow sense, including at best some commonplace remarks regarding staging. Numerous journal articles with a comparative focus are mostly restricted to a more or less updated variant of motif history or to comparisons between single works of specific authors. Highly sophisticated new approaches to great dramatic authors of that age, such as, e.g., Stephen Greenblatt's publications on the Elizabethan theatre,[5] have considered the questions raised by early modern

---

[4] As to the intellectual depth of the *Celestina*, which is from my view one of the most relevant texts of European early modernity, see my "Mittelalterlich kosmische Ordnung und rinascimentales Bewußtsein von Kontingenz: Fernando de Rojas' *Celestina* als Inszenierung sinnfremder Faktizität (mit Bemerkungen zu Boccaccio, Petrarca, Macchiavelli und Montaigne)," in: Gerhart von Graevenitz and Odo Marquardt, edd., *Kontingenz* (München: Fink, 1998), pp. 152–173.

[5] Stephen Greenblatt, *Shakespearean Negotiations: The Circulation of Social Energy in Renaissance England* (Oxford: Clarendon Press, 1988).

theatre from the perspective of one particular "national" culture; exogenous sources, mainly Italian and French, are taken into consideration, if applicable, but the perspective as a whole is not comparative. This applies as well, *mutatis mutandis*, to Antonio Maravall's research on the Spanish Golden Age drama.[6] Maravall considers the *corral* theatres as part of a propaganda system; that is in principle a hypothesis worth being considered, but his focus on Spanish drama of that age entails certain limitations with regard to this thesis. Walter Benjamin's essay on German baroque drama is still a source of inspiration,[7] as is Albrecht Schöne's monograph on emblem books and German baroque drama,[8] which was the first publication to draw attention to the close links between drama and the visual culture of that age. — So far, however, there has been no systematic discussion of early modern drama as a phenomenon pertaining to the entirety of western and central European societies of that age. The main desiderata of the DramaNet project are: 1) a thoroughly comparative perspective; 2) a consideration of drama/theatre beyond the confines of literary discourse in the traditional sense; 3) a "strong" hypothesis regarding the societal function of early modern drama; 4) an integration of the data available in the cultural field into the general historical dynamic of that age: the rise of England and France, decay of Spain, contradictory tendencies, but mainly stagnancy in the rest of Europe, including the German territories.

In terms of theory, the project is investigating the productivity of the metaphor of culture as a virtual network. The metaphor is conceived in the first place with regard to this specific field, early modern drama, but its aims at the same time go beyond the limits of the age and the genre that are the focal points of this project.

Post-modernist theorising of larger cultural contexts replaced the structuralist standard metaphor of the tree by the metaphor of the rhizome (Deleuze/Guattari).[9] The main progress in this replacement was the overcoming of the concepts of strictly defined hierarchies and of unidirectional processes that are implied by the tree metaphor. The problem inherent to the rhizome concept is that it seems to suggest a "naturalistic," biology-inspired model of cultural processes, which nevertheless may follow a logic that is independent of the general patterns of the evolution of life. Cultural artefacts differ from biological entities

---

6 José Antonio Maravall, *Teatro y literatura en la sociedad barroca* (Barcelona: Ed. Crítica, 1990).
7 Walter Benjamin, *The Origin of German Tragic Drama* [*Ursprung des deutschen Trauerspiels*, 1928], trans. John Osborne (London: Verso, 1977).
8 Albrecht Schöne, *Emblematik und Drama im Zeitalter des Barock* (München: Beck, 1964).
9 Gilles Deleuze and Félix Guattari, *A Thousand Plateaus: Capitalism and Schizophrenia*, trans. Brian Massumi (Minneapolis: University of Minnesota Press, 1987), pp. 3–25.

in that they do not necessarily follow a pre-stabilised programme (encoded in the genes), but are rather subject to relatively free decisions made by humans.[10] — The rhizome concept, whose provisional merits shall not be contested, may have its weakest point in being still all too structuralist, notwithstanding its claims to being post-structuralist: a rhizome is a non-hierarchical, de-centred structure; on the other hand, however, it is an on-going replication of one basic pattern that remains identical to itself during the processes of replication. — The third point to be raised critically is the question of the transformation of (visible) forms, that is, of entities consisting of large quantities of elementary units. In the realm of biological life these transformations occur, but the mutation of genes and the possibly ensuing coming into being of new species are relatively rare; they happen within chronological frames that transcend the regular human existence. Culture, on the other hand, is characterised by rapid and erratic change in phenomena; if there is stability at all, it is to be found neither in the pheno- nor in the genotype, but rather in function. — In short, if the notion of rhizome is applied to the cultural sphere, its shortcomings are the problem of agency, the overestimation of standardising with regard to the elementary units of cultural structures and the undervaluation of morphic change as a distinctive characteristic of cultural evolution.

The metaphor, or rather, metonymy of circulating social energy introduced by Stephen Greenblatt with regard to modelling cultural processes has the advantage of accounting for the high degree of flexibility of the corresponding processes. The risks implied by this concept seem to converge in two points: the question of whether such circulation happens freely, according to a largely non-causal logic (contingency) and on behalf of an immanent propulsive potential of the material concerned ("social energy") or whether it is dependent on structures that enable it to a greater degree than is suggested by the assumption of an inherent energy. The latter alternative points towards the complex of questions revolving around the problem of agency: such structures may be established or not; they may be enhanced or rather be restricted; they may be extended or rather interrupted. — The high relevance of the problem of agency and especially of exerting pressure, in one way or another, on the circulating social energies becomes all the more visible as one transcends the analysis of "national" circuits: how are we to account for the incontestable differences to be observed with regard to, e.g., early modern English and Spanish drama (theatre,

---

[10] I do not wish to engage here with the discussion of whether "free will"/ "free decisions" are illusions by which we try to hide from ourselves that we are only carrying out natural programmes; making culture my theme, I will stick to observable surface phenomena and consider nothing but the observable logic of their development.

respectively)? What is "different" in the processes of circulation and where does the difference originate from? And, perhaps the most important point: what are the consequences of these differences, with regard to culture in the narrow sense (literature and, in this case, theatre) and with regard to culture at large, that is, society? — The second point in Greenblatt's approach that might be worth reconsidering is that he posits the "separation of artistic practices from other social practices."[11] This separation is crucial with regard to the recipients' perspective (the most famous narrative text of that age, the *Quijote*, deals exactly with this problem, in the sense that it presents a hero who seems to be not capable of or not willing to operate this separation). But to what extent should we separate artistic material and other cultural material with regard to processes of transfer and circulation? Of course, there is a separation as far as the materialised forms are concerned; paintings and "pragmatic" manufactured goods may travel on one ship, but as material forms they are distinct and travel as distinct items. This separation seems much more difficult to establish in terms of conceptual forms: what exactly is transferred when a dramatic text is "exported" to another country or even just to another town within the same country? Firstly, of course, a specific text, but along with it, as shall be argued here, all the non-artistic cultural forms and concepts it is made up of (philosophical, theological, anthropological, juridical, political discourses, etc.). Cultural dynamics are to a large extent based on this specific feature: organised forms ("works," artistic as well as non-artistic) are not only transported themselves, but rather along with the whole range of cultural material they contain. — The main desiderata of the DramaNet project with respect to theory are: 1) a concept that accounts for the specificity of cultural processes with regard to "natural" processes; 2) a model that enables and favours transnational comparisons; 3) an approach that allows for an adequate consideration of the problem of agency, and 4) a frame that opens up possibilities for the discussion of literary phenomena as simultaneously separate from and part of a larger discursive scenario, or cultural practices respectively.

The DramaNet project is an attempt to move beyond the existing concepts just referred to by investigating the explanatory potential of the metaphor I indicated above. I will briefly outline the main implications of this new concept.

A network is a non-hierarchical structure without a centre. It does not originate spontaneously, however, or by means of an extra-human, evolution-driven process. It is produced by humans and created for intention-driven purposes. These intentions may be fulfilled or not. If they are not fulfilled, the net may be destroyed by those who constructed it. Very frequently, though, network

---

[11] Greenblatt, *Shakespearean Negotiations*, pp. 12 f.

structures that do not evolve according to initial expectations assume other, often unforeseen and in that sense potentially "revolutionary" functions. — As soon as they exist, even net structures functioning according to initial purposes come to transport not only the material for the circulation of which they were created, but other, at times completely heterogeneous material as well. This happens frequently without being noticed, at least for some time. "Innovation" is in most cases a consequence of such an unnoticed transfer of heterogeneous material that would have been rejected, had it been noticed.

Network structures may be set up everywhere and anywhere. Apart from the will to set them up, they do not need any further specified substratum. The only requirement is to have the means (money, labour force) to construct and entertain them. A net has no entelechical form. Networks are never complete. They are not created once and for all. Net structures may thus extend and ramify to regions completely unknown to those who set them up initially.

Cultural networks are a specific variant of network structures. They may have a stable material substratum or not; in any case, they need a material substratum, but not necessarily a stable one. "Culture" in this context is conceived in the broadest possible way, that is, in the etymological sense (from Lat. *colere*) of all activities by which humans transform the nature-given habitat. Culture understood as a specific trait of humans differs from elementary processes of customising the natural habitat that can be observed with animals, in the sense that it exists in two different registers bound to each other—as material forms and as conscious concepts that inform the respective forms or can be extrapolated from them. The cultural net primarily contributes to transferring these conceptual forms. The material forms may "travel" as well (paintings, statues, books), but not necessarily in order to produce cultural activity and exchange. — The circulation of conceptual forms also needs a material substratum in order to take place. Most frequently, this material substratum comprises circulating humans (merchants, warriors, courtiers or diplomats, future spouses, religious officials, academics, artists).

The movement of material mediated by cultural net structures is not unidirectional. It will remain to be explored whether this aspect can be better accounted for by conceiving cultural nets as being organised according to circuit structures or whether it is more apt to assume them to be shaped according to a highway pattern. The advantage of the latter alternative would be that in such a structure, inverse movement of the transferred material is possible but not compulsory, mandatory or necessary. Total reciprocity and complete absence of hierarchies as a feature of culture seems to be as problematic an assumption as the obsolete metaphor of culture as a tree.

Since they are constructed by humans, cultural network structures are subject to the human will for their transport capacity. They may be extended and enlarged, or, rather, parts of them may be enlarged. They may be restricted or interrupted temporarily, or even be destroyed completely. The material may be allowed to float freely, or it may be submitted to a more or less systematic scrutiny and then allowed to travel on or not, or partly so. Control agents are not contingent upon the material floating in the net, they obey an external logic. If control agents are not changed from time to time, they may be affected by the scrutinised material and thus fall short of their duties. The control logic may be belief-driven, power-driven or money-driven. It may be an illusion that movements within the cultural net are driven by "immanent" quality standards.

Typically, the types of control logics I have just apostrophised do not exist in "pure" versions, but as specific and varying constellations of the three components; in almost all observable cases, there are internal frictions between the components. Much cultural difference, in the age to be considered but in other ages and places as well, seems to result from differing overall control logics. In the early modern as in the present-day world, different concepts of what the "right" control logic is or should be may have led and may still lead to "culture clashes."

Circulating material may be withdrawn from the net at any given point. As soon as withdrawn, the material is shaped into formally defined entities by humans (individuals or groups of humans). In case the material is language-based, the first step of this formal shaping is the homogenising of differing symbolic codes (languages). The levels of further formal organisation typically attained differ dramatically. The formal entities ("works") are then "used" with regard to different functions, mainly didactics, entertainment and reflection.

Since they exist in a material as well as in a conceptual mode, the formal entities originating from the cultural net are inconsumable. After having been "used" they continue to exist, in some cases both in the material and the conceptual mode (paintings, books), but in any case in the conceptual mode. They are then re-absorbed by the material floating in the net and continue their potentially endless travel.

As is true with regard to "physical" nets (e.g. road networks), the floating material may circulate in different degrees of formal organisation, from the level of "raw material" up to the level of organised entities capable in certain cases of being auto-motive within the net. The fact that the material floating in cultural nets is not homogeneous (in the sense of not being formally standardised) is a plea for discarding the metaphors of web or grid that could be considered as well. Highly organised entities may keep that level of formal consistency when reabsorbed by the net after having been used, or may be decomposed into the components out of which they were assembled.

Literary texts would, according to this perspective, become a configuration of cultural material organised with regard to all three functional dimensions mentioned above (didactics, entertainment and reflection). The relative weight of each purpose would vary from work to work and would be subject to reassessment from the perspective of different recipients. *Pragmatic* cultural texts,[12] in contrast, would be characterised by either one of these functions. There may be traces of the non-dominant functions in pragmatic texts as well (e.g. the pleasurable, in a way "entertaining" presentation of a philosophical text or of a religious sermon). This latter point and the aspect, mentioned above, that different purposes inform a literary text to different degrees may account for the affinities between certain literary and certain non-literary texts, mainly philosophical or religious. "Literature" as strictly distinct from the other discourses is not a phenomenon, it is an ideal concept, and we should even consider the possibility that it came up only with the rise of philosophical aesthetics (Kant, *Critique of Judgment*), that is, at the end of the eighteenth century.

What may be the possible results of such a new approach to early modern European drama? Firstly, it would automatically free the texts and the actual practices from being considered within the boundaries of national cultures. Evident common traits could be explained as originating from the participation in one common network structure and need no longer be explained by way of almost always highly speculative assumptions about this or that book having been available to this or that author at a given place in a given moment. Transculturality would thus become the standard case, "nationality" of cultural artefacts would be considered the particular case to be explained according to the control logics outlined above (mainly: power- or belief-driven attempts to restrict the floating material available at a given place at a given moment). Common traits between spatially or temporally separated works of art would no longer be difficult to explain. Reception in later times or in remote regions could be accounted for according to the three basic control mechanisms mentioned above. Circulating material may thus be considered exoteric or esoteric, depending on the times and places where it is assessed. Fundamental formal standards that can be observed in all European "national" cultures could be accounted for by considering the

---

[12] I will not discuss the question of scientific texts nor of those texts, such as, e.g., political treatises, that first emerged as separate text corpora particularly in this period. All theoretical problems involved are addressed in a satisfactory fashion within Niklas Luhmann's thesis of modernity as a period of ever-growing functional specialisation, that is, as separation of discursive sub-fields, which in former periods constituted the one general discursive field (the latter term according to Michel Foucault, *The Archaeology of Knowledge and the Discourse on Language* [*L'Archéologie du savoir*, 1969], trans. A. M. Sheridan Smith [New York, NY: Pantheon Books, 1972], pp. 31–76; as to Niklas Luhmann see *Observations on Modernity* [*Beobachtungen der Moderne*, 1992], trans. William Whobrey [Stanford, CA: Stanford University Press, 1998]).

floating of the material as taking place to differing degrees of formal organisation: "shaping" need not necessarily start at the basic level whenever a quantity of material is extracted from the net in order to be shaped. (Relative) difference with regard to form could be explained with the possibility of imposing whatever form on the material floating in the net.

Theatre performances are based on literary texts, or, at least, on a précis of a possible literary text. As cultural (arte)facts they differ, though, from texts. The reception situation is not individual, it is collective. The actual artefact is mediated by language and vision. Sound and, eventually, scent are additional channels of mediation. The shared experience of reception, the engagement of all the ("indirect") senses[13] and the fusion of the arbitrary (symbolic) and the iconic sign systems result, with the recipient, in a sense of being overwhelmed or, rather, it is the major intention of the cultural practice we call theatre as well as of its modern variants, film and television, to bring about this effect.

The main characteristic of early modern drama as a cultural practice, that is, as theatre, is its historically unprecedented impact. It reaches a broad audience that neither traditional elitist nor popular culture could draw, and its being stripped of ritual contexts enhances the "emotional" impact on the individual recipient incommensurably; ritual performances, such as, e.g., religious drama or the ritual of religious service, entail processes of automatisation[14] because of their repetitive structures. As such, early modern theatre is the site of an immensely increased speed as well as the intensification of processes of cultural transfer. Consequently, it may have been used to shape or reshape intra-individual and thus societal patterns of connecting cultural material ("mental habits," "mentalities").

On the other hand, as a non-ritual cultural practice, early modern theatre cannot rely on a pre-stabilised audience that would be obliged to attend, as, e.g., religious service could, at least in that age. Any attempt at shaping mentalities has thus to be based on structures of enticement. Visual effects ("magic," "marvel"), love and laughter are the cultural resourses typically extracted from the net in order to effect enticement. It is one salient trait of early modern drama as a mass medium that these resourses are combined indiscriminately with "serious" material extracted from the net (religious, philosophical, moral discourses). The boundaries of classical drama theory (Aristotle) are systematically transgressed; exceptions from this general rule (the French seventeenth-century stage) have to be carefully considered.

---

13 Meaning: with the exclusion of touch and taste.
14 In the sense of the term as introduced by the Russian formalists.

The fact that it is dependent on language differentiates (early modern) theatre from other performative cultural practices that could be sensibly subsumed under the heading "mass culture" as well, such as e.g. ancient gladiator fights, medieval and Renaissance festival culture (courtly and popular) or modern sport events. One could perhaps come up with the thesis that events and performances with a mass appeal produce social cohesion as such, or are at least intended to do so. Theatre as a specialised variant includes language, that is: *specific* meaning. Language-based performative practices that are presented in order to be consumed by a given public are thus apt to produce cohesion and then to steer, as it were, the body social into one specific direction. It seems to be mainly the specificity of this steering capacity that differentiates theatre from the other performative practices mentioned above.[15]

The great experiment of an early mass culture was put into practice in different variants in different countries. In England it was an anticipation of phenomena that became ubiquitous in the twentieth century. France opted for a traditionally disciplined variant of drama during this period, keeping genres, and thus discourses and audiences, separate. Only comedy (Molière) was part of an all-encompassing, quasi-egalitarian mass culture as briefly characterised above. In Spain there is the remarkable phenomenon of an immensely successful theatre-as-mass medium, which was literally destroyed and cut off the cultural net by authoritarian means at the end of the seventeenth century. On the German stage of that age, there was little readiness to make use of the entire material circulating in the cultural net. Selection processes were executed in a particularly rigid way, and they were much more belief-driven than in other European countries of the time, with the exception of Poland.

---

15 Sport events, for example, could be conceived—beyond the integrative function, which seems characteristic of all performative practices—as instruments of implementing a spirit of competition amongst those who attend and watch. Gladiator fights may have a (highly desirable) "brutalising" function within the social and cultural structure of an empire based on physical, military force. Court festivals might implement an attitude of admiration with reference to the person who enabled them to take place, that is, the prince or monarch (etc.).

Part I: **Transnational Aspects of European Drama**

M. A. Katritzky
Stefanelo Botarga and Pickelhering: Fishy Italian and English Stage Clowns in Spain and Germany

Juliet's wishful pronouncement on the name of the rose applies even less to comic stage names than to flowers.[1] Cultural expectations shape every aspect of our perceptions, and the funny business of early modern travelling actors is enhanced by well-chosen stage names; even more so if they have strong regional associations. With reference to new textual and iconographic evidence, this article focuses on the origins, transnational diffusion and significance of two stage names based on fish specialities with specific regional associations: as names, as Italian and English stage roles and as popular stock festival costumes, both within their Spanish- and German-speaking host regions, and beyond.

---

1 William Shakespeare, *Mr William Shakespeares comedies, histories, & tragedies: Published according to the True Originall Copies* (London: Iaggard & Blount, 1623), p. 59 (*Romeo and Juliet*[, 2.2.43 f.]: "[T]hat which we call a Rose, / By any other word would smell as sweete").

Note: My thanks to the organisers and participants of events at which earlier versions of this work were presented and discussed: Martin Procházka: *Renaissance Shakespeare/ Shakespeare Renaissances*, International Shakespeare Association 9th World Congress, Prague, July 2011 (ISA Seminar 17: *Shakespearean Players in Early Modern Europe*, co-chaired with Pavel Drábek); Volker Bauer and my Herzog August Bibliothek and Theater Without Borders friends and colleagues: *Borders and Centres: Transnational Encounters in Early Modern Theatre, Performance and Spectacle*, Theater Without Borders Annual Workshop 2012 at the Herzog August Bibliothek, Wolfenbüttel, May 2012; Friedemann Kreuder: *Cartographies of the European Past: Nation, Region, Trans-Nation* (The Presence of the Past: European Cultures of Memory, International Summer Schools 2010–2012, IPP Performance and Media Studies, keynote: "Transnational Discourses on Travelling Stages: Fishy Funny Business with Mediterranean Botarga and North Sea Pickle Herring"), Johannes Gutenberg Universität Mainz, July 2012; Hiram Kümper and Vito Gironda: *Gleichheit/ Ungleichheit* (220023-2. Teil-GK-SoSe 2012: "Equality/ Inequality: On and Around Early Modern European Travelling Stages"), Universität Bielefeld, July 2012; Joachim Küpper, Gautam Chakrabarti, Leonie Pawlita and Madeline Rüegg: *Theatre Cultures within Globalising Empires: Looking at Early Modern England and Spain*, DramaNet, Freie Universität Berlin, November 2012: this text version submitted 25 March 2013). For supporting this research, my thanks also to The Open University Arts Faculty Research Committee and the Herzog August Bibliothek and its staff and Fellows, most especially Ulrike Gleixner, Jill Bepler, Volker Bauer, Ulrich and Birgit Kopp, Asaph Ben-Tov, Bob and Pauline Kolb, Cornelia Niekus Moore and Charlotte Colding Smith (Herzog August Bibliothek Visiting Fellowship, Summers 2011, 2012).

https://doi.org/10.1515/9783110536881-002

Widespread opportunities for long-term co-ordinated professional acting were developed only during the sixteenth century, by actors who introduced many of the significant features of organised professional drama as we know it today, including year-round availability of performances, the participation of female as well as male actors, and above all the trans-regional mobility of performing groups. Theatre was an important part of medieval life in every European region. But the profession of wandering minstrel was economically challenging. Such entertainers faced widespread civic and church disapproval, expressed in harsh, unpredictable legal restrictions. Not least, these restrictions reflected strict calendar regulations prohibiting the year-round performance required by professionals wishing to earn their living on the stage. Court-, community- and above all Church-controlled feasts and fasts, of diverse length and type, punctuated and defined the early modern festive year. They restricted the activities of performers to specific dates and seasons, centred around the major Church feasts. Although the exact dates and regulations varied from one region to another, these excluded Lent and the other fasting days on which it was compulsory to eat fish rather than meat. During the medieval period, organised theatre largely consisted of amateur performances. Their actors were men and boys who belonged to schools and universities, city guilds, church congregations or courts. They returned to their studies or occupations when the performance was over. Increasingly, some of these amateur actors thought about ways of making performing a more economically secure long-term career prospect. By the mid-sixteenth century, musicians and entertainers were signing contracts to band together in formal groups with ambitious cultural and economic aims.

Although no European region was without its own characteristic amateur performance culture, not every region was equally successful in exporting professional players. By the late seventeenth century, actors of many nations routinely toured Europe. During the late sixteenth century and early seventeenth century, the situation was very different. Viable transnational brands of professional theatre were then mainly exported from two European language areas, to audiences in two broadly overlapping geographic host regions. Firstly, from the mid-sixteenth century onwards, the *commedia dell'arte* developed by male and female actors speaking the conglomerate of regional dialects that form the basis for the modern Italian language was performed in the Mediterranean regions. Secondly, from the 1580s onwards, itinerant professional all-male acting troupes from the English-speaking islands started touring European countries in the North Sea regions. Despite the disruptions of the Thirty Years' War, they exported their "English comedy" to mainland Europe for over a century.

Long expensive journeys required considerable financial incentives, and players who travelled had to be flexible enough to accommodate local regulations, confessional practice and linguistic barriers. For all these reasons, the Italian actors generally travelled to France and Spain, performing a repertoire addressing Catholic audiences, while the English actors favoured the German-speaking regions, mostly offering Protestant repertoires. Both Italian and English troupes developed innovative promotional strategies for challenging the traditional restrictions of the Christian festive year, and for encouraging prominent court and civic patrons to finance their travel expenses. Patronage was key. Wealthy French, Italian and Habsburg rulers recommended Italian players from one court to another with Habsburg family connections. Close relations between Queen Anne (wife of King James of England and sister of King Christian of Denmark) and the rulers of many northern European courts provided a ready-made patronage network for travelling English players. Troupes also modified their travel plans to accommodate lucrative non-performing economic activity. Many smaller *commedia dell'arte* troupes used free outdoor performances of the type that flourished in warm, dry southern climates to promote medical goods and services. English actors, especially those enjoying court patronage, often had diplomatic duties, or dealt in arms, musical instruments, luxury goods or cloth, either between courts or at the large trade fairs.

Germany's reputation as an attractive, lucrative hub for international itinerant performers, established in the late sixteenth century, was increasingly damaged by the Thirty Years' War, which devastated central Europe from 1618 to 1648.[2] The Mediterranean and North Sea regions were linked by the Habsburg lands. Strenuous political attempts to bring England into the Habsburg fold repeatedly foundered. In 1558 following the childless death, after four years of marriage, of King Philip II of Spain's Catholic second wife, Queen Mary I of England (daughter of Henry VIII and Philip's great-aunt Catherine of Aragon), his suit was rejected by Elizabeth I, Mary's half-sister and Protestant successor. In 1623, continued Spanish insistence on Prince Charles' conversion to Catholicism finally led King James I to abandon his decade-long negotiations to marry his heir to Philip II's granddaughter, the *infanta* María Ana. During the early modern period, Spain and Germany imported rather than exported professional drama. Through its wealthy courts, Europe-wide cultural contacts and international business centres, the Habsburg Empire established itself as the great early modern contact zone for professional Italian and English travelling troupes. The Inquisition's persecution of actresses made Spain an increasingly unattractive destination for

---

2 Pavel Drábek and M. A. Katritzky, "Shakespearean Players in Early Modern Europe," in: Bruce R. Smith, ed., *The Cambridge Guide to the Worlds of Shakespeare*, 2 vols. (Cambridge/New York: Cambridge University Press, 2016), vol. 2 (*The World's Shakespeare, 1660–present*), pp. 1527–1533.

mixed gender Italian troupes after 1586, and women were definitively banned from Spanish stages in 1596.[3]

Stefanelo Botarga and Pickelhering, the two fish-inspired comic stage names of early modern itinerant actors under consideration here, both have very specific regional associations. One derives from the Mediterranean delicacy *botargo*, the other from the North Sea speciality *Bückelhering* or pickle herring. Stefanelo Botarga is a stock role created around 1570 by an Italian actor in Spain. Pickelhering, the most popular stage clown of the early seventeenth-century English actors in the German-speaking regions, was created somewhat later.[4] The *Oxford English Dictionary* documents two definitions of the term "pickle herring."[5] Since the fifteenth century, it has denoted a specific type of preserved herring, a popular fish speciality in North Sea regions of The Netherlands, England, Germany and Scandinavia. A second meaning, of "a clown, a buffoon," recorded in Germany from c. 1610, officially entered common English usage only in the eighteenth century. Rare but notable much earlier occurrences linked to this second usage occur in the works of several prominent English dramatists and writers, such as Gabriel Harvey (1593),[6] Thomas Dekker (1607)[7] or William Shakespeare, whose eponymously windy and flatulent old drunkard Sir Toby Belch in *Twelfth Night*, written around 1601, robustly curses "these pickle herring."[8]

As well as the meanings of "fish" and "clown," a third definition was explored by John Alexander, in an article of 2003 linking the expression to a particular

---

[3] Teresa Ferrer Valls, "La representación y la interpretación en el siglo XVI," in: Javier Huerta Calvo, ed., *Historia del teatro español*, 2 vols. (Madrid: Gredos, 2003), vol. 1, pp. 239–267, pp. 260–263.

[4] On Pickelhering (and on a fish-based comic stage name not here considered, Stockfisch), see Katritzky, "Pickelhering and Hamlet in Dutch Art: The English Comedians of Robert Browne, John Greene, and Robert Reynolds," *Shakespeare Yearbook* 15 (2005), pp. 113–140, p. 120; Katritzky, "'A Plague o' These Pickle Herring': From London Drinkers to European Stage Clowns," in: Martin Procházka, Michael Dobson, Andreas Höfele, and Hanna Scolnicov, eds., *Renaissance Shakespeare, Shakespeare Renaissances: Proceedings of the Ninth World Shakespeare Congress* (Newark: University of Delaware Press, 2014), pp. 159–170.

[5] "pickle-herring, n.," in: John A. Simpson, ed., *Oxford English Dictionary*, 3rd ed. (Oxford: Oxford University Press, 2000–in progress), *Oxford English Dictionary Online*, http://www.oed.com/view/Entry/143422 (retrieved: 19 April 2012).

[6] Gabriel Harvey, *Pierces Supererogation or A new prayse of the Old Asse: A Preparatiue to certaine larger Discourses, intituled Nashes S. Fame* (London: Iohn VVolfe, 1593), sig. Ff4v (quoted below).

[7] Thomas Dekker, *A knights Coniuring. Done in earnest: Discouered in Iest* (London: William Barley, 1607), sig. Lr (quoted below).

[8] Shakespeare, *Comedies, histories, & tragedies*, p. 258 (*Twelfe Night, Or what you will*, 1.5).

type of heavy social drinking in early modern Holland.[9] My researches interrogate ways in which disputed pre-eighteenth-century English usages of the expression "pickle herring" relate to its adoption as a stage name. Using this third definition as a key to their interpretation, I draw on previously unconsidered archival documents to support "pickle herring" as a term associated with heavy drinkers. But I identify this usage's origins not in seventeenth-century Holland but in a quite specific sixteenth-century English location, Southwark in the 1580s.

The earliest undisputed English use of Pickelhering as a generic comic stage name is in 1656, by Richard Flecknoe, who may have seen professional English actors during his 1650 visit to the Brussels court of Beatrix of Lorraine.[10] In the German-speaking regions it occurs already in two instrumental medleys transcribed in a Linz organ manuscript of c. 1611. The initial bars of one, "Tantz Pückelhäring," are based on music for "Nobodyes Gigge" composed by Richard Farnaby, an English lutenist employed at the North German court of Wolgast in the 1620s.[11] The Wolfenbüttel court's close family connections with English royalty made it a favoured destination for English players, who were based there for many years from the 1590s. Wolfenbüttel archival court records of around 20 May 1615 confirm Pickelhering as the stage name of the English actor George Vincent.[12] Pickelhering is named and depicted as a clown role in a collection of play-texts based on performances by the English players in Germany, published in Germany in 1620,[13] and in two German broadsheets of 1621,[14] and Netherlandish Pekelharing performers are also recorded from 1621.[15]

---

9 [Robert] John Alexander, "The Dutch Connection: On the Social Origins of the Pickelhering," *Neophilologus* 87 (2003), pp. 597–604.
10 Richard Flecknoe, *The Diarium, or Journall: Divided into 12 Jornadas in Burlesque Rhime or Drolling Verse* (London: Henry Herringman, 1656), sig. A3v; Katritzky, *Women, Medicine and Theatre, 1500–1750: Literary Mountebanks and Performing Quacks* (Aldershot/Burlington, VT: Ashgate, 2007), p. 153.
11 John M. Ward, "The Morris Tune," *Journal of the American Musicological Society* 39.2 (1986), pp. 294–331, pp. 306 f.; Alexander, "Will Kemp, Thomas Sacheville and Pickelhering: A Consanguinity and Confluence of Three Early Modern Clown Personas," *Daphnis* 36 (2007), pp. 463–486, pp. 467 f.
12 Niedersächsisches Hauptstaatsarchiv, Hannover, Kammerrechnungen Cal. Br. 21, Nr. 1756, fol. 49r; see Willem Schrickx, "'Pickleherring' and English Actors in Germany," *Shakespeare Survey* 36 (1983), pp. 135–147, p. 139; Schrickx, *Foreign Envoys and Travelling Players in the Age of Shakespeare and Jonson* (Wetteren: Universa, 1986), pp. 235–238.
13 [Fridericus Menius, ed.,] *Engelische Comedien vnd Tragedien Das ist: sehr schöne / herrliche vnd außerlesene / geist- vnd weltliche Comedi vnd Tragedi Spiel / Sampt dem Bickelhering* (s.l., 1620).
14 Katritzky, "Pickelhering and Hamlet," pp. 129 f., figs. 4 and 5.
15 Gregor J. M. Weber, "'t Lof van den Pekelharingh: Von alltäglichen und absonderlichen Heringsstilleben," *Oud Holland* 101.2 (1987), pp. 126–140, p. 139, n. 28.

Updated renaming perhaps accounts for the Pickle Herring role of the Revesby sword play, cited by some scholars as evidence for this stage name's pre-Shakespearean English provenance. Regardless of the date of the performance practice it actually reflects, the Revesby sword play's earliest known manuscript (dated 1779 and first published only in 1889) is plausibly identified as "an eighteenth-century composite."[16] Possibly, the popularity of visiting English actors inspired Andreas Gryphius to give the name Pickelhäring to the equivalent character to Shakespeare's Bottom in *Absurda comica oder Herr Peter Squentz*, his 1658 version of the Pyramus and Thisbe episode familiar from *Midsummer Night's Dream*. Other specialists have suggested that the Pickelhering name was popularised by *Faustus*, which Baron Waldstein saw performed by English comedians in Strasbourg as early as 1592.[17] By 1604, when the first edition of Marlowe's *Faustus* features "Pickle-herring" as a proper name, the term clearly evoked much more than simply fish for English theatre audiences. According to traditional scholarship, when the sin Gluttony introduces himself to Dr Faustus as the Godson of "Peter Pickle-herring,"[18] this name refers to a "carnivalesque social type" with "a craving for [...] herring,"[19] and to the use of Lenten fish symbolism, of the type reflected in Pieter Bruegel's *Battle of Carnival and Lent* of 1569 and early modern derivations by lesser artists.[20]

In addition to carnival associations, the complex London social connotations of Christopher Marlowe's use of the name "Peter Pickle-herring" suggest the negative usage of the word "pickle," in the sense of a regrettable chaos or mess, as

---

16 Thomas Fairman Ordish, "Morris Dance at Revesby," *The Folk-Lore Journal* 7.5 (1889), pp. 331–356; Michael J. Preston, "The Revesby Sword Play," *The Journal of American Folklore* 85.335 (1972), pp. 51–57, p. 57.
17 Julian Hilton, "Pickelhering, Pickleherring and What You Will," in: Jean Pierre Vander Motten, ed., *Elizabethan and Modern Studies: Presented to Professor Willem Schrickx on the Occasion of His Retirement* (Gent: Seminarie voor Engelse en Amerikaanse Literatuur, R.U.G., 1985), pp. 131–142, p. 134.
18 Christopher Marlowe, *The Tragicall History of D. Faustus* (London: Thomas Bushell, 1604), sig. C4v.
19 Alexander, "Will Kemp," p. 466; see also Alexander, "Ridentum dicere verum (Using Laughter to Speak the Truth): Laughter and the Language of the Early Modern Clown 'Pickelhering' in Geman Literature of the Late Seventeenth Century (1675–1700)," in: Albrecht Classen, ed., *Laughter in the Middle Ages and Early Modern Times: Epistemology of a Fundamental Human Behavior, its Meaning, and Consequences* (Berlin/New York: De Gruyter, 2010), pp. 735–766, p. 766; Frederick B. Jonassen, "The Meaning of Falstaff's Allusion to the Jack-a-Lent in *The Merry Wives of Windsor*," *Studies in Philology* 88.1 (1991), pp. 46–68, p. 55, pp. 59 f.
20 For *Carnival and Lent* depictions, see Katritzky, *The Art of Commedia: A Study in the Commedia dell'Arte 1560–1620 with Special Reference to the Visual Records* (Amsterdam/New York: Rodopi, 2006), pp. 422–424, plates 86–88.

in 1565, when Hozjusz notes that a group of disputing theologians "[...] left the matter in as euell a pyckell as they founde it."[21] Previously unrecognised is their direct reference to an actual historical figure, whose nickname came to the attention of the community of actors, dramatists and writers working and socialising in late sixteenth-century Southwark. This is the Flemish beer brewer Peter Van Durant, resident in the Southwark parish of St Olave's, whose will of 25 September 1584, identifies him as "Peter van Durant alias Picklehearinge" (confirmed in the *marginalia* as "Petri van Durant alias Picklehering").[22] Decades before its theatrical adoption is recorded in Europe, "Pickelhering" is thus documented as the nickname of a Flemish resident of Southwark. A short walk downstream the River Thames from London's Southbank theatre district, St Olave's Parish was commonly known as "Pickle Herring" until its wholesale destruction in 1999 to make way for City Hall, the present headquarters of the Greater London Authority. Several of its streets, buildings and landmarks had evidently acquired the Pickleherring name by 1596, by when "John Welshaw, a brewer, had taken a house and yard 'on backside at Pikell Herringe'."[23] By 1612, documents are referring to the local quay as "Pekelharing Kay."[24]

Tavern owners have always known that cheap salty snacks promote the sale of alcohol. In early modern London, social drinking required salted meats and fish, especially herrings, then classified by three colours: green, white and above all red. Green, or fresh herrings were not economically viable, as they spoiled faster than they could be distributed. Traditionally, Londoners consumed cheap preserved herrings as the red—or smoked—herrings now known as kippers and bloaters, and the white herrings preserved with salt but without smoke. A third method of preserving herrings, the Flemish "pickled herring," was introduced to London only in the late sixteenth century. Alexander Addlehead, a fictional Scot featured by the pseudonymous Philip Foulface, offers the God Bacchus "[...] a dozen of red herrings to season his mouth before he sat downe to taste his

---

21 Stanisław Hozjusz, *A most excellent treatise of the begynnyng of heresyes in oure tyme* [*De origine haeresium nostri temporis*], trans. Richard Shacklock (Antwerp: Æg. Diest, 1565), fol. 23r.
22 National Archives, Kew, London (Records of the Prerogative Court of Canterbury: Will Registers, Ref. PROB 11/67/312). See also William Rendle, "Pickell Heringe," *Notes and Queries* 7 (1886), p. 209; Rendle and Philip Norman, *The Inns of Old Southwark and Their Associations* (London/New York: Longmans, Green, 1888), p. 36.
23 P. 32.
24 Isobel Davies, "Seventeenth-Century Delftware Potters in St Olave's Parish, Southwark," *Surrey Archaeological Collections Relating to the History and Antiquities of the County* 66 (1969), pp. 11–31, p. 12, p. 15.

liquor,"²⁵ and Thomas Nashe writes of "[...] some shooing horne to pul on your wine, as a rasher of the coles, or a redde herring [...],"²⁶ and elsewhere notes, "Heere I bring you a redde herring, if you will finde drinke to it, there an ende [...]";²⁷ in 1600, Cornwallis refers to "a pickled Herring to bring on drinke."²⁸ Possibly, the Southwark brewer Peter Van Durant earned his nickname "Pickelhering" by promoting in his Southwark beer taverns this common staple food of Flanders, still viewed as an exotic promoter of alcoholic consumption as late as the 1580s by Londoners.

Many impoverished, hungry drinkers damaged their health by overindulging in cheap beer tavern herrings. Most notoriously, the English writer Robert Greene's death on 3 September 1592 was attributed to a surfeit of Flemish pickled herrings and German white wine. The sorry circumstances of his death made a deep impression far beyond his immediate circle, and were gloatingly mocked by his literary arch-enemy Gabriel Harvey. Harvey deplored Greene's gluttonous and sinful lifestyle, his illegitimate son Fortunatus (mockingly dubbed Infortunatus by Harvey), who died in 1593,²⁹ and his "[...] infamous resorting to the Banckeside, Shorditch, Southwarke, and other filthy hauntes [...]."³⁰ Deriding the habitual heavy drinking of Greene's immediate circle, Harvey mocks Thomas Nashe's fondness for "a goblet of *rennish wine* [...] a *pickle-herring*" and his "notorious surfett of pikle herring," and dismisses the man himself as a "*Pickle-herring clarke*" whose publications are "[...] but lenten stuff, like the old pickle herring[.]"³¹ Robert Greene's death informs many publications of the 1590s. Particularly striking are the conversations in Hell between deceased writers and actors in which Thomas Dekker has the recently deceased Thomas Nashe identify

---

25 Philip Foulface, *Bacchvs Bovntie, Describing the debonaire dietie of his bountifull godhead, in the royall obseruance of his great feast of Pentecost* (London: Henry Kyrkham, 1593), sig. Cv.
26 Thomas Nashe, *Pierce Penilesse, his svpplication to the Diuell* (London: I[ohn] B[usbie], 1592), sig. Fr.
27 Nashe, *Nashes Lenten Stuffe, Containing, the Description and first Procreation and Increase of the towne of Great Yarmouth in Norffolke: With a new Play neuer played before, of the praise of the Red Herring* (London: N[icholas] L[ing] and C[uthbert] B[urby], 1599), sig. A3r.
28 William Cornwallis, *Essayes* (London: Edmund Mattes, 1600), essay 43, sigs. Ee4r–Gg2v, sig. Ee5v.
29 Lori Humphrey Newcomb, "Greene, Robert (*bap.* 1558, *d.* 1592)," in: Henry Colin Grey Matthew and Brian Harrison, eds., *Oxford Dictionary of National Biography* (Oxford: Oxford University Press, 2004), online ed., ed. Lawrence Goldman, 2008, http://www.oxforddnb.com/view/article/11418 (retrieved: 11 September 2011).
30 Harvey, *Fovre Letters, and certaine Sonnets: Especially touching Robert Greene, and other parties, by him abused: But incidently of diuers excellent persons, and some matters of note* (London: John Wolfe, 1592), pp. 9 f., quote on p. 10.
31 Harvey, *Pierces Supererogation*, sig. Ff4v and pp. 61–63; italics in the original.

his own cause of death with that of his friend Greene, by "[...] invey[ing] bitterly (as he had wont to do) against dry-fisted Patrons, accusing them of his vntimely death [...]" because if they had not short-changed him he would "[...] not so desperately haue ventur'de his life, and shortend his dayes by keeping company with pickleherrings [...]."[32] An oblique reference of 1600 to Robert Greene as a "worthy" drunkard "[...] whom diuers Dutchmen held full deare, / Was stabb'd by pickeld Hearings & strong Beere[.]"[33] suggests that the circle of writers and actors around Robert Greene and Thomas Nashe may have habitually frequented the Southwark taverns of Flemish brewers such as Peter "Pickle-herring" Van Durant.

Even before around 1610, when the stage clown created in Germany by the English actors was formally named Pickelhering, many English literary usages linked the term to Southwark associations of heavy social drinking. In the writings of Harvey, Rowlands, Dekker, Marlowe and Shakespeare, the term "pickle(d) herring(s)" alludes not simply to the fish, but also to the sinful gluttony and clownish, red-nosed, boisterous folly of the heavy drinkers in Southwark's Pickle Herring district, and the Dutchmen who provided its beer and Flemish pickle-herrings. A chain of historical evidence links the culinary use of the term "pickled herring"—via late sixteenth-century allusions to drinking associations in an area close to London's Globe Theatre—to its seventeenth-century theatrical use on mainland Europe as the name of the comic stage clown Pickelhering. A persuasive new link in this chain is provided by Peter van Durant's will of 1584. Sustained mockery of Robert Greene's death from too much alcohol and pickled herring, by Gabriel Harvey and other writers, ensured that van Durant's nickname sealed Southwark's legendary reputation: for extremes of alcoholic excess that were sinful—sometimes even fatal. In short, this reconsideration of the term "Pickelhering" provides valuable contextualisation for its choice as a comic stage name by the English actors in early seventeenth-century Northern Europe, by confirming its establishment as a popular London nickname in the 1580s.

The *commedia dell'arte*'s international stars generated pan-European interest. A possible influence on the English actors' choice of Pickelhering is the success of an earlier fish-inspired stage name, Stefanelo Botarga, whose Italian creator acted mainly in Spain. A German festival book recording a Düsseldorf court wedding of 1585 suggests both the extent of the late sixteenth-century German fashion for Italian *commedia dell'arte* performances at court weddings

---

32 Dekker, *A knights Coniuring*, sig. Lr.
33 Samuel Rowlands, *The Letting of Hvmovrs Blood in the Head-Vaine: With a new Morissco, daunced by seauen Satyres, vpon the bottome of Diogines Tubbe* (London: W[illiam] F[erbrand], 1600), Satyre 6, sigs. E6r–E8r, sig. E8r.

and the unprecedented impact of Botarga.[34] Because of their linguistic barriers and unpredictable weather conditions, the German-speaking regions were an unattractive commercial prospect for speculative tours by anything larger than modest Italian troupes of the type supporting charlatans and quack doctors. This ensured that, North of the Alps, full-strength mixed-gender Italian troupes of upwards of ten players, performing full-length *commedia dell'arte* plays, represented a prestigious badge of international cultural sophistication, limited to the wealthiest and most highly educated patrons. German noblemen unable to afford the status symbol of inviting full-strength Italian troupes to their courts found other ways of incorporating elements of the *commedia dell'arte* into their festivals.

On Tuesday 18 June 1585, guests enjoyed a costumed running at the ring, staged at the Düsseldorf court of Duke Wilhelm von Jülich, Cleve and Bergen, during the third of eight days of festivities for the marriage of his heir, Prince Johann Wilhelm, to Princess Jakobine von Baden.[35] Eight of the nine competing groups of knights chose to wear nationally or classically inspired masquerade costume such as that of Moors or Persians, mermaids or Amazons. Drawing on very recent developments in Italian professional acting, the ninth tournament group caused something of a sensation through its novel choice of stage costume, and specifically that of the central comic master-servant pair of the *commedia dell'arte*, the elderly Venetian Magnifico, and his rustic servant, Zanni. While the festival book of the 1585 Düsseldorf wedding does not depict the *commedia dell'arte* group as such, it does depict the parade that opened their tournament. According to its text, the six knights of the ninth group entered in two rows. Three knights in front were costumed in the red underclothes, red berets and black cloaks worn by the *commedia dell'arte* masters; three knights behind them were costumed in the unbleached wide cut sailor trousers of their servants. Such masquerade groups were typically mounted on thoroughbred horses, led by court musicians playing military instruments such as drums or trumpets. But this group had more surprises for their judges and audience. They entered perched on

---

34 Dietrich Graminaeus, *Beschreibung derer Fürstlicher Güligscher [e]tc. Hochzeit so im jahr Christi tausent fünffhundert achtzig fünff am sechszehenden Junij vnd nechstfolgenden acht tagen zu Düsseldorff mit grossen freuden, Fürstlichen Triumph vnd herrligkeit gehalten worden* (Cölln: [Gras], 1587).
35 The ninth tournament entry is described on sigs. Pv–Rr. Alberto Martino partially transcribes sigs. Q2r–v ("Fonti tedesche degli anni 1565–1615 per la storia della Commedia dell'arte e per la costituzione di un repertorio dei *lazzi* dello Zanni," in: Martino and Fausto de Michele, eds., *La ricezione della Commedia dell'Arte nell'Europa centrale 1568–1769: Storia, testi, iconografia* [Pisa/Roma: Serra, 2010], pp. 13–68, p. 17).

donkeys loaded with bales of hay, led by two professional actors, Italian *buffoni* costumed as a Venetian Magnifico and his servant, Zanni. The six suspiciously foreign-looking knights completed the formalities of tournament greetings, including an unusually lengthy interrogation by the judges, before being permitted to compete at the running of the ring. Meanwhile, the two Italian professional actors entertained the spectators with all manner of comic routines, or *lazzi*, of the *commedia dell'arte*. Some mocked chivalrous customs, such as the accepted ways of mounting and dismounting a tournament horse, others relied heavily on singing and acrobatics, in which, the official record of this court festival here assures us, the Italians excel "above all other nations." While the Venetian Magnifico played tricks with his cloak, the Zanni kept altering his "strange, large hat [...] in different ways."[36] The duo also sang comic Italian songs to a viola and played numerous ridiculous tricks with a rustic farmyard rake or harrow, of a type illustrated in the central vignette of a late sixteenth-century print by Ambrogio Brambilla depicting nine *lazzi*.[37]

Although Diederich Graminaeus, author of the official published festival book, does not name the two Italian professionals within its description of their performance, he does identify each of the six German knights in this masquerade both by their own name and by their chosen stage name:

> Otto Wildt Rheingraff / so sich *Tofano Dacon Gentelomo de Venetia*, Herr Carl Graff zu Zollern / *Stephanello putarcho Il Consilier dela signioria de Venetia*, Herr Philips Marckgraff zu Baden un[d] Hochberg, *Pantalion de Bisoignosi gentilomo de Venetia*. Die drey folgende aber / Herr Jacob Marckgraff zu Baden / *Il Senior Petrolin*. Der Edler und Ehrenfester Niclaß Pickadel / *Il Senior Ioan Carotta*, auch Albrecht Thuen / so sich *Il Senior Rauanel* genant.[38]

Graminaeus here indicates that the masquerade was organised by one of the knights riding in the front row, the then 38-year-old Duke Karl von Hohenzollern (1547–1606). Elsewhere, he lists the complete entourages of all the major wedding guests, and provides a possible identification for the professional *buffoni*, as the two servants named as: "Jacob the Italian and his companion" in the entourage of the bride's brother, Karl's distant relative Margrave Philip.[39] As well as Philip, Karl's group included a second Catholic Margrave of Baden, his first cousin Jacob,

---

36 See Graminaeus, *Beschreibung*, sigs. Q2r–v; my translation ("einem seltzamen grossen Huth / denselben er mit vielfeltiger enderung zu gebrauchen gewist [...] Haben sich auch mit singen und springen erzeigt / wie dann vor allen anderen sich alsolche Nation einzustellen weiß / den Preiß zuerhalten").
37 Reproduced in Katritzky, *The Art of Commedia*, p. 395, plate 54.
38 Graminaeus, *Beschreibung*, sigs. Qr–v; emphasis in the original.
39 Sig. C5v ("Jacob der Welß und sein gesellen").

whose entourage included this masquerade's three remaining noblemen: Jacob's chief steward, Claß von Pickadel, Albrecht Thun von Newburg and Rheingraf Otto zu Kyrburg, brother of Duke Karl's future daughter-in-law Juliane Ursula von Salm.[40] Philip took the generic name of the old master, or Venetian merchant, of the *commedia dell'arte* (Pantalon) and Jacob the stage name of one of its most successful servants (Pedrolino). The remaining three knights who accompanied Karl took the stage names of a *commedia dell'arte* master (Tofano) and servants (Zan Carotta, Zan Ravanel) whose originators are unknown, although they are named in playtexts and popular publications of the time.[41] Graminaeus's interpretation of this masquerade refers to virtuous government, while hinting at a distaste for professional performers and revealing that the three knights who took the parts of the comic servants were costumed in "variously coloured clothes, including red caps and grey hats which they liked to keep changing and altering into different shapes, according to their preference."[42]

Duke Wilhelm of Bavaria, first cousin of Margrave Philip, chose Duke Karl to represent him at the 1585 Düsseldorf wedding.[43] In 1568, both Karl and his father were present at the festivities for Wilhelm's own wedding, at the Munich court of his father. Karl was then a trusted twenty-year-old Munich courtier. Duke Karl's father, who from the age of 12 grew up at the Madrid court of his godfather,

---

40 See Katritzky, *Healing, Performance and Ceremony in the Writings of Three Early Modern Physicians: Hippolytus Guarinonius and the Brothers Felix and Thomas Platter* (Farnham/Burlington, VT: Ashgate, 2012), p. 343 (Diagram 2b).
41 Tofano is a stock role of *commedia dell'arte* scenarios (e.g., Flaminio Scala, *Il Teatro delle Fauole rappresentatiue, overo La Ricreatione Comica, Boscareccia, e Tragica: Divisa in Cinquanta Giornate* [Venezia: Pulciani, 1611], Day 24: "Il Finto Tofano," pp. 69–71). Sixteenth-century texts naming Zan Carotta and Ravanel transcribed by Vito Pandolfi (*La Commedia dell'Arte: Storia e testo*, ed. Vito Pandolfi, 6 vols. [Firenze: Le Lettere, 1957–1961]) include, for both: *Il Lachrimoso Lamento che fe Zan Salcizza, e Zan Capella, Inuitando tutti i Filosofi, Poeti, e tutti i Fachi delle ualade, à pianzer la morte di Zan Panza di Pegora, alias Simon Comico Geloso* (Venezia: Al Segno della Regina, 1585) (in: *La Commedia dell'Arte*, vol. 1, pp. 219–226); *Opera nuova Nella quale si contiene vno insonio, che ha fatto il Zanni Bagotto, in lingua Bergamasca* (s.l., 1576) (in: *La Commedia dell'Arte*, vol. 1, pp. 257–261); Bartolomeo Rossi, *Fiammella Pastorale* (Paris: Abel L'Angelier, 1584) (in: *La Commedia dell'Arte*, vol. 2, pp. 96–120, p. 113); for Ravanel only: *Pronostico nvovo sopra l'anno presente, composto per il vostro amoreuolissimo Missier Rauanel Astrologo Bergomensis* (Venezia: In Frezzaria al Segno della Regina, 1581) (in: *La Commedia dell'Arte*, vol. 1, pp. 205–208).
42 Graminaeus, *Beschreibung*, sig. Ee2r; my translation ("[...] in underschiedlicher farben Kleidung / als mit roden Kappen, / grawen Hühten die man offtermahl nach wolgefallen in vielfeltiger gestalt enderen und umbwechselen möchte [...]."); sig. Ee3v.
43 Sigs. Dv–D2r.

Emperor Charles V,[44] was the guest of honour in Munich, representing King Philip II of Spain. The 1568 wedding festivities included comic interludes performed by Italian *buffoni*, and the earliest substantially documented *commedia dell'arte* performance. This was staged by Munich court musicians, including the renowned Flemish choir master Orlando di Lasso as the Venetian Magnifico and the Neapolitan tenor singer Massimo Troiano as his servant Zanni.[45] The *commedia dell'arte* performances of the 1568 Munich wedding evidently made a deep and lasting impression on Duke Karl. They influenced his choice of *commedia dell'arte* masquerade costumes in 1585, and again in 1598. Karl's 1598 masquerade costumes, wrongly described as specific types of regional costume in Jakob Frischlin's court-sponsored printed festival book description,[46] are correctly identified as those of various *commedia dell'arte* servants by Felix Platter, who attended the 1598 festival in his capacity as court physician to the bride's brother-in-law.[47] Platter's account reveals that, costumed as Zan Badello, Duke Karl organised a tournament entry of ten knights, including himself, all costumed as variants of the Zanni, or comic *commedia dell'arte* servant. The only participant of Karl's 1585 masquerade who also joined him at the 1598 tournament was Reingraf Otto. Duke Karl had abducted his future wife, Jacob of Baden's widow, in 1590, and by 1598, Philip of Baden had also died.

In 1585, Duke Karl masqueraded not under the name of a *commedia dell'arte* servant, but a Venetian master, Stephanello Putarcho. Successful Italian *commedia dell'arte* actors typically specialised for many years in one part, often played under their own personal stage name. The stage name Stefanelo Botarga was created by the Italian professional actor Abagaro Frescobaldi, whose father was a Florentine merchant resident with his family in Padua at his birth. His three sisters were aged 32, 26 and 24 years old at their father's death around 1568, suggesting birth dates for Abagaro and his brother during the 1530s or 1540s. Frescobaldi was already using the stage name Botarga by the time of his earliest recorded performances, in Padua in 1568 and 1571.[48] He toured Iberia with his

---

44 Ernst Georg Johler, *Geschichte, Land- und Orts-Kunde der souverainen teutschen Fürstenthümer Hohenzollern, Hechingen und Sigmaringen: Beiträge zur Geschichte von Schwaben* (Ulm: Stettin, 1824), pp. 48 f.
45 Katritzky, *The Art of Commedia*, pp. 54–58.
46 Jakob Frischlin, *Drey schöne und lustige Bücher von der Hohenzollerischen Hochzeyt* [1599], ed. Casimir Bumiller (Konstanz/Eggingen: Isele, 2003), pp. 222 f., p. 240.
47 Felix Platter, *Tagebuch: (Lebensbeschreibung) 1536–1567*, ed. Valentin Löscher (Basel/Stuttgart: Schwabe, 1976), pp. 499–501. On the 1598 masquerade, see also Katritzky, *The Art of Commedia*, p 47, pp. 96–102; Katritzky, *Healing, Performance and Ceremony*, pp. 117–126.
48 María del Valle Ojeda Calvo, "Otro manuscrito inédito atribuible a Stefanelo Botarga y otras noticias documentales," *Criticón* 92 (2004), pp. 141–169, p. 144, p. 165.

own troupe in the 1580s, and before that with the renowned *commedia dell'arte* troupe of the Roman actress Barbara Flaminia and her husband Alberto Naseli of Ferrara, who respectively performed under the stage names Hortensia and Zan Ganassa.[49] In the late 1560s, Flaminia was the star of her troupe, staging competitive performances at the court of Mantua with the troupe of her great rival, Vincenza Armani.[50] In 1568, the two troupes amalgamated and Flaminia left to join the troupe of Naseli, whose comic performances were also attracting considerable attention by 1570, when he and an actor playing the Spaniard Ernandico entertained guests at a court wedding in Ferrara by engaging in a mock battle at the end of a banquet.[51] A treatise of 1634 on acting, by the *commedia dell'arte* actor Nicolò Barbieri (stage name: "Beltrame"), includes Arlecchino and Ganassa among its rare named references to contemporary performers: "La Spagna prima si seruiua delle nostre Italiane, e i Comici vi faceuauo assai bene: Arlicchino, Ganaßa & altri hanno seruito la felice memoria di Filippo secondo, & si fecero ricchi; ma doppo quel Regno ne hà partorito tante, che ne riempie tutti quei gran Paesi, & ne manda anche molte Compagnie in Italia."[52] Fifteen years later, in 1649, Giovan Domenico Ottonelli quotes this passage in a section of his lengthy theatrical treatise. Unfavourably comparing Italian with Spanish actors, he notes here that Barbieri told him that during a visit of 1644 to Florence a Florentine had passed on first-hand reports of Ganassa's troupe that he had heard around the year 1610, from older Spanish colleagues in Seville who (although Lope de Vega celebrates Ganassa's bawdy *lazzi*)[53] expressly praised the Italian troupe for its uncharacteristic lack of obscenity:

---

49 Ojeda Calvo, *Stefanelo Botarga e Zan Ganassa: Scenari e zibaldoni di comici italiani nella Spagna del Cinquecento* (Roma: Bulzoni, 2007), pp. 85–90.
50 Katritzky, *The Art of Commedia*, p. 86, p. 201, p. 246.
51 Angelo Solerti and Domenico Lanza, "Il teatro ferrarese nella seconda metà del secolo XVI," *Giornale storico della letteratura italiana* 18 (1891), pp. 148–185, p. 159; Robert Henke, *Performance and Literature in the Commedia dell'Arte* (Cambridge/New York: Cambridge University Press, 2002), p. 83.
52 Nicolò Barbieri, *La Svpplica: Discorso famigliare [...] Diretta a quelli, che scriuendo, ò parlando trattano de' Comici* (Venetia: Marco Ginammi, 1634), p. 80–81. Despite continuing confusion on this issue, it seems most unlikely that Naseli ever played the role of Harlequin, which was first developed by Tristano Martinelli (on this point, see also Maria Grazia Profeti, "Ganassa, Bottarga e Trastullo in Spagna," in: Anna Maria Testaverde and Alberto Castoldi, eds., *Zani Mercenario della Piazza Europea: Giornate Internazionali di Studio, Bergamo 27–28 Settembre 2002* [Bergamo: Moretti & Vitali, 2003], pp. 178–197, pp. 181 f.).
53 Norman D. Shergold, "Ganassa and the 'Commedia dell'Arte' in Sixteenth-Century Spain," *Modern Language Review* 51 (1956), pp. 359–368, p. 363.

[...] Ganassa, Comico Italiano, e molto faceto ne' detti, andò là con vna Compagnia di Comici Italiani, e cominciò à recitare all'vso nostro: e se bene egli, come anche ogni altro suo compagno, non era bene, e perfettamente inteso, nondimeno con quel poco, che s'intendeua, faceua ridere consolatamente la brigata; onde guadagnò molto in quelle Città, e dalla pratica sua impararono poi gli Spagnuoli á fare le Comedie all'vso Hispano, che prima non faceuano. Tutto questo io accetto per vero, e credo, che, come Ganassa cercaua di apportar vtile, e diletto co' suoi gratiosi motti, e recitamenti priui di oscenità, così gli Spagnuoli impararono à fare Comedie modeste, e non oscene.[54]

Naseli and Flaminia's troupe consolidated the fashion for *commedia dell'arte* at German court weddings, tentatively pioneered in Munich in 1568, by performing at the imperial Habsburg wedding festivals of 1570. Having played at the 1570 Prague proxy wedding festivities for Emperor Maximilian II's daughter Anna, to Philip II, they followed Anna's sister Elisabeth, betrothed to Charles IX, to Paris; performing en route at her proxy wedding festivities at the imperial Diet of 1570 in Speyer.[55]

Frescobaldi, possibly already with Naseli's troupe for up to three years when Philip II called them from Paris to Madrid in 1574, was touring Iberia with them by 1574. When he played Stefanelo Botarga to Naseli's Zan Ganassa, the duo created an immensely popular master-servant double act, celebrated in and beyond Spain. Diverse textual and visual records of Frescobaldi, with or without Naseli, include a madrigal referring to "Zanni o Stefanello" by Antonfrancesco Grazzini ("Il Lasca," 1503–1584),[56] Adriano Banchieri's "Stefanello Botarga Chiozotto, mercante da fichi secchi" of 1601,[57] the Venetian merchant "Stefanel" or "Stefanel Bottarga" in Flaminio Scala's *scenari* collection of 1611,[58] and

---

54 Giovan Domenico Ottonelli, *Della Christiana Moderatione del Theatro Libro Secondo, detto La Solvtione de' Nodi* (Firenze: Gio. Antonio Bonardi, 1649), p. 37.
55 Armand Baschet, *Les comédiens italiens à la Cour de France sous Charles IX, Henri III, Henri IV et Louis XIII d'après les lettres royales, la correspondance originale des comédiens, les registres de la trésorerie de l'épargne et autres documents* (Paris: Plon, 1882), pp. 24 f., pp. 41 f.; Karl Trautmann, "Italienische Schauspieler am bayerischen Hof," *Jahrbuch für Münchener Geschichte* 1 (1887), pp. 193–312, pp. 228–230; Otto G. Schindler, "Comici dell'Arte bereisen Europa: Ein Abriss," *Maske und Kothurn* 50.3 (2005), pp. 7–17, p. 9; Schindler, "Comici dell'Arte alle Corti austriache degli Asburgo," in: Martino et al., eds., *La ricezione della Commedia dell'Arte*, pp. 69–143, pp. 73–87.
56 Antonfrancesco Grazzini, *Le Rime Burlesche edite e inedite*, ed. Carlo Verzone (Firenze: Sansoni, 1882), p. 297 (Madrigal 33, v. 25); Kathleen Marguerite Lea, *Italian Popular Comedy: A Study in the Commedia dell'Arte, 1560–1620, with Special Reference to the English Stage*, 2 vols. (Oxford: Clarendon Press, 1934), vol. 1, p. 250.
57 See Ojeda Calvo, *Stefanelo Botarga e Zan Ganassa*, p. 142.
58 Scala, *Il Teatro delle Fauole rappresentatiue*, Days 23: "Il Portalettere," pp. 66–68, and 27: "La Mancata Fede," pp. 78–81; Lea, *Italian Popular Comedy*, vol. 2, p. 482. Possibly influenced by Botarga are various references to the old Venetian master "Stefano caragolo Venetiano," by

popular prints featuring "Pantalone and Stefanello"[59] or, in the *Recueil Fossard*, "Stephanel Bottarga."[60] From 1581 onwards, Frescobaldi's impact on Iberian performance practice became even more direct. Naseli and Flaminia continued touring Spain until they returned to Italy in 1584.[61] In 1581, instead of following them to Madrid, Frescobaldi married the newly widowed Spanish actress Luisa de Aranda, and took the place of her late husband, Juan Granado, co-leading Aranda's Spanish acting troupe around Valladolid, Valencia, Madrid and Seville. The latest records cited in connection with the couple's activities date to 1588 in Spain and Frescobaldi's signature is said to be absent from a lost document of 1604 recording Aranda's sale of the family home in Valladolid, leading Ojeda Calvo to suggest that she was then already a widow.[62] However, a record that has escaped attention in this context possibly indicates that Frescobaldi's career continued into the seventeenth century, outside Spain, where the commercial theatres were closed down completely in the late 1590s, before being permitted to reopen in 1600, with even greater restrictions on actresses. Jean Héroard, personal physician to Louis XIII, records that for a week or so after seeing the Accesi, the Mantuan court troupe of Italian professional actors, perform at Fontainebleau in August 1608, the then seven-year-old French Dauphin selected his daily palace password from their stage names. Having already chosen the names Fritellino and then Pantalone:

> Le 15 [August 1608], vendredi [...] Il donne pour mot du guet: *Colo*, c'étoit le nom de l'un des comédiens. [...] Le 17 [...] [I]l donne pour mot du guet: *Doctor*, personnage de la comédie. Le 18 [...]. [I]l donne le mot *Piombino*, qui étoit un comédien. Le 19, mardi [...]. Il donne pour mot *Stefanello*, après s'être fait nommer tous ceux qu'il avoit donnés les jours précédents.[63]

---

his servant "Zan Buratino Bergamasco," as "M. Strofanel," "M. Stronfanel" or "M. Stefanello" in a play of 1613 by Giovanni Sinibaldi (*Gl'otto assortiti comedia: Nova, piacevole, & ridicolosa* [Venetia: Giovanni Alberti, 1613], fol. 28r, fols. 34r–v, fol. 44v, fol. 47r).
59 Katritzky, *The Art of Commedia*, p. 596, plate 308 (*Il Trionfo de Carnavale nel paese de Cucagna*).
60 Pierre Louis Duchartre, *The Italian Comedy* (New York: Dover, 1966), p. 333 (*Recueil Fossard* 36).
61 Bernardo José García García, "L'esperienza di Zan Ganassa in Spagna tra il 1574 e il 1584," in: Testaverde et al., eds., *Zani Mercenario della Piazza Europea*, pp. 131–155, pp. 134–136, p. 143.
62 "Otro manuscrito inédito atribuible a Stefanelo Botarga," p. 165; Ojeda Calvo, *Stefanelo Botarga e Zan Ganassa*, pp. 89 f.
63 *Journal de Jean Héroard sur l'enfance et la jeunesse de Louis XIII (1601–1628)*, eds. Eudore Soulié and Edouard de Barthélemy, 2 vols. (Paris: Firmin Didot, 1868), vol. 1, pp. 351–353 (see also Baschet, *Les comédiens italiens*, pp. 182–184 and Lea, *Italian Popular Comedy*, p. 281, p. 482).

Either Frescobaldi's stage name had already been taken over by a younger Italian professional by 1608,[64] or he himself was then touring France with the Accesi troupe.

One trademark characteristic of *commedia dell'arte* performances is their mastery of improvisation. Many *commedia dell'arte* actors based their pre-rehearsed improvised speeches on memorable dialogue. The best actors collected, wrote down and memorised useful texts in personal notebooks known as *zibaldoni*. Two manuscripts, variously written in the Venetian dialect, maccaronic Latin, Spanish or Catalan, recording a wealth of texts of particular relevance to the *commedia dell'arte* Venetian merchant were discovered in the 1990s in the Royal Library of Madrid and identified as being compiled by Frescobaldi during the 1580s, by María del Valle Ojeda Calvo, who published her edition of one of them in 2007.[65] As the only known *zibaldoni* belonging to a *commedia dell'arte* actor in the role of the old master, Frescobaldi's manuscripts provide valuable insights into typical "improvised" speeches of the Pantalone figure, which they refer to by various names, including "Stefanello" and "Botarga." A major source for Frescobaldi's *zibaldoni* is Andrea Calmo's comic *Lettere* (already plundered by dramatists such as Giovan Battista Cini and Domenico Bruni); others include political writers such as Macchiavelli or Castiglione, playwrights such as Ludovico Dolce or Giovan Battista Giraldi, and Spanish writers such as Melchior de Santa Cruz or Diego Hurtado de Mendoza.[66] Ojeda Calvo cites Cesare Rao as a possible influence on the "second-hand erudition" of such "literary piracy," identified by her as the dominant working method not just of Botarga, but of early modern *commedia dell'arte* actors as a whole.[67] Rao is the editor of the only known text outside Botarga's own *zibaldone* associated with the actor, a comic lament to Ganassa's loss of his friendship with a deceased louse published in 1585. This

---

[64] The actor Giovan Giorgio is thought to have revived the role of Ganassa on the Spanish professional stage from 1592 to 1603 (Jaime Sánchez Romeralo, "El supuesto retorno de Ganassa a España," *Quaderni ibero-americani* 67–68 [1990], pp. 121–131; Profeti, "Ganassa, Bottarga e Trastullo," p. 179).
[65] Ojeda Calvo, *Stefanelo Botarga e Zan Ganassa* ("Lo zibaldone di Stefanelo Botarga [Ms. II-1586]," pp. 181–590).
[66] Ojeda Calvo, "Stefanelo Botarga: un pirata della letteratura," in: Testaverde et al., eds., *Zani Mercenario della Piazza Europea*, pp. 156–177, p. 157, pp. 164 f.; Ojeda Calvo, "Otro manuscrito inédito atribuible a Stefanelo Botarga," pp. 144–147, p. 154; Ojeda Calvo, *Stefanelo Botarga e Zan Ganassa*, pp. 113–129, pp. 168 f.
[67] Ojeda Calvo, "Stefanelo Botarga: un pirata della letteratura," pp. 171 f.; Ojeda Calvo, *Stefanelo Botarga e Zan Ganassa*, pp. 124 f., p. 140.

"Lament of Ganassa and Botarga" (on the death of a louse)[68] confirms the two roles as variants of the Italian professional stage's central servant-master pair and offers a particularly clear example of the "plagiarised literary collage" and wide literary reading required to underpin and refresh their improvised dialogue. A recycled update of Ortensio Lando's burlesque "Oratione di Puccio nella morte d'un suo pedocchio" (first published in Venice in 1549, in *Sermoni funebri de' vari authori nella morte de diversi animali*), its ultimate classical sources most notably include Lucian of Samosata's consummate Greek exercise in Menippean parody, *Encomium of the Fly*, widely celebrated via Leon Battista Alberti's ironic Renaissance Latin mediation, *Musca*.[69]

Pastoral and satiric fragments based on classical sources feature heavily in Frescobaldi's *zibaldoni*; religious plots and characters, beyond one mystery play fragment and a dramatised *Ave Maria*, hardly at all.[70] This amply bears out the complaints of two Spanish Jesuits whose anti-theatrical attacks, approvingly citing attempts by the early Christian fathers to have actresses banned from Rome, appear to target the activities of Naseli's troupe. In 1593, liberally quoting early churchmen, Pedro de Ribadeneyra, who accompanied Philip II to England during his marriage to Mary Tudor in the 1550s, condemns:

> [...] estas representaciones, Pestilencia de la republica[,] [...] Catedra de pestilencia, escuela de incontinencia; obrador de luxuria; horno de Babylonia[,] [...] Fiesta delos demonios[,] [...] inuencion del demonio, para corromper y destruyr el genero humano. En otra, [...] compara[n]do el teatro (q[ue] es lugar de las representaciones) con la carcel [...]. [...] Grandes males hazen las comedias en las ciudades [...]. [...] [L]as mugercillas que representan comunme[n]te son hermosas, lasciuas, y que han vendido su honestidad, y co[n] los meneos y gestos de todo el cuerpo, y con la boz bla[n]da y suaue, con el vestido y gala a manera de Sirenas, encantan, y transforma[n] los hombres en bestias [...].[71]

In 1589, Juan de Pineda accuses foreign comedians, "especially the Italians," of provoking Spaniards to great sinfulness by rejecting the opportunity to showcase virtuous Catholic saints such as Catherine, Agnes or Lucy, in favour of plots

---

68 Cesare Rao, *L'argvte, et facete lettere:[...] Nelle qvali si contengono molti leggiadri Motti, & solazzeuoli Discorsi* (Trento: Marc'Antonio Pallazzolo, 1585), fols. 98r–99r ("Lamento di Giovanni Ganaßa, con M. Stefanello Bottarga suo Padrone"); Shergold, "Ganassa and the 'Commedia dell'Arte'," p. 363; Henke, *Performance and Literature*, p. 83.
69 On which, see Jean-Claude Margolin, "L'influence de Lucien sur les 'Propos de table' d'Alberti," *Revue belge de philologie et d'histoire* 51.3 (1973), pp. 582–604, p. 587, pp. 598–604.
70 Ojeda Calvo, "Nuevas aportaciones al estudio de la *Commedia dell'arte* en España: el *zibaldone* de Stefanello Bottarga," *Criticón* 63 (1995), pp. 119–138, p. 123.
71 Pedro de Ribadeneyra, *Tratado de la Tribvlacion: Repartido en dos libros* (Alcalá: Iuan Iñiguez de Lequerica, 1593), fols. 63r–64r, fol. 70v.

based on classical pagans such as "Medea and Jason, Paris and Helen, Aeneas and Dido, and Pyramus and Thisbe."[72]

Pineda's references to classical pastoral lend added weight to an account of Ganassa which has largely escaped the attention of theatre historians, although musicologists cite it as exemplifying the professional musician Domenico Pietro ("Pedro") Cerone of Bergamo's first-hand and anecdotal knowledge of "Peninsular theorists and practitioners."[73] Having spent around a decade in Spain, in 1603 Cerone (c. 1566–1625) was appointed musician to the court of Naples and priest at the church of SS. Annunziata. Here he finalised his weighty treatise on music; aligned with moralising didactic Counter-Reformation principles and dedicated to Philip III, it was published in Castilian, for Spanish Empire readership, in 1613.[74] An early section, explaining that those who abuse music do not deserve to be called musicians, opens with a consideration of Ganassa, a troupe-leader known to have hired local musicians while in Catalonia.[75] Here, Cerone offers valuable insights into the stage practice of the troupe with which Frescobaldi toured Iberia during the 1570s, confirming the importance of pastoral music, singing and dancing in their performances, their use of rustic instruments such as hurdy-gurdies, and the judgmental distaste with which church and court musicians then viewed the commercial stage-based activities of "such wild musicians":

> No ay Sacristan ni moço de Choro, que de buena gana no affeyte con el honroso titulo de Musico. Este mal vso vino à notar Ganassa comediante Italiano, quando en las postreras comedias, que recitò en la ciudad de Barzelona en Cataluña, represento vna Pastoral; adonde entre los otros diuersos personajes, introduxo à vnos pastores que dançauan, otros que tañian la gayta, y otros instrumentos rusticos, y à otros que cantauan à su Dios versos de alabança: y entre ellos auia vn porquero, que tañia vn cuerno, el qual discurendose quien lo auia hecho mejor, dixo: *Nosotros los Musicos merecemos guirlandas texidas por mano del nuestro PAN*. Por cierto grande bofetada diò entonces Ganassa à los Cantores de oydia, que tan facilmente se vsurpan el nombre de Musico; introduziendo en su comedia vn vil porquero tañedor de cuerno, que tan desuergonçadamente se vsurpasse el nombre

---

72 Juan de Pineda, *Primera parte de los treynta y cinco dialogos familiares de la Agricvltura Christiana* (Salamanca: Pedro de Adurça, y Diego Lopez, 1589), fols. 349v–350r (Dialogo 15, para.26), fol. 350r; my translation ("especialmente de los Italianos"; "[gozando de los cuentos] de Medea y de Iason, y de Paris y Helena, y Eneas y Dido, y de Piramo y Tisbe [...]").
73 Robert Stevenson, "[Review:] *El Melopeo Tractado de Musica Theorica y Practica* by Pedro Cerone," *Journal of the American Musicological Society* 24.3 (1971), pp. 477–485, pp. 480 f.
74 Enrique Alberto Arias, "Cerone as Historian," *Anuario Musical* 58 (2003), pp. 87–110, pp. 89 f.
75 As recorded, for example, in his contract of 1581 with two Castilian musicians (John V. Falconieri, "Historia de la 'Commedia dell'Arte' en España," *Revista de Literatura* 11 (1957), pp. 3–37 & 12 (1958), pp. 69–90, p. 26; Shergold, "Ganassa and the 'Commedia dell'Arte'," p. 362; García García, "L'esperienza di Zan Ganassa in Spagna," p. 138, p. 150).

de Musico. Paresceme que à tal termino à llegado este mal vso, que solo falta, que estos iñorantes se pongan en comunidad con los virtuosos Maestros y eccelentes Musicos; y que en sus conuersaciones y platicas salgan con vn preambulo de *Nosotros Musicos*: ygualando el cantar del cueruo, al del ruynseñor: y comparando el faber del torpe asno, al de la prudente y sabia raposa.[76]

Cerone's disapproval of professional actors, and concern to distance the emerging professions of music from the distinctively costumed Italian actors in Spain, resurfaces a few pages further on. Here, he emphasises that true musicians reject deforming acrobatics, vanities and fooling, and especially strange costumes of the type which, according to St Bernard, indicate bad practice.[77]

Stefanelo Botarga's influence persisted far beyond his own period. The pimento red costume of the *botarga* features repeatedly in the poetry of Francisco de Quevedo y Villegas.[78] Several of Lope de Vega's writings allude to Ganassa and Estefanelo or Botarga. Botarga costume is worn as a stock Spanish festival disguise in his play *Las ferias de Madrid*[79] and throughout the seventeenth century, and at least once by the great playwright himself. At the 1599 double wedding of the recently deceased Philip II's son, King Philip III of Spain, to Margarita of Austria, and Philip III's sister Isabella to Margarita's cousin, Albert of Austria, Lope de Vega, in his Botarga costume and mounted on a mule laden with meat, himself symbolised Carnival. Lent was represented by his servant, carrying fish and wearing a turban hung with eels and sardines.[80]

Food was a major source for comic stage names and it is worth examining Botarga and Pickelhering in the context of the foods that gave them their names: the North Sea fish speciality *Bückelhering* and the Mediterranean fish speciality

---

[76] Domenico Pietro Cerone, *El Melopeo y Maestro, tractado de mvsica theorica y practica: en que se pone por extenso, lo que vno para hazerse perfecto Musico ha menester saber[,] [...] repartido en XXII Libros* (Napoles: Iuan Bautista Gargano y Lucrecio Nucci, 1613), Libro primero, chap. 22: "De como ay vnos que se vsurpan el nombre de Musico, no siendo meriteuoles del nombre de Cantor," pp. 64–66, pp. 64 f.

[77] Libro primero, chap. 28 "Quales condiciones ha de tener el buen Maestro," pp. 74 f., p. 75.

[78] Francisco Gómez de Quevedo y Villegas, *Poësias de Don Francisco de Quevedo Villegas, [...] Tercera Parte* (Brusselas: Francisco Foppens, 1670), p. 281 (*Thalia, Musa sexta*, soneto 53: "Burlase del Camaleon, moralizando satiricamente su naturaleza"), p. 338 (*Thalia, Musa sexta*, romance 17: "Los Borrachos celebres," pp. 337–339), p. 448 (*Thalia, Musa sexta*, romance 88: "Matraca de los Paños, y Sedas," pp. 443–449), p. 449 (*Thalia, Musa sexta*, romance 89: "Pavura de los Condes de Carrion," pp. 449–451).

[79] Félix Lope de Vega y Carpio, *Segvnda Parte de las Comedias de Lope de Vega Carpio* (Valladolid: Iuan de Rueda, 1611), fols. 334r–365v, fol. 362v.

[80] Shergold, "Ganassa and the 'Commedia dell'Arte'," pp. 363–366; Valls, "La representación y la interpretación," pp. 259 f.; Profeti, "Ganassa, Bottarga e Trastullo," pp. 185 f.

botargo. Joseph Addison, writing in 1711 about food-based stage names, recognised their national significance as an important aspect of their comicality, writing of stage clowns:

> [T]here is a Set of merry Drolls, whom the common People of all Countries admire [...]: I mean those circumforaneous Wits whom every Nation calls by the Name of that Dish of Meat which it loves best. In *Holland* they are termed *Pickled Herrings*; in *France, Jean Pottages*, in *Italy, Maccaronies*; and in *Great Britain, Jack Puddings*. These merry Wags, from whatsoever Food they receive their Titles, that they may make their Audiences laugh, always appear in a Fool's Coat, and commit such Blunders and Mistakes in every Step they take, and every Word they utter, as those who listen to them would be ashamed of.[81]

This pragmatic early eighteenth-century approach, associating the origins of food-based clown names with favourite national dishes, or with culinary practices during Carnival and Lent, is still broadly accepted by most modern theatre specialists. According to Ralf Haekel, for example, "Most clown names signify foods." "Pickelhering derives from the English 'pickled herring,' that is from preserved herrings."[82]

Let me complicate this a little by proposing another, rather more speculative, influence that, by contrast, has received little or no attention in this context. It concerns what I refer to as "literary anthropologies": preserved and modified cultural memories of paraethnographic records such as the descriptions of monstrous or marvellous foreign races recorded by the classical writers Alexander the Great and Pliny.[83] Literary anthropologies supplied a template for the expectations of colonial explorers deep into the seventeenth century. Early modern Europeans were intensely aware not just of their own continent, but of the startling expansion of the known world into new continents undocumented by Biblical or classical sources. Rather than viewing these new discoveries with fresh eyes, their expectations of New World inhabitants were profoundly shaped by literary anthropologies. The map of the New World in the 1561 edition of Sebastian Münster's great cosmography of the whole known world, first published in 1552, hints at this process when it names South America "Atlantis" and indicates the presence of *anthropophagi* or cannibals there. It explicitly draws on literary anthropologies

---

81 Joseph Addison, "Editorial," *The Spectator* 1.47 (24 April 1711), pp. 1–2.
82 Ralf Haekel, *Die Englischen Komödianten in Deutschland: Eine Einführung in die Ursprünge des deutschen Berufsschauspiels* (Heidelberg: Winter, 2004), p. 236, p. 236, n. 602; my translation ("Die meisten Namen des Narren bezeichnen Speisen."; "Pickelhering leitet sich vom englischen 'pickled herring', also von gepökeltem Hering ab [...].").
83 Katritzky, "Literary Anthropologies and Pedro González, the 'Wild Man' of Tenerife," in: John Slater, Maríaluz López-Terrada, and José Pardo-Tomás, eds., *Medical Cultures of the Early Modern Spanish Empire* (Farnham/Burlington, VT: Ashgate, 2014), pp. 107–128.

to describe and depict a whole range of Old and New World "Indians," each identical to one or another of the familiar classical literary anthropologies. Some are physically distinctive, such as hairy satyrs or wild people, those who use one foot as a sun-shade, one-eyed or two-headed peoples, the Blemmyes (whose heads were located on their chests), the Dog-heads, the long eared ones, pygmies, mermaids or Amazons. As well as the *anthropophagi* or cannibals, those distinguished primarily by dietary rather than physical characteristics include the *astomi*, who nourished themselves by smelling apples, and the *ichthyophagi* or fish-eaters, these latter variously identified by classical anthropologists as Ethiopian or Persian.[84] An account of them in the early medieval *Liber monstrorum* provides insights into why early modern illustrators often depicted them hairy and unclothed, much as they then depicted wild men of the woods:

> [I]n India next to the Ocean we have learnt of a certain race of humans hairy in their whole body, who are said to live on water and raw fish, covered in natural nakedness only by bristles like wild animals. And the Indians call them Ichthyophagi, and they are not only accustomed to the land, but dwell in streams and ponds and mostly next to the river Epigmaris.[85]

After the Reformation, regional fish-eating practices acquired complex layers of connotations in the light of diverging Catholic, Lutheran and Calvinist fasting regulations.[86] Early modern fasting regulations were not always transparent. In 1549, for example, compulsory Friday fish-eating was reinstated in some Protestant regions of Northern Germany. To decrease the risk of being caught and punished by the authorities for not observing fish fasts when dining at inns during the 1590s, the Swiss physician Thomas Platter the Younger sometimes ordered forbidden foods such as duck, meat or eggs to be served to him in a private dining room. While visiting London in Autumn 1599, he was surprised to learn that Protestant England still observed both the traditional Lenten fish fast, and year-round weekly two-day fish fasts.[87] The exact extent of any impact of cultural

---

84 Gordon Lindsay Campbell, *Strange Creatures: Anthropology in Antiquity* (London: Duckworth, 2006), pp. 86 f.
85 *Liber monstrorum: Latin–English*, in: Andy Orchard, *Pride and Prodigies. Studies in the Monsters of the Beowulf-Manuscript* (Toronto: University of Toronto, 2003), pp. 254–315, p. 269 ("Et in India iuxta Oceanum pilosum toto corpore quoddam genus humanum didicimus, qui in naturali nuditate setis tantum more ferino contecti crudis cum aqua piscibus ita uiuere dicuntur. Quos Indi Ichthyophagos appellant. Qui non tantum in terris adseti, sed fluminibus ac stagnis et iuxta amnem Epigmaridem maxime demorantur." p. 268).
86 My thanks to Bob Kolb and Charlotte Colding Smith for helpful discussions on this point.
87 Thomas Platter d. J., *Beschreibung der Reisen durch Frankreich, Spanien, England und die Niederlande 1595–1600*, ed. Rut Keiser, 2 vols. (Basel/Stuttgart: Schwabe, 1968), vol. 2, p. 824; Katritzky, *Healing, Performance and Ceremony*, p. 66.

memories of classical fish-eaters, or practices of religious fish fasts, on fish-based early modern clown names is unclear, as is any cross-influence between stage names chosen by Italian or English actors. However, given their perceived links with religious fasting practices, fish-based stage names undoubtedly provided excellent opportunities for pointed covert theatrical references to national and confessional variations in religious practices.[88]

Early modern theatre and print culture acknowledge strong connections between the clear class divide in early modern London fish-eating and social drinking habits. Prince Hal bemoans the wanton extravagance of Falstaff's "intolerable" consumption of *"Item*, Anchoues and Sacke after Supper ii.s.vi.d,"[89] while one of George Wilkins' dramatic dialogues notes that a newly wealthy character "[...] feedes now vppon Sacke & Anchoues [...],"[90] and for Ben Jonson, "[...] a dish of pickled Saylors, fine salt Sea-boyes, shall relish like *Anchoues*, or *Caueare*, to draw downe a cup of *nectar*, in the skirts of a night."[91] John Marston contrasts "good meate, *Anchoues, cauiare*" with "bottle ale & red Herrings,"[92] and *Pasquils Iestes* emphasises the lowly status of beer and herrings when evoking "[...] a certaine Alehouse or Inne, where couetous wretches [...] feede vpon browne bread, and red Herrings."[93] While poor folk ate North Sea herring with their beer not just during fish fasts, but as an everyday food staple, wealthy drinkers accompanied their after-dinner wine with exotic preserved fish specialities, of the type available in the four London wine bars personally vetted by the indefatigable John Taylor, for his exhaustively comprehensive "rough guide" of 1636 to London's drinking venues. All run by Dutchmen, they sold Rhine wines accompanied by salted meats, pickled herrings, anchovies, caviar and *botargo*.[94] Tuna or cod roe

---

88 On the religious and philosophical context of the *commedia dell'arte*, see Katritzky, *Healing, Performance and Ceremony*, esp. chaps. 14–15, pp. 245–282; Matt Cawson, "Corporeality and Subversion in Post-Renaissance Italy: The Inquisition and the Commedia dell'Arte," *Platform* 7.1 (2013), pp. 26–41.
89 Shakespeare, *Comedies, histories, & tragedies*, p 60 (*1 Henry IV*, 2.4). N.B. The currency notation refers to two shillings and sixpence, equivalent to 30 pennies, or twelve and a half new pence, or one eighth of a pound.
90 George Wilkins, *The Miseries of Inforst marriage: As it is now playd by his Maiesties Seruants* (London: George Vincent, 1607), sig. E4r.
91 Ben Jonson, *Neptvnes Trivmph for the return of Albion* (s.l., 1623), sig. C2v.
92 John Marston, *What You Will* (London: Thomas Thorpe, 1607), sigs. C2r, F2v–3r.
93 *Pasquils Iestes: Mixed with Mother Bunches 'Merriments'* (London: John Browne, 1609), sig. F2r; see also Thomas Dekker, *Blurt master-constable: Or The Spaniards night-walke As it hath bin sundry times priuately acted by the Children of Paules* (London: Henry Rockytt, 1602), sig. B3v.
94 John Taylor, *Taylors travels and circvlar perambvlation, through [...]the Famous Cities of London and Westminster: [...] with an Alphabeticall Description, of all the Taverne Signes [...]* (London: A[ugustin] M[atthews], 1636), sig. D7r.

that has been preserved by being pressed, dried and salted, and traditionally manufactured in Mediterranean regions such as Iberia, France and Italy, *botargo* is perhaps most familiar to contemporary northern Europeans as the main ingredient of taramasalata. Like pickled herring, it is typically served with alcoholic drinks, in which context it is praised by writers such as François Rabelais,[95] John Fletcher ("Andrew: There's a Fishmongers boy with Caviar Sir, / Anchoves and Potargo, to make ye drinke.")[96] and Samuel Pepys. One "very hot" moonlit June evening in 1661, the diarist Pepys, who served *botargo* to specially favoured guests, sat out in his London garden until midnight with his distinguished naval colleague Sir William Penn "[...] talking and singing and drinking of great drafts of Clarret and eating botargo and bread and butter till 12 at night, it being moonshine. And so to bed – very near fuddled."[97] If the most popular stock comic role of the English actors derives from cheap herrings, it is unsurprising that one of the wealthy masters of the *commedia dell'arte* takes his stage name from the expensive fish delicacy *botargo*. For both, the strong link with excessive alcoholic consumption offers clues to their attraction as comic stage names.

This consideration of specific new documentation and possible influences of literary anthropologies and religious fasting traditions indicates new perspectives on the transnational adoption of fish-based stage names, and contributes to moving the debate beyond the simple food-clown formula by informing and complicating the connection between fish speciality and comic stage name. Similar themes featured in the stage names of different European regions, and on *commedia dell'arte* and English travelling stages the names chosen by actors reflected local considerations of their home and host nations. The most celebrated fish-based Italian stage name was created in Spain and refers to Mediterranean *botargo*. Whether or not cultural memories of classical fish-eaters influenced this choice of clown name, or even whether Stefanelo Botarga's success in Spain in the 1580s—great enough to have registered by 1585 in German festival culture—influenced the English actors, they in turn created a popular clown in the early seventeenth-century German-speaking regions named after North Sea pickled herring. The impetus for these stage names clearly came neither directly nor solely from the fish itself. Rather than simply reflecting vague late medieval

---

95 François Rabelais, *Gargantua and Pantagruel*, trans. Sir Thomas Urquhart and Pierre Le Motteux, *Everyman's Library* (London: David Campbell Publishers, 1994), p. 30, p. 70, p. 778.
96 John Fletcher, *The Elder Brother A Comedie: Acted at the Blacke Friers, by his Maiesties Servants* (London: I[ohn] W[aterson] and I[ohn] B[enson], 1637), sig. E2v.
97 Samuel Pepys, *The Diary of Samuel Pepys: a new and complete transcription*, ed. Robert Latham and William Matthews, 11 vols. (London: Bell and Hyman, 1970–1983), vol. 2 (1971), *1661*, p. 115.

pan-European links between foolery and carnivalesque foods, early modern fish-based stage names complicate culinary connotations with darker literary and other cultural and anthropological associations that stretch back into the classical past, and created opportunities for coded religious, political and social comment on the travelling stages of early modern Europe.

Tatiana Korneeva
The Art of Adaptation and Self-Promotion: Carlo Gozzi's *La Principessa filosofa*

Carlo Gozzi's *teatro spagnolesco* can serve as a particularly enlightening example for a reflection on, and re-evaluation of, the wide-ranging influences of early modern Spanish theatrical practices on the geographical and cultural spaces conquered by this empire. The eighteenth-century Venetian playwright (1720–1806), also referred to as the Italian Shakespeare due to the irregular and extravagant character of his dramatic production,[1] adapted about twenty comedies from the Spanish drama of the *Siglo de Oro* for the Italian stage. Better known for his avantgarde theatrical fables, from 1767 Gozzi found not only a new source of inspiration in Spanish comedies, but also, as he saw it, a way to renew and revitalise Italian theatrical practice more generally.[2] The playwright himself considered this part of his dramatic production to be no less important than his highly successful *Fiabe teatrali* (written and performed in 1761–1765) and even claimed in the preface to one of his Spanish comedies that "[...] se si vorrà scrivere una storia veridica de' nostri Teatri, [...] si dovrà fare [...] menzione [...] del mio nuovo genere tratto dagli argomenti Spagnuoli" [whoever decides to write the true history of our theatres should mention [my] new genre based on Spanish scenarios].[3]

Whereas Gozzi's Spanish plays have so far remained largely unknown to the general public, there has been a revival of research interest in his adaptations of Spanish drama, thanks to the recent discovery of an extraordinary family archive containing 9500 unpublished folios and manuscripts that shed new light on the composition process of the playwright's theatrical and theoretical writings.[4] The

---

[1] Giuseppe Baretti, *An Account of the Manners and Customs of Italy: With Observations on the Mistakes of Some Travellers, with Regard to that Country* [1768], in: Baretti, *Opere*, ed. Franco Fido (Milano: Rizzoli, 1967), pp. 611–646, p. 628.

[2] Carlo Gozzi, *La più lunga lettera di risposta che sia stata scritta inviata da Carlo Gozzi a un poeta teatrale italiano de' nostri giorni*, in: *Opere edite ed inedite del Co: Carlo Gozzi*, 14 vols. (Venezia: Zanardi, 1801–1804), vol. 14, pp. 3–168, p. 54.

[3] Gozzi, Preface to *I due fratelli nimici*, in: *Opere del Co: Carlo Gozzi*, 8 vols. (Venezia: Colombani, 1772–1774), vol. 5, pp. 283–287, pp. 286–287.

[4] Gozzi's adaptations from Spanish comedies suffer from the fact that only a small percentage of these plays are available in modern, scholarly editions (*I due fratelli nimici*, in: *Opere: Teatro e polemiche teatrali*, ed. Giuseppe Petronio [Milano: Rizzoli, 1962] and *Le droghe d'amore*, ed. Camilla Guaita [Milano: Cuem, 2006]), and none of them is regularly performed in theatres. After the discovery of the playwright's archive in 2004 and its subsequent acquisition by the Biblioteca Nazionale Marciana in Venice Gozzi's *teatro ispano-veneto* has begun to attract the scholarly

theoretical conceptualisation of the metaphor of culture as a net enabling the multi-directional circulation of material forms and cultural artefacts (a metaphor whose productivity and explanatory potential are elucidated by the essays in this volume) can provide further insights into Gozzi's adaptations and, in a broader sense, into the complex relationships between Italian and Spanish dramatic practices. This new approach to the study of drama allows to show how Spanish materials were diffused and made available in mid-eighteenth-century Venice and to highlight the process of transculturalisation. Drawing on the concept of culture as a dynamic net, as outlined by Joachim Küpper,[5] I will address the question of what is transferred with the dramatic text and what is altered in the process of adaptation. Moreover, a case study of one of Gozzi's Spanish comedies, *La Principessa filosofa, o sia Il controveleno* [The Princess Philosopher, or the Antidote] (1772), and its source text, *Desdén con el desdén* [Disdain Meets With Disdain] (1654) by Agustín Moreto y Cabaña (1618–1669), will raise a further question in my investigation, namely: did the conceptualisation of intellectual property develop differently in the field of dramatic literature compared to non-dramatic forms? In drawing my conclusions, I will argue that the entangled history of the performance of Gozzi's play is particularly illuminating in endeavouring to understand the impact of authorial agency on the circulation of cultural artefacts.

Gozzi and the Cultural Net

Let me start with some preliminary considerations on why Gozzi's adaptations from Spanish drama of the *Siglo de Oro* lend themselves to being examined in terms of the circulation of theatrical material within the cultural net. First of all, Spain was the dominant power in Italy in the early modern period and played a significant role in its history during the *Seicento*. Cultural and political encounters between Italy and Spain were the order of the day, with numerous exchanges of authors, playwrights and theatre troupes. Even when Spanish rule in Italy gave way to Austrian domination in 1715, the interchanges between the two countries continued well into the eighteenth century. Gozzi's own encounter with Spanish

---

attention it merits. See especially the collections of essays dedicated to these plays by Susanne Winter, ed., *Carlo Gozzi: I drammi 'spagnoleschi'* [Heidelberg: Winter, 2008] and Javier Gutiérrez Carou, ed., *Metamorfosi drammaturgiche settecentesche: Il teatro 'spagnolesco' di Carlo Gozzi* [Venezia: lineadacqua, 2011]).
5 For the conceptual framework of the DramaNet project approach, see the chapter by Joachim Küpper in this volume.

culture was enabled by general factors, such as the diffusion of travel writings by Italian tourists visiting Spain[6] and the settlement of Jesuits in Italy,[7] as well as more personal circumstances, such as his friendship with the major Venetian scholar of Spanish literature, Giovanni Battista Conti,[8] and the playwright's collaboration with Antonio Sacchi's itinerant troupe, which at the beginning of their relationship had just returned from Portugal.

Along with these exchange processes, which brought about Gozzi's encounter with Spanish drama, the lively intra-European circulation of texts and performances should also be taken into consideration. Indeed, although Gozzi's *Principessa filosofa* remains faithful to the Spanish original, its title shifts attention onto the single character, away from Moreto's emphasis on the action, revealing similarities with both Molière's 1664 *comédie-ballet*, *La princesse d'Elide*, and Pietro Chiari's comedy, *Alcimena principessa delle isole Fortunate* (1750). Another possible source for Gozzi's play is Luigi Riccoboni's *Rebut pour Rebut* (1717), first staged in Paris by the troupe of the Nouveau Théâtre Italien. Moreover, Gozzi may have also been familiar with the Italian sixteenth-century adaptations of Moreto's play by Antonio Parrino (*Amare e fingere*, 1675) and Arcangelo Spagna (*Lo sdegno con lo sdegno si vince*, 1709).[9] The Italian reception of Spanish theatre in the eighteenth century can be therefore defined in terms of a dynamic contextual network, in which the relationships between texts were often mediated by both French dramatic culture and the native Italian tradition. Considering the Venetian theatrical

---

[6] Particularly relevant in this regard are Giuseppe Baretti's *Lettere familiari a' suoi tre Fratelli, Filippo, Giovanni, e Amedeo* from Portugal and Spain (1762–1763) and *A Journey from London to Genoa: through England, Portugal, Spain, and France* (1770). Baretti was Gozzi's friend and admirer, and after he made his way back from England to Italy via the Iberian Peninsula, he most likely gave the playwright an enthusiastic account of Spanish drama (Piermario Vescovo, "'Alcune reliquie de' teatrali spettacoli spagnuoli': Da uno 'spagnolismo' a un altro," in: Winter, ed., *Carlo Gozzi*, pp. 57–71). Indeed, he considered Lope de Vega and Calderón among the greatest of poetic geniuses, describing their works as original, forceful and elegant (Baretti, *Opere*, pp. 647 f.; Robert Bufalini, "The Lapidation of Giuseppe Baretti and the Invective of His *Lettere familiari* from Portugal and Spain," *Modern Language Notes* 125.1 (2010), pp. 141–152, p. 151).

[7] One of these Jesuits, Cristoforo Tentori, was the tutor to Almorò Tiepolo's family, to which Gozzi's mother belonged. See Franco Fido, *La serietà del gioco: Svaghi letterari e teatrali nel Settecento* [Pisa: Pacini Fazzi, 1998], chap. 4.2 "I drammi spagnoleschi," pp. 130–158, p. 134.

[8] Enrico Carrara, *Studio sul teatro ispano-veneto di Carlo Gozzi* (Cagliari: Valdes, 1901), p. 9; Vittorio Cian, *Italia e Spagna nel secolo XVIII: Studi e ricerche* (Torino: S. Lattes, 1896), pp. 42–46; Fido, *La serietà del gioco*, p. 134.

[9] On Gozzi's sources for *La Principessa filosofa*, see Monica Pavesio, "*Rebut pour Rebut-Ritrosia per ritrosia*: un canovaccio del *Nouveau Théâtre Italien* di Luigi Riccoboni come possibile fonte de *La principessa filosofa* di Gozzi," in: Winter, ed., *Carlo Gozzi*, pp. 193–206; Maria Grazia Profeti, "Gozzi e l'"informe e stravagante teatro spagnolo'," in: Winter, ed., *Carlo Gozzi*, pp. 23–41, p. 31.

milieu's extreme receptiveness to cultural material of any kind, the adaptations from Spanish Golden-Age drama provided Gozzi with a means to link his plays to a wider network of literary, ideological and social texts.

"Una idea da me rovesciata e riedificata a mio modo"

The metaphor of the cultural net is thus particularly useful in describing the interconnected networks of production and consumption in which the theatrical texts were enmeshed. Given that the adaptation of drama involves not only a translation from one language to another but also from one theatrical practice to another, it is vital to address the question of what changes were made in the process of adapting the play for the *genio italiano* [the Italian genius] and the *gusto natio* [national taste].

Moreto's *Desdén con el desdén* is a typical love comedy in which three noblemen vie for the attention of the princess of Barcelona. Diana, the lady in question, is disdainful and intellectually opposed to love and marriage. However, one of her suitors, Carlos, succeeds—with the help of his servant, the *gracioso* Polilla—in winning her affection. His strategy consists in repaying Diana's disdain with his own apparent disinterest, and, indeed, the princess swallows the bait. Wounded by Carlos's seeming aloofness, Diana hence resolves to have him fall in love with her. She is thus led into the trap devised by Carlos, and when he takes the decisive step of his plan by feigning interest in her lady-in-waiting, Diana is irretrievably lost.

These tangled situations of the Spanish play appealed to Gozzi, who considered theatre the "recinto di divertimento" [enclosure of diversion].[10] He borrowed Moreto's entire plotline of a princess who rejects marriage and thus threatens the social order, as well as the principal motifs of love and feigned disdain. However, although Gozzi was willing to acknowledge his debts to Moreto, he also insisted, in the preface to his adaptation, on the radical difference between his comedy and those of his predecessors:

> *El Desden con el desden*: Commedia di D. Agostino Moreto, m'ha dato l'argomento per questo Dramma. Moliere ha rubata l'idea della sua *Principessa d'Elide* al Moreto, ma egli ha

---

[10] For Gozzi's definition of theatre as "recinto di divertimento" or "recinto di passatempo," see the prefaces to *Il Fajel* ("Prefazione del Traduttore," in: *Il Fajel: Tragedia del Sig. D'Arnaud tradotta in versi sciolti dal Co: Carlo Gozzi* [Venezia: Colombani, 1772], pp. 5–36, esp. p. 32) and *I due fratelli nimici* (p. 284).

Note: The heading of this section is taken from Gozzi, *La più lunga lettera di risposta*, p. 36.

fatto un'opera che punto non ha che fare colla mia *Principessa filosofa*. Il confronto è facile. Si troverà, che'l mio Dramma è differentissimo e nell'ossatura, e ne' dialoghi dal *Desden con el desden* del Moreto, e dalla *Principessa d'Elide del Moliere* [...].[11]

[*El Desdén con el desdén*, a comedy by D. Agostino Moreto provided me with an argument for this drama. Molière stole the idea for his *Principessa d'Elide* from Moreto and wrote a work that has nothing to do with my *Principessa filosofa*. The comparison is easy: my play is very different both in structure and in its dialogues from both Moreto's *Desdén con el desdén* and Molière's *Principessa d'Elide* (...).]

In his *Memorie inutili* [*The Useless Memoirs*] (1797), Gozzi distances himself again from his sources, claiming that he "trass[e] dal fondo delle Commedie spagnole molti Drammi, [...] enunziando sempre que' Drammi come tratti, e non come tradotti" [I drew on many Spanish comedies, always specifying that my works were inspired by them and not translated from them].[12] On numerous other occasions, Gozzi challenges his critics and invites them to look for the differences between his plays and their originals.[13] Let us follow the playwright's lead and explore what makes Gozzi's adaptation so different—*differentissimo*—from the source texts, where the playwright even claims that if someone tried to revive and stage Molière's translation of Moreto's comedy, it would not enjoy the same success as his own play (p. 149). Since both Moreto's and Gozzi's plays are essentially comedies of character, and it is indeed the *dramatis personae* who engage the audience's imagination and are responsible for the plays' aesthetic effects, I will focus on how the relationships between the principal characters—the princess Teodora, her suitor Don Cesare (the counterparts of Moreto's Diana and Carlos) and their intermediary, Giannetto (the equivalent of the *gracioso* Polilla)—are treated in the Italian adaptation.

---

[11] All quotations from Gozzi's play are taken from the *editio princeps*: Gozzi, *La Principessa filosofa, o sia Il controveleno*, in: *Opere del Co: Carlo Gozzi*, vol. 5, pp. 145–280 (here "Prefazione," pp. 147–148). Hereafter, page numbers will be cited parenthetically. All translations are my own.

[12] Gozzi, *Memorie inutili*, edd. Paolo Bosisio and Valentina Garavaglia, 2 vols. (Milano: LED, 2006), vol. 2, part 3, "Lettera confutatoria da me scritta l'anno 1780, e indirizzata a Pietro Antonio Gratarol a Stockholm," p. 825. Hereafter, followed by chapter, page, and then volume number in arabic numerals. Unless otherwise noted, all translations are mine.

[13] See, for example, the preface to *Il pubblico secreto*, in: *Opere edite ed inedite*, vol. 6, p. 5: "[s] commetto, che l'opera mia è differente molto da quella di Calderone, e da quella del Cicognini" [I bet my work is very different from that of both Calderón and Cicognini].

Poetics of Adaptation

Moreto's Carlos is a courtly character conscious of his social importance and duties. He also possesses a profound knowledge of human behaviour and the mechanisms of desire. Indeed, Carlos falls in love with Diana despite her merely ordinary beauty ("una hermosura modesta"[14]), because for the first time in his life he is unable to get what he wants. He explains that "Que aunque sea la codicia / de más precio lo que alcanza / que lo que se le retira, / sólo por la privación / de más valor lo imagina" [Because even though we may desire what we can obtain more than what is withheld from us, only because we are deprived of the latter, we imagine it to be of greater value].[15] Realising that only the challenge which the unattainability of the desired object represents for his own ego will shake the princess's indifference, Carlos decides to feign disinterest in Diana's charms.

Gozzi's Don Cesare appears to be the complete opposite of his Spanish forebear. As he confides to Giannetto, he is hopelessly in love with the princess of Barcelona and completely overwhelmed by the force of his feelings:

> DON CESARE: Tento con te uno sfogo
> D'un'affanno angoscioso, e che m'uccide
> Omai chiuso nel seno. Io sono, amico,
> Straziato il core, oppresso dall'angoscia
> Sol per colei, che prima nominasti.
> (*s'appoggia ad una spalla di Giannetto piangendo*)
> (p. 154)

> [DON CESARE: In you I seek the release
> For the painful grief that is killing me,
> Now locked in my bosom. My heart, my friend,
> Is tortured and burdened with anguish
> Only for her, whom you mentioned earlier.
> (*crying, he leans on Giannetto's shoulder*)]

Don Cesare also lacks the intelligence and spirit of initiative of his Spanish counterpart, and the unpromising beginning of the courtship of Donna Teodora leaves him in a state of profound melancholy, as revealed by the very first stage direction in the opening scene of the first act: "D. Cesare starà sedendo innanzi, appoggiato con un gombito ad un tavolino, con una guancia alla mano, immerso in

---

14 Agustín Moreto, *El desdén, con el desdén*, ed. Enrico di Pastena, *Biblioteca clásica* (Barcelona: Crítica, 1999), v. 84. Quotations from the play are followed by line numbers, referring to this edition. Unless otherwise noted, all translations are mine.
15 Vv. 264–268. Translation is from Raymond R. MacCurdy, ed., *Spanish Drama of the Golden Age: Twelve Plays* [New York, NY: Appleton-Century-Crofts, 1971], p. 585.

una profonda malinconìa" [D. Cesare is sitting leaning forward, his elbow on a small table and his hand on his cheek, in a state of profound melancholy] (p. 151). Giannetto, the go-between between Don Cesare and the object of his affections, therefore has to devise a plan whereby the unfortunate lover can get the better of the princess. Thus, whereas Moreto preserves the dignity of Carlos' character, Gozzi transfers the intellectual qualities of the noble protagonist to the low figure of the Venetian servant.

Giannetto, like his Spanish counterpart, the *gracioso* Pollila, is thus constantly at the centre of the dramatic action, performing a dual function: on the one hand, he is the playwright and the stage director who controls the role-playing of the other characters and, on the other, he is the spectator-commentator of their actions. As playwrights, Giannetto and Polilla are responsible for bringing the destined couples together, whereas the role of providing commentary on the dramatic action enables them to communicate with the audience more than other characters. However, if Polilla's metaphorical language creates a linguistic substructure underlying the surface plot, Giannetto's function is to entertain, using his Venetian dialect and his Pantalone-like manners to engage a theatre-going public seeking only entertainment and laughter ("Volli da questo Dramma lontane le nostre maschere, sostituendo però il carattere d'un Veneziano faceto per ridur l'opera più intesa dall'universale, è più popolare"; [I wanted to keep the *commedia dell'arte* stock characters away from this play, and I thus substituted for them the figure of the funny Venetian fellow in order to make the work more universally understandable and more popular]).[16]

Both Moreto's Diana and Gozzi's Teodora reject courtship and concomitantly marriage. They thus fall outside the norm, because by refusing to fulfil their social duty of guaranteeing political succession in their kingdoms, the heroines try to impose a pattern of conduct alien to a person of their rank. Diana is not really a comic character, however, since the question she is raising is a serious one, namely, whether a woman is free to choose her course in life without interference from tradition and social conventions.[17] Compared to her Spanish counterpart, Gozzi's Teodora is a much less complex character, since her position regarding marital relationships recalls more that of Turandot, the ultra-feminist from Gozzi's homonymous fairy-tale play, the exotic princess who exudes hostility and disdain for the male sex.

---

16 Gozzi, Preface to *La Principessa filosofa*, p. 148.
17 Bruce W. Wardropper, "Moreto's *El Desdén con el Desdén*: The 'Comedia' Secularized," *Bulletin of Hispanic Studies* 34 (1957), pp. 1–9, p. 3.

Like Carlos, Diana never allows passion to get the better of her: even when she admits that her love for her suitor has been aroused by jealousy of her cousin Cintia, she is still able to reason effectively. Her Italian counterpart also considers herself aloof and self-controlled, but in the *scène probante* (Act 2 scene 2), where Gozzi measures the positions of his protagonists and prepares them for yet another meeting, which further modifies their personalities, the stage directions reveal that Donna Teodora is no more than an irritable and short-tempered woman: "invasata alquanto" [rather possessed] (p. 186), "riscaldata" [heated] (p. 187), "smaniosa per [...] so noncuranza" [stung by his disinterest] (p. 189), "fiera," "collerica" [imperious, choleric] (p. 196), "sorpresa, e un poco riscaldata" [surprised and a little bit warmed up], "più riscaldata" [more warmed up], "un poco attonita" [a little bit astonished], "irritata" [irritated], "smaniosa" [mad] (p. 199), "[s]ento dell'ira" [in a transport of anger], "con ilarità affettata" [with feigned hilarity] (p. 201), "agitata sforzandosi alla calma" [agitated but forcing herself to remain calm], "collerica" [choleric], "riscaldata" [warmed up], "rabbiosa" [furious] (p. 202). Gozzi goes on burlesquing and ridiculing his heroine in this scene, which is one of the most delightful in Moreto's comedy: in the garden where Diana tried to seduce her ostensibly disdainful suitor by singing to him, Teodora is presented as sitting "in una positura di cochettismo" [in a flirtatious posture] (p. 228) with "un'abito da giardiniera, pittoresco, bizzarro, e modestamente lascivo" [a picturesque peasant dress, bizarre and modestly lecherous] (p. 226).

Another important difference between Teodora and Diana consists in the explanations provided by the two playwrights as to why their heroines find the idea of marriage so intolerable. In Moreto's version, it is Diana's extensive study of ancient mythology and philosophy that has led her to a false understanding of love as responsible for all the world's troubles,[18] and to her resultant challenging of the social order.[19] Moreto, however, does not condemn the learned woman as such, but rather his heroine's misinterpretation of the function of knowledge, and intellectual activity disconnected from real life. Indeed, Polilla's use of antiquated and Macaronic Latin indicates the death of the classical learning which Diana cherishes.[20]

Gozzi modernises the sources from which Teodora's convictions are derived: it is not just her reading of ancient fiction, but especially her encounter with modern French Enlightenment philosophy that has made the princess an "illuminata",

---

18 Moreto, *El desdén, con el desdén*, vv. 440–450, vv. 824–827, vv. 828–884.
19 Frank P. Casa, "Diana's Challenge in *El desdén con el desdén*," *Romanistisches Jahrbuch* 23 (2010), pp. 307–318, pp. 317 f.
20 Janet B. Norden, "Moreto's Polilla and the Spirit of Carnival," *Hispania* 68.2 (1985), pp. 236–241, p. 239.

the enlightened one ("GIANNETTO: La ga la vovana de esser filosofa; la vol renderese particular con dei novi sistemi; la vol superar tutti i talenti del secolo" [GIAN.: She has the will to be a philosopher; she wants to be unique, conversant with new systems, she wants to surpass all the talents of the century] (p. 157); "TEODORA: Secol felice, illuminate menti / Voi l'uom studiaste, e a me la traccia apriste / Della scienza al ver [...]"; [TEOD.: Happy age, enlightened minds, / you studied man and opened for me the way / of true science] (pp. 176–177)). However, the validity of Enlightenment thought is likewise questioned through the character of Giannetto, Gozzi's spokesperson, who also ironically calls himself a philosopher, although insisting on the practical aspect of his wisdom: "GIAN.: Mi no go letture, nè studio, ma spero de esser più filosofo della Principessa Teodora. Studio i caratteri, osservo le cause, e i effetti, che le produse sui anemi, e cavo delle dottissime conseguenze" [GIAN.: I do not read nor do I study, but I hope to be more of a philosopher than the princess Teodora. I study the characters, I observe the causes and the effects that they produce on the human soul, and deduce the most intellectual consequences] (p. 158).

Over the course of the play, Giannetto argues that Donna Teodora's philosophical principles exhibit a dangerous rhetorical emptiness, or at least an inability to connect words with concrete human experiences. The character of Teodora thus incarnates all the Enlightenment ideas that the playwright himself criticised throughout his entire theatrical production: the spirit of tolerance, freedom of discussion and argument, the desire to overcome traditional socio-economical values, and the ungrounded abstraction of the *philosophes*' system of reasoning.[21] Donna Teodora's refusal to marry can also be seen in this light, since it undermines the structure of the patriarchal family and dissolves established hierarchies, and can be considered as Gozzi's counter-Enlightenment critique of the *philosophes*, who cared little about politics, society or any issue of national importance.

Moreover, whereas Moreto allows his protagonists to argue their cases (indeed, Diana and Carlos spend most of their time challenging each other's positions on the questions of love, gratitude and free will),[22] Gozzi's Donna Teodora is repeatedly attacked and ridiculed by the other characters, who blame her enlightened

---

21 On the anti-*philosophe* discourse in Europe, see Darrin M. McMahon, *Enemies of the Enlightenment: The French Counter-Enlightenment and the Making of Modernity* (Oxford: Oxford University Press, 2001), esp. pp. 189–201.

22 Frank Casa ("Diana's Challenge," p. 308) has pointed out that a primary element of Moreto's dramatic technique consists in setting off two or more characters to confront each other. Already the title, *Desdén con el desdén*, hints at the existence of two equal forces destined to mutual annihilation in order to allow a positive force of love to emerge.

education for the princess's views. Her lady-in-waiting exclaims that she is "matta, è matta, è matta" [mad, mad and mad] (p. 178), suggesting that Enlightenment philosophy is itself tantamount to madness. Teodora's father, Don Riccardo, allows her to do as she pleases, but he too sees her rejection of marriage as a manifestation of insanity ("RIC.: Avrai delle ragion fondate, e forti / Per difendere in te quell'avversione, / Che follia sembra in ver"; [RIC.: You have your reasons, valid and strong, / To defend your aversion (towards marriage), / which in reality seems to be a madness] (p. 174)), while Giannetto calls the princess a "fanatica" [fanatic] (p. 159).

This radical departure from the Spanish source makes one suspect that Gozzi may have had very personal reasons for this denigration and mockery of Enlightenment principles, for which Teodora serves as a mouthpiece. The antagonistic and militant character of Gozzi's literary production came from a lifelong habit of contesting and countering other authors' work and lent itself well to his self-posturing. Indeed, his *Fiabe teatrali* originated from debates on the reform of the comic theatre and provided Gozzi with a potent weapon to wage war against his rival playwrights, Carlo Goldoni (1707–1793) and Pietro Chiari (1712–1785), whom he saw as guilty of transforming everyday life into material for the stage. When *La Principessa filosofa* was performed in 1772, both of Gozzi's enemies had already left Venice. However, according to the playwright, the political and cultural life of the city was no less under threat from numerous "impostors" who were invading the Venetian stage with translations from French bourgeois drama.[23] One of them, who also happened to be a woman, was especially responsible for spreading dangerous Enlightenment ideas in Italy through her productions of French didactic drama. Gozzi's new enemy was Elisabetta Caminer Turra (1751–1796), and it is certainly no coincidence that *La Principessa filosofa* was originally staged precisely at the moment when the first volume of Caminer's *Composizioni teatrali moderne* (1772–1774), a compilation of her adaptations from French theatre, appeared in a printed edition.

To summarise the points I have made thus far: the main differences between Gozzi's play and its source consist first of all in the significant alteration of Moreto's ideological message, which is particularly evident in the portrayal of the female protagonist. While Moreto's play is centred on the right and wrong ways of understanding philosophy and applying it to everyday life, Gozzi's *teatro spagnolesco* provided the playwright with a space where he could self-consciously reflect on contemporary trends in the literary field and counteract the "pernicious" influence of Enlightenment ideas.

---

[23] On the anti-French function of Gozzi's adaptations from Golden Age Spanish theatre and their counter-Enlightenment message, see Gozzi, *La più lunga lettera di risposta*, pp. 9, 34, 45, 54.

Secondly, the difference between the Spanish source text and its Italian adaptation stems from the construction of the *dramatis personae*. As I pointed out, the transformation of the *gracioso* into the figure of "Veneziano faceto" [funny Venetian fellow][24] Giannetto clearly shows the adaptation of the Spanish play to the tastes of Venetian audiences. Moreover, whereas Moreto's delightful comedy is distinguished by the psychological finesse with which the lovers' relationships are portrayed, Gozzi tends to extreme psychological simplification of his protagonists. His disdainful princess of Barcelona and her suitor represent another variant of the Chinese princess Turandot and her lover Calaf, whereas Giannetto is, if not exactly the *commedia dell'arte* mask of Pantalone, then a modernised version of him. The simplification of characters is also evident in the secondary figures of Cesare's rivals, who appear ridiculous since they come to Barcelona not in search of love, nor to conquer the princess, but because of a frivolous desire to court women (p. 154). Overall, the simplification of the characters' psychology combined with the story of disturbed social order and the final re-establishment of balance made of Gozzi's adaptation a reproduction of his theatrical fables in another guise.

This raises another important question, namely how to explain the immediate and tremendous success that Gozzi's comedy enjoyed,[25] considering, on the one hand, its extremely polemical character and the easily recognisable targets of his satire, and, on the other hand, the fact that the playwright resorted to the Spanish material precisely out of the necessity to refurbish his repertoire based on the marvellous, whose novelty had worn off and whose popularity had declined.

Author's Pen, Actor's Voice

One possible explanation for the play's success is that Gozzi was working not only with the source text, but he was also tailoring the *dramatis personae* to the abilities of his acting troupe. For example, the homonymy of the play's protagonist and the actress who played her, Teodora Ricci (1750–ca. 1806), suggest that the playwright is sincere when he claims in his memoirs that he studied and probed the minds of his performers while constructing every single role in his "poetic caprices":

---

24 Gozzi, Preface to *La Principessa filosofa*, p. 148.
25 Ibid., p. 147: "Egli ha cagionato un'irruzion favorevole del Pubblico, e si volle replicato a furore diciotto sere" [(The play) caused an auspicious stir among the audience, and was repeated with immense success eighteen times].

> [...] studiai, e penetrai filosoficamente tanto bene gli spiriti, e i caratteri de' miei soldati, che *tutte le parti da me scritte* ne' miei capriccj poetici teatrali, composte con la mira all'anima dei miei personaggi e a quelli addossate, erano esposte sul Teatro per modo che sembrava che uscissero da' loro proprj cuori naturalmente, e per ciò piacevano doppiamente.[26]
>
> [I studied and grasped philosophically the spirits and the characters of my soldiers so well that I composed all the parts in my poetic theatrical caprices with the aim of fitting them to the souls of my actors. Indeed, once presented in the theatre, these parts seemed to come so naturally from their hearts that they were doubly pleasing to the public.]

Indeed, if we compare the behaviour of Donna Teodora with the description of Ricci that Gozzi provides in his memoirs, the female protagonist seems to mirror the neurasthenic and impetuous temperament of the actress who, in her later years, suffered from a disease of the nerves and died in a mental hospital:

> Impetuosa e fervida di temperamento, e ambiziosa per se medesima come un Lucifero, ella fremeva, piangeva, entrava nel letto colla febbre leonina, bestemmiava il momento in cui aveva accettato di entrare nella Compagnia del Sacchi, e di venire a Venezia. [...] Fu allora che, avendo conosciuto il di lei carattere, composi il mio Dramma della *Principessa Filosofa* per formarle una parte che stesse bene al suo dosso.[27]
>
> [Of fervid and impetuous disposition, and as ambitious as a Lucifer, she trembled, cried and went to bed with a leonine fever, cursing the moment she had agreed to enter the Sacchi company and come to Venice. It was then that, having come to understand her character, I wrote my play, *The Princess Philosopher*, in order to compose for her the role that would suit her well.]

It is thus highly probable that the success of the play and of the performer—who after the first performance immediately attained the status of la "stella più splendente tra le Comiche" [the most resplendent star among comic actresses], "una Attrice inarrivabile nella bravura"[28] [an actress unsurpassable in her skills]—was due largely to the fortunate consonance between the character and the actress, who hurled herself into the emotionally charged passages, with which she identified.

It is also no coincidence that Gozzi, the fierce defender of improvised comedy, chose not to make use of the *commedia dell'arte* stock characters ("[v]olli da questo Dramma lontane le nostre maschere"), nor that Giannetto is the only figure who somehow resembles the type of Pantalone. The playwright decided to modernise this mask character, turning him into the figure of "Veneziano faceto," because of the actor, Giambattista Rotti, a relatively recent arrival in Sacchi's company. Rotti joined the troupe in 1769, on his return from Vienna, where he had been employed as a copyist of Metastasio and had performed the Goldonian repertoire. Thus,

---

26 Gozzi, *Memorie inutili*, part 2, chap. 1, vol. 2, p. 420; my italics.
27 Ibid., part 2, chap. 9, vol. 2, p. 462.
28 Ibid., part 2, chap. 10, vol. 2, p. 466.

Gozzi's decision to eliminate the masks was also guided by the necessity to adapt the role to the actor, who brought an abundance of Goldonian characterisation to his performances in the troupe. It is also worth mentioning that, after his return to Italy, Rotti translated Beaumarchais's *Les deux amis, ou Le négociant de Lyon*.

Such tailoring of the *dramatis personae* to the performers' individual skills and previous experiences is also evident in the parts of Donna Teodora's suitors, Don Gastone and Don Alfonso, which were entrusted to the actors Luigi Benedetti and Francesco Bartoli. Both specialised in the role of the "second lover," but they were both also translators and dramatists. Indeed, Benetti distinguished himself with his excellent performance in the role of Milord Bonfil in Goldoni's *Pamela* and with his co-translation into Italian (with Antonio Sacchi) of the Spanish comedy, *Offender colla finezza* by Girolamo Viglayzan.[29] Francesco Bartoli, Teodora Ricci's husband, composed five comedies and tragi-comedies, which were regularly staged by the Sacchi troupe, and in 1773, at the request of the *capocomico*, he adapted *Il Finto Muto, ovvero il Mezzano de' proprj affronti*[30] from the Spanish original. Bartoli also authored *Le Notizie istoriche de' comici italiani* (1782), the work that for the first time placed actors rather than playwrights at the centre of attention, and seeks to acknowledge their "diritto di essere considerati persone di spirito per il magistero della loro arte, e di avere qualche luogo fra i letterati, come autori di commedie e tragedie" [their right to be considered people of intellect for the mastery of their art and to have a place among the men of letters as the authors of comedies and tragedies].[31] Bartoli offers a sincere and reliable description of the environment of the comic actors, and also provides the following portrait of Sacchi, the director of Gozzi's troupe:

> Non è il Sacco solamente un Comico materiale, ma è d'un ingegno non spoglio di cognizioni, specialmente intorno alla Storia Universale, mostrandosi nelle conversazioni di dotte persone illuminato, ed erudito; oltre di ciò egli possiede la lingua Francese, e la Spagnola, e nelle occasioni di dover mettere in Scena qualche nuova rappresentazione, o Comica, o Tragica che sia, sa molto bene istruire i suoi Comici, insegnando ad essi il vero modo di eseguire con puntualità, ed accuratezza.[32]

---

29 Biblioteca Nazionale Marciana di Venezia, Fondo Gozzi, 9.10, c. 9r; see also Giulietta Bazoli, "La vita spettacolare dei testi," in: Gutiérrez Carou, ed., *Metamorfosi drammaturgiche*, pp. 129–145, p. 136.
30 Bazoli, *L'orditura e la truppa: Le Fiabe di Carlo Gozzi tra scrittoio e palcoscenico* (Padova: Il Poligrafo, 2012), p. 255.
31 Quoted in Rosalba Milan, *Francesco Bartoli: Arte e Teatro nell'Italia del Settecento* (Rovigo: Minelliana, 1990), p. 57.
32 Francesco Bartoli, *Notizie istoriche de' Comici italiani intorno all'anno MDC fino a' giorni presenti: Opera ricercata, raccolta, ed estesa da Francesco Bartoli bolognese accademico d'onore clementino*, 2 vols. (Padova: Conzatti, 1782), vol. 2, p. 148.

[Not only is Sacchi a comedian but he also has a mind not entirely stripped of knowledge, especially on the topic of Universal History, and in conversations with learned people, he shows himself to be well-educated and erudite. Moreover, he masters the French language and the Spanish, and on occasions when he has to stage a new performance, whether comic or tragic, he knows very well how to instruct his comic actors, teaching them the true way of punctual and accurate execution.]

Bartoli's description thus shows how far removed the *capocomico* was from the cliché of the ignorant director of the comic troupe, solely motivated by financial considerations. Indeed, it was Sacchi who, aware of the necessity to meet the demands of an insatiable theatrical market, brought the works of Golden-Age Spanish drama to Gozzi's attention, as the playwright himself points out in his memoirs: "[i]l Sacchi mi mandava tratto tratto de' fasci di quelle strane, e mostruose opere di quel Teatro; la maggior parte erano da me scartate, e rifiutate" [Sacchi sent me one bundle after another of those strange and monstrous works of that Spanish theatre; I rejected or discarded most of them].[33] In claiming for himself the merit of accepting or refusing the scripts, the playwright is skirting the fact that the idea of revamping the company's repertoire through the Spanish adaptations was as much Sacchi's as his own. Indeed, Bartoli's accounts, as well as the profiles of the actors engaged in the production of *La Principessa filosofa*, show that their role in the choice of repertoire and in the success of the productions was much more decisive than Gozzi was willing to acknowledge. These profiles also testify to the emergence of the new figures of the comic actor and the *capocomico*, who were well-educated and highly professional, attentive to the smallest details of what would appear on stage.

"Comica Famigliola": Actors-Translators-Creators

The mid-eighteenth-century theatre industry was thus a collective product of joint authorship by playwrights and actors, infinitely adaptable to both the tastes of the public and the abilities of theatre troupes. In fact, for Bartoli, Italian theatre practice was characterised by this intense collaboration between dramatists and actors, which ultimately generated the audience's interest in theatrical performances. In his correspondence with Giuseppe Baretti, Gozzi himself explains (and complains) that "[s]e nel cartello d'invito esposto da questa Truppa, non si leggono i nomi loro [...], sono perduti tosto due terzi de' concorrenti al loro

---

33 Gozzi, *Memorie inutili*, part 2, chap. 20, vol. 2, p. 542.

Teatro"[34] [if one does not see their names on the playbill (...), two thirds of theatre-goers are irretrievably lost].

Yet, on the many pages of his memoirs and theoretical works dealing with the genesis and poetics of his theatre,[35] Gozzi robs his actors of any description of their artistic profiles and even removes their names.[36] Apart from his portrayal of Teodora Ricci (who was not only Bartoli's wife, but also happened to be the playwright's lover), Gozzi remains silent regarding the specific contribution of his players to Italian and European theatrical culture. Especially symptomatic in this respect is Gozzi's silence concerning Rotti (who brought Goldonian characterisation to Sacchi's company) and the purely caricatural portrait of Bartoli:

> [...] buona persona, e che prima di fare il Comico, aveva fatto il Librajo. Quell'arte aveva lasciato in lui una spezie di fanatismo letterario. Leggeva tutto il giorno, e tutta la notte, e scriveva de' grossi volumi da porre alle stampe, co' quali, diceva egli, d'essere certo di fare un grosso guadagno, e delle investite per sè ed eredi. La sua indefessa, faticosissima sterile applicazione, lo alienava dalle cure domestiche, delle quali lasciava il peso, e la direzione alla Moglie, niente chiedendo per sé, e niente badando alle sue scarpe rotte, e alle sue calzette infangate, forse per imitare un filosofo.[37]
>
> [(...) a good man, who before becoming a comic actor, was a book agent. That art left in him a species of literary fanaticism. He read all day and night and wrote big volumes to be submitted to publishers with which—he used to say—he was certain of making a huge profit, and investments for himself and his heirs. His tireless, exhausting and sterile work alienated him from household chores, the burden of which he left to his wife, asking nothing for himself and caring nothing about his broken shoes and his muddy socks, perhaps in order to imitate a philosopher.]

However, not only does Gozzi not acknowledge the merit of his actors as translators, dramatists and practically as his co-authors, but the few mentions of them in his writings are also accompanied by disparaging descriptions of the comic troupe with which the playwright collaborated for more than twenty years:

> Cotesta truppa [...] è composta quasi interamente di stretti parenti a tale, ch'ella si può chiamar più una comica famiglioula, che una comica Truppa. La morigeratezza ne' costumi di questa *brigatella*, la gratitudine, ch'ella sa dimostrare, come si deve credere, a' doni utili,

---

34 Gozzi, *Lettere*, ed. Fabio Soldini, *I giorni* (Venezia: Marsilio, 2004), p. 114.
35 See in particular the *Manifesto* to the Colombani edition (1772), *Il Ragionamento ingenuo e storia sincera dell'origine delle mie dieci Fiabe teatrali* (1772), and *La più lunga lettera di risposta* (1804), the last detailed authorial analysis of Gozzi's theatrical works.
36 In order to find specific information on Francesco Rotti or the *innamorati* Luigi Benedetti and Petronio Zanarini, we have to look at Bartoli's extensive annotations or Goldoni's *Mémoires*.
37 Gozzi, *Memorie inutili*, part 2, chap. 12, vol. 2, p. 478.

> che le vengono fatti, il merito nell'arte sua, le preghiere di soccorsi, la persecuzione, [...] non mi lasciarono fermare il pensiero in tutto di abbandonarla.[38]

> [This troupe (...) consists almost entirely of close relatives, so that it would be more precise to call it a comic family than a comic troupe. However, the moderation in the costumes of this *brigatella*, the gratitude that it duly demonstrates for the useful gifts bestowed on it, the merit in its artistic skills, the insistent prayers for help, the persecution (...) did not allow me to consider abandoning it altogether.]

> Tutto il resto della Compagnia, nel tempo ch'io presi a soccorrerla, ed a prendere prattica con quella, era di vecchi, di vecchie, di figure infelici abili, di personaggi agghiacciati, di ragazzi, e ragazze inesperti.[39]

> [All the rest of the company, during that time when I began to help and hang around them, consisted of old men and women, unhappy figures, appalling characters and inexperienced boys and girls.]

Even more astonishing is that Gozzi's general silence concerning his players and his dismissive descriptions of their inadequate abilities in his memoirs and prefaces are to be found side by side with references to the "friendly assistance" that the playwright generously grants them free of charge.[40] But while Gozzi wants to make it seem as if Sacchi's troupe was languishing in a crisis of ideas after its return from Portugal, in reality it was a company of the first rank in the panorama of European theatre, endowed not just with excellent performers but also with its own creative playwrights.

Self-Promotion, Authorial Agency and the Cultural Net

What conclusions can be drawn from the analysis of the events surrounding the adaptation of Moreto's *Desdén con el desdén* for the Italian stage and the staging of Gozzi's *Principessa filosofa*? First of all, it is apparent that in no other domain is the question of authorial agency as central as it is in the theatre, and nowhere

---

38 Gozzi, Preface to *Zeim, re dei Genj*, in: *Opere edite ed inedite*, vol. 4, pp. 5–17, pp. 6 f.
39 Gozzi, *Memorie inutili*, part 2, chap. 1, vol. 2, p. 417.
40 See Gozzi's *Appendice al* Ragionamento ingenuo, in: Gozzi, *Il ragionamento ingenuo*, ed. Alberto Beniscelli, *Testi della cultura italiana* (Genova: Nolan & Costa, 1983), p. 95: "Il nuovo genere, con cui, dopo il genere fiabesco, immaginai di soccorrere con utilità nel teatro l'italiana truppa comica del Sacchi, lo volli trarre dagli argomenti del teatro spagnolo" [The new genre—which, following the fairy-tale genre, I imagined would be of some utility in the theatre of Sacchi's Italian comic troupe—I wanted to draw from the themes of the Spanish theatre].

is it more problematic. Gozzi's silence on his actors' contribution to the creative process leads one to think that it might be worth revisiting Michel Foucault's influential essay "What is an Author?" but to do so in order to consider the alternative question of "*where* is the author?" and to ask how the conceptualisation of intellectual property for dramatic literature developed differently to the way it did for non-dramatic forms. Whereas the first of these questions is of a more rhetorical nature, I will attempt to answer the second one in my concluding remarks.

The example of Gozzi's *teatro spagnolesco* illustrates two parallel processes that took place in mid-eighteenth-century Venice. On the one hand we witness the professionalisation of actors, and on the other hand the growing preoccupation of playwrights with crafting their own distinctive authorial identity. Gozzi's self-fashioning and self-promotion in the prefaces to his plays and his memoirs serve as a solid illustration of these processes, precisely because, despite his own repeatedly expressed a lack of interest in having his dramatic works printed or in receiving any personal acknowledgement or financial compensation,[41] his paratextual silence on the performing troupe's contribution to the creative process makes it clear that Gozzi was in fact preoccupied with legitimising his dramatic production and with reinforcing his position on the literary Parnassus.

But, if the early modern theatre as a site of textual production was largely incompatible with various strategies of individualisation, and the absence of clearly defined notions of dramatic authorship constituted the norm rather than the exception,[42] what was it that nevertheless led to the emergence of the concepts of intellectual property and authorship in eighteenth-century dramatic

---

[41] For a far-reaching discussion of the rhetorical strategies that Gozzi repeatedly deploys to feign his resistance to having his theatrical works printed and the playwright's paratextual statements about the transposition of plays from the stage to printed form in the Colombani edition, see Anna Scannapieco, *Carlo Gozzi: la scena del libro* (Venezia: Marsilio, 2006).

[42] According to Stephen Orgel, "What is a Text?," *Research Opportunities in Renaissance Drama* 24 (1981), pp. 3–6, "that the authority of a text derives from the author [...] is almost never true" (p. 3) in the case of Renaissance dramatic texts: "A play was a collaborative process, with the author by no means at the centre of the collaboration. The company commissioned the play, usually stipulated the subject, often provided the plot, often parcelled it out, scene by scene, to several playwrights. The text thus produced was a working model, which the company then revised as seemed appropriate. The author had little or no say in these revisions: the text belonged to the company, and the authority represented by the text—I am talking about the *performing* text—is that of the company, the owners, not that of the playwright, the author." (ibid.) See also Anny Guimont, "La comedia en colaboración: recursos escénicos y teatralidad en *Caer para levantar*," *Bulletin of the Comediantes* 49 (1997), pp. 319–336, on collaborative writing in Spanish Golden Age theatre, with specific reference to Moreto's comedies.

literature—which, at least as far as Italy is concerned, can be considered a liminal case for early modern drama?

My answer to this question is that in this period we witness a significant change in the perception and the role of theatre, in that it began to be recognised as a privileged site for social debate and a powerful means of reform. Of course, theatrical performances have always been imbued with transgressive or subversive potential. However, Gozzi's extremely polemical self-posturing, the deployment of his theatrical fables and the Spanish adaptations to counteract the influence of the Enlightenment (and to wage war against those who were disseminating it in the Italian theatre of the day—Carlo Goldoni, Pietro Chiari, Elisabetta Caminer) testifies less to the personal characteristics of the playwright than to the fact that theatre had become a social and cultural tool capable not only of commenting on, but of influencing and changing reality.

To use Gozzi's own words (which are not dissimilar from Diderot's statements on the matter), theatre took the place of the pulpit, becoming "un pergamo [...] più efficace a rovesciare le teste, che non è un pergamo della Chiesa per raddrizzarle" [a Pergamon that is more efficient in turning heads than a pulpit of the church is in straightening them].[43]

Moreover, Gozzi's case also seems to illustrate several points that have to be addressed in order to develop the notion of culture as a dynamic net into a working concept, namely: what is the role of authorial agency in the circulation of forms and artefacts? How does authorial agency, or what Foucault famously termed "the author's function," determine the circulation and the subsequent performances of dramatic texts? Gozzi's reduction of collaborative activity to his sole authorship can be seen as the manifestation of the playwright's determination to control the circulation of his theatrical production. As Foucault states, "[t]he author's name [...] indicates the status of th[e] discourse within a society and a culture"[44] and it is simultaneously used as an anchor for interpreting a text. In other words, the author performs the function of a controlling mechanism, since a discourse that comes equipped with an author's name is not immediately consumed and forgotten.[45] Indeed, if we consider the "Gozzi myth" and the "Gozzi vogue" created by the German Romantics, the Venetian playwright was undoubtedly successful in establishing an enduring artistic reputation. Foucault, however, goes on to claim that authorial agency has a restraining function in "the free circulation, the free manipulation, the free composition, decomposition, and recomposition

---

43 Gozzi, *La più lunga lettera di risposta*, p. 50.
44 Michel Foucault, "What Is an Author?" trans. Josué V. Harari, in: *The Foucault Reader*, ed. Paul Rabinow (New York, NY: Panteon Books, 1984), pp. 101–120, p. 107.
45 Ibid., p. 114.

of fiction."[46] But does this assertion remain valid with regard to texts that are performed? Theatre is a live art and notoriously ephemeral, and the German and Austrian reception of Gozzi's tales and of his Spanish plays, ranging from high-quality productions by gifted directors (such as Friedrich Wilhelm Gotter or Friedrich Ludwig Schröder) to the abrupt decline not in quantity or variety of forms but in the quality of productions,[47] clearly testifies to the fact that the determination of concepts of authorial intellectual property in the mid-eighteenth century did not exercise any controlling influence on the dramatic texts that were modified or even deformed in their subsequent circulation and performance.

Although it is hardly possible to establish the impact and the exact extent of the playwright's agency by examining the production of a single playwright or even a single national culture, the events surrounding the staging of *La Principessa filosofa* and the history of the performances over the centuries of Gozzi's theatrical works in general seem to demonstrate that Foucault's claim concerning the restraining function of the author in the free circulation of artworks within the cultural net does not hold true for theatrical works.

---

46 Ibid., p. 119.
47 Gozzi's plays have been adapted as melodramas, musical plays, operas and operettas. See Hedwig Hoffmann Rusack, *Gozzi in Germany: A Survey of the Rise and Decline of the Gozzi Vogue in Germany and Austria, with Especial Reference to the German Romanticists* (1930; repr. New York, NY: AMS Press, 1966), pp. 56 ff.

Robert Henke
From Augsburg to Edgar: Continental Beggar Books and *King Lear*

Framed by his brother Edmund as an aspiring patricide, Edgar in Shakespeare's *King Lear* suddenly finds himself a fugitive, a wanted man with only a moment to reinvent himself, following Gloucester's orders to bar all seaports and town gates.[1] His speech of auto-transformation works as a transparent, Brechtian assumption of a fictional role that is "*not* this, *but* that" as he deliberately dons his character before our eyes, exposing its artificiality and constructedness, even as, at the end of the speech, he declares the transformation complete:

> EDGAR:
> I heard myself proclaimed,
> And by the happy hollow of a tree
> Escaped the hunt. No port is free, no place
> That guard and most unusual vigilance
> Does not attend my taking. While I may scape
> I will preserve myself, and am bethought
> To take the basest and most poorest shape
> That ever penury in contempt of man
> Brought near to beast. My face I'll grime with filth,
> Blanket my loins, elf all my hair in knots
> And with presented nakedness outface
> The winds and persecutions of the sky.
> The country gives me proof and precedent
> Of Bedlam beggars, who, with roaring voices,
> Strike in their numbed and mortified bare arms
> Pins, wooden pricks, nails, sprigs of rosemary;
> And with this horrible object, from low farms,
> Poor pelting villages, sheepcotes and mills,
> Sometime with lunatic bans, sometime with prayers,
> Enforce their charity. Poor Turlygod, poor Tom,
> That's something yet: Edgar I nothing am.[2]

Edgar resolves to perform for his life, and the performance becomes all the more telling because his "fictional" role of mad, vagabond beggar draws significantly from the actual position in which he suddenly finds himself: homeless, and thus

---

[1] William Shakespeare, *King Lear* [c. 1605–1606], ed. Reginald A. Foakes, The Arden Shakespeare, 3rd Series (London: Thomson Learning, 1997), 2.1.80.
[2] 2.2.172–192.

living under the elements and at the mercy of charity; exiled; persecuted, and under intense surveillance. The role of Poor Tom is short on the kind of ruse and guile common to the English rogue books and long on sheer, naked (almost literally) performance: one vulnerable person beseeching another with the simple, but total art of the body and its theatrical projections and prostheses, which include make-up (griming his face with mud), costume (the semi-nakedness of a loin cloth), voice ("roaring voices," "lunatic bans," "prayers") and gesture ("[s]trike in their numbed and mortified bare arms"). Creating a radically "poor theatre" out of practically nothing, Edgar shifts with nothing more and nothing less than what lies before him in his dispossessed state. The self-mutilation that Edgar either announces he will perform, or enacts directly before us during the speech, when coupled with his later chaotic but coherent narrative of sin, devil possession and penance, can be productively understood in the context of late medieval religious, penitential discourse as it was articulated by the figure of the vagabond beggar in various fourteenth- to sixteenth-century continental texts. Three salient aspects of Poor Tom's performance should be emphasised: 1) the elementally corporeal, bare nature of his performance—a minimalist virtuosity and asceticism worthy of Jerzy Grotowski's "holy" actor; 2) the rhetorical nature of a performance designed to "[e]nforce [...] charity"—one that if governed by trickery, operates by marshalling the full range of vocal and bodily rhetorical resources towards the end of persuading for charity; 3) the pervasively religious aura of the figure and the performance: an unsettling mixture of devil haunting, penitence, curse ("lunatic bans") and blessing ("prayers").

Critics have long pointed to two English rogue books, John Awdeley's 1561 *The Fraternity of Vagabonds* and Thomas Harman's 1566 *A Caveat for Common Cursitors*, as possible sources for Edgar's particular type, the "Abraham Man," who has left or escaped from Bethlem, or "Bedlam" Hospital: London's hospital for the mentally ill. Calling himself "Poor Tom," according to Awdeley's extremely brief text, the Abraham Man "feigneth himself mad," and "walketh bare-armed and bare-legged"[3] or, as Edgar puts it, with "presented nakedness" and a mere blanket cast over his loins. For Harman, the swindler's repertoire consists of an oral-formulaic collection of terrible tales about how he has been beaten in Bedlam or some prison, just as Poor Tom obscurely alludes to having

---

3 Good editions of both Awdeley's and Harman's texts may be found in Arthur F. Kinney, ed., *Rogues, Vagabonds, and Sturdy Beggars: A New Gallery of Tudor and Early Stuart Rogue Literature* (Barre, MA: Imprint Society, 1973), pp. 91–101 (*The Fraternity of Vagabonds*); pp. 109–153 (*A Caveat for Common Cursitors, Vulgarly Called Vagabonds*). The quotation is from Kinney, ed., *Rogues, Vagabonds, and Sturdy Beggars*, p. 91.

been whipped, "stocked, punished and imprisoned."⁴ Harman's Abraham Man, like Poor Tom who haunts "low farms, / [p]oor pelting villages, sheepcotes and mills," is a specifically *rural* character, whose own dispossession reflects the very poverty of the "pelting" countryside in this period of agricultural calamity as analysed by Marx. (And compared to almost all other early modern English dramatists, whose background was predominantly urban, the Stratford-raised Shakespeare might have actually seen some of these rural types.) Just as Edgar, as a "horrible object," resolves to "[e]nforce [...] charity," the Abraham Man accosts farmers' houses and demands succour of its terrified inhabitants with, in Harman's words, "fierce countenance."⁵

But despite these salient points of contact with Shakespeare's Poor Tom, the English texts somewhat miss the mark in their emphasis on the Abraham Man's ruse and craft: a quality shared by almost all of the English frauds. So Harman deems a certain Stradling (his exhibit A for the Abraham Man) to be "the craftiest and most dissemblingest Knave," who is capable "with his tongue and usage to deceive and abuse the wisest man that is."⁶ In claiming that the Abraham Man can "pick and steal, as the upright man or Rogue,"⁷ Harman tends to collapse his designated subject into the general, overriding archetype of the dissembling rogue. Harman's rogues are almost infinitely resourceful (except when they are being unmasked by the author himself or another authority), but in body, voice, gait, gesture, make-up and costume they are less performatively virtuosic than the continental beggars of the catalogues. Stephen Greenblatt, of course, relates Poor Tom's verve to the performative bravado of contemporary exorcists, as anatomised by Samuel Harsnett in his 1603 *A Declaration of Egregious Popish Impostures*: a long-acknowledged source for the names of the devils Edgar claims to be possessing him.⁸ Both kinds of texts aim to debunk fraud: Harman's rogues bamboozle their victims regardless of religious confession (and with almost no reference to religious aura or rhetoric); Harnett sharply divides the world between credulous Catholics naïve enough to be taken in by the hocus-pocus incantations of the exorcist and the grotesque gyrations of the possessed; and wily Protestants shrewd enough to see through the exorcist's cheap tricks. But both the Harman and Harsnett texts pose the question of belief or disbelief more starkly, I would

---

4 Shakespeare, *King Lear*, 3.4.130 f. For Harman on the "Abraham Man," see Kinney, ed., *Rogues, Vagabonds, and Sturdy Beggars*, pp. 127 f.
5 P. 127.
6 P. 128.
7 P. 127.
8 Stephen Greenblatt, *Shakespearean Negotiations: The Circulation of Social Energy in Renaissance England* (Berkeley: University of California Press, 1988), pp. 94–128.

propose, than is appropriate for Poor Tom, who conjures up an intermediate field of performance and reception between belief and doubt, in which the truly skeptical position might be to acknowledge that the ostensive charlatan, might, after all, be telling the truth.

The English rogue books, in fact, appear to derive from a German tradition. Sebastian Brant's 1494 *Das Narrenschiff*, published in the same city as the *Basler Betrügnisse* (Basle) and translated into English by Alexander Barclay in 1509, describes in chapter 63 manifold types of beggars surely taken from other German texts, but cast in an even harsher and more censorial tone: false miracle mongers, relic sellers, cripples, epileptics and others. Bronisław Geremek argues that Robert Copland's *Highway to the Spital-House* (c. 1535–1536), which describes both "deserving" and "undeserving" types of the poor lodging in a hospice, was directly influenced by Barclay's translation of Brant's text.[9] It may have been the case that the English writers took the idea of beggar types from *Das Narrenschiff* and (for those who could read German) from one of the myriad and frequently reprinted versions of the 1509/10 *Liber Vagatorum* or other German texts. They may well have fused the beggar idea with the notion of the vagabond-rogue that they could have absorbed from *Till Eulenspiegel*, translated into English in 1548, and that later in the sixteenth century they would have received from translated Spanish picaresque novels. The rogue tended to eclipse the beggar.

In fact these and other German texts, and a 1484–1486 Latin manuscript from Italy, capture the particular melding of religious enchantment and disenchantment operative in Poor Tom better than the almost completely a-religious and altogether debunking English texts. If Shakespeare, according to Debora Shuger, may draw on neo-medieval notions of economic redistribution for King Lear's "Poor naked wretches" speech, the idea of the beggar informing Poor Tom may be more cognate with this late medieval, continental discourse than it is with the aggressive Protestant texts of Harman and others.[10]

To be sure, these late medieval/early modern German and Latin texts scarcely aim to hallow their subjects, deemed frauds meriting both exposure and punishment. But they emerge from continental geographical and temporal contexts in which the public might just as easily believe as disbelieve the itinerant beggar posing as (or actually being?) a hermit, priest, friar, relic-seller, indulgence monger, baptised Jew, survivor of religious persecution or tormented soul

---

9 Bronisław Geremek, *Les fils de Caïn: L'image des pauvres et des vagabonds dans la littérature européenne du XVe au XVIIe siècle*, trans. Joanna Arnold-Moricet et al. (Paris: Flammarion, 1991), p. 68.
10 See Debora K. Shuger, "Subversive Fathers and Suffering Subjects: Shakespeare and Christianity," in: Donna B. Hamilton and Richard Strier, edd., *Religion, Literature, and Politics in Post-Reformation England, 1540–1688* (Cambridge: Cambridge University Press, 1996), pp. 46–69.

practicing penance and seeking redemption. There is a fascination, unlike anything invoked by the English texts, with both the performative aura of the beggars and their capacity to elicit feelings ranging from credence and compassion to disgust and disbelief. Tellingly, as Lee Palmer Wandel notes in a detailed iconographical study, the many title-pages fronting the frequently recycled *Liber Vagatorum* present beggars without editorial intervention, representing them as genuinely poor and disabled as they solicited alms.[11] The images used for the *Liber Vagatorum* reflect a general southern German tendency to depict a greater ethical range (i.e., the subjects are not all undeserving frauds) in the visual field relative to the textual arena: the Nuremberg artist Barthel Beham in 1524 published a broadsheet depicting different kinds of beggars, some of which are represented as undeserving of their fates.[12] The author of the *Liber Vagatorum*, and Martin Luther in a preface written for a 1528 edition of the text, declare their own vulnerability; they have themselves been victims of these charismatic charlatans, whose performances have evidently exercised a peculiar power. If Shakespeare, in *As You Like It*, can take an easy target of Protestant skepticism such as the hermit—excoriated in Spenser's *Faerie Queene* as a cunning fraud—and render him a plausible holy man, then he might also reverse, or at least complicate the valence of vagabond beggars who evoked the religious fears and hopes of their publics.

The *Liber Vagatorum* derives from a long line of German beggar catalogues that actually have their origins not in literature, but in municipal registers. They arise at precisely the same time (the fourteenth century) and place (southern Germany) where the first early modern European poor laws were devised. What unites these early German texts, their development and flowering in Italy and Germany, and the late English catalogues of Awdeley and Harman, is the persistent, indeed obsessive impulse to name, typify and categorise beggars and vagabonds. Faced, for the first time, with numbers of poor so great that one could not possibly know each of their names, the problem of identification became paramount—and it was easier to think in terms of categories than individuals. If, following the new poor laws, one was compelled to evict itinerant beggars out of the city back into the devastated countryside to a fate of probable starvation, it was easier if you believed these individuals were evil imposters wrongly diverting the scarce resources of charity from the deserving, and local poor. To the terrifying prospect of squadrons of beggars invading European cities beginning in the late

---

11 Lee Palmer Wandel, *Always Among Us: Images of the Poor in Zwingli's Zurich* (Cambridge: Cambridge University Press, 1990), p. 103.
12 Pp. 101–104.

fifteenth century, the beggar books satisfied a kind of blessed rage for order: the comfort of categorising and rationalising the dizzying and threatening multitude.

Such an account, admittedly psychological and speculative, is not incongruent with Geremek's more historical and discursive explanation: "This procedure is the effect of the method of medieval teaching, which relies upon the principle of classifying by means of enumeration."[13] The very method of analysis into disparate categories, with talismanic names distinguishing one indigent group from another, thus derives for Geremek from figures such as the Carolingian scholar Alcuin. As with medieval bestiaries, one comes to know the unknown through the known. Still, Geremek, and other historians of poverty such as Brian Pullan who have addressed this issue,[14] insist that the beggar catalogues are hardly written out of whole cloth, concluding that "there is no doubt that [...] [such judiciary documentation] is based on real facts."[15] For all their evident literary verve, the clerks at Augsburg and Basle were responding to *something*. The insistent and practical need to distinguish between two fundamental groups of beggars—those deserving and those undeserving of charity—could have easily been expanded to an extension and multiplication of categories beyond the practical binary one.

Many details of the beggar catalogues simply have the ring of truth. They describe wretched performers exploiting both the "aura" and the simple convenience of liminal spaces around churches, such as doors and thresholds, in ways that match archival documents. The large number of religious frauds detailed in the continental books (again, at variance with the English rogue catalogues) reflects the pervasive presence, especially in fourteenth, fifteenth and early sixteenth centuries, of itinerant religious who either were fraudulent or easily gave off the appearance of so being, and thus came under attack from reformers such as Martin Luther. Additionally, they evoke a world, also congruent with archival documents, in which a very thin line obtained between itinerant entertainers (musicians, acrobats, storytellers, actors) and vagabond beggars. What most plausibly matches the beggar catalogues and real life, however, is that the need for identity transformation and fictional role playing—what Edgar experiences in the "happy hollow of a tree"—appears to be all but structured into the poor laws. In Milan, as Giovanni Liva has demonstrated, special attention was devoted to identifying and persecuting "foreigners" in liminal places, such as seaports, city

---

[13] Geremek, *Les fils de Caïn*, p. 75.
[14] Brian Pullan, "Poveri, mendicanti e vagabondi (secoli XIV–XVII)," in: *Storia d'Italia: Annali*, vol. 1: *Dal feudalesimo al capitalismo*, edd. Ruggiero Romano and Corrado Vivanti (Torino: Einaudi, 1978), pp. 981–1047, p. 1013.
[15] Geremek, *Les fils de Caïn*, p. 77. ("[I]l ne fait pas de doute [...] qu'elle [la documentation judiciaire] repose sur des faits reels.")

entrances, boats travelling near borders and inns. Fiction, however, provided a way out for the starving beggar with his wits still about him. The controls, argues Liva, "ignored the fact that it was very easy [...] to give a false name," whence a late seventeenth-century edict fining any foreigner who had tricked the authorities by "altering their declarations of first and last name, country or the place from where they came."[16] Itinerant improvisation, taking on various roles and identities in order to survive to the next day, exaggerating, distilling, reversing and transforming the raw facts: this was the stuff of existence as the disciplinary screws of the authorities tightened around the poor. The life of the street and the art of the disciplining beggar books may have worked in mutually reinforcing ways. Illiterate beggars were clearly not reading the new literature, but those involved in the discourse and practice of enforcement may have been, and actual beggars could have played into the discursive categories prepared for them.

Early German Texts

In the 1342 Augsburg municipal register account of five fraudulent beggar types, four out of the five trade on specifically *religious* motifs, all featuring virtuosic one-on-one performance techniques rather than the criminal networking characteristic of the English rogue books and German and Spanish picaresque novels. Anticipating a category from Teseo Pini's *Speculum Cerretanorum*, the *Hürlentzer* posed as Jews baptised—presumably in a serial fashion—to Christianity. The *Clainnier*, or false pilgrims, cleverly exploit the liminal spaces bordering churches, as do several of the types from *Liber Vagatorum*. The *Grentzier*, the only one of the five types not given an explicitly religious function, feign sickness. The *Münser* pose as Capuchin monks and the self-flagellating *Serpner*, as penitents.[17] In just a year, the Augsburg categories expand to nine, broadening the range of penitential performance techniques. Included in the added categories are the *Fopperin*, "die nement sich unsinne an"[18] [who call themselves mad]. Another category of

---

16 Giovanni Liva, "Il controllo e la repressione degli 'oziosi e vagabondi': La legislazione in età spagnola," in: Danilo Zardin, ed. *La città e i poveri: Milano e le terre lombarde dal Rinascimento all'età spagnola* (Milano: Jaca Book, 1995), pp. 291–332, p. 311.
17 Friedrich Kluge, *Rotwelsch: Quellen und Wortschatz der Gaunersprache und der verwandten Geheimsprachen* (Strasbourg: Karl S. Trübner, 1901), p. 1; Geremek, *Les fils de Caïn*, p. 78. Kluge provides editions of the Augsburg registers, *Die Basler Betrügnisse der Gyler* and several other texts preceding the *Liber Vagatorum*.
18 Kluge, *Rotwelsch*, p. 2.

pilgrims, the *Mümser*, drag chains; the *Sinweger* repent having killed their family relatives; and the *Spanvelder* mutilate their legs in order to simulate wounds.[19]

Apart from a 1350 Breslau document that catalogues eleven types of petty criminals, and a 1381 municipal register in Constance that provides the names (or nicknames) and salient characteristics of notorious brigands,[20] the next major German text, and quite possibly the chief textual antecedent of the c. 1509 *Liber Vagatorum*, is an important fifteenth-century report from Basle. Like the Augsburg catalogues, *Die Basler Betrügnisse der Gyler* issues from municipal registers—texts with an avowedly documentary aim. According to Friedrich Kluge, three nearly identical copies of the text survive: one from a book of municipal depositions dating 1411–1463 (and probably written between 1430 and 1444); the second as a text added to a judicial statute of 1457; and the third as an insertion of the Basle chronicle of Johann Knebel in 1479.[21] The multiplicity of texts, as Bronisław Geremek argues, suggests the wide interest and dissemination of this particular text and those like it.[22] As well as furnishing a likely source of the *Liber Vagatorum*, the *Basler Betrügnisse* may well explain the transmission from Germany to Italy of the beggar catalogue genre. Teseo Pini, the Italian vicar and author of the late fifteenth-century *Speculum Cerretanorum*, served under Bishop Girolamo Santucci (1427–1494), who was sent by Pope Sixtus IV to Germany, where he stayed until 1478. As Piero Camporesi argues, "[it] is very probable [...] that in one of the returning legate's chests also travelled the manuscript of *Die Basler Betrügnisse der Gyler*, which constituted the nucleus of the *Liber Vagatorum*: pages that were not turned in vain" by Santucci.[23]

The *Basler Betrügnisse*, consisting of twenty-six to thirty categories depending on the version, constitutes a major expansion of the genre, reprising a few of the Augsburg types but adding many more, versions of which will be recycled in the *Liber Vagatorum* (and a few in the *Speculum Cerretanorum*).[24] (Generally, types often resurface in these texts under altered or altogether different names.) Several categories (*Grantener, Sweiger, Valkentreiger, Brasseln*) practice the kind of self-mutilation and the application of grotesque substances to the body that we have observed, and which is cognate with Poor Tom's striking of his "numbed and

---

19 Ibid.; Geremek, *Les fils de Caïn*, pp. 78 f.
20 Kluge, *Rotwelsch*, pp. 2 f.; Geremek, *Les fils de Caïn*, pp. 79 f.
21 Kluge, *Rotwelsch*, p. 9.
22 Geremek, *Les fils de Caïn*, p. 80.
23 Piero Camporesi, "Introduzione," in: Camporesi, ed., *Il libro dei vagabondi: Lo* Speculum Cerretanorum *di Teseo Pini,* Il vagabondo *di Rafaele Frianoro e altri testi di 'furfanteria'* (Torino: Einaudi, 1973), pp. IX–CLXXV, p. CLX.
24 Kluge, *Rotwelsch*, pp. 8–16; Geremek, *Les fils de Caïn*, pp. 80–84.

mortified bare arms" with various sharp objects. As in all the continental texts, much attention is given to religious fraud: the converted Jew (*Vermerin*, following the *Hürlentzer* of the Augsburg registers), the relic seller (*Theweser*), the pilgrim (*Klamerierer*, following Augsburg), the false priest (*Galatten*) and others. Anticipating a somewhat fuller development in the *Liber Vagatorum*, the *Spanfelder* seem particularly apposite to Poor Tom: arriving into a town, they deposit their clothes, kneel nakedly in front of churches and shake with cold and utter fearful cries. The *Krochere*, who also prostrate themselves naked before churches, clarify the penitential nature that is merely implicit in many of the other types: desiring to expiate their sins they sit naked in front of a church and beseech those passing by to whip them. It is the *Vopper* (expanding from the *Fopperin* of the 1343 Augsburg register), however, who most strikingly evoke Poor Tom, conjuring a spectacle like nothing to be found in the English texts. The *Vopper* are divided into two types: the first tear apart their garments. The second, the *Vopper, die da ditzent*, claim that they have been possessed by a demonic spirit, and only an offering on behalf of a saint will deliver them.[25] The overall tone of the *Basler Betrügnisse* is relentlessly harsh and censorial, and no accompanying visual imagery softens the blow, but, in its elaboration of the performative techniques and narratives of the types well beyond what is indicated in the Augsburg entries, it points the way to the *Liber Vagatorum*.

Liber Vagatorum

The *Liber Vagatorum: Der Betler Orden* was a seminal text, published in countless editions, under three different titles, from 1509 to 1755.[26] In this German text, the beggar catalogue reaches its mature form, and it is hard to imagine cosmopolitan English writers not being aware of it. Martin Luther, who actively advocated for the reformation of poor relief along with his campaign against the mendicant orders, wrote a preface to a 1528 edition—a version that was frequently republished.

Of all the types described in the *Liber Vagatorum*, the *Schwanfelder* (elaborated from the *Spanfelder* of the *Basler Betrügnisse*) seem particularly apposite to

---

25 Kluge, *Rotwelsch*, pp. 13 f.
26 For a German-English edition of the *Liber Vagatorum*, see David Biron Thomas, ed., *The Book of Vagabonds and Beggars: With a Vocabulary of Their Language and a Preface by Martin Luther*, trans. John Camden Hotten (London: The Penguin Press, 1932). For bibliographic details regarding the *Liber*, see Geremek, *Les fils de Caïn*, p. 53.

Poor Tom, for their implicit "stage directions" of divestiture, shaking from cold, self-mutilation with sharp plants and supplication:

> Das sind betler wenn sie in ein stat kommen so lassen sie die klaider in den herbergen und sitzen für die kirchen bey nackend und zittern jamerlichen vor den lewten das man wenen sol sie leyden grossen frost so haben sie sich gestochen mit nesselnsamen und mit andern dingen das sie sunckel werden.[27]

> [These are beggars who, when they come into town, leave their clothes at the inn and then sit down naked in front of churches, and shake miserably in front of the people in order to make them think that they suffer from terrible cold. They prick themselves with nettles and other things to make themselves shake.]

Here, and throughout the text, religious fraudulence plays centre stage. The *Lossner*, who like Poor Tom claim to have been in prison, carry their chains still with them as a continual sign of penitence governed by the vows they have made to various saints. Even more performatively virtuosic penitents are the *Klenckner*, who at church doorways or religious gatherings bemoan their past captivity at the hands of the infidels and "umb deren [der Heiligen] willen sie mit grosser jaemerlicher klagen der stymm bitten und haischen"[28] [for the sake of the saints with loud, mournful cries of their voice supplicate and beg]. The *Vagierer*, wandering scholars who profess to know the black arts, are explicitly called "devil conjurers" ("beschwerer der tewfel")[29] for their capacity, according to the author, of unleashing devilish powers. The *Dobisser*, or false anointers, exploit the credulence of simple farmers by touching them with images of the Virgin or of saints; like the canny *Schlepper* (along with the *Kammesierer*, false priests) they make profit from donations of worship materials (candles, altar cloths, etc.) that they presumably need for their unholy masses. The *Deutzer*, feigning sickness, beseech alms to go on pilgrimage on behalf of "this or that" saint.[30] A *Veranderin*, a woman who purports to have converted from Judaism (cf. the Augsburg *Hürlentzer*), will reward charity by telling the credulous donor the fate of their father or mother in the afterlife.

All of the *Liber's* mendicants, with one exception, are "*Veranderen*": changers and shape shifters. The only unambiguously good category in the catalogue is that of the *Breger*: "[D]as sind petler die kain zaichen von den heyligen oder wenig an inen haben hangen und kommen schlechtlich und einfaltigklich für

---

[27] Thomas, ed., *The Book of Vagabonds*, pp. 102 f.
[28] Pp. 74 f.
[29] Pp. 84 f.
[30] Pp. 92 f. ("Das sind petler die sind lang kranck gelegen (als sie sprechen) und haben ein schwer fart verhaissen zu dem heyligen und zu ihenem.")

die lewt gangen und haischen das almosen umb gottes und unser lieben frawen willen[.]"³¹ [They have no or very few tokens of the saints hanging about them and proceed clumsily and simply up to people and beg alms for God's or the Holy Virgin's Sake]. They are "one-sided" ("einfaltigklich") and pose no threat because their appearance matches their reality. The author grudgingly concedes that in some cases aid may also be given to the second group, the *Stabeylern*: vagrants who work the country from one saint's shrine to the next, with dozens of saints' tokens hanging from their hats and cloaks. But here we are already plunged into the world of theatrical deceit, semiotic confusion (the very problem that the beggar catalogues are supposed to alleviate), and what might be called "a war of signs." ³²

If the clothes of the *Stabeyler*, cluttered with tokens of all the saints, are made of one hundred pieces like that of the mythical Harlequin, their verbal repertoires can similarly be seen as "rhapsodic," or stitched together, in the manner of oral compositions performed by actors, singers and storytellers. In fact, much of the *Liber Vagatorum* goes to enumerating the typical narratives deployed in the imposters' street theatre, as with the *Lossner*, close readers of late medieval romance or contemporary captivity narratives: "These are knaves who say they have lain in prison six or seven years, and carry the chains with them wherein they lay as captives among the *infidel* [...] and they have forged letters, as from the princes and lords of foreign lands [...]."³³ Typical speeches recorded in the *Liber Vagatorum* are presented in an oral-formulaic manner, with alternative phrases enumerated at various insertion points.

Liber Vagatorum recounts one after another prodigious feat of acting: acting designed to move the hearts and minds of gullible bystanders to charity via pity or terror. Masters of theatrical *techné*, these travelling actors exploit the full gamut of performance semiotics, enlisting the signs of costume, make-up extending through the entire body, gesture, stance, facial expression, gait, non-verbal voice and sound, a rich verbal repertoire of speeches and stories, props, even occasionally addressing the senses of touch and smell. Even more impressive than the *Dützpetterin*, beggar women who can feign both miscarriages and pregnancy,

---

31 Pp. 68 f.

32 For a semiotic analysis inspired by Foucault's *Discipline and Punish*, see William C. Carroll, *Fat King and Lean Beggar: Representations of Poverty in the Age of Shakespeare* (Ithaca, NY: Cornell University Press, 1996), pp. 44 f.

33 Thomas, ed., *The Book of Vagabonds*, p. 73; italics in the original. ("Das sind pettler die sprechen sie seyen vi. oder vii. jar gefangen gelegen und tragen die ketten mit inen darin sie gefangen sind gelegen unter den unglaubigen [...] und haben das loebsaffot aus frembden landen von dem fürsten und von dem herrn [...]."; p. 72.)

is the male variant: men who feign to be pregnant. The false women lepers, or *Junckfrawen*, deftly combine make-up and intense physical acting, as do the *Grantner*, afflicted with the falling sickness of St. Vitus. Close attention is given to the make-up, prostheses and foul substances used by the histrionic frauds, which match the swampy eco-spheres inhabited by Poor Tom: the *Schweiger* besmear horse dung onto their arms and legs; the *Seffer* coat themselves with a foul type of salve. If we think of the actor playing Gloucester rather than the fictional character, Shakespeare's play is again invoked by the destitute, but also sanctified *Zickische*, or blind men, who take cotton, apply a blood-like substance to it and attach it to their eyes with a kerchief. All in all, the *Liber Vagatorum*, by far the single most important early modern beggar catalogue from an international perspective, provides an exhaustive and compelling account of destitute performative techniques (certainly exaggerated, but not without a basis in reality), drawing from a very minimalist and raw form of theatre.

Speculum Cerretanorum

Not much is known about the life of Teseo Pini, the author of *Speculum Cerretanorum*, who appears to have been a vicar from Urbino, and also involved in the legal profession, both as a doctor in law and as a judge. As we have pointed out, there is a strong possibility that Pini may have had access to the *Basler Betrügnisse der Gyler* through his superior, Girolamo Santucci, who had lived in Germany during the 1470s and in whose library was included a manuscript treatise in Latin on "cerretani": the very term, of course, used by Pini..[34] To be sure, there were also important Latin and Italian texts available to Pini on the figure of the *cerretano*, *ciarlatano* and *vagabondo*, such as the fifteenth-century humanist Flavio Biondo's *Italia Illustrata* (composed 1448–1453), which provides an account of the origins and practices of the *cerretani* to which Pini is clearly indebted.[35] Piero Camporesi speculates that the *Speculum*, probably written between 1484 and 1486, may not have been published because of the author's death, although it does appear to have circulated in manuscript. Ironically, it was only due to an act of blatant plagiarism by the Roman Dominican priest Giacinto de'Nobili, who used the pen name of Rafaele Frianoro, that Pini's work ever saw the light of day. Frianoro translated the text from Latin to Italian, changed the names of popes

---

34 For this manuscript, see Camporesi, "Introduzione," p. CLXII.
35 P. CXIV.

and other historical figures to fit his own time, and shifted from the first to the third person whenever Pini narrated *in propria persona*.

Resting squarely within the censorial bounds of the beggar book, Pini certainly continues to represent almost all vagabond beggars as fraudulent, but the discourse around poverty is somewhat more cosmopolitan and many-sided than that of the German texts. The *Biantes*, used alternatively as a generic name for the vagabonds and for one sect, are said by Pini to derive their name from Bias of Priene, a sixth-century BC philosopher considered one of the Seven Sages, and, while not explicitly a Cynic, famous for sayings such as "I carry all my things with me." Several of the categories closely match the picture of the Cynic sage, living naked under the elements, in a way congruent with Poor Tom. So Pini's *Cocchini*: "[D]icti sunt a quatiendo, qui per hiemem nudi vadunt, quasi sua quatientes membra, stridentes dentibus, ut maiorem vim frigoris se concepisse ostendant. Ii prae se ferunt nihil praeter egestatem nuditatemque habere [...]."[36] [Are so called from the shaking, for those who go about naked through the winter, shaking their arms and legs, gnashing their teeth, in order to show that they suffer from the tremendous force of the cold. They claim to have nothing more than their nudity and poverty.]

Similarly, the *Apezentes* "dicunt se nihil praeter victum concupiscere, spernere vinum et nuditatem amare [...]." [Say that they desire nothing but minimal sustenance, spurning wine and loving nudity].[37] A striking sign that Pini extends the bare beggar catalogue into a wider discursive terrain is provided by his entry for the rebaptised Jews, or *Iucchi*: a surprisingly recurrent category that appears in the Augsburg registers, the *Basler Betrügnisse* and the *Liber Vagatorum*. Pini is the first to give these figures a social context related to the contemporary problem of poverty: [H]i fingunt se quondam fuisse Iudeos ditissimos fenerario quaestu, et visiones vidisse terribiles, miraculaque inaudita et pene incredibilia proferunt, quibus allecti, more Apostoli, dimisisse talentum et omnia que habebant, ut Christum pauperem sequerentur pauperes et perfecti [...].[38] [These pretend to have once been Jews made extremely rich by usury, but who, having seen horrible visions, and astonishing and incredible miracles which they recount, have been drawn, in the same way as the Apostles, to give up all their possessions and, perfected in poverty, to follow the poverty of Christ.]

---

36 Teseo Pini, *Speculum Cerretanorum*, in: Camporesi, ed., *Il libro dei vagabondi*, pp. 3–77, p. 40.
37 Ibid.
38 Pp. 44 f.

Within the bounds of a late medieval anti-Semitic discourse, these fraudulent opportunists point to a genuine critique of usury, and advocacy of radical Christian economics as an antidote.

As with the German texts, most of the imposters traffic in religious motifs, but the various religious transactions performed by the beggars are considerably more articulated in the Latin text. Several of Pini's fraudulent beggars, posing as priests, conduct the Mass itself (in exchange, of course, for palpable reward) and generally Pini's charlatans can be seen to perform the various speech-acts and transactions of the Holy Office. The first specific type described by Pini, the *Biantes*, are called such for their general claim to *bless* ("vel quia beatitudinem promittunt")[39]—just as poor Tom can dispense prayers as well as "lunatic bans." The *Affratres*, or false friars, deceitfully bedecked in priestly habit, both *confess* and *absolve*, cannily pinching the Mass offerings for their unholy uses. Selling counterfeit *indulgences*, the *Biantes* promise to procure spiritual benefits for one's ancestors in hell or purgatory. Several of the types offer to audiences the spiritual gift of *witness*: the *Acatosi* claim to have been captives of the Turks or Saracens, bearing and brandishing chains to prove it, testifying to the endurance of their faith under the harsh deprivations they experienced in prison, where they still have relatives. Several categories perform the vicarious expiation, and perhaps the homeopathic cure, of compelling physical *penitence*, especially the *Affarfantes*:

> Fingunt enim multa miracula dicentes se magna perpetrasse flagitia divinoque quodam nutu morbo aliquo percussos et voto obtinuisse morbi liberationem, ut peccatum suum et gratiam eis factam cunctis gentibus paenitendo nuntiarent; percutiunt enim nudum corpus suum aliquibus levibus catenis, [...] aiunt oportere eos talem agendo paenitentiam totum peragrare orbem.[40]

> [They claim to have witnessed many miracles, saying that they have committed terrible sins and were stricken by a terrible infirmity from God, they were liberated from the infirmity by a vow they made to God that as a penance they would travel the world witnessing before all of the people to their sin and to the great mercy of God, striking their bodies with light chains of iron.]

In these kinds of penitential performances and generally throughout the *Speculum Cerretanorum*, a high degree of physical virtuosity is required: from the *Acadentes*, who simulate falling; from the *Atrementes*, or "Tremblers"; from the Tarantulists, or *Attarantati*, who vibrate and shake their heads, tremble at the knees,

---

39 P. 18.
40 Pp. 31 f.

sing and dance, flutter their lips, and shriek and agitate like mad people. Vocal virtuosity seems to be a particular hallmark of Pini's charlatans: the *Asciones*, who like the *Attarantati* pretend to be mad, "[n]ihil petunt sed inarticulatas voces emittunt, nutuque quid velint indicant"⁴¹ [ask for nothing but utter forth inarticulate sounds, indicating what they want simply by moving their heads]. And the performative nature of their activity is made even more clear here than in the German texts, with a fuller picture provided of the piazza arena of performance and the public credulously flocking to see them. Of the *Spectini*, it is said that "[...] homines feminaeve ad eorum contiones confluant non minori delectatione quam ad videndum spectacula cucurrissent."⁴² [Both men and women flock to their assemblies with no less pleasure than if they were running to comedies.] The *Alacrimantes*, or Weepers, and the *Acadentes* (Fallers), take care only to perform when large crowds have collected. Interestingly, many of Frianoro's minor additions have to do with filling out the performative context—in his version, the *Aca[p]tosi* clear out a performative space in the piazza with the very power of their strange cries in Arabic and Hebrew.⁴³ Still, as we have seen here, the Latin text of Pini that Frianoro appropriated was already rich in performative detail.

Poor Tom

Although Poor Tom does not exactly position himself in the liminal zone of a sacred space, like the *Schwanfelder* and so many other beggar types described in the catalogues, he invokes spiritual aura through other means. If the exorcism intertexts also informing Poor Tom, as Stephen Greenblatt has argued, point to the "sham theatricality" projected from Samuel Harsnett's debunking, dis-enchanting point of view, so do those of the fraudulent beggar, which describe Edgar's chief object: to "enforce charity."⁴⁴ Poor Tom might be seen as performing a kind of auto-exorcism, but it is put to the service of his fictional superobjective of supplication. The devils tormenting him are tantamount to furious, soul-possessing sins—"of lust, as Obidicut; [...] Mahu, of stealing; Modo, of murder"⁴⁵—that he must expiate, with the help of the Ten-Commandments-style platitudes that

---

41 P. 34.
42 P. 41.
43 See Rafaele Frianoro, *Il vagabondo ovvero Sferza de' bianti e vagabondi* [1640], in: Camporesi, ed., *Il libro dei vagabondi*, pp. 79–165, p. 115.
44 Greenblatt, *Shakespearean Negotiations*, pp. 94–128.
45 Shakespeare, *King Lear*, 4.1.62–64.

he spouts ("obey thy parents, [...] commit not with man's sworn spouse")[46] and the bystander's charity. In Edgar's fiction, the destitute speaker has fallen into poverty for unbridled womanising, dicing, stealing and greed: sins that expose the opulence and inequities of the wealthy. Poor Tom, according to his own crazed but actually coherent narrative, had been a court servant "proud in heart and mind" who "served the lust of my mistress' heart and did the act of darkness with her [...]. Wine loved I deeply, dice dearly; and, in woman, out-paramoured the Turk [...]."[47] Poor Tom's devil discourse, rather than merely rehearsing mad snatches from Harsnett, inscribes the demons into a densely poetic, if also formulaic narrative of the sin, moral repentance and spiritual charity familiar in the narratives of sham beggars.

In Edgar's extended, auto-stage direction, he enumerates the forms, postures and techniques of the actor's body as he prepares to play Poor Tom. First, he applies facial make-up, liming his face with grime. Next, he attends to costume, or rather anti-costume, taking off all of his clothes but a loincloth (as the mad Lear, in his "Cynic" imitation of this "learned Theban," will try to do later: "Off, off, you lendings: come, unbutton here."[48]). Then, he applies a kind of debased wig, tangling and matting his hair. A "roaring voice" will be his fallback vocal register, and then, as so many of the beggar books detail, he marks his body with signs of mutilation. Ambiguously sacred, or *sacré*, in the French sense, Poor Tom can both curse and bless: he will have prepared both curses, or "lunatic bans," and prayers in the fashion of itinerant beggars building up verbal repertoires.

From his first appearance out of the hovel to the point an act later when he casts aside the role—not accidentally just after his father gives a powerful speech on charity and redistribution—Edgar performs for his life. Deftly melding gesture and voice, his frozen shaking beats to the time of senseless speech: "O do, de, do, de, do, de [...]."[49] and "Humh"[50]—both added to the Folio text as possible incorporations of the actor's improvisations. Poor Tom frequently utters the kind of fearsome, non-verbal sounds frequently described in the beggar books: "Alow, alow, loo, loo!"[51] and "suum, mun, nonny."[52] Wild, grotesque, violent motions could easily complement lines like "The foul fiend bites my back"[53] and deictically rich

---

46 3.4.78–80.
47 3.4.83–90.
48 3.4.106 f.
49 3.4.57 f.
50 3.4.46.
51 3.4.76.
52 3.4.97.
53 3.6.17.

utterances fire the actor's gestic invention: "*There* could I have him now, and *there*, and *there* again, and *there*."[54] (Here again the Folio text, by adding the fourth "there," may be incorporating actor's improvisations.) Grotesque head movements might accompany Poor Tom's declaration that he will "throw his head"[55] at the imaginary dogs that Lear has conjured for the trial scene, and we can generally guess that Poor Tom has mastered the body language of the suppliant beggar, as he explicitly begs: "Do Poor Tom some charity, whom the foul fiend vexes."[56]

What might be a quintessential instance of sham theatricality, of course, turns out to have immense power—power for many critics, viewers and readers of the play and for the play's internal audience members. Edgar's particular rendition of a beggar, with the powerful gestic, kinetic and vocal features described above, captures something like the athletic and ascetic actor of Jerzy Grotowski's "poor theatre," with Edgar taking "poor" in an even more literal sense than the Polish director-theorist. For Grotowski, the figure of the naked, suffering, vulnerable actor, stripped of the distractions of stage lighting, props and even costume, is fundamentally compelling in a way that returns us to the elemental power of theatricality itself. We might then consider the representation of a beggar to be the Ur-role, or ground fiction, of the actor himself. Actors can play the full gamut of human experience, and reveal to us the constructed nature of societal roles: a revelation which may carry either conservative overtones, as with the stable balance of *Pobre* and *Rico* in the neo-medieval system of Calderón's *El gran teatro del mundo* (c. 1633–1636), or radical implications in Hamlet's upsetting observation that the body of a dead beggar serves "politic worms"[57] as well as that of a king.

The effect of Poor Tom on the play's internal audiences, especially King Lear and Gloucester, is both traditional and radical, in that Christian theology, especially from patristic and medieval sources, traditionally advocated the redistribution of wealth in ways entirely inimical to early capitalism. Poor Tom draws much of his power, symbiotically, from his association with the dispossessed king on the heath; like Lear, he has elected to "outface / The winds and persecutions of the sky." Lear's powerful "Poor naked wretches" speech may be literally prompted by his sudden designation of the Fool as "houseless poverty"[58] as he sends him into the hovel. While the Fool is inside the roofless shelter, and before

---

54 3.4.60 f.; my italics.
55 3.6.62.
56 3.4.59.
57 Shakespeare, *Hamlet*, ed. Harold Jenkins, The Arden Shakespeare, 2nd Series (London: Thomson Learning, 2005), 4.3.20.
58 Shakespeare, *King Lear*, 3.4.26.

Poor Tom has emerged, Lear utters the speech, which conjures the state of dispossessed vagabonds like Poor Tom so aptly that it appears to function as his cue.

> LEAR:
> Poor naked wretches, wheresoe'er you are,
> That bide the pelting of this pitiless storm,
> How shall your houseless heads and unfed sides,
> Your looped and windowed raggedness, defend you
> From seasons such as these? O, I have ta'en
> Too little care of this. Take physic, pomp,
> Expose thyself to feel what wretches feel,
> That thou mayst shake the superflux to them
> And show the heavens more just.[59]

It is as though Lear is already responding to Poor Tom, in a speech that sublimely melds notions of traditional, medieval charity with radical arguments for economic redistribution. As Debora Shuger has argued, "'superflux' is a Shakespearean coinage, a translation of a technical term from medieval canon law referring to that portion of a person's income or goods that is *owed* to the poor."[60] In fact, at the time when *King Lear* was written many were challenging some of the more draconian elements of the new poor laws implemented throughout Europe by appealing to Greek patristic writers such as St. John Chrysostom and medieval writers such as Aquinas, who each argued that greed and hoarding were tantamount to robbery and that economic redistribution was a moral imperative. The continental beggar books, censorial though they are, reflect a late medieval/early modern world when the poor laws were not yet written in stone, when it was especially difficult to tell whether an itinerant "holy man" might be swindling or saving your soul, and when begging, increasingly untethered from large charitable institutions, was a performance. The *Basler Betrügnisse*, *Speculum Cerretanorum* and *Liber Vagatorum* also beckon us to the world of Poor Tom.

---

59 3.4.28–36.
60 Shuger, "Subversive Fathers and Suffering Subjects," p. 53; italics in the original.

Part II: **Intercultural Connections between English and Spanish Drama**

Leonie Pawlita
Dream and Doubt: Skepticism in Shakespeare's *Hamlet* and Calderón's *La vida es sueño*

The resurgence of ancient skepticism in the sixteenth and seventeenth centuries represents one of the critically formative phenomena of the cultural history of the early modern period. This essay seeks to explore how both William Shakespeare's *Tragedy of Hamlet, Prince of Denmark*, written around the year 1600, as well as Pedro Calderón de la Barca's most famous *comedia*, *La vida es sueño* [Life Is a Dream], published in 1636, have incorporated elements deriving from this influential philosophical discourse, as well as the related epistemological and ethical questions regarding contemporary discussions of skepticism, or, in other words, why and how these plays dramatise the fundamental epistemological question of skepticism in early modern Europe.[1] A further emphasis of the analysis will be on

---

[1] For a comparative study on the two dramas that focuses on the aspect of skepticism, see already Joachim Küpper, "*Hamlet*, by Shakespeare, and *La vida es sueño*, by Calderón, or the Problem of Scepticism," *Germanisch-Romanische Monatsschrift* 58 (2008), pp. 367–399; see, furthermore, Küpper, "*La vida es sueño*: 'Aufhebung' des Skeptizismus, Recusatio der Moderne," in: Küpper and Friedrich Wolfzettel, edd., *Diskurse des Barock: Dezentrierte oder rezentrierte Welt?* (München: Fink, 2000), pp. 383–426; for *Hamlet* in particular see Verena Olejniczak Lobsien, *Skeptische Phantasie: Eine andere Geschichte der frühneuzeitlichen Literatur* (München: Fink, 1999), esp. pp. 102–126. With respect to skepticism in Shakespeare's famous tragedy, see, moreover, among others, Millicent Bell, *Shakespeare's Tragic Skepticism* (New Haven, CN/London: Yale University Press, 2002), pp. 29–79; Graham Bradshaw, *Shakespeare's Scepticism* (Brighton: Harvester Press, 1987), pp. 95–125; Stanley Cavell, *Disowning Knowledge in Six Plays of Shakespeare* (Cambridge/New York, NY: Cambridge University Press, 1987), pp. 179–192; John D. Cox, "Shakespeare and the French Epistemologists," *Cithara* 45 (2006), pp. 23–45; Aaron Landau, "'Let me not burst in ignorance': Skepticism and Anxiety in *Hamlet*," *English Studies* 82 (2001), pp. 218–230; Christoph Menke, "Tragödie und Skeptizismus: Zu *Hamlet*," *Deutsche Vierteljahrsschrift für Literaturwissenschaft und Geistesgeschichte* 75 (2001), pp. 561–486. Regarding studies on the aspect of skepticism in *La vida es sueño*, see, in addition, among others, Anthony J. Cascardi, *The Limits of Illusion: A Critical Study of Calderón* (Cambridge/New York, NY: Cambridge University Press, 1984), pp. 11–23; William Egginton, "Psychoanalysis and the Comedia: Skepticism and the Paternal Function in *La vida es sueño*," *Bulletin of the Comediantes* 52 (2000), pp. 97–122; Everett W. Hesse, "The Role of Deception in *La vida es sueño*," in: Bruno M. Damiani, ed., *Renaissance and Golden Age Essays in Honor of D. W. McPheeters* (Potomac, MD: Scripta Humanistica, 1986), pp. 120–129; Andrés Lema-Hincapié, "¿Existir en sueño o en vigilia? Las respuestas de Calderón y Descartes," *Daimon* 34 (2005), pp. 53–68; Bárbara Mujica, "Calderón's *La vida es sueño* and the Skeptic Revival," in: Arturo Pérez-Pisonero and Ana Semiday, edd.,

aspects of the topic of dream, present in both dramas, which will be considered in connection with the elements of skepticism thematised in the texts. Before entering into the discussion of the plays—on the basis of some central scenes—, however, I shall first briefly outline the philosophical and historical frame of reference.

In *The History of Scepticism*, the historian of philosophy Richard Popkin emphasised an extensive skeptical, i.e. "Pyrrhonian[,] crisis" (*"crise pyrrhonienne"*) pervading early modern Europe, in particular at the beginning of the seventeenth century.[2] In attempting to overcome this crisis, that is, in confronting skepticism, important impulses emerged that became decisive for the configuration of modernity. At the latest, the publication in 1562 of the first Latin translation of the basic systematic exposition of Pyrrhonian skepticism—named after the legendary figure Pyrrho of Elis (c. 365–275 BCE)[3]—written by the Greek physician and philosopher Sextus Empiricus in the second century CE ensured a wide dissemination and reception of this philosophical current.[4] The central elements and terms of

---

Texto y espectáculo: Nuevas dimensiones críticas de la 'comedia' (New Brunswick, NJ/El Paso: SLUSA, 1990), pp. 23–32; Henry W. Sullivan, "*Tam clara et evidens*: 'Clear and Distinct Ideas' in Calderón, Descartes, and Francisco Suárez, S. J.," in: Alva V. Ebersole, ed., *Perspectivas de la comedia*, 2 vols. (Valencia: Estudios de Hispanófila, 1978), vol. 2, pp. 127–136.
2 See Richard H. Popkin, *The History of Scepticism: From Savonarola to Bayle*, 3rd ed. (Oxford/New York, NY: Oxford University Press, 2003), pp. 3–98, esp. pp. 3–43.
3 Of this Greek philosopher, who participated in the campaigns of Alexander the Great into India, mainly anecdotal information has been passed down; as we can read in Diogenes Laertius' account of Pyrrho: "He denied that anything was honourable or dishonourable, just or unjust. And so, universally, he held that there is nothing really existent, but custom and convention govern human action; for no single thing is in itself any more this than that. He led a life consistent with this doctrine, going out of his way for nothing, taking no precaution, but facing all risks as they came, whether carts, precipices, dogs or what not, and, generally, leaving nothing to the arbitrament of the senses; but he was kept out of harm's way by his friends who [...] used to follow close after him." (Diogenes Laertius, [*Vitae et sententiae philosophorum*, Book 9, chap. 11, 61–69] *Lives of Eminent Philosophers: Greek-English*, trans. Robert Drew Hicks, 2 vols. [London: Heinemann; New York, NY: Putnam's Sons, 1925], pp. 474–483, p. 475 [62])
4 The 1562 edition, published by Henri Estienne, was followed by Gentian Hervet's Latin publication of Sextus' complete works in 1569. The Greek original of the *Pyrrhoneioi Hypotyposeis* was published in 1621, and at the end of the sixteenth century parts of an English version appeared, the first translation into a modern vernacular language. (See Popkin, *History of Scepticism*, pp. 18 f.) But already in the Middle Ages Sextus' writings were known. In fifteenth-century Italy, Greek manuscripts circulated among humanistic intellectuals. (See, for instance, Luciano Floridi, *Sextus Empiricus: The Transmission and Recovery of Pyrrhonism* [Oxford/New York, NY: Oxford University Press, 2002], pp. 13–25, regarding the transmission in the Middle Ages; also pp. 25–51, regarding the reception in the Renaissance, and esp. pp. 27–35, regarding the rediscovery by the Italian humanists). Popkin writes: "From the mid-fifteenth century onward, with the discovery of

classical skeptical thinking set forth in Sextus Empiricus' *Outlines of Pyrrhonism*, are as follows: *isosthenia*, the equally balanced co-presence of opposing arguments; *epoché*, the suspension of judgement that follows from *isosthenia*, that is, from the undecidability, or the impossibility of recognising the truth of a statement; and *ataraxia*, the tranquil state of mind that, according to the skeptics, can be attained fortuitously by practising *epoché*.[5] The skeptical argumentation is characterised by assuming consistent relativity; it thus continually casts doubt on any claim of absoluteness. The skeptics' argumentative repertoire is provided by the famous skeptical *tropoi*, the so-called "tropes" or "modes of suspension of judgement." These are argumentative schemes designed to demonstrate relativity. In most cases, they emphasise that sensory perception cannot provide a basis for certain knowledge.[6] In anticipation of what is to come later in my readings of

---

manuscripts of Sextus' writings, there is a revival of interest and concern with ancient skepticism and with the application of its views to the problems of the day." (*History of Scepticism*, p. **xx**). For a study that focuses on the aspect of skepticism in medieval times, see Dominik Perler, *Zweifel und Gewißheit: Skeptische Debatten im Mittelalter*, 2nd ed. (Frankfurt a.M.: Klostermann, 2012). In addition to Popkin's study, see, for the influence of skepticism in sixteenth-century Spain, the account given in Maureen Ihrie, *Skepticism in Cervantes* (London: Tamesis, 1982), pp. 19–29, and for the reception in England, see William M. Hamlin, *Tragedy and Scepticism in Shakespeare's England* (Basingstoke/New York, NY: Palgrave Macmillan, 2005), pp. 29–115.

5 See Sextus Empiricus, Πυρρώνειοι ὑποτυπώσεις/ *Outlines of Pyrrhonism: Greek-English*, ed. and trans. Robert Gregg Bury, in: *Sextus Empiricus*, ed. and trans. R. G. Bury, 4 vols. (London: W. Heinemann; Cambridge, MA: Harvard University Press, 1933–1949), vol. 1, Book 1, 1–12, pp. 2–9, and Book 1, 25–29, pp. 18–21. See, for instance: "Scepticism is an ability, or mental attitude, which opposes appearances to judgements in any way whatsoever, with the result that, owing to the equipollence of the objects and reasons thus opposed [ἰσοσθενής], we are brought firstly to a state of mental suspense [ἐποχή] and next to a state of 'unperturbedness' or quietude [ἀταραξία]." (Book 1, 8, pp. 6 f.); "'Equipollence' [ἰσοσθενής] we use of equality in respect of probability and improbability, to indicate that no one of the conflicting judgements takes precedence over any other as being more probable. 'Suspens[ion of judgement]' [ἐποχή] is a state of mental rest, owing to which we neither deny nor affirm anything. 'Quietude' [ἀταραξία] is an untroubled and tranquil condition of soul." (Book 1, 10, pp. 6–9); "[...] [T]hey [the skeptics] suspended judgement; and they found that quietude [ἀταραξία], as if by chance, followed upon their suspense [ἐποχή], even as a shadow follows its substance." (Book 1, 29, pp. 20 f.) All references in this essay to the *Outlines of Pyrrhonism* are from Bury's bilingual edition. The following more recent English editions of the *Hypotyposeis*, however, are to be noted and have been consulted as well: Sextus Empiricus, *Outlines of Scepticism*, edd. and trans. Julia Annas and Jonathan Barnes (Cambridge/New York, NY: Cambridge University Press, 2000); Sextus Empiricus, *The Skeptic Way: Sextus Empiricus's* Outlines of Pyrrhonism, ed. and trans. Benson Mates (Oxford/New York, NY: Oxford University Press, 1996).

6 See Sextus Empiricus, *Outlines of Pyrrhonism*, Book 1, 36–163, pp. 24–93, for the ten "tropes of *epoché*" attributed to Aenesidemus (first century BCE). As Sextus summarises at the beginning: "They are these: the first, based on the variety in animals; the second, on the differences

the plays, I shall quote from the fourth of the ten tropes listed in Sextus' *Outlines of Pyrrhonism*, which states that, because the results of sensory perceptions vary according to different conditions, i.e. according to the mental or physical state of the perceiver at the moment of perception—such as sleeping or waking, drunkenness or sobriety, motion or rest, young or old age—, making a reliable judgement about the "reality status" of the perceived is impossible. The following applies with respect to the waking state, sleeping and dreaming:

> Sleeping and waking [...] give rise to different impressions, since we do not imagine when awake what we imagine in sleep, nor when asleep what we imagine when awake; so that the existence or non-existence of our impressions is not absolute but relative, being in relation to our sleeping or waking condition. Probably, then, in dreams we see things which to our waking state are unreal, although not wholly unreal; for they exist in our dreams, just as waking realities exist, although non-existent in dreams.[7]

The dream argument would become centrally important in René Descartes' (1596–1650) well-known use of and attempt to overcome skepticism[8]—an aspect I will also come back to in the discussion of the dramas.

The core argument of Pyrrhonism is doubt concerning the reliability of sense perception. The skeptical assumption that our perception is relative opposes Aristotelian epistemology, which claims that all knowledge begins with perception and that we are able, by means of the senses governed by reason, to arrive at a true, objective view of the world. From a skeptical point of view, no reliable statements can be made about reality: the world does not actually have to *be* as it

---

in human beings; the third, on the different structures of the organs of sense; the fourth, on the circumstantial conditions; the fifth, on positions and intervals and locations; the sixth, on intermixtures; the seventh, on the quantities and formations of the underlying objects; the eighth, on the fact of relativity; the ninth, on the frequency or rarity of occurrence; the tenth, on the disciples and customs and laws, the legendary beliefs and the dogmatic convictions." (Book 1, 36 f., p. 25) In addition, Sextus gives the five modes of suspension of judgement attributed to Agrippa (first century CE), "on disagreement," "on regress *ad infinitum*," "on relativity," "on hypothesis," and "on circular reasoning" (Book 1, 164–177, pp. 94–101), another list of two tropes (Book 1, 178 f., pp. 100–103) and a catalogue of "skeptic expressions" [φωναί] (Book 1, 187–209, pp. 106–125), all these providing argumentative instruments to set up equipollence.

7 Book 1, 104, p. 63; on trope 4 on the whole, see Book 1, 100–117, pp. 58–69.

8 See René Descartes, *Meditationes de prima philosophia* [1641], in: *Œuvres de Descartes*, edd. Charles Adam and Paul Tannery, 13 vols. (Paris: Cerf, 1897–1913), vol. 7, esp. Meditatio 1, pp. 17–23, esp. pp. 19 f.; Descartes, *Meditations on First Philosophy*, in: *The Philosophical Writings of Descartes*, trans. John Cottingham, Robert Stoothoff and Dugald Murdoch, 3 vols. (Cambridge/New York, NY: Cambridge University Press, 1984–1991), vol. 2, pp. 1–62, First Meditation, pp. 12–15, esp. p. 13.

appears to us.⁹ The questions and problems posed by skepticism are not only concerned with the field of knowledge but also extend to ethics and praxis. From the perspective of the skeptics, the state of not knowing is in no way a shortcoming; on the contrary, it is brought about deliberately and encountered by refraining from judgement with serenity. The central question of how one is to behave in the face of uncertainty or how a skeptical attitude is to be integrated into practical life is answered by the Pyrrhonists—whose goal is to lead a carefree, completely undogmatic life—as follows: one must adhere to the world as one finds it; to what is accepted in the community in which one finds oneself living. With respect to undertaking necessary action, one must orient oneself by everyday experience and by following tradition and custom.¹⁰

The revival of Pyrrhonian skepticism in the early modern period is not only situated within a humanistic interest in ancient literature and philosophy, but occurred in particular against the backdrop of a period marked by massive changes, the loss of previous certainties and new epistemological challenges. Notably, the discovery of new continents beginning in 1492 cast doubt on traditional categories explaining the world. One was faced (from a European perspective) with previously unknown territories not mentioned in the Bible¹¹ and

---

9 See Sextus Empiricus, *Outlines of Pyrrhonism*, Book 1, 18–22, pp. 12–17.
10 See Book 1, 17, pp. 12 f.; Book 1, 22–24, pp. 16 f.; Book 1, 26–30, pp. 18–21; Book 1, 226, pp. 138 f. The second tradition of ancient skepticism should also be mentioned, known as "Academic skepticism," which was formulated and developed in the Platonic Academy from the third to the first century BCE. The significant distinction between the two ancient forms of skepticism is that the skepticism of the Academics is universal and absolute—the knowledge of truth is considered in principle impossible—, while for the Pyrrhonians, however, it is universal and relative. Thus, according to Sextus, the adherents of Academic skepticism are not perceived as "skeptics," but as "negative dogmatists." According to Popkin, this distinction was also adapted in the context of the reception of skepticism in the early modern age when, in the sixteenth and seventeenth centuries the terms "skeptic" and "Pyrrhonian" were used synonymously by most contemporaries. A momentous modification (also in terms of its reception) that Academic skepticism developed from a principled rejection of truth and certainty and from the concomitant assumption that even deception is in principle not to be excluded, was the substitution of the certainty criterion with the criterion of "credibility" or "probability" (πιθανότης, *probabilitas*). With this move, both "judgements" about the world and practical action were oriented according to probabilities. The distinction of ideas by degrees of credibility and a detailed examination of their subject allow to a certain extent a provisional "understanding" of reality, only when the verified is credible or likely as opposed to true rather than false. This holds a thoroughly constructive potential in terms of scientific conceptualisations. (See the explanations given in the *Outlines of Pyrrhonism* on the differences between the skeptics and the Academic philosophy: Book 1, 220–235, pp. 132–145, esp. Book 1, 226–231, pp. 138–143; see Popkin, *History of Scepticism*, pp. xvii f. and p. xx).
11 Regarding this aspect, see Küpper, "The Traditional Cosmos and the New World," *MLN* 118 (2003), pp. 363–397. See also already Küpper, "*La vida es sueño*," p. 416, for pointing to

with inhabitants of this "new world" who had unheard-of cultures, knowledge and belief systems. The discovery of America, the circumnavigation of the globe by Magellan (1519–1522) and the definitive end of the Ptolemaic worldview later brought about by the Copernican hypothesis, advanced in the work of Galileo and completed by Kepler's findings, namely, the proof that the earth was a sphere and not at the centre of the universe meant that doubts about the reliability of sense perception—and thus Aristotelian epistemology—, the main argument of skepticism, gained in virulence. In the area of faith, through the Reformation's questioning of the status of the church and the criterion of tradition, the sole valid authority for truth was shaken. Given an emerging pluralism in the fields of science, philosophy and religion, the arguments of the skeptics appeared to be a mode of addressing the uncertainty of one's own time, an uncertainty centred on the reliability of sensory perception.

This applies not only to the realm of philosophy and religion. The reception of classical Pyrrhonism can be understood as a phenomenon extending far beyond philosophy into almost all discourses, affecting the whole of Europe and ubiquitous in early modern culture. As I will try to show in the following pages, looking first at *Hamlet* and then at *La vida es sueño*, the challenges generated by skepticism in the intellectual debates of the seventeenth century also concerned the drama of the time and triggered different ways of confronting and "answering" them.

The *Hamlet* source material derives from Norse mythology and was recorded in writing in the *Historiae Danicae* of Saxo Grammaticus at the end of the twelfth century. However, it is the expanded version of the story—expanded in particular through moralising commentaries—in François de Belleforest's popular *Histoires tragiques* (1559–1582) that is generally regarded as one of Shakespeare's immediate sources.[12] Although constitutive elements of the plot (fratricide, "incestuous marriage," feigned madness and execution of a long-delayed revenge) are present, there is no ghost. Fengon—the equivalent character to

---

the significance of the discoveries in the context of the reception of skepticism; see in this regard also Popkin, *History of Scepticism*, p. 98.

12 It is the third *histoire* of the fifth volume, published for the first time in 1570, of the seven-volume collection of "tragic stories," which Belleforest wrote between 1559 and 1582, initially as a continuation of the translation and adaptation of Bandello's *Novelle* begun by Pierre Boaistuau and published in 1559 under the title *Histoires tragiques*. For the sources of *Hamlet*, see Harold Jenkins, "Introduction," in: William Shakespeare, *Hamlet*, ed. Harold Jenkins, The Arden Shakespeare, 2nd Series (London: Thomson Learning, 2005), pp. 1–159, pp. 82–112, esp. pp. 85–89 (Saxo Grammaticus), pp. 89–96 (Belleforest), pp. 82–85 and pp. 97–101 (*Ur-Hamlet* and *The Spanish Tragedy*).

Shakespeare's Claudius—murders Amleth's father in public; consequently, there is no doubt as to the identity of the murderer.[13] In *Hamlet*, however, the protagonist, having returned to the Danish court of Elsinore from his place of study in Wittenberg because of his father's sudden death, first and only learns of the murder from the ghost: "GHOST: 'Tis given out that, sleeping in my orchard, / A serpent stung me—so the whole ear of Denmark / Is by a forged process of my death / Rankly abus'd—but know, thou noble youth, / The serpent that did sting thy father's life / Now wears his crown."[14]

Ghost figures were by no means uncommon on the stage of the time. A significant influence came from the reception of Seneca's tragedies in the sixteenth century.[15] As is well known, Thomas Kyd's *The Spanish Tragedy* (printed in 1592) also contains the element of the ghost figure and in reports on performances of the so-called *Ur-Hamlet*, the appearance of a ghost is highlighted as well. In numerous plays of Shakespeare's oeuvre, there are aspects of the "supernatural," and also specifically in the form of ghosts (consider *Richard III* or *Julius Caesar*).

It is not the figure of the ghost itself in *Hamlet* that is relevant in Shakespeare's modification of the source material, but its problematic reality status; the doubts about the reality of the ghost and of his words are directly connected to the central motif of the play: Hamlet's hesitation over carrying out the revenge called for by the spirit of his father. Thus, two key aspects in the context of the discussion related to skepticism are brought into play: firstly, the field of epistemology, the question of the possibility of identifying what is perceived via the senses as "certain"—this is doubted by the skeptics and represents one of their main arguments; secondly, the area of praxis (which is connected to the former complex of problems), the question of whether and how a specific action is possible when facing uncertainty.

---

13 See François de Belleforest, *Histoires tragiques. Histoire* 108 [1604]: "Avec quelle ruse Amleth qui, depuis, fut roi de Danemark, vengea, la mort de son père Horwendille, occis par Fengon son frère et autre occurrence de son histoire," in: Christian Biet, ed., *Théâtre de la cruauté et récits sanglants en France (XVIe–XVIIe siècle)* (Paris: Laffont, 2006), pp. 509–545, p. 513. Even if Amleth is still a child at the time of the act, the code of honour commits him to avenge the murder of his father as soon as he has reached manhood. His feigned madness serves to gain time and to lull the murderer, who took possession of his victim's throne, empire and wife, into a false sense of security (see p. 515 f.).
14 William Shakespeare, *Hamlet*, 1.5.35–40. All references to the play are from Shakespeare, *Hamlet*, ed. Jenkins, and are subsequently given parenthetically in the text.
15 See already Frederic W. Moorman, "The Pre-Shakespearean Ghost," *Modern Language Review* 1 (1906), pp. 86–95, esp. p. 89 f.; on ghostly apparitions in Elizabethan theatre, see also Stephen Greenblatt, *Hamlet in Purgatory* (Princeton, NJ/Woodstock: Princeton University Press, 2001), pp. 151–204 (chap. 4 "Staging Ghosts").

The question of the ghost's "ontological" status is virulent from the play's outset. In the opening scene of the drama, the sentinels are waiting together with Horatio for his appearance at midnight:

> HORATIO: What, has *this thing* appear'd again tonight?
> BARNARDO: I have seen nothing.
> MARCELLUS: Horatio says *'tis but our fantasy*,
> And will not let belief take hold of him,
> Touching this *dreaded sight* twice seen of us.
> Therefore I have entreated him along
> With us to watch the minutes of this night,
> That if again this *apparition* come,
> He may approve our eyes and speak to it.
> HORATIO: Tush, tush, 'twill not appear.
> (1.1.24–33; my italics)

The problem of classifying the perceived continues, as the spirit actually appears twice in the further course of the scene, only to vanish again shortly afterward without responding to the words of Horatio (1.1.43–54, 1.1.128–146). At no point is he clearly identified with the late king; only a similarity is emphasised several times (see 1.1.43–46, 49–53, 61–67, 113). The uncertainty, perceived as threatening, about the cause and significance of the "apparition"[16] evokes attempts at interpretation, which draw upon mythical explanations and include the current political and military situation.[17] There are explicit references to the realm of speculation ("HOR.: So have I heard and do in part believe it." 1.1.170; "MAR.: Some say that [...]" 1.1.163); and the uncertainty about what is seen manifests itself in the irritated exclamations, as the ghost disappears in the mist of dawn: "BAR.: 'Tis here. / HOR.: 'Tis here. / MAR.: 'Tis gone." (1.1.145–147).

Horatio decides to inform Hamlet about what he believes he has seen;[18] but even before the ghost is mentioned in their conversation in the second scene of the first act, Hamlet says: "My father—methinks I see my father— / HOR.: Where,

---

16 See, e.g., "HOR.: [...] It harrows me with fear and wonder." (1.1.47).
17 It is only a few weeks' time since the sudden and mysterious death of King Hamlet. Denmark is now making evident preparations for war, the cause of which remains unknown to the public (1.1.73–82). Horatio states that, according to rumours, an attack from Norway is imminent; Young Fortinbras is said to intend recapturing the areas that his father had lost in the battle against King Hamlet (1.1.83–110). The ghost is interpreted on the one hand as a "portentous figure" (1.1.112), as an ominous sign of the future of the state (1.1.72), in which parallels are drawn to the mysterious events that supposedly took place before the death of Caesar in ancient Rome (1.1.16–128); on the other hand, it is connected with *topoi* based on popular beliefs about apparitions (see, e.g., 1.1.139–141, 154–170).
18 "HOR.: This spirit, dumb to us, will speak to him." (1.1.176).

my lord? HAMLET: In my mind's eye, Horatio." (1.2.184 f.) This reference to the internal senses, that is, to the realm of the imaginary, of vision and the dreamlike is relevant against the backdrop of Hamlet's "actual" encounters with his father's ghost (in 1.4–5 and 3.4), to the extent that there is no certainty as to whether these encounters have reality status (that is, they are perceived by the outer senses), or whether they too happen only in Hamlet's "mind's eye." The distinction between external and internal sense perception ("fantasy") is frequently thematised in the play, most prominently in Horatio's reaction to the first appearance of the ghost: "BAR.: Is not this something more than fantasy? / [...] / HOR.: Before my God, I might not this believe / Without the *sensible and true avouch / of mine own eyes.*" (1.1.57–61; my italics).

Hamlet is incredulous ("'Tis very strange." 1.2.220) and unsettled ("but this troubles me." 1.2.224) by the report of his friend and the guards and asks detailed questions regarding the appearance of the apparition.[19] Nevertheless, the scene closes with the statement: "HAM.: My father's spirit—in arms! All is not well. / I doubt some foul play." (1.2.255 f.).[20] The vague assumption that something is going wrong, that "foul play" is at work, becomes concrete only when Hamlet is "in direct contact" with the ghost, who clearly calls what happened a crime: "GHOST: I am thy father's spirit, / [...] / If thou didst ever thy dear father love—/ HAM.: O God! / GHOST: Revenge his foul and most unnatural murder. / HAM.: Murder!" (1.5.9–26). The exclamation of Hamlet following the revelation of the murderer (1.5.35–40), "O my prophetic soul! My uncle!" (1.5.41), repeats not only the dimension of inner perception ("in my mind's eye"), but also implies the possibility of a prognosticating dream. A potential prophetic dream narrative here would thus be shortened radically—condensed to a verse.[21] Hamlet's first reaction to the appearance of the ghost is also noteworthy. Not Hamlet, but Horatio is the one who sees the spirit: "Look, my lord, it comes." (1.4.38) and interprets its gesture: "It beckons you to go away with it" (1.4.58); finally Hamlet: "It waves me forth again. I'll follow it. / [...] / Go on, I'll follow thee." (1.4.68–79). Hamlet

---

19 See 1.2.226–242, e.g., "Arm'd, say you?" (l. 226), "From top to toe?" (l. 227), "What look'd he, frowningly?" (l. 230).
20 The uncertainty felt by the protagonist in face of the constellation of the early and unexpected death of his father and the rapid subsequent marriage of his mother to his uncle—now in possession of the crown—and the perceived unease about these events are articulated very clearly already at earlier stages; see Hamlet's first monologue, 1.2.129–158, esp. 132–134 and 150–158; his conversation with Horatio, esp. 1.2.174–183; his first scene with Gertrude and Claudius, 1.2.64–129, esp. 68–75.
21 See Marjorie B. Garber, *Dream in Shakespeare: From Metaphor to Metamorphosis* (New Haven, CN/London: Yale University Press, 1974), p. 95.

does not recognise the ghost as his father in the first place, he says that he rather exhibits a "questionable shape" (1.4.43), and, starting to talk to him, *names* him: "[...] I'll call thee Hamlet, / King, father, royal Dane. O answer me." (1.4.44 f.)[22] When Hamlet finally follows the apparition, Horatio states with some concern: "He waxes desperate with imagination." (1.4.87).

Throughout the entire play, Hamlet is the only person who hears the ghost speak. That the ghost's words are attributable to Hamlet's imagination is thus a possible, plausible, if not obvious assumption. This may in particular be illustrated by considering the fourth scene of act three, where Old Hamlet's Ghost appears one last time. In the famous "closet scene," only the protagonist sees and hears him, in contrast to Gertrude.[23] The queen can interpret the behaviour of her son only within the model of mental illness ("Alas, he's mad." 3.4.106; "This is the very coinage of your brain. / This bodiless creation ecstasy / is very cunning in." 3.4.139–141). The aspect of madness or delusion represents a prominent and complex theme in Shakespeare's play, so that even the feigned madness must be considered a relevant variable in the plot—as Hamlet declares at the end of the first act: "[...] I perchance hereafter shall think meet / To put an antic disposition on" (1.5.179 f.). Claudius' ambition is to determine the reason for "Hamlet's transformation" (2.2.5; see 3.1.2–4). However, simulation, in the sense of deceiving the outside world and internal sensory deception are not always clearly separable in relation to Hamlet's remarks and behaviour.[24]

Although Hamlet accepts the charge of the ghost to avenge the murder of his father (see 1.5.29–31, 95–112), he does not take action. The doubts about the credibility of the ghost—and thus the foundation of the revenge entrusted to him, Claudius' actual guilt—remain;[25] they culminate in the assumption that the

---

[22] See also Küpper, "*Hamlet* and *La vida es sueño*," p. 384, as well as pp. 380–384, regarding the role of the ghost in the scenes discussed above.

[23] "HAM.: [...] What would your gracious figure? / [...] / GHOST: Speak to her, Hamlet. / HAM.: How is it with you, lady? / QUEEN: Alas, how is't with you, / That you do bend your eye on vacancy, / And with th'incorporal air do hold discourse? / [...] / [...] Whereon do you look? / HAM.: On him, on him. [...] / [...] / [...] Do not look upon me, / Lest with this piteous action you convert / My stern effects. [...] / [...] / QUEEN: To whom do you speak this? / HAM.: Do you see nothing there? / QUEEN: Nothing at all; [...] / HAM.: Nor did you nothing hear? / QUEEN: No, nothing but ourselves. / HAM.: Why, look you there, look how it steals away. / My father, in his habit as he liv'd! / Look where he goes even now out at the portal." (3.4.105–138).

[24] In this respect, Hamlet's encounter with Ophelia, immediately after the central monologue (3.1.89–163), and the scene of the funeral (5.1.210–294) should be mentioned.

[25] On the one hand, to Horatio: "[...] Touching this vision here, / It is an honest ghost, that let me tell you." (1.5.143 f.), and on the other, when he "sees" the ghost for the first time: "Be thou a spirit of health or goblin damn'd, / Bring with thee airs from heaven or blasts from hell, / Be thy

apparition of his dead father may have been a demon, a deception of the devil: "[...] The spirit that I have seen / May be a devil, and the devil hath power / T'assume a pleasing shape, yea, and perhaps, / Out of my weakness and my melancholy, / As he is very potent with such sprits, / Abuses me to damn me. [...]" (2.2.594–599).[26]

Hamlet's consciousness of the precarious reality-status of the ghost and thus his doubts about the reliability of his senses—Joachim Küpper calls him "the prototype of the contemporary sceptical intellectual"[27]—manifests itself in the plan to obtain certainty by other means concerning what has happened: "[...] I'll have grounds / More relative than this. The play's the thing / Wherein I'll catch the conscience of the King." (2.2.599–601). As he states:

> [...] I have heard
> That guilty creatures sitting at a play
> Have, by the very cunning of the scene,
> Been struck so to the soul that presently
> They have proclaim'd their malefactions.
> For murder, though it have no tongue, will speak
> With most miraculous organ. I'll have these players
> Play something like the murder of my father
> Before mine uncle. I'll observe his looks;
> I tent him to the quick. If a do blench,
> I know my course. [...]
> (2.2.584–594)

This, however, contradicts Hamlet's previous observation:

> Is it not monstrous that this player here,
> But in a fiction, in a dream of passion,
> Could force his soul so to his own conceit
> That from her working all his visage wann'd,
> Tears in his eyes, distraction in his aspect,
> A broken voice, and his whole function suiting
> With forms to his conceit? And all for nothing!

---

intents wicked or charitable, / Thou com'st in such a questionable shape / That I will speak to thee. [...]" (1.4.40–44), and, in a similar way, after its disappearance: "O all you host of heaven! O earth! What else? / And shall I couple hell? [...]" (1.5.92 f.).

26 First, the category of "demonic dream" should be mentioned here. The "power of the devil" resides in the manipulation of the inner perception, so that Hamlet may have been tricked by a supposedly "well-intentioned" form—the spirit of his dead father—but one that harbours deeply evil intentions in reality. Secondly, Hamlet's self-confessed melancholy is noteworthy in view of his disposition toward a highly active imagination.

27 Küpper, "*Hamlet* and *La vida es sueño*," p. 389.

> For Hecuba!
> What's Hecuba to him, or he to her,
> That he should weep for her? What would he do
> Had he the motive and the cue for passion
> That I have? [...]
> (2.2.545–556)

Hamlet had previously instructed one of the arriving actors in the second act to recite a monologue from an *Aeneid*-play,[28] where Aeneas tells Dido about Priam's slaughter (see 2.2.427–444). The clearly visible and convincing emotionality of the actor when he speaks of Pyrrhus' murder of Priam and especially the lamentation of Hecuba, refer not only to the "power" of the theatre and the craft of acting, but also to the ability of human beings to fake emotions ("What's Hecuba to him, or he to her[?]") and likewise to conceal them. The awareness of the possibility of simulation and dissimulation is in contrast to the notion of being able to obtain certainty about something based on the appearance of the gestures of a person ("I'll observe his looks; / I tent him to the quick. If a do blench, / I know my course.").[29] In anticipation of what will be staged in the following, Hamlet thus articulates his doubts that the "test" of Claudius that is to be staged will provide certainty. The protagonist does not, however, content himself with this structure of *isosthenia*. He continues his search for certainty. "*The Murder of Gonzago*" (3.2.134–254), the play to be performed before the royal court, dramatises the core of what "motivates and plagues" the protagonist—the circumstances of his father's death; it is used in the form of an "experiment," Horatio being instructed as an observer of second order.[30]

---

[28] The passage mirrors basic motifs of Shakespeare's play; the representation in *Hamlet* differs, however, from the version of Vergil, as well as from contemporary dramatic versions, for example, *The Tragedy of Dido* (1594) by Christopher Marlowe and Thomas Nashe (see Jenkins, "Longer Notes," in: Shakespeare, *Hamlet*, pp. 421–571, pp. 477–481).

[29] See Küpper, "*Hamlet* and *La vida es sueño*," pp. 388 f.

[30] "HAM.: There is a play tonight before the King: / One scene of it comes near the circumstance / Which I have told thee of my father's death. / I prethee, when thou seest that act afoot, / Even with the very comment of thy soul / Observe my uncle. If his occulted guilt / Do not itself unkennel in one speech, / It is a damned ghost that we have seen, / And my imaginations are as foul / As Vulcan's stithy. Give him heedful note; / For I mine eyes will rivet to his face, / And after we will both our judgements join / In censure of his seeming." (3.2.75–87). Hamlet not only arranges the performance (HAM.: We'll hear a play tomorrow. / [*To First Player*] [...] Can you play *The Murder of Gonzago*? / FIRST PLAYER: Ay, my lord. / HAM.: We'll ha't tomorrow night [...]" 2.2.530–534), but also supplements the script with a short speech he wrote himself ("[...] a speech of some dozen or sixteen lines, which I would set down and insert in't [...]." 2.2.535 f.). What these "dozen or sixteen lines" may be, or if they are to be found in the "play within the play" at all, is debated (see the editor's notes as well as Jenkins, "Longer Notes," pp. 481 f.,

When the murder finally takes place on stage, the performance is interrupted ("OPHELIA: The King rises. / [...] POLONIUS: Give o'er the play. / KING: Give me some light. Away." 3.2.259–262). Although Hamlet feels at first entitled to derive the proof of guilt from the behaviour of the king ("HAM.: O good Horatio, I'll take the ghost's word for / a thousand pound. Didst perceive?" 3.2.280 f.), Horatio's neutral statements, which do not refer to any specific reaction of Claudius, show no certainty in this regard ("HOR.: Very well, my lord. / HAM.: Upon the talk of poisoning? / HOR.: I did very well note him." 282–284). What is crucial, however, is that Hamlet introduces the "murderer" as "nephew to the King" (3.2.239). This puts the reason for Claudius' abrupt leaving of the performance up for discussion: he might not have seen the scene as an allusion to his own crimes, but rather to a potential assassination attempt by his nephew Hamlet. It is also noteworthy that during the "dumb-show" that precedes *The Murder of Gonzago*, whose plot it anticipates and which illustrates the poisoning in the garden, there is no reaction to be seen on the part of the royal couple.[31] Claudius himself reveals that he is guilty of murdering his brother only in a soliloquy in the following scene ("O, my offence is rank, it smells to heaven; / It hath the primal eldest curse upon't– / A brother's murder. [...]" 3.3.36–38).[32]

In this way the true circumstances of his father's death remain hidden from Hamlet until the end of the play. Ultimately, he kills his uncle—just before his own violent death. But this is done only after the fatally wounded Laertes informs him of Claudius' intrigue concerning their duel and his plans concerning (Young) Hamlet's murder (see 5.2.316–333). Evidence about the reality status of the ghost and his words, about Claudius' guilt and thus the justification for revenge are not

---

p. 507). Ultimately, however, and in particular regarding the interpretative approach pursued here, this is not of high relevance.

31 Especially since the allusion to the murder of Hamlet's father appears quite explicit there. As the stage direction says: "The trumpet sounds. A dumb show follows. Enter a King and a Queen very lovingly, the Queen embracing him and he her. She kneels and makes show of protestation unto him. He takes her up and declines his head upon her neck. He lies him down upon a bank of flowers. She, seeing him asleep, leaves him. Anon comes in another Man, takes off his crown, kisses it, pours poison in the sleeper's ears, and leaves him. The Queen returns, finds the King dead, makes passionate action. The Poisoner with some Three or Four comes in again. They seem to condole with her. The dead body is carried away. The Poisoner woos the Queen with gifts. She seems harsh awhile, but in the end accepts his love." (3.2.133/134)

32 His pangs of conscience are already indicated at the beginning of this act: "POL.: 'Tis too much prov'd, that with devotion's visage / And pious action we do sugar o'er / The devil himself. KING: [*aside*] O'tis too true. / How smart a lash that speech doth give my conscience. / The harlot's cheek, beautied with plast'ring art, / Is not more ugly to the thing that helps it / Than is my deed to my most painted word. / O heavy burden!" (3.1.49–54).

obtainable by Hamlet until his own end—for the protagonist, there is no "solution" to this dilemma, it remains a constellation of skeptical *isosthenia*.

Hamlet's doubt is universal and radical. Later in Descartes the initially adopted possibility of a malicious deception caused by a "geniu[s] [...] malignu[s]"[33] is excluded by the axiomatic authority of a benevolent God;[34] but for Hamlet the aspect of potential demonic deception remains virulent ("The spirit that I have seen / May be a devil").[35] While the radical skeptical doubt in the argument of the *Meditationes* will serve to overcome skepticism,[36] the staging of the uncertainty in *Hamlet* does not lead to a proclamation of solid evidence, nor does it result in a propagation of Pyrrhonian serenity—quite the contrary. This manifests itself through the disastrous and gloomy end of the drama (Horatio is the only survivor; two families have been extinguished; Denmark will be captured by Norway under Fortinbras). And the protagonist's attitude of *epoché* leads to no *ataraxia* whatsoever. Hamlet himself qualifies his hesitation again and again as highly problematic[37] and continues the search for certainty over large parts of the play. Completely in the spirit of Hamlet's remark at the end of the first act, "The time is out of joint. [...]" (1.5.196), uncertainty and ambiguity characterise Shakespeare's drama as a whole and are, so to speak, focused on the protagonist: "[...] Hamlet findet sich in einer Situation radikalen Ordnungsverlusts und des Zusammenbruchs aller bisherigen Gewißheiten." [Hamlet finds himself

---

33 "Supponam igitur non optimum Deum, fontem veritatis, sed genium aliquem malignum, eundemque summe potentem, & callidum, omnem suam industriam in eo posuisse, ut me falleret: putabo coelum, aërem, terram, colores, figuras, sonos, cunctaque externa nihil aliud esse quam ludificationes somniorum, quibus insidias credulitati mea tetendit[.]" (Descartes, *Meditationes*, pp. 22 f.) ["I will suppose therefore that not God, who is supremely good and the source of truth, but rather some malicious demon of the utmost power and cunning has employed all his energies in order to deceive me. I shall think that the sky, the air, the earth, colours, shapes, sounds and all external things are merely the delusions of dreams which he has devised to ensnare my judgement." (Descartes, *Meditations*, p. 15)]
34 See Descartes, *Meditationes*, pp. 34–52 (Meditatio 3), esp. pp. 41–52, pp. 53–62 (Meditatio 4), esp. p. 53, pp. 63–71 (Meditatio 5), esp. pp. 65–71, esp. p. 71, see also pp. 79 f. and p. 90; Descartes, *Meditations*, pp. 24–36 (Third Meditation), esp. pp. 28–36, pp. 37–43 (Fourth Meditation), esp. p. 37, pp. 44–49 (Fifth Meditation), esp. pp. 45–49, esp. p. 49, see also p. 55 and p. 62.
35 In his short comparison between Shakespeare and Descartes, John D. Cox sets Descartes' "demon hypothesis" in relation to *Macbeth*, however ("Shakespeare and the French Epistemologists," p. 32 f.).
36 See, e.g., Descartes, *Meditationes*, pp. 71–90 (Meditatio 6), esp. pp. 78–80, pp. 89 f.; see also p. 25, p. 27, pp. 28 f., pp. 34 f., pp. 37–40, pp. 68–71; Descartes, *Meditations*, pp. 50–62 (Sixth Meditation), esp. pp. 54–56, pp. 61 f.; see also pp. 16 f., p. 18, pp. 19 f., p. 24, pp. 25–28, pp. 47–49.
37 See, e.g., Hamlet's soliloquy following the "player's scene," 2.2.544–601, 544, 566–583; see also 4.4.32–66.

in a situation radically deprived of order and all previous certainties], as Verena Lobsien puts it.³⁸ This is also in close connection to the treatment of the dream in the play and in particular in its central monologue "To be or not to be" (3.1.56–88). The contemplation of death and use of the metaphorical dream concept in this context expresses that there are only probabilities, no certainties for Hamlet. "[...] To die—to sleep, / No more; [...] / [...] / [...] 'tis a consummation / Devoutly to be wish'd. To die, to sleep; / *To sleep, perchance to dream*—ay, there's the rub: / For in that sleep of death what dreams may come" (3.1.60–66; my italics). At the end of life is sleep; but *perhaps* the life after death harbours comparable, if not immensely more difficult, hellish suffering than earthly life.³⁹ That "the dread of something after death" not only ultimately outweighs the known evils to which man is exposed in this life, but also has an influence on his actions or non-action, is indicated in the last verses of the monologue.⁴⁰ Confronted with the question of carrying out the revenge on Claudius or not, while being uncertain concerning his guilt, it is the fear of eternal damnation that makes the eponymous hero decide against taking action. Continuing this line of thought, to gain certainty becomes an enterprise of even vital dimensions.

La vida es sueño is supposed to have been written around thirty-five years after Shakespeare's play was composed and it is embedded in the cultural-historical context of Counter-Reformation Spain. The resulting "different treatment" of skepticism becomes all the clearer when reading it against the backdrop of *Hamlet*.

Although there is a traditional prophetic dream used in the beginning, or rather in the plot's prehistory, the focus of Calderón's drama is not on actual dreams. Clorilene, Segismundo's mother, while pregnant, had repeatedly dreamed of giving birth to a "monstrosity"—"un monstruo en forma de hombre" ["a bold / monster in human shape"],⁴¹ "[la] víbora humana del siglo" ["the

---

38 Olejniczak Lobsien, *Skeptische Phantasie*, p. 105.
39 "But that the dread of something after death [...] / [...] puzzles the will, / And makes us rather bear those ills we have / Than fly to others that we know not of?" (3.1. 78–82).
40 "Thus conscience does make cowards of us all, / And thus the native hue of resolution / Is sicklied o'er with the pale cast of thought, / And enterprises of great pitch and moment / With this regards their currents turn awry / And lose the name of action. [...]" (3.1. 83–88).
41 Pedro Calderón de la Barca, *La vida es sueño* [1636], ed. Ciriaco Morón, 31st ed., *Letras Hispánicas* (Madrid: Cátedra, 2008), v. 672. All references to Calderón's play are to this edition and will be cited parenthetically by verse numbers in the text. The English translation is taken from Calderón, *Life Is a Dream/ La vida es sueño: A Dual-Language Book*, ed. and trans. Stanley Appelbaum (Mineola, NY: Dover Publications, 2002).

human viper of the age"] (v. 675)[42]—who would kill her, as we learn in the long speech given by the aging King Basilio (vv. 589–843, see vv. 660–675). We also learn that, indeed, Clorilene died in childbirth. His wife's dream and death form part of several dismal omens and observations related to Segismundo's birth,[43] which lead Basilio to the prognostication that his only son and rightful heir to the throne would become an arrogant, cruel man and tyrannical ruler bringing disaster to the country and eventually overthrow and kill him.[44] He spreads news in the kingdom that the newborn child had died and has his son secretly kept as a prisoner in a tower in the mountains. There he has him raised by Clotaldo, the king's confidant, without Segismundo knowing anything of his royal birth (vv. 738–759). When the son is an adult, Basilio decides to test him. The father wishes to find out whether or not the prophecy is true: "quiero examinar si el cielo / [...] / o se mitiga o se temple / por lo menos, y vencido / con valor y con prudencia / se desdice;" (vv. 1102–1110) ["I wish to determine whether heaven / [...] / can be assuaged, or at least / mollified, and whether, overcome / by merit and wisdom, / it can go back

---

42 Regarding the image of the "viper," see the interpretation in Frederick A. de Armas, "The Serpent Star: Dream and Horoscope in Calderón's *La vida es sueño*," *Forum for Modern Language Studies* 19 (1983), pp. 208–223, pp. 210–212.

43 "BASILIO: [...] [L]os cielos / se agotaron de prodigios. / [...] / [N]ació en horóscopo tal, / que el sol, en su sangre tinto, / entraba sañudamente / con la luna en desafío; / [...] / El mayor, el más horrendo / eclipse que ha padecido / el sol, después que con sangre / lloró la muerte de Cristo, / éste fue; [...] / [...] / Los cielos se escurecieron, / temblaron los edificios, / llovieron piedras las nubes, / corrieron sangre los ríos. / En este [...] / mortal planeta o signo / nació Segismundo dando / de su condición indicios, / pues dio la muerte a su madre [...]" (vv. 662–704) ["BAS.: (...) (T)he heavens / exhausted their miracles(.) / (...) / (H)e was born at such an astrological conjunction / that the sun, tinged with its blood, / was fiercely entering / into a joust with the moon(;) / (...) / The greatest, most terrifying / eclipse ever suffered by / the sun from the time when it bloodily / bewailed the death of Christ / was this one(;) (...) / (...) / The sky was darkened, / buildings shook, / the clouds rained stones, / the rivers ran blood. / Under this (...) / fatal planet or sign / Segismundo was born, giving / an indication of his nature, / because he killed his mother."]

44 "Bas.: Yo, acudiendo a mis estudios, / en ellos y en todo miro / que Segismundo sería / el hombre más atrevido, / el príncipe más cruel / y el monarca más impío, / por quien su reino vendría / a ser parcial y diviso, / escuela de las traiciones / y academia de los vicios; / y él, de su furor llevado, / [...] / había de poner en mí / las plantas, y yo rendido / a sus pies me había de ver: / [...] / siendo alfombra de sus plantas / las canas del rostro mío." (vv. 708–725) ["BAS.: I, referring to my books, / found in them, and in all things, / that Segismundo would be / the most insolent man, / the most cruel prince, / and the most impious monarch, / through whom his kingdom would come / to be fragmented and divided, / a school for treason / and an academy of vice; / and that he, carried away by his fury, / (...) / would one day set his foot / on me, and that I, surrendering / would find myself groveling before him / (...) / the gray hairs of my beard / serving as a carpet to his feet."] See also vv. 604–606, vv. 612–643, for Basilio as a scientist and the basis for his prognosis, the science of astrology.

on its word;"].⁴⁵ If the prince proves to be a good ruler contrary to the prediction, he will ascend the throne.⁴⁶ Should he, however, "haughtily, boldly, insolently, / and cruelly give[s] free rein / to his vices" ("soberbio, osado, atrevido / y cruel con rienda suelta / corre el campo de sus vicios" vv. 817–819), he will be imprisoned forever (vv. 824 f.).⁴⁷ For the purpose of this test, Segismundo is drugged with a narcotic and brought to the palace in order to rule.⁴⁸

The discussion of the play's central theme already stated in its title starts at this point and is intimately connected to the drama's concern with the contemporary debate about skepticism.⁴⁹ Calderón's *comedia* advances the core skeptical thesis of the unreliability of the senses with a firmly established element in the skeptics' repertoire, namely the problem of being able to distinguish between the state of dreaming and of wakefulness, which refers verbatim to the fourth trope of Sextus Empiricus mentioned above. The mode of representation used to put skepticism on stage is, structurally speaking, a sort of play-within-a-play, a play whose protagonist is not aware of his role. Segismundo's skepticism and the related questions concerning the ethical-practical realm are generated only

---

45 J. Küpper interprets "[...] Basilio as a literary model of emerging Empiricism [...]." ("*Hamlet* and *La vida es sueño,*" p. 398): "Basilio's procedural mode can be summarized as follows: first observing nature, then trying to systematize the data and organize them according to the principle of causality [...], and finally, based on this analysis, venturing a prognostication in order to control future contingency. [...] [T]he aim pursued by Basilio [...] [is] to reduce possible misfortune [...]." (ibid.). In view of the "message" of the play—this should be mentioned already— Basilio represents one of those figures who "fail." In this way, the concept of "modernity" (for which he stands) is also "rejected" through the plot development of the play (see on this aspect pp. 396–399 and esp. Küpper, "*La vida es sueño,*" pp. 392–399). The philosophical basis of this strain of modern epistemology emerging in the seventeenth century is skepticism (the reference point being primarily the second tradition of ancient skepticism, Academic skepticism): sensory perception can deceive; hence, the results are always subject to potential revision. If Calderón's play formulates a critique of the emerging, modern paradigm of empiricism, it is also an implicit criticism of (here: Academic) skepticism.

46 "Bas.: [...] siendo / prudente, cuerdo y benigno, / desmintiendo en todo al hado / que dél tantas cosas dijo, / gozaréis el natural / príncipe vuestro [...]" (vv. 808–813) ["(...) if he is / prudent, sane, and beneficent, / and completely gives the lie to the prophecy / that said all those things about him, / you will enjoy the presence of your / natural prince (...)"].

47 In the latter case, Astolfo and Estrella, the king's nephew and niece, will ascend the Polish throne as a royal couple (vv. 831–835).

48 See Clotaldo's account, vv. 989–1087.

49 This concerns the play's main plot with its protagonist Segismundo. However, see also how already Clotaldo, after his first conversation with Rosaura (dressed as a man and carrying his sword), is faced with doubts about the reliability of his sensory perception linked to the question of the (morally) right action, ultimately taking a classic skeptical position, i.e. abstaining from taking a decision and from taking action, vv. 395–468.

by the orchestration of his father, who undertakes this approach so he can tell his son (in the event that he fails the test) that his experience as a ruler had only been a dream.[50]

When Segismundo, disoriented and confused, awakens in the royal palace, he says the following:

> SEGISMUNDO:
> ¡Válgame el cielo! ¿Qué veo?
> ¡Válgame el cielo! ¿Qué miro?
> Con poco espanto lo admiro,
> con mucha duda lo creo.
> ¿Yo en palacios suntuosos?
> ¿Yo entre telas y brocados?
> ¿Yo cercado de criados
> tan lucidos y briosos?
> ¿Yo despertar de dormir
> en lecho tan excelente?
> ¿Yo en medio de tanta gente
> que me sirva de vestir?
> Decir que sueño es engaño,
> bien sé que despierto estoy.
> ¿Yo Segismundo no soy?
> Dadme, cielos, desengaño.
> [...]
> Pero sea lo que fuere,
> ¿quién me mete en discurrir?
> Dejarme quiero servir,
> y venga lo que viniere.
> (vv. 1224–1247)

---

[50] See the whole passage, vv. 1120–1149, in whose last verses Basilio supplements the measure using the play's title metaphor, formulated here for the first time, which will in the course of the play, and in view of the "transformation" of the protagonist, become increasingly relevant, being itself subject to a change in meaning ("podrá entender que soñó / y hará bien cuando lo entienda, / porque *en el mundo*, Clotaldo, / *todos los que viven sueñan*." [vv. 1146–1149; my italics] ["he will be able to surmise that it was a dream; / and it will be a good thing for him to realize, / because in this world, Clotaldo, / everyone who lives is a dreamer"]). Even if the corresponding meaning within the context of the Segismundo plot still remains to be discussed, it may be noted that, according to the reading supported here, this reference to "life is a dream" stands in connection to the skeptical notion of the indistinguishability of waking and sleeping. If Basilio implies that because of this it would be irrelevant whether Segismundo lives in a palace or in a prison, this can be seen as a reference to the skeptics' moral indifferentism. The problem here is in particular—and this represents from the play's point of view a configuration directed against skepticism—that Basilio applies this indifference only to the life of his son but not to himself, since the aim of his own actions is to prevent being deprived of his status.

[SEG.: Heaven help me! What's this I see? / Heaven help me! What do I behold? / I marvel at it with little fear, / but I believe it only with great doubt. / I in a luxurious palace? / I amid fabrics and brocade? / I surrounded by such well-dressed, / energetic servants? / I awakening from sleep / in such an excellent bed? / In the midst of so many people / helping me to dress? / To say I'm dreaming is mistaken, / I know very well I'm awake. / Am I not Segismundo? / Heavens, clarify my confusion! / (...) / But, whatever it may be, / who's forcing me to ponder it? / I want to let myself be served, / come what may.]

On account of the entirely new situation in which he finds himself, Segismundo doubts the reality of his sensory impressions. In a classic skeptical manner, he wonders if he is awake or dreaming. Then he interjects that the perceptions that appear so doubtful to him could not be a dream, since he knows with certainty that he is awake. Attempting to reassure himself, he asks whether he might not be himself, not Segismundo. His current perceptions cannot be reconciled with his life until that point, with his existence as a prisoner in the tower, because after all Segismundo does not know at this time that he is a prince.[51] In order to gain certainty, the protagonist attempts, somewhat unsuccessfully, to construct the argument that Descartes would later advance to refute the skeptical dream trope. Based on the examination of whether continuity can be established between perceptions appearing doubtful at the moment and the life led up to that point, the dreaming and the waking state can be held distinct from each other according to Descartes' argumentation.[52] Gripped by uncertainty, Segismundo pleads to heaven in a ritual and formulaic way for *desengaño*, that is, to be freed of his possible delusion. However, the "right way" implicitly suggested from the perspective of the play is first abandoned by Segismundo. Pondering further about whether he is dreaming or awake appears to him to be irrelevant, but regarding his actions the conclusion he draws is to enjoy to the fullest the amenities and comforts that he subjectively perceives as real ("Pero sea lo que fuere, / ¿quién me mete en discurrir? / Dejarme quiero servir, / y venga lo que viniere." vv. 1244–1247). The following scene in the palace is characterised by Segismundo's violent actions

---

51 As the "director" Basilio says, later he will be informed by Clotaldo of his royal descent and the circumstances that led to his life in isolation (vv. 1268–1294).
52 See Descartes, *Meditationes*, pp. 89 f. ("Cum vero eae res occurrunt, quas distincte, unde, ubi, & quando mihi adveniant, adverto, earumque perceptionem absque ulla interruptione cum tota reliqua vita connecto, plane certus sum, non in somnis, sed vigilanti occurrere." p. 90); Descartes, *Meditations*, pp. 61 f. ("But when I distinctly see where things come from and where and when they come to me, and when I can connect my perceptions of them with the whole of the rest of my life without a break, then I am quite certain that when I encounter these things I am not asleep but awake." p. 62). The references to the skeptical "dream trope," and the connection to Descartes' argumentation, are already to be found in Küpper, "*La vida es sueño*," esp. pp. 399 f., p. 400, n. 46, p. 401, n. 50.

aimed at fulfilling his desires.[53] In short, he does not pass the test arranged by his father. Consequently, Basilio has him transported back to his prison while putting him to sleep once again. When he awakens in this familiar environment and is convinced by Clotaldo that what he experienced in the palace was just a dream (vv. 2092–2108), the doubts about the reliability of his sensory perception increase compared to the selective uncertainty experienced the first time he awoke. In terms of perception, he cannot distinguish between his current experience and the experience in the palace that has been explained to him by Clotaldo as a dream, so he ponders the possibility that he is dreaming even now: "SEG.: [...] si ha sido soñado, / lo que vi palpable y cierto, / lo que veo será incierto; / y no es mucho que rendido, / pues veo estando dormido, / que sueñe estando despierto." (vv. 2102–2107) ["(...) if what I saw palpably and surely / was just a dream, / what I see now is probably doubtful; / and it wouldn't be a surprise that, / if I see clearly while asleep, / I should dream while awake."][54]

The conclusion drawn by him consists in the skeptical thesis of fundamental doubt concerning the reliability of sensory perception. This is expressed metaphorically in Segismundo's famous monologue at the end of the second *jornada*. All of life is a dream, concludes the protagonist: "¿Qué es la vida? Un frenesí. / ¿Qué es la vida? Una ilusión, / una sombra, una ficción, / y el mayor bien es pequeño, / que toda la vida es sueño, / y los sueños, sueños son." (vv. 2182–2187) ["What is life? / A frenzy. / What is life? An illusion, / a shadow, a fiction, / and our greatest good is but small; / for, all of life is a dream, / and even dreams are dreams."].[55]

---

53 These radically self-centred actions (following the passage quoted above and the "maxim" uttered later, "Nada me parece justo / en siendo contra mi gusto." [vv. 1417 f.] ["Nothing seems right to me / if it goes against my grain."]), initially staged as a consequence of Segismundo's indissoluble doubt about the reality status of his perceptions and conveying to that extent a critique of skepticism, include one murder (vv. 1422–1431), three attempted killings (e.g., vv. 1680–1693) and one attempted rape (vv. 1624–1667). Regarding the implication of hedonism, see Küpper, "La vida es sueño," pp. 406 f. See also Everett W. Hesse's description: "Since no 'desengaño' is forthcoming to relieve the anxiety arising from his inability to explain his predicament, he [Segismundo] finds it easier to allow his behavior *to follow the pleasure principle* [...]." ("The Role of Deception," pp. 121 f.; my italics).
54 See the similar line of argument in Descartes' first *Meditatio* (Descartes, *Meditationes*, p. 19; Descartes, *Meditations*, p. 13), and more explicit in the sixth *Meditatio* (Descartes, *Meditationes*, p. 77; Descartes, *Meditations*, p. 53). See also the reference in Küpper, "La vida es sueño," p. 401, n. 47. Furthermore, see the respective passage in Montaigne's *Apologie* (Michel de Montaigne, *Apologie de Raimond de Sebonde*, Essais 2:12 [1580–1588], in: *Les Essais*, edd. Jean Balsamo, Michel Magnien, Catherine Magnien-Simonin, and Alain Legros, Bibliothèque de la Pléiade [Paris: Gallimard, 2007], pp. 458–642, pp. 633 f.).
55 According to J. Küpper's apt interpretation: "[...] [Segismundo] draws a conclusion that we could understand as the transition from the literal meaning of the concept of 'dream' to a

But the play does not stop at this reference to the basic tenet of skepticism. It is Clotaldo who reminds Segismundo that epistemological uncertainty does not suspend the validity of basic ethical norms: "Segismundo, que aún en sueños / no se pierde el hacer bien." (vv. 2146 f.) ["CLOTALDO: Segismundo, because even in dreams / good deeds are never wasted."][56]

When Segismundo is freed from the tower at the beginning of the third *jornada* by rebels who seek to prevent foreign rule and install the legitimate successor on the throne, he is once again faced with the problem of adequately classifying his perception. And due to his previous experience, he also considers to be an illusion what he is experiencing now: "SEG.: [...] Ya / otra vez vi aquesto mesmo / tan clara y distintamente / como agora lo estoy viendo, / y fue sueño. [...]" (vv. 2348–2352) ["(...) Once before / in the past I saw the very same thing / just as clearly and distinctly / as I see it now, / and it was a dream."].[57]

---

metaphorical one. If, indeed, we cannot trust our sensory perceptions to distinguish the real from the unreal (or fictitious), if 'life' ('*la vida*') is 'una ilusión, una sombra, una ficción,' then the proposition 'toda la vida es sueño' [...] is true, not in the sense that one would always be dreaming, but in the sense that everything we experience is unreliable. One could call this step in Segismundo's intellectual development the stage of classical Pyrrhonian Scepticism, that is, of radical doubt." ("*Hamlet* and *La vida es sueño*," p. 372; see also Küpper, "*La vida es sueño*," pp. 401 f.).

56 In anticipation of the discussion below of the third *jornada*, the play's Christian-Catholic frame should be pointed out. In Bárbara Mujicas words: "The truth comes to Segismundo not through reflexion or observation but through revelation. Clotaldo, the teacher, articulates God's message, even though he does not identify it as such: 'aún en sueños / no se pierde el hacer bien' [...]. Man must act, for it is through his actions that he will be judged after death." ("Calderón's *La vida es sueño* and the Skeptical Revival," p. 29). See also Segismundo's first verses ("Es verdad; pues reprimamos / esta fiera condición, / esta furia, esta ambición, / por si alguna vez soñamos." vv. 2148–2151 ["It's true, then: let me restrain / my fierce nature, / my fury, my ambition, / in case I ever dream again."]), which show his readiness now to suppress those impulses to which he gave way uncontrollably during the palace episode. See, moreover, vv. 2158–2164, vv. 2168–2177, for the evocation of images of the transience of earthly goods and all worldly existence, and vv. 2156 f., for an allusion to the horizon of the Christian afterlife.

57 "SEG.: [...] [S]é / que toda esta vida es sueño, / idos, sombras, que fingís / hoy a mis sentidos muertos / cuerpo y voz, siendo verdad / que ni tenéis voz ni cuerpo; / que no quiero majestades / fingidas, pompas no quiero, / fantásticas ilusiones / [...] / Para mí no hay fingimientos; / que, desengañado ya, / sé bien que *la vida es sueño*." (vv. 2320–2343; italics in the original) ["(S)ince I know / that all of this life is a dream, / away with you, you shadows that today / pretend to my numbed senses / that you have a body and a voice, / though the truth is you have neither voice nor body; / for I don't want majesty / that is feigned, I don't want pomp / that is imagery, illusions / (...) / For me there is no more pretense, / because now, undeceived, / I know perfectly well that *life is a / dream*."]. When one of the soldiers attempts to dispel Segismundo's suspicion of deception by referring, as an indication of the reality of their undertaking, to the large number of his subordinates whom he can *see* by looking out in the mountains (vv. 2344–2348), Segismundo

Nevertheless, after initial hesitation (see vv. 2307–2352), the Polish prince decides to comply with the request of the soldiers and to march against the army of his father in the struggle to establish his legitimate rule. He decides to act. This action, however, is no longer subordinate to satisfying his own desires, but is undertaken in the general public interest;[58] Segismundo thus reconfirms the lesson taught by Clotaldo: "SEG.: [...] sea verdad o sueño, / obrar bien es lo que importa; / si fuere verdad, por serlo; / si no, por ganar amigos / para cuando despertemos." (vv. 2423–2427) ["(...) whether it's reality or a dream, / to do good is what matters; / if it should be reality, just because it is good; / if not, for the sake of winning friends / for the time when we awaken."][59] It is the "*obrar bien*," "to do good; to do right," which the protagonist elevates to a maxim of his actions. And this imperative applies in waking as well as in dream states. The dream-life metaphor now refers to the Christian metaphysical framework of this world and the hereafter. And the implication of the Counter-Reformation dogma is that one's actions on earth (in the state of dream) are decisive for the afterlife which is the "real" waking state.

The liberation by the soldiers, as well as the subsequent encounters and events,[60] are ultimately able to substantiate for Segismundo that what had happened in the palace was reality and not just a dream. But he does not interpret this evidence as a guarantee of certainty, in the sense of the continuity argument later developed by Descartes. From Segismundo's perspective, there is no reliable distinction between reality and dream, reality and illusion, truth and deception,

---

replies with the lines quoted above—using a formulation that also features prominently in the context of Cartesian philosophy. Segismundo's expression of doubt refers to the unreliability of perception: even if this is "clear and distinct," it does not convey any certainty concerning the ontological status of what is perceived and may just as well turn out to be a deception. For Descartes, however—and this difference is crucial—, the formulation "clear and distinct" (*clare et distincte*) occurs in the context of the requirements for the concepts linked to the guarantors of certainty, the innate ideas. See, e.g., Descartes, *Discours de la méthode* [1637], in: *Œuvres de Descartes*, vol. 6, pp. 1–78, pp. 11–22, esp. p. 18 (Descartes, *Discourse on the Method*, in: *The Philosophical Writings of Descartes*, vol. 1, pp. 111–151, pp. 116–122, esp. p. 120); Descartes, *Principia philosophiae* [1644], in: *Œuvres de Descartes*, vol. 8:1, p. 21 f. (Descartes, *Principles of Philosophy*, in: *The Philosophical Writings of Descartes*, vol. 1, pp. 193–291, p. 207 f.); Descartes, *Meditationes*, pp. 35–40 (Descartes, *Meditations*, pp. 24–28). See in this respect Henry W. Sullivan's analysis ("*Tam clara et evidens*") and also Küpper, "*La vida es sueño*," p. 408, n. 71.

58 "SEG.: Vasallos, [...] / [...] en mí lleváis / quien os libre, osado y diestro, / de extranjera esclavitud. / Tocad al arma [...] / [...] / Contra mi padre pretendo / tomar armas [...]" (vv. 2373–2380) ["Vassals, (...) / (...) in me you have / a man who will boldly and skillfully free you / from foreign servitude. / Sound the alarm (...) / (...) / I intend to take arms / against my father (...)"].

59 See also vv. 2359–2372, vv. 2399–2401.

60 See the encounters with Clotaldo (vv. 2387–2427) and esp. with Rosaura (vv. 2690–3015).

original and copy.⁶¹ Even the momentary realisation that the experience in the palace was not a dream but reality could be the result of a universal deceit (in the sense of the *genius malignus* hypothesis later proposed by Descartes).⁶²

One can understand the doubt as it is presented in *La vida es sueño* using Descartes' term "hyperbolic doubt."⁶³ The result of overcoming skepticism by means of rhetoric, undertaken in Descartes, leads to rationalism, which lays the ground for modernity.⁶⁴ In Calderón, skepticism is not overcome epistemologically (epistemologically, the *comedia* ultimately stands in continuity with Pyrrhonism), but in terms of moral philosophy in line with Catholic dogmatics. The certainty question is repositioned: the question of whether sensory perception is reliable or not is irrelevant to earthly life. Of relevance is the dimension of the beyond, which is the place of true life, of certainty, of the waking state (a category that does not exist from a skeptical perspective). Orientation for the disoriented is provided by Christian faith and the moral-theological principles for practical action as taught by the Church: it is the "obrar bien," the right course of action, through which man can "earn" the "true life" after death. Segismundo formulates this lesson as follows:

> [...] ¡con mis razones propias
> vuelvo a convencerme a mí!
> Si es sueño, si es vanagloria,
> ¿quién, por vanagloria humana,
> pierde una divina gloria?
> [...]
> [...] si sé

---

61 See vv. 2938–2949: "¿[...] [T]an parecidas / a los sueños son las glorias, / que las verdaderas son / tenidas por mentirosas, / y las fingidas por ciertas? / ¿Tan poco hay de unas a otras / que hay cuestión sobre saber / si lo que se ve y se goza, / es mentira o es verdad? / ¿Tan semejante es la copia / al original, que hay duda / en saber si es ella propia?" ["Are glories (...) / so similar to dreams / that real ones / are considered fictitious / and feigned ones true? / Is there so little difference between them / that it's questionable knowledge / whether what one sees and enjoys / is a lie or the truth? / Is the copy so similar / to the original that doubt arises / as to which is which?"]
62 See Küpper, "*La vida es sueño*," p. 404, n. 57; Lema-Hincapié, "¿Existir en sueño o en vigilia?," p. 59, who both compare the Basilio of the first and second acts with Descartes' "demonic deceiver."
63 Descartes, *Meditationes*, p 89 ("hyperbolicae [...] dubitationes"); Descartes, *Meditations*, p. 61 ("exaggerated doubts"). With regard to Calderón's representation in *dramatic* form, the "play-within-the-play"-like structure is a crucial element: Segismundo's skeptical doubts about the reliability of his senses are triggered by means of Basilio's staged artificial dream.
64 It should be recalled that Cartesian autonomous realism ultimately also only works if one excludes the thesis of a "malicious demon" as ruler of the world.

> que es el gusto llama hermosa
> que la convierte en cenizas
> cualquiera viento que sopla,
> acudamos a lo eterno,
> que es la fama vividora,
> donde ni duermen las dichas,
> ni las grandezas reposan.
> (vv. 2967–2985)

[I convince myself (...) / with my own reasoning! / If it's a dream, if it's vainglory, / who, in exchange for human vainglory, / would lose a divine glory? / (...) / (...) if I know / that pleasure is a lovely flame / that is turned to ashes / by any wind that blows, / let us look to eternity, / which is everlasting fame / where good fortune does not sleep / and grandeur does not take repose!]

In relation to the position toward skepticism taken in the *comedia*, I would like to mention two further aspects. It is the insight granted to Segismundo that makes him become a good Catholic Christian and Christian ruler, rather than a skeptical adherence to the "traditions of the ancestors" (in this case: Catholicism). In accordance with the Christian concept, Segismundo's attitude is an activist one, which stands in marked contrast to the skeptical course of non-action. In keeping with the genre, the ending of the *comedia* is harmonious, with the new ruler Segismundo subordinating his own wishes to the "general good" and the restoration of order.[65]

---

[65] The "reformed" Segismundo not only curbs his anger against his father (after having defeated the king's army, he submits to Basilio, who in turn transfers the crown to his son [vv. 3146–3253]), he also renounces his own desire for Rosaura and finally orders Astolfo to marry her (vv. 2958–2992, vv. 3005–3015, vv. 3255–3261); he himself will take Estrella as bride (vv. 3278–3287). At the end of the play, the kingdom is pacified, rule is stable, lost honour is restored through marriage, the dynastic problem is resolved by another marriage of convenience. With regard to the aspect of *prudentia* (the virtue that in traditional Christian moral theology primarily determines the *hacer bien*, the good action on earth), see, e.g., in more detail the already mentioned third encounter between Segismundo and Rosaura, here vv. 2950–2993. What is presented there is once again the temptation to allow moral indifference to prevail and to give in to *passio*, sensual desire; to put it plainly, Segismundo, as in the palace scene, again thinks of raping Rosaura (vv. 2954–2962). With the transformed Segismundo, however, *ratio* gains the upper hand ("Mas ¡con mis razones propias / vuelvo a convencerme a mí!" [vv. 2967 f.]) on the basis of the insight: "¿quién, por vanagloria humana, / pierde una divina gloria?" (vv. 2970 f.); "acudamos a lo eterno" (v. 2983). According to Tridentine dogma, for the baptised, it is possible to resist sinful temptation by using God-given reason. One could also say that reason (of the baptised) is able to control the will successfully. Suppressing his own desire, Segismundo now wants to restore Rosaura's honour and to pursue his intention to regain the crown (vv. 2986–2993); as royal ruler he will marry her off to the person with whom she has had a (secret) affair in the past.

Calderón composed two other plays with the same title as his famous *comedia* discussed here. A first version of the *auto sacramental* called *La vida es sueño* originated around the same time as the *comedia*, and a second version, provided with a *loa*, was written by Calderón in his later period, on the occasion of the Corpus Christi celebration in Madrid in 1673. This latter was first printed in 1677 in the *Primera parte de autos sacramentales*.[66] The dream-*auto* cannot be discussed in detail here and it is not intended to interpret it as an allegorical explanation for the *comedia*. In order to contextualise (and substantiate) what has been argued above, some remarks concerning the *auto* may be made. The *auto sacramental* is especially suited to shed light on the reasons why Calderón addresses skepticism in his best-known work and why he gave this treatment precisely the direction found in the *comedia*.

The *auto* renders immediately evident that an author of the Counter-Reformation ultimately cannot help but take a skeptical position as far as epistemology is concerned: with regard to the most sublime of the truths of faith, the real presence of Christ in the consecrated bread and wine, the senses do not lead the way to truth, they deceive and not only occasionally, but systematically. What the believer sees and tastes is bread (and wine).[67]

---

66 See Fernando Plata Parga, "Introducción," in: Calderón, *La vida es sueño: Edición crítica de las dos versiones del auto y de la loa*, ed. Plata Parga, *Teatro del Siglo de Oro: Ediciones críticas* (Kassel: Reichenberger; Pamplona: Universidad de Navarra, 2012), pp. 11–64, pp. 25–27, pp. 35–38 and pp. 45–47. The performance of the *autos sacramentales* formed part of the celebrations in worship of the Eucharist and the mystery of transubstantiation. The doctrine of transubstantiation, reaffirmed in the resolutions of the Council of Trent—the (permanent) real presence of Jesus Christ's body and blood in the consecrated substances of bread and wine—is one of the Catholic Church's dogmas most disputed by Protestantism. See *Canones, et decreta sacrosancti oecvmenici, et generalis Concilii Tridentini svb Pavlo III, Ivlio III, Pio IIII, Pontificibvs max[imis]* (Mediolanum: Antonius Antonianus, 1564), Sessio 13, 11 October 1551: "Decretum de sanctisimo Eucharistiæ Sacramento," fols. 29v–32r, esp. Caput 1 "De reali præsentia Domini nostri Iesu Christi, in sanctisimo Eucharistiæ Sacramento," fols. 29v–30r, Caput 4 "De transubstantatione," fol. 30v, Canones 1, 2, 4 and 8, fols. 31v–32r; *The Canons and Decrees of the Sacred and Œcumenical Council of Trent: Celebrated under the Sovereign Pontiffs Paul III, Julius III, and Pius IV*, trans. James Waterforth (London: Dolman, 1848), Session the Thirteenth, 11 October 1551: "Decree concerning the most holy sacrament of the Eucharist," pp. 75–84, esp. chap. 1 "On the real presence of our Lord Jesus Christ in the most holy sacrament of the Eucharist," p. 76, chap. 4 "On Transubstantiation," p. 78, Canons 1, 2, 4 and 8, pp. 82 f. This doctrine stipulates that sensory perception is unable to distinguish between a consecrated host and non-consecrated bread and wine, but that the former is different from the latter in "essence" or "substance," and therefore also in their effective power; according to Catholic dogma, the reception of the Eucharist is of fundamental importance for the salvation of the soul.

67 With regard to this *auto sacramental* it is in particular the *loa* that has to be mentioned. Set in the context of the dogma of Eucharistic transubstantiation, it represents an allegorically drama-

In terms of praxis, however, to adopt the ancient skeptics' indifference and "acquiescence in that which is" as a guideline for action would be unacceptable from a Christian point of view, as is evidenced not least by the *auto La vida es sueño*, whose action follows the genre's typical basic structure of Creation, Fall and Redemption.[68] For that "which is," is a fallen world; and adhering to it would

---

tised critique of the reliability of sensory perception and, related to this, the accentuation of the relevance of faith (and tradition). The allegorical figures of the five senses (Vista, Oído, Olfato, Gusto and Tacto) enter into an archery competition, their target being the Host and Chalice hanging at the top of a Cross. Vision, Smell, Touch and Taste fail, only Hearing succeeds and hits the target, because: "Oído: La Fe que allí hay cuerpo y alma / y carne y sangre me ha dicho; / y pues sentido de Fe / es solamente el Oído, / crea el Oído a la Fe / y no a los demás sentidos. / Que si la Vista, el Olfato, / el Tacto y el Gusto han visto, / tocado, olido y gustado / pan, es porque no han creído / que solos los accidentes / duran en aquel divino / milagro de los milagros, / [...] / no la substancia de pan, / pues con poder infinito / transubstanció la substancia / del pan en carne y del vino / en sangre[.] [¿][q]ui[e]n es la misma / verdad que imperiosa dijo: / 'Este es mi cuerpo y mi sangre' / con alma y vida[?] [...]" [Hearing: Faith has told me that there are body and soul / and flesh and blood; / and since the sense perception that belongs to Faith / is Hearing alone, / will the sense of Hearing believe Faith / and not what the other senses tell. / If the senses of Vision, Smell, / Touch and Taste have seen, / touched, smelled and tasted / bread, it is because they did not believe / that only the accidents / remain in this divine / miracle of miracles, / (...) / but not the substance of bread, / since by means of infinite power / transubstantiated the substance / of the bread into flesh and that of the wine / into blood he who is the same / truth as the one that (with soul and life) imperiously said: / 'This is my body and my blood' / (...).] (Calderón, *Loa para el auto intitulado* La vida es sueño, in: Calderón, *La vida es sueño: Las dos versiones del auto y de la loa*, pp. 83–101, vv. 223–244; my translation). On the unreliability of sensory perception in the context of the sacrament of the Eucharist, see Thomas Aquinas, *Summa theologiæ* 3^a q. 75 a. 5, esp. co., ad. 2 and ad. 3 (Thomas Aquinas, *Summa Theologiæ: Latin Text and English Translation, Introductions, Notes, Appendices and Glossaries*, ed. Thomas Gilby, 61 vols. [London: Blackfriars/Eyre & Spottiswood; New York, NY: McGraw-Hill, 1964–1973; repr. Cambridge/New York, NY: Cambridge University Press, 2006], vol. 58: *The Eucharistic Presence (3^a 73–78)*, ed. and trans. William Barden, pp. 72–77, esp. pp. 74 f., pp. 76 f.).

68 See Calderón, *Auto sacramental intitulado* La vida es sueño *[segunda versión; 1673]*, in: Calderón, *La vida es sueño: Las dos versiones del auto y de la loa*, pp. 105–199. For a small insight and contextualisation of what follows, I give a brief summary of the *auto*: The Four Elements (Agua, Aire, Tierra, Fuego) fight against each other, until Poder [Power], Sabiduría [Wisdom] and Amor [Love] (the Three Persons of the Holy Trinity) appear. These announce the creation of El Hombre [Man]. He will be endowed with Entendimiento [Understanding], by means of which he is capable of distinguishing between good and evil, and with Albedrío [free Will], which makes him able to act according to the bad as well as to the good. He will be able to rule and control the Elements and, furthermore, to gain Gracia [divine Grace] as a wife, if he passes the test: El Hombre will be brought to a splendid palace without him knowing of his role as God's crown prince; if he does not behave well, but in an arrogant and disobedient way, he will be expelled. La Sombra [Shadow/Darkness] and El Príncipe de las Tinieblas [The Prince of Darkness; Lucifer] lament on the occasion of the creation of Man. El Hombre is released from the prison of Non-mean to fall prey to sin. Christian ethics is decidedly activist; according to the Catholic view, seizing the possibility to oppose sin and to accept God's grace is placed in the (free) will of the (baptised) individual. But this "will to do the good" ultimately eludes all knowing. The right and good action is not based on knowledge; it is based on a higher, non-rational insight, the truth of which remains epistemologically unconfirmed and can attain persuasive power only rhetorically. Considering that Segismundo at the end of *La vida es sueño* is, within the limits of earthly possibility, a happy man, there is an implicit promise that the *obrar bien* not only guarantees otherworldly happiness, but also allows for a certain contentment already in one's earthly existence.

Drawing on DramaNet's theoretical conceptualisation of culture as a network, the revival of ancient skepticism in early modern Europe is an example of the extraction of floating material available in the cultural net. As this essay illustrates, the usage of this material pertained also to the two great theatre cultures of the time.[69]

Despite all their significant differences—in terms of genre, date of origin, linguistic and cultural context, or ideological agenda—both plays stage Pyrrhonian skepticism's basic assumption of the unreliability of sensory perception,

---

being, accompanied by Gracia who carries a torch. In the palace, El Hombre is amazed to find himself acclaimed, but soon full of pride he insists on his own free will and freedom of action. The advice and warnings given by Entendimiento seem a nuisance to him, and he prefers to turn to pleasure and Albedrío's flattery. Sombra and El Príncpe de las Tinieblas (now Pecado [Sin]), in disguise, offer him a poisoned apple. Entendimiento warns him of the disastrous deceptiveness of his senses and wants him to use reason, while Albedrío encourages him to pursue sensory delights. El Hombre hurls Entendimiento down a rock (with the help of Albedrío) and eats the apple, then he falls into a deathlike sleep. When El Hombre awakes in his dark prison, he wonders whether all this has been a dream. But he is now put in chains and when he calls Luz/Gracia [Light/Grace] Sombra appears. El Hombre recognizes the dimension of the afterlife (the awakening), which includes the recognition of the all-determining principle of the eternal (or: The Eternal) and the necessity to submit to this principle and to act according to its laws. He gets back Entendimiento and Albedrío, Albedrío being forcibly brought up by Entendimiento and laid at El Hombre's feet. El Hombre pleads with Poder for forgiveness. Sabiduría appears in human nature in the guise of a foreign wanderer and frees El Hombre from his chains, putting them on herself. Sombra and El Príncipe attack the prisoner, whom they mistake for El Hombre, with tree-branches, but fall down dead at the feet of Sabiduría/Christ on the cross. Finally, Agua supplies the element for baptism and each of the other Elements supplies some part of what will become the Eucharist. In order to be able to act "in the dream of life" according to the "laws of the Eternal" so that the "awakening" will not occur in the "prison of Darkness," El Hombre is accompanied by Entendimiento, Albedrío and Luz/Gracia (The Light of Grace); through the ritual repetition in the sacrament of the Eucharist he can always again participate in the grace conferred on him by the divine self-sacrifice.

69 For the concept and terminology, see the article by Joachim Küpper in this volume.

which ultimately also shows once more that this question was a problem that challenged thinkers from all over Europe in that era. The quest for certainty, the symptom of the time, so to speak, became more and more virulent particularly in the first half of the seventeenth century;[70] Descartes' project is only the most conspicuous symptom of the attempt to overcome skepticism with the intention to establish a firm basis of certainty, of *knowledge*, a philosophical foundation for the scientific exploration of the world.

In both *Hamlet* and *La vida es sueño* the theatrical device of the play-within-the-play is used to bring skepticism and the problems linked to it to the stage. The two dramas are not limited to merely staging the basic skeptical argument, but try to go further. The questions concerning epistemology are linked to the ethical dimension, raising fundamental questions of moral philosophy that the two plays approach and "answer," though in very different ways. In Calderón's treatment of skepticism, the focus is, ultimately, on religious didactics. In the sense of a "method" anticipating on a very abstract level the approach of Descartes, the doubt regarding sensory perception is exaggerated in *La vida es sueño* with the aim of preparing the recipients to accept the play's final argument committed to the Counter-Reformation project. From the perspective of the eternal world, the question of whether a distinction can be made between dream and reality is dismissed as irrelevant, in favour of the relevance of (ethical) action; the action has an effect, for better or for worse, in relation to the life in the world beyond. At the end of the *comedia* there is neither skeptical *epoché*, nor epistemology, but, rather, the certainty of religious dogma. In *Hamlet*, however, there is no "solution" provided for the problem posed by the basic skeptical argument; the play remains ambivalent in this regard. To that extent, it is an "open," modern text. Shakespeare does not raise the epistemological question from a dogmatic Christian standpoint, and he gave the material the form of a tragedy. As optimistic as the outcome is for the Polish prince presented in Calderón's drama, so disastrous is it for Shakespeare's Danish prince. In its consequences, skepticism, as it comes to be represented in *Hamlet*, is destructive. The ancient skeptics' "promise" of tranquil *epoché* (which is endorsed, for instance, by the serene humanism of Montaigne) is depotentiated and becomes substituted by despair. It is ultimately *not* possible to abdicate from sure knowledge of what *is*—in this way, Shakespeare's play certainly does not present any solutions; but it clearly formulates a desideratum, without, however, pointing out the direction where its fulfilment may be found.

---

70 See Popkin, *History of Scepticism*, esp. pp. 97–99.

Madeline Rüegg
The Patient Griselda Myth and Marriage Anxieties on Early Modern English and Spanish Stages

The Patient Griselda myth tells the story of a marquis who is reluctant to get married, but, under pressure from his subjects, agrees to take a wife and chooses a poor young country girl for her virtues. Once married, he doubts his wife's perfection and therefore tests her for more than ten years by taking away her children, pretending to have them killed, and by repudiating her. Finally, the marquis asks her to prepare his second wedding with a young noble lady. This second wedding never occurs, since the marquis finally reveals that the bride and her brother are Griselda's children; what is actually celebrated is the family reunion and Griselda's patience. This tale, which to our modern perceptions may appear horrible, fascinated Europe from the late fourteenth century until the nineteenth century, as the many translations and adaptations it underwent attest.[1]

I consider the Patient Griselda narrative an early modern European myth both in the specific Aristotelian sense of *mythos*, i.e., a story of some length that is easily remembered, with a beginning, middle and end, which can be used as a plot or argument for drama, and the more general meaning of a story belonging to a wider network of stories constituting the mythology of a given culture at a certain point in time. I here follow William G. Doty's definition of mythology:

> A mythological corpus consists of (1) a usually complex network of myths that are (2) culturally important, (3) imaginal (4) stories, conveying by means of (5) metaphoric and symbolic diction, (6) graphic imagery, and (7) emotional conviction and participation (8) the primal, foundational accounts (9) of aspects of the real, experienced world and (10) humankind's roles and relative statuses within it.
>
> Mythologies may (11) convey the political and moral values of a culture and (12) provide systems of interpreting (13) individual experience within a universal perspective, which may include (14) the intervention of suprahuman entities as well as (15) aspects of the natural and cultural orders. Myths may be enacted or reflected in (16) rituals, ceremonies, and dramas, and (17) they may provide materials for secondary elaboration, the constituent

---

[1] There are later adaptations, the most recent I am aware of being an American sequel presenting Griselda's daughter about to get married and trying to make sense of her mother's life-story (Tinney Sue Heath, *The Patience of Griselda* [e-book: Callihoo Publishing, 2011]). However, the tale has today clearly lost its previously enormous appeal.

https://doi.org/10.1515/9783110536881-006

mythemes (mythic units) having become merely images or reference points for a subsequent story, such as a folktale, historical legend, novella, or prophecy.[2]

I do not here have enough room for a thorough analysis of how the Patient Griselda story fits these criteria—and some obviously do not apply, such as number (8), "primal and foundational accounts"—but I will briefly demonstrate that most of these features can be identified when considering the artistic life of the story from its first known occurrence in the Italian Renaissance to the early modern period.[3]

Although it may not yet have functioned or been recognised as a myth when it initially appeared in Italy as the last *novella* of Giovanni Boccaccio's *Decameron* (written around 1353), its subsequent literary—oral and written—and iconographic life[4] gradually enabled the mythification of the Patient Griselda story at the European level.[5]

---

[2] William G. Doty, *Mythography: The Study of Myths and Rituals*, 2nd ed. (Tuscaloosa, AL: University of Alabama Press, 2000), pp. 33 f.
[3] For Doty, a myth does not need to meet all the above criteria, but a "sufficient number of common features among those of the definition to be recognisable as 'myth'" (*Mythography*, p. 33).
[4] For an analysis of the figure of Griselda in select representations in the pictorial arts see Judith Bronfman, *Chaucer's* Clerk's Tale: *The Griselda Story Received, Rewritten, Illustrated* (New York, NY/London: Garland Publishing, 1994), esp. chap. 5, pp. 93–124.
[5] Igor Candido links Boccaccio's *novella* with the myth of Psyche and Eros: "Boccaccio costruisce [...] il personaggio di Griselda su quello di Psiche, perfezionando il suo modello da un punto di vista morale. [...] il confronto tra Griselda e Psiche implica in chiave allegorica il superamento della seconda da parte della prima" [Boccaccio constructs [...] the character of Griselda on that of Psyche, perfecting his model from a moral point of view [...] the comparison between Griselda and Psyche implies in allegorical terms that the former surpasses the latter] (Igor Candido, "Amore e Psiche dalle chiose del *Laur.* 29.2 alle due redazioni delle *Genealogie* e ancora in *Dec.* X, 10," *Studi sul Boccaccio* 37 (2009), pp. 171–196, p. 195; my translation). He concludes that "[r]iscritta nella novella di Griselda, la *fabula* di Amore e Psiche assolveva alla stessa funzione che aveva nel suo contesto originale, consolare le donne ristrette dai voleri di padri, fratelli e mariti, tutti gli uomini segnati dall'esperienza della peste, ma nell'*exemplum* di una donna [...] Boccaccio [...] additava, alla fine del suo capolavoro, l'ideale di perfezione raggiungibile dall'anima umana" [rewritten in Griselda's *novella*, the *fabula* of Love and Psyche assumes the same function it had in its original context: comfort women restrained by the wills of fathers, brothers and husbands, all the men scarred by the experience of the plague, but in the *exemplum* of a woman [...] Boccaccio points out at the end of his masterpiece the ideal of perfection that a human soul can reach] (Candido, "Amore e Psiche," p. 196; my translation). Although Marina Warner rightly stresses that "[e]very telling of a myth is part of that myth: there is no ur-version, no authentic prototype, no true account" (Marina Warner, *Six Myths of Our Time: Little Angels, Little Monsters, Beautiful Beasts, and More* [New York, NY: Vintage Books, 1995], p. 13), I treat Boccaccio's text not as a myth but as the starting point from which Psyche and Eros's myth was reshaped to suit European-Christian culture and ideology—in other words mythology; and the *novella* would have to undergo a hundred and

From its original claimed purpose of representing a "matta bestialità"[6] or "foolish cruelty," according to Dioneo, the *novella*'s narrator, it became an edifying tale of the perfect Christian under Petrarch's pen in his 1373 Latin translation, "De obedentia [sic!] et fide uxoria" (*Seniles*, 17, 3). Since Petrarch's version, not only did the Italian story gain popularity at the European level, as the translations into many vernacular languages attest, but artists also started to represent some scenes from the story in paintings. In addition, probably under the influence of the title Petrarch gave the story, many of the literary and pictorial realisations of the tale were associated with wedding celebrations or marital life. The Catalan Bernat Metge dedicated his *Valter e Griselda* (1388) to Isabel de Guimerà with the hope of strengthening her already virtuous behaviour as a wife. The French Philippe de Mézière is the author of *Le Livre de la vertu du sacrement de mariage et du reconfort des dames mariees* (c. 1384–1389), which contains among other exemplary stories that of Griselda, and whose title makes explicit the didactic purpose of this collection of tales in relation to marriage. Mézière is also thought to have composed the first theatrical adaptation of the story, *L'Estoire de Griseldis* (1395), which may have been written to promote a marriage between Richard II of England and the French Isabella of Valois, given Mézière's implication in the match, and the fact that his richly illustrated manuscript provides nineteen pictorial representations of several scenes from the story.[7] In fifteenth-century Italy, common wedding gifts were *cassoni* or wooden chests decorated with paintings, which in the 1480s and 1490s frequently represented Griselda.[8] The anonymous Spanish "treatise" (as the author calls it), *Castigos y doctrinas que un sabio daba a sus hijas*, written in the fifteenth century, also uses the story of Griselda as an *exemplum* of wifely behaviour. *La historia de Griseldis Marquesa de Saluces: a exemplo de las dueñas casadas: prouocandolas a obediencia paciencia y constancia y a toda virtud* (anonymous, printed in 1544), as its title indicates, is addressed to wives and aims to teach them "obedience, patience and constancy and all virtues."

These are a few examples. During the fifteenth and the sixteenth centuries more adaptations and pictorial reproductions appeared not only in England,

---

fifty years of rewritings, translations, adaptations and iconographic representations to become, from an Italian story, an early modern European myth.
6 Giovanni Boccaccio, *Decameron* [1353], ed. Vittore Branca, 2 vols. (Torino: Einaudi, 1992), vol. 2, p. 1233.
7 See *L'Estoire de Griseldis* [1395], ed. Barbara Mary Craig (Lawrence, KS: University of Kansas Publications, 1954), pp. 4 f.
8 See Ellen Callmann, "The Growing Threat to Marital Bliss as seen in Fifteenth-Century Florentine Paintings," *Studies in Iconography* 5 (1979), pp. 73–92.

France, Spain and Italy, but all across Europe. These numerous rewritings,[9] and the fact that the simple mention of Griselda's name in any of its spellings (Grissild, Grissel, Griseldis, etc.) sufficed to evoke her story and her exemplarity, attest to the cultural importance of the story.[10] The above-mentioned examples of the story's artistic realisations being linked with marriage show that not only is it grounded in the real world, but it displays women's role in marital relationships as patiently obedient to their husbands, thereby conveying culturally-constructed moral values regarding the ceremony and ritual of marriage, taken as a lifelong commitment in which women are subordinate to men. In other words, by the early modern period Griselda had become the archetype of the patient, obedient and meek—that is to say ideal—wife, and her story a myth aimed at maintaining social order and gender hierarchy.

Consequently, at the turn of the sixteenth to seventeenth century, in an age in which the Reformation and the Counter-Reformation still debated the social and religious status of marriage, it seems only natural that Thomas Dekker, Henry Chettle and William Haughton in England and Félix Lope de Vega Carpio in Spain should have turned to the Patient Griselda myth to theatrically engage with the socio-political issue of the marital union.

Given that French versions in particular influenced some of the English and Spanish rewritings and translations, it is difficult to find a precise source or the specific textual realisation(s) of the myth on which the English and Spanish writers based the early modern plays I wish to analyse: Dekker, Chettle and Haughton's *The Pleasant Comedy of Patient Grissel* composed towards the end of 1599 and printed in 1603; and Lope de Vega's *El ejemplo de casadas o prueba de la paciencia* written between 1599 and 1603 and printed in 1615 in Madrid and in 1616 in Barcelona.[11]

---

[9] For a survey of all the adaptations of the story in Europe and beyond from the fourteenth until the twentieth century, see Raffaele Morabito, "La diffusione della storia di Griselda dal XIV al XX secolo," *Studi sul Boccaccio* 17 (1988), pp. 237–285.
[10] To mention but a few examples of the appearance of Griselda's name in early modern literature: William Forrest in 1558 wrote a hagiographical poem on the life of Catherine of Aragon renaming her "Grisild" (*The History of Grisild the Second*); in Shakespeare's *The Taming of the Shrew*, Petruccio claims that Catherine "[f]or patience [...] will prove a second Grissel" (William Shakespeare, *The Taming of the Shrew* [1623]: *Texts and Contexts*, ed. Frances Elizabeth Dolan [Boston, MA/New York, NY: Bedford Books of St. Martin's Press, 1996], 2.1.288).
[11] Regarding the date of the play, see Marie-Françoise Déodat-Kessedjian and Emmanuelle Garnier, "Prólogo," in: Félix Lope de Vega Carpio, *Comedias de Lope de Vega: Parte V* [1615], ed. Marie-Françoise Déodat-Kessedjian and Emmanuelle Garnier (Lleida: Milenio, 2004), pp. 35–48, pp. 35 f.

However, these plays still attest to a cultural transfer from Boccaccio's Italian text into Spanish and English cultures. While the story had achieved cultural relevance all across Europe by the end of the sixteenth century, it still bore many features of its Boccaccian realisation, especially in terms of the Aristotelian *mythos* or plot that I have summarised above: the storyline and its various narremes[12] of a wife of poor origins whose obedience and patience are tested by the taking away of her children, repudiation and active participation in the preparation of her husband's second wedding are clearly identifiable in both plays. At the same time, the *novella* underwent processes of acculturation or nationalisation, that is to say, both plays display English and Spanish traits, respectively.

In the English comedy the plot is all the more recognisable since not only the Italian setting in the town of Saluzzo and the surrounding area, but also the only three names Boccaccio gave to characters in the *novella* are preserved, though in English form. Following a tradition starting with Chaucer's retelling of the story in the *Clerk's Tale*, which turned Griselda's name first into Grisilde and, from the 1560s, into Grissil or Grissel, Dekker, Chettle and Haughton's Griselda is called Grissil. The same tradition has Gualtieri, the marquis, become alternatively Walter, Gautier or Gualter; the latter is the name retained by the playwrights. Griselda's father, Giannucole, in English rewritings becomes Janicola or Janicle; the former is the name used by Dekker, Chettle and Haughton.

The playwrights open their plays with a hunting scene in which the marquis's courtiers, Mario, Lepido and his brother, the marquis of Pavia, complain that Gualter promised to get married on this day but does not seem to be willing to keep his promise. The marquis actually leads them to Grissil's home. She is not a shepherdess but the daughter of a basket-maker and she has a servant, Babulo, the play's fool, and a brother, Laureo. Gualter asks both Janicola's and Laureo's consent to marry Grissil. When all agree to the match—Grissil included— the marquis not only brings his bride to his palace in Saluzzo but also invites the entire family to come and reside with them. As Grissil is about to give birth to twins, Gualter starts testing her. He first pretends to be angry at her by claiming that his subjects despise her for being low-born, and treats her worse than his own servants. Then, he banishes her family from court. When Grissil gives birth to her daughter and son, he continues his testing: he repudiates her and sends his wife and children back to the countryside. Shortly afterwards, Gualter orders Furio, his faithful servant, to go and take the babies from Grissil and to

---

12 I use narreme as the smallest unit of narration of prose narratives (e.g. Boccaccio's *novelle*), as well as of plays, following Helmut Bonheim's application of the term to drama in order to identify common narrative patterns from one play to another (see Helmut Bonheim, "Shakespeare's Narremes," *Shakespeare Survey* 53 [2000], pp. 1–11).

pretend to kill them while actually bringing them to Pavia to have them raised by his brother. Finally, he asks Grissil and her family to come back to Saluzzo to prepare his second wedding, which never takes place since the bride and her brother are Grissil's children. The marquis reveals who they are and celebrates Grissil's patience and restores her father's, brother's and servant's place at court. In addition Dekker, Chettle and Haughton devised two contrasting subplots with completely new material not present in any previous versions of the myth. The first one presents a Welsh lady, Gwenthyan, a widow and a shrew, once married to the marquis's late cousin, who marries a Welsh knight, Sir Owen ap Meredith. Their married life offers a parody and comic counterpart to Grissil's trials. In the second subplot, Julia, the marquis's sister, is courted by several suitors but prefers to remain a virgin and all the more so as she witnesses the married lives of the Welsh couple and that of her brother and Grissil.

Thus, while Dekker, Chettle and Haughton acknowledge and keep the Italian setting of the myth and create new characters to whom they give Italian names (Mario, Lepido, Babulo Furio, etc.), the English writers stick to the anglicised spellings derived from the reception of the story in England for the characters of Griselda, her father and the marquis. Moreover, the dramatists accentuate the British coloration of the myth by introducing the Welsh figures of Sir Owen ap Meredith and Lady Gwenthyan, as counterparts for Gualter and Grissil. Welsh characters were common on the early modern English stage, especially for comic purposes as is the case here. The unlikely presence of the Welsh couple in Saluzzo and the name changes into Grissil, Gualter and Janicola suggest that the Griselda myth had by then become part of English literary tradition and had acquired English traits.

Lope de Vega, while clearly using the myth as his basic plot structure, went further than the English playwrights in the process of acculturation: unlike any previous Spanish versions of the myth, he situated the *comedia*'s action on the Iberian Peninsula, in Catalonia, and gave Spanish names to all the characters: Griselda becomes Laurencia; Gualtieri, the marquis, becomes the Conde "Enrico de Moncada;"[13] and Griselda's father Giannucole is now Lauro.[14]

---

[13] All references to the play come from Lope de Vega, *El ejemplo de casadas y prueba de la paciencia*, in: *Comedias de Lope de Vega: Parte V*, pp. 51–133, and will be cited parenthetically by verse number in the text; here v. 29. All the translations are mine.

[14] For more on the myth's realisations in Spain, see Caroline Brown Bourland, "Boccaccio and the *Decameron* in Castilian and Catalan Literature," *Revue Hispanique* 12 (1905), pp. 163–189, 211–214; Isidoro Pisonero del Amo, "Un motivo boccacciano: 'La paciente Griselda' en la literatura española," in: Pedro Peira, ed., *Homenaje a Alonso Zamora Vicente*, 5 vols. (Madrid: Castalia, 1992), vol. 3, pt. 2, pp. 221–241; Juan Carlos Conde, "Un aspecto de la recepción del

The *comedia* begins with Enrico's courtiers entreating him to get married. Although he promises he will do so, he delays the moment of choosing a wife by going hunting and by giving audience to prisoners hoping to obtain his grace. The latter activity has no precedent in other Spanish versions of the tale and expands the myth's engagement with social issues, since the cases presented to the Conde all concern marriage. After pardoning all the prisoners, Enrico goes hunting again and then meets Laurencia. He immediately determines to marry her, which he does after obtaining both her and her father's consent. After Laurencia gives birth to a daughter and sometime later to a son, Enrico starts testing her by asking his servant Tibaldo to take away her daughter in order to have the child killed. The Conde then asks Laurencia for his son and pretends to have him too killed. Shortly afterwards, Enrico repudiates her and sends her back to her father. After spending several years in the countryside with her father, an additional character absent from previous rewritings, the widowed prince of Bearn, having heard of Laurencia's virtues, sends her a messenger to ask for her hand. At the same time another messenger arrives from Enrico's court to bid her to come back to the Conde's castle and prepare his second wedding. Laurencia rejects the prince of Bearn's offer on the grounds that she is still Enrico's wife and leaves to take care of the marriage celebration. Enrico's second nuptials never take place since he reveals that his supposed bride and her brother are Laurencia's children. The family is reunited and Laurencia's patience greatly praised.

By moving the myth's setting from Italy to Spain and giving his characters new Spanish names and titles, Lope turns Griselda and the marquis into Spanish figures. He even makes them appear to belong to Iberian history by setting the play during the time of the Third Crusade (1189–1192), in which Enrico is said to take part with the real historical figures of the English king Richard the Lionheart and the Spanish king Alfonso VIII. Though the latter did not actually take part in the Crusades, he was famous for his successful battle of the Navas de Tolosa against the Moors in 1212 during the Reconquista and, thus, helps to endow the play with an aura of national chronicle and legend. Consequently, through this process of nationalisation, Lope turns the Italian story into a Spanish legend.

The theoretical framework elaborated by the DramaNet research group, which considers culture as a net, helps us to consider the source problem from a new perspective and provides a metaphoric explanation of how Lope and Dekker, Chettle and Haughton, though separated in spatial terms, worked on plays presenting the same story. Culture, understood as "conscious concepts" and their

---

Decameron en la Península Ibérica, a la sombra de Petrarca. La historia de Griselda," *Cuadernos de Filología Italiana* Special Issue (2001), pp. 351–371.

"material forms,"[15] when envisaged through the metaphor of a net, in which these concepts and their material forms float without a necessarily clear starting point and circulate beyond national borders or within countries, allows for a better understanding of how the Griselda myth could be used in England and Spain at the same time. This story was readily available as a concept, plot or set of narremes and in material forms (books, manuscripts, paintings) not only within the respective English and Spanish cultural nets but also within the European cultural net. Therefore, Lope de Vega, Dekker, Chettle and Haughton could easily have come across the story in one of its oral, written or pictorial realisations and chose to shape it into a *comedia* and an Elizabethan play, respectively. In addition, this shaping process produced similarities, which the cultural net can also account for, despite inherent generic differences between early modern Spanish theatre and English drama.

By comparing these two plays I wish to demonstrate that, firstly, it is significant that they both freely elaborate the myth's treatment of marriage more than any previous version; and, secondly, that they used similar techniques, which belonged to English and Spanish literary traditions or cultural nets, to address social anxieties about the life-changing nature of marital commitment. My analysis, therefore, focuses on some of the additional material rather than on the main story of the myth.

Both Lope's and Dekker, Chettle and Haughton's works introduced new characters. These are mainly stock figures extremely common in early modern English and Spanish drama, which they could have picked up either by simply attending or reading plays by other contemporary dramatists or from their knowledge of classical Latin drama.[16] The English playwrights and Lope also enlarge the Griselda myth with new episodes or subplots. While this additional dramatic material can in both cases be related in terms of narremes to other contemporary plays, indicating their thematic affiliation with English and Spanish literary traditions or cultural nets respectively, in the English play the affiliation is also

---

15 See Joachim Küpper's article in this volume.
16 Although little is known about Haughton's or Chettle's education, Dekker most likely attended grammar school, where he could have become familiar with Latin authors. At any rate Dekker's mastery of Latin is attested by his English translation of the Latin poem *Grobianus* by Friedrich Dedekind (see John Twyning, "Dekker, Thomas [c. 1572–1632]," in: Henry Colin Grey Matthew and Brian Harrison, edd., *Oxford Dictionary of National Biography* [Oxford: Oxford University Press, 2004], online ed., ed. Lawrence Goldman, 2008, http://www.oxforddnb.com/view/article/7428 [retrieved: 14 June 2012]). Lope's proficiency in Latin and thorough knowledge of classical literature is well attested by his Jesuit education and numerous references to Latin and Greek authors throughout his work.

formal, given that, like Elizabethan drama in most of its instances, it presents a complex dramatic structure with a main plot and two subplots. Finally, in terms of literary language, both in *Patient Grissil* and *El ejemplo de casadas*, a rhetoric of the monstrous or grotesque is used in order to exorcise through laughter anxieties about getting married. Monstrosity and the grotesque were commonly employed in early modern Spanish and English literatures, especially in satirical writings, such as those of Quevedo or Gracián in Spain,[17] whose works Lope could have read; and Dekker was himself a satirist who made use of such metaphorical language, especially of the grotesque, in his pamphlets, following an early modern English tradition of pamphleteers who used these rhetorical techniques as means of denouncing contemporary vices by enhancing their repulsive features and/or making them appear comic.[18]

The topic of marriage, in the early modern period, is at the centre of many writings of various natures—literary and non-literary: sermons, ballads, conduct books, laws, plays etc. As a rite of passage and a central device that structures society, marriage has attracted much attention over the centuries, all the more so during certain transitional periods such as the sixteenth and seventeenth centuries, when the Reformation brought radical changes to religious rituals and doctrine.

On the one hand, following Lutheran and Calvinist arguments that virginity is not holier than marriage and that marriage was ordained by God for all men and women without exception,[19] Protestant England started allowing priests to marry during Edward VI's reign, but prohibited it again during Mary I's Catholic rule and made it lastingly lawful under Elizabeth as part of the Thirty-Nine Articles of Religion (1563),[20] which also denied marriage's sacramental status and redefined it as a civil contract.[21] On the other hand, Catholic Europe, to which Spain belonged, convened at the Council of Trent (1545–1563) to condemn Protestant-

---

[17] For the specific use of the monstrous as a satirical device in Gracián and Quevedo, see Jorge Checa, "Figuraciones de lo monstruoso: Quevedo y Gracián," *La Perinola: Revista de investigación quevediana* 2 (1998), pp. 195–211.
[18] For the use of the grotesque in early modern English literature, see Neil Rhodes, *Elizabethan Grotesque* (London: Routledge, 1980); and Kathryn Michelle Brammall, "Monstrous Metamorphosis: Nature, Morality, and the Rhetoric of Monstrosity in Tudor England," *The Sixteenth Century Journal* 27.1 (1996), pp. 3–21.
[19] See Theodora Ann Jankowski, *Pure Resistance: Queer Virginity in Early Modern English Drama* (Philadelphia, PA: University of Pennsylvania Press, 2000), p. 11.
[20] Gwendolyn Bridges Needham, "New Light on Maids 'Leading Apes in Hell'," *The Journal of American Folklore* 75. 296 (1962), pp. 106–119, p. 107.
[21] Christine Peters, "Gender, Sacrament and Ritual: The Making and Meaning of Marriage in Late Medieval and Early Modern England," *Past and Present* 169. 1 (2000), pp. 63–96, pp. 77–78.

ism as a heresy, to reaffirm Catholic doctrine and to redefine some of its aspects, including marriage. While the decrees of the Council restated the more elevated status of virginity and chastity, the necessity of celibacy for priests, the sacramental nature of matrimony and its indissolubility even in the case of adultery, they also revised marriage doctrine to solve the problem of clandestine unions. The Council took a series of measures to achieve greater control over marriage and its lawfulness: it rendered obligatory the publication of bans and the public enactment of betrothal sanctified by a priest at the church doors and removed the obligation of parental consent to produce a valid union, thereby endowing both men and women with complete freedom of choice of partner—a necessary freedom, given that any sacrament has to be willingly accepted and performed, if the person is an adult, in order to be valid.[22] For Protestants, on the contrary, parents' approval was indispensable.

However, many European Catholic countries had civil laws countering the Tridentine decree and requiring parental consent for marriages. The application of the Council of Trent's decisions was far from smooth and led to legal conflicts within some families whose elders tried to impose marital unions on unwilling children.[23] In Protestant England similar familial tension could arise when children married "clandestinely" through spousals only, that is to say, by exchange of vows *per verba de praesenti* in front of a witness: while spousals even without parents' approval were enough to make a marriage legal, according to civil law, as Barnett and Mary Sokol explain, marriage by spousals only was "viewed as an offence by both society and Church law. [...] especially families [...] deplored the excessive freedom [...] allowed a bride and groom."[24]

Regarding marriage's indissolubility, most Protestants thinkers were more flexible than Catholics, usually considering adultery a ground for divorce, and allowing spouses to separate—that is to say, to live under different roofs, yet not remarry—on various grounds such as impotence or insanity, among others.[25] In practice, however, as Barnett Jerome and Mary Sokol explain:

---

[22] Gabriela Carrión, *Staging Marriage in Early Modern Spain: Conjugal Doctrine in Lope, Cervantes, and Calderón* (Lewisburg, PA: Bucknell University Press, 2011), p. xiii.
[23] See Ignacio Arellano and Jesús María Usunáriz, edd., *El matrimonio en Europa y el mundo hispánico: Siglos XVI y XVII* (Madrid: Visor Libros, 2005); Jesús María Usunáriz and Rocío García Bourrellier, edd., *Padres e hijos en España y el mundo hispánico: Siglos XVI y XVIII* (Madrid: Visor Libros, 2008).
[24] Barnett Jerome Sokol and Mary Sokol, *Shakespeare, Law, and Marriage* (Cambridge: Cambridge University Press, 2003), pp. 14 f.
[25] David L. Smith, "Divorce and Remarriage From the Early Church to John Wesley," *Trinity Journal* 11. 2 (1990), pp. 131–142, pp. 138–140; Sokol et al., *Shakespeare, Law, and Marriage*, pp. 140–142.

> In early modern England once a man and woman were validly married they remained bound to each other for as long as they lived, for better or worse, because divorce in its modern sense was not available. If a marriage failed the church courts were sometimes able to grant an order for one of two kinds of divorce, but neither corresponds to the modern law of divorce. Firstly, the church courts could grant a divorce *a vinculo matrimoni*. Here a marriage was annulled if the courts found a "dirimentary impediment" making the marriage void *ab initio*—it had never existed. The parties could then be free to marry again. Secondly, the church courts could make an order for a divorce *a mensa et thoro*. Here husband and wife were freed from their legal duty to cohabit, but they were not free to remarry. This kind of divorce more nearly corresponds to modern judicial separation.[26]

In addition, it was extremely rare that someone actually separated or obtained a marriage annulment, mainly because financially these were expensive to obtain, and socially marriage breakdown brought dishonour and shame, as Elizabeth Foyster has demonstrated.[27]

As far as ritualistic practices were concerned, not only was there no fixed rule and a lot of diversity in practices, but as Christine Peters demonstrates, the liturgical changes regarding marriage initiated by the Reformation in England were either not very specifically Protestant or had little impact on the laity's representation of marriage: for example, English Protestants' transfer of the ceremony inside the church building was a phenomenon that could also be observed in Catholic France.[28]

As regards Catholic and Protestant advice literature, Peters also remarks that the constitution of marriage as a civil contract was accompanied by much insistence on its holiness and blessedness, and the fact that spouses had to "live well" in order to achieve salvation, if, and only if, one was touched by God's grace. Such were conceptions that were similar to Catholic admonitions to spouses to behave properly.[29] As Kathleen Davies argues, the English Protestant and European Catholic treatises on marriage, which aimed to educate the laity on the purposes and lawfulness of marriage, how to choose a wife, how to be a good wife or husband and how marriage was to be hierarchised—the husband being head of the family and the wife his subordinate—did not significantly differ, except for some rare Protestant invectives against virginity.[30]

---

26 P. 139.
27 Elizabeth Ann Foyster, *Manhood in Early Modern England: Honour, Sex and Marriage* (London/New York, NY: Longman, 1999), esp. pp. 10–13.
28 Peters, "Gender, Sacrament and Ritual," pp. 77–80.
29 P. 77.
30 Kathleen M. Davies, "Continuity and Change in Literary Advice on Marriage," in: Richard Brian Outhwaite, ed., *Marriage and Society: Studies in the Social History of Marriage* (London: Europa Publications Limited, 1981), pp. 58–80.

This suggests that early modern Catholics and Protestants had converging views on various theoretical aspects of marriage: providing more children, i.e. Christians for God's service; a means to avoid lechery; and the perpetuation of the divine order of things, in which the wife is subjected to her husband's will. Additionally, in practice, similar conflicts about the choice of spouses could arise as much in Spain as in England; and while divorce was prohibited in Catholic countries, reformed England did not socially favour it, despite the existence of legal means of separation.

As a consequence, similar anxieties regarding marriage could arise in both Spain and England. Thus the Patient Griselda myth, with its long recognised didactic potential to teach women how to be meek, obedient and most of all patient wives, as well as its initial attention to a ruler's reluctance to get married, could serve similar purposes regarding marriage on both the Protestant English and Catholic Spanish stages.

The Comedy of Patient Grissil and the *Ejemplo de Casadas* freely enlarge the tale in order to address the question of embracing marital status, and the implications of marriage for an individual and for her or his family or the larger community. This issue raises anxiety in more than one character in these plays in so far as, according to the Freudian definition, it generates "a particular state of expecting the danger or preparing for it, even though it may be an unknown one."[31]

Marriage, as anthropologists from Van Gennep onwards have commented, is a social enterprise and not an individual's freely made choice: it is influenced by one's family and/or community and has repercussions on one's life and on one's community.[32] Contemplating the consequences of marriage on one's life or social group can generate anxieties in the individual entering matrimony as much as in members of her or his circle of close relations.

Among the possible anxieties this could produce, I will first consider the fear experienced by subjects whose ruler refuses to marry, an anxiety the early modern Spanish and English audiences may have shared.

Lope de Vega opens his play with his Conde acknowledging the validity of his subjects' marriage petition in terms of succession: he says, "Vasallos, yo os agradezco / vuestra justa pretensión; / deseo la subcesión" (vv. 1–3) [Vassals, I thank you / for your request; / I want succession]. Similarly, Dekker, Chettle and

---

[31] Sigmund Freud, *Beyond the Pleasure Principle* [*Jenseits des Lustprinzips*, 1920], in: *The Standard Edition of the Complete Psychological Works of Sigmund Freud*, edd. and trans. James Strachey, Anna Freud, Alix Strachey and Alan Tyson, 24 vols. (London: The Hogarth Press, 1955), vol. 18, p. 12.
[32] See Arnold Van Gennep, *Les rites de passage* (Paris: Libraire Critique Emile Nourry, 1909), esp. chap. 7, pp. 165–207.

Haughton's first scene presents the marquis's brother and courtiers complaining that their lord is carelessly hunting instead of answering the various neighbouring rulers' offers of their daughters or other female relatives in marriage: "This day you vowed to wed: but now I see, / Your promises turne all to mockerie,"[33] reproaches the marquis of Pavia, Gualter's brother; Lepido, his courtier, continues, "This day your self appointed to giue answere / To all those neighbour-Princes, who in loue / Offer their Daughters, Sisters and Allies, / In marriage to your hand." (1.1.22–25).

These two opening scenes reveal that, as a ruler, the marquis or Conde cannot choose not to marry without provoking discontent. Moreover, as the English playwrights only imply and Lope explicitly states, what is at stake in a ruler's marriage is his succession. If a king died without an heir, his realm would face wars, which would destroy and divide the country until one among various, more or less legitimate pretenders to the throne emerged victorious. Yet, in both plays, the subjects' fear is ungrounded because Gualter and Enrico are young and still have time to find a wife and have legitimate children to succeed them after their death.

Although Spanish successions had occurred quite smoothly for more than a century when Lope's play was composed (c. 1599–1603), the fact that Philip II died in 1598 may have awakened anxieties, even though he was succeeded by his 22-year-old son, Philip III: the new king was not married when he inherited the throne; and it had taken his father more than fifty years and four marriages to have a son who would survive him.

The opening scene of the *Ejemplo de casadas* stresses the importance that a ruler provide an heir, as we have seen, which is echoed twice in the third act, in two passages not present in previous versions of the myth. First, after Laurencia is sent back to her father, Enrico wishes to embark on a crusade. His courtiers, Floriano and Celio, try to persuade him to stay and ask for a papal dispensation in order to remarry: "FLORIANO: Sin sucesión nos dejas" [FLO.: You leave us without succession]; "CELIO: [...] Mira, señor, en qué aflicción nos dejas" [CEL.: [...] Look, my lord, in what affliction you leave us]; "FLO.: [...] escribe al Santo Padre que disponga / por causa tan ligítima" [FLO.: (...) write to the Holy Father to have him decide on this legitimate case] (vv. 2200, 2203, 2213 f.). Secondly, when the prince of Bearn appears, he explains that his wife is dead and that he has no heir, but twice promises his courtiers, Rosardo and Anselmo, that he will remarry to provide them with a rightful heir: "casarme y daros prometo / ligítima sucesión"

---

[33] All references to the play come from, Thomas Dekker, Henry Chettle, William Haughton, *Patient Grissil* [1603], in: *The Dramatic Works of Thomas Dekker [c.1590–1629]*, ed. Fredson Bower, 4 vols. (Cambridge: Cambridge University Press, 1953), vol. 1, pp. 207–298, and will subsequently be given in parenthesis in the main body of the text; here 1.1.20 f.

[I promise to get married and give a legitimate succession], he affirms and reiterates, a few lines later, "y os daré a todos contento, / y sucesión a mi estado" [and I will give you all satisfaction, / and succession for my estate] (vv. 2267–68, 2275–76). Lope may have, thereby, been trying to encourage his new king to marry and quickly have children.

On the other hand, England was facing a much more problematic situation: in 1599, when Dekker, Chettle and Haughton wrote their comedy, the Queen, Elizabeth I, was already 66 years old, unmarried, refusing to get married and undoubtedly a post-menopausal woman. She additionally did not want to name a successor, and continued to refuse to do so until she was on her deathbed. To write or speak about the succession was punishable by a year's imprisonment; and anyone daring to question her political abilities was equally in danger of prison.[34] Therefore, playwrights had to be careful if they wished to address this delicate issue. This may explain why Gualter is never really unwilling, reticent or afraid of getting married, unlike Lope's Conde Enrico. The marquis's initial carelessness about marriage is a mere joke he plays upon his courtiers. Although he briefly protests that his brother and his courtiers wish to force his "free thoughts into the yoake of loue, / To grone vnder the loade of marriage," which he calls a "burthen" (1.1.61 f., 63), he has actually already made up his mind to marry Grissil: he had seen her before and courted her for a while (as we learn in Act 1 scene 2).

However, Dekker, Chettle and Haughton still seem to address the controversial issue of Elizabeth's lack of an heir, not to convince the queen to have children, since this was beyond hope, but to ridicule her egoistic cult of virginity and suggest she should have been more far-sighted and married to secure her succession with legitimate offspring. Therefore, they employ a group of stock characters who could easily be grafted onto Griselda's story in a typically Elizabethan subplot: Julia, the marquis's sister, a virgin unwilling to get married, and her suitors, Farneze, Onophrio and Urcenze. From her very first appearance in Act 2 scene 1, she rejects wedlock on the grounds that she deems it "a kinde of hell" (l. 259) and compares it to war: "You may well call that a combat, for indeede marriage is / nothing else, but a battaile of loue, a friendly fighting, a kinde of / fauourable terrible warre" (2.1.273–75). Julia also claims, "I deale by marriage as some *Indians* doe the Sunne, adore it, / and reuerence it, but *dare not* stare on it, for *feare* I be starke / blinde" (2.1.276–78; my italics, except for "*Indians*"). These metaphors underline her anxiety, yet she has so far no reason

---

34 See Cyndia Susan Clegg, *Press Censorship in Elizabethan England* (Cambridge: Cambridge University Press, 1997), p. 32.

to fear: Julia has never entered wedlock, and she has not witnessed yet what married life is for the other couples of the play, Gualter and Grissil, and Sir Owen and Lady Gwenthyan. Julia prefers to remain unmarried because, apparently following Catholic doctrine, she values virginity over marriage: "sweet virginitie is that inuisible God-head that turns vs / into Angells, that makes vs saints on earth and starres in heauen: / heere Virgins seeme goodly, but there glorious." (2.1.263–65)

Julia is an Italian lady, sister to the marquis and not an English queen, in other words, removed from Elizabeth by her nationality and political position, but of equal rank and gender. Moreover, her Catholic arguments, placing virginity above the married status, can be read as a rhetorical gesture comparable to Elizabeth's self-fashioning as a Virgin Queen. Elizabeth I used the cult of the Virgin Mary, appropriating Marian poetics and pictorial representations, and combining these with her symbolic marriage to her nation as a device that allowed her to "receive the adulation of her subjects as the universal object of a Petrarchan religion of love, one that pervaded ballads, pageants, and dramatic entertainments" (as John King nicely summarises).[35] Similarly, Julia employs her plea for virginity as a means to disdain her suitors, while encouraging them to follow her "religion of love": "In heauen is no / wooing yet all there are louely: in heauen are no weddings yet al /there are louers" (2.1.265–67). The marquis's sister enjoys the power she has over her suitors and treats them like pets: "oh for a Drum to summon all my louers, my / suiters, my seruants together" (ll. 177 f.), she wishes in Act 4 scene 3, to which they answer in echoing terms: "FARNEZE: I appeare sweet mistresse without summons. / ONOPHRIO: So does *Onophrio*. / URCENZE: So does *Vrcenze*." (ll. 179–181)

Julia is no queen; but her ridiculous power over no less ridiculous followers clearly parodies Elizabeth I and her handling of her court and worshippers.

In addition, the virginity of the marquis's sister is presented as anomalous and monstrous. In Act 2 scene 1, trying to make sense of Julia's rejection of lovers and marriage, Farneze says: "Then I perceiue you meane to leade apes in hell" (l. 257). As Gwendolyn Needham comments, this English expression most likely "originated in Protestant feeling against celibacy" and "[b]y its prediction of punishment in hell, the proverb expresses not mere derogation, but condemnation of celibacy as a positive evil."[36] "In proclaiming the doom of the unmarried," Needham further contends, in its secular meaning "the proverb implicitly argues

---

[35] John N. King, "Queen Elizabeth I: Representations of the Virgin Queen," *Renaissance Quarterly* 43.1 (1990), pp. 30–74, p. 30.
[36] Needham, "New Light on Maids," pp. 106 f.

for the perpetuation of the race, recognizes the social and economic necessity of woman's prompt marriage, and criticizes wayward female nature."³⁷ The proverb casts Julia either as a barren woman followed by apes that stand as substitute children, or as a monstrous mother who gave birth to apes in hell. As Needham reminds:

> As subman, the ape was believed capable of intercourse with woman and ever ready to ravish her. A symbol of sin and sexuality, the ape was often placed in contrast with the unicorn, the symbol of chastity and of Christ. As a fool, the ape's imitative nature permitted his representing all kinds of follies as well as vices—a valuable instrument for humor and satire.³⁸

Furthermore, Julia's suitors can also be likened to apes, for they can barely be differentiated from one another and some of their cues (such as those previously cited) echo or mimic each other. Thus, they might become the apes Julia will lead in hell.

Association of celibacy with monstrosity was not uncommon in the early modern period. If not monstrous, virginity was at least considered unnatural or anomalous by Protestant thinkers. Luther, in his "Sermon at Merseberg" (1545), states: "Who commanded you to vow and swear something which is contrary to God and his ordinance, namely, to swear that you are neither a man or a woman, when it is certain that you are either a man or a woman, created by God."³⁹ Thomas Becon, in his preface to the 1541 edition of the English translation of Heinrich Bullinger's *Der christliche Ehestand*, writes: "Lette other prayse suche [i.e. those who vow to remain virgins] as maye iustly seme to be monsters of nature for theyr sterrilite and barrennes."⁴⁰ Moreover, as Theodora Jankowski argues, Elizabeth I was indeed an "anomalous" figure, as a "Virgin Queen *and* eternally desired love object"⁴¹—a definition which perfectly suits Julia (except for the royal title).

---

37 P. 110.
38 P. 112.
39 Martin Luther, "Sermon at Merseburg [1545]," in: *Luther's Works*, edd., Helmut T. Lehmann and Jaroslav Pelikan, 55 vols. (St. Louis, MO: Concordia Publishing; Philadelphia, PA: Fortress Press, 1958), vol. 51: *Sermons I*, ed. and trans. John W. Doberstein, p. 362, quoted in Jankowski, *Queer Virginity*, p. 11.
40 Heinrich Bullinger, *The golde[n] boke of christen matrimonye* (London: Joh[a]n Mayler, 1542), sig. A3r. This book went into nine editions until 1575 (see Needham, "New Light on Maids," p. 109). For an extended analysis of this passage see Eric Joseph Carlson, "Clerical Marriage and the English Reformation," *Journal of British Studies* 31.1 (1992), pp. 1–31, p. 9.
41 Jankowsky, *Pure Resistance*, p. 13.

Consequently, Dekker, Chettle and Haughton seem to have employed the marquis's sister, on the one hand, to parody Elizabeth's cult of virginity and thereby exorcise social anxiety concerning her succession by turning this fear into laughter over the cause of the situation—the Queen's refusal to marry and have children—and, on the other hand, more generally, to ridicule those who shun love and are afraid of marriage.

However, as the play unfolds, yet another interpretation emerges: Julia's fears gradually appear more grounded and comprehensible, so she becomes the voice of men and women oppressed by marital life. Julia, throughout the play, occupies the position of witness and judge, contemplating and drawing moral conclusions about the marquis's cruel testing of Grissil and about Gwenthyan and Sir Owen's comical fight over the right to rule over their marriage. Gwenthyan being a shrew and Sir Owen a braggart knight, the display of their married life gives way to much humorously staged tension. Julia's particular position, aside from the action, transforms her into an audience member within the play, a function she shares with her suitors. Julia and her followers even acknowledge their status as spectators: Urcenze predicts that the union between Gwenthyan and Sir Owen will be a conflict, calling it a "welch tragedie" (2.1.230); and Julia refers to the "enterlude" (4.3.173) when speaking of the episode in which Gwenthyan dresses in rags and serves some beggars the banquet prepared for the marquis and his court. The audience is, thereby, invited to identify with Julia; and some members of the audience may have shared her fear and rejection of marriage, a fear reinforced by her witnessing the other characters' marital behaviour throughout the play.

Moreover, Julia's status as spectator-within-the-play makes her a suitable character to begin the comedy's tripartite epilogue. Interrupting her brother and preventing him from reciting the conclusion of the play and celebrating Grissil's patience, she says:

> Nay brother your pardon awhile: besides our selues there are
> a number heere, that haue beheld *Grissils* patience, your owne
> tryals, and Sir *Owens* sufferance, *Gwenthians* frowardnes, these
> Gentlemen louertine, and my selfe a hater of loue: amongst this
> company I trust there are some mayden batchelers, and virgin
> maydens, those that liue in that freedome and loue it, those that
> know the war of mariage and hate it, set their hands to my bill,
> which is rather to dye a mayde and leade Apes in hell, then to liue
> a wife and be continually in hell. (5.2.275–283)

Here Julia tries to use the proverb "to lead apes in hell" to serve her own interest, like Beatrice in Shakespeare's *Much Ado About Nothing*. As Needham remarks: "[Beatrice] declares that the predicted punishment applies no more to lively maids than to gay bachelors. Delivering her apes to the devil at the gate, she will 'away to St. Peter for the heavens: he shows me where the bachelors sit, and there live we as merry as the day is long' [...]."[42]

Julia gestures towards a similar attitude and employs the proverb as a self-asserting means to express her determination to remain a virgin and oppose those who favour marriage: she prefers "to dye a mayde and leade Apes in hell, then to liue a wife and be continually in hell." The phrase helps Julia in stressing through an epistrophe ("in hell") that, in her opinion, marriage is for women an extremely painful and inescapable experience. "Society tolerated a high level of violence against wives as a normal feature of domestic relations," as Sara Mendelson and Patricia Crawford explain.[43] Moreover, a wife's belongings—financial and material—were her husband's. So it was harder for women not only to find the means to start legal action against their husbands, but also to obtain a separation *a mensa et thoro*. Even if neither the shrewish Gwenthyan nor the cruelly mistreated Grissil wish to be separated from their spouse, Julia expresses her impression that, regardless, there is no way out of marriage, and that wedlock is, thus, a hellish torment on earth.

However, the proverb also punishes Julia with everlasting life in hell. While she acts as the voice of men and women oppressed by marriage, and of wives in particular, the dramatists undermine her plea for freedom, probably to avoid an accusation of sedition or of being Papists.[44] Such a plea was contrary to Protestantism, which condemned all forms of celibacy. Therefore, Julia does not speak the last words: Gwenthyan silences her and accuses her of "abus[ing] yong mens and damsels" and scaring them away from "good sportes and honorables states" (5.2.285, 286). And the conclusion of the play falls to Sir Owen, who gets tangled up in his plea for patience in marriage:

> [...] if sir *Owen* was
> not patient, her Latie had not beene pridled, if *Grissill* had not
> beene patient her cozen *Marquesse* had not been pridled: well now
> if you loue sir *Owens* Latie, I hobe you loue Sir *Owen* too, or is grow
> mighty angry, Sir *Owen* loue you as God vdge mee out a cry, a
> terrible teale, doe you heare now, they pray awl that haue crabbed

---

42 Needham, "New Light on Maids", p. 112 (the quote from Shakespeare comes from: William Shakespeare, *Much Ado About Nothing* [1600], ed. Claire McEachern, The Arden Shakespeare, 3rd Series [London: Thomson Learning, 2006], 2.1.41–44).
43 Sara Heller Mendelson and Patricia Crawford, *Women in Early Modern England: 1550–1720* (Oxford: Oxford University Press, 1998), p. 140.
44 For more on Elizabethan censorship of Catholic and "papistical books" see Clegg, *Press Censorship*, chap. 4, pp. 79–102.

husbands and cannot mend them, as *Grissils* had, and awl that
haue fixen wiues, and yet is tame her well enough as sir *Owen*
does, and awl that haue scoldes as sir *Owen* does, and awl that loue
fair Laties as sir *Owen* does, to sed her two hands to his pill, and
by God shall haue sir *Owens* heard and soule in his pellie: and so
God saue you all. *Man gras wortha whee, Man gras wortha wee.*
[i.e. My grace is to you] God night Cozens awl. (5.2.301–313)

Sir Owen's comic confusion can be interpreted as an attempt to remind the audience that marital problems should be laughed at, and should not generate anxieties. Yet, Julia's voice may have resonated past Sir Owen's last words and made a favourable impression on the audience, among those spectators who may have preferred to remain bachelors and virgins, either because they were Catholic or as a life choice without any religious motivation, simply because they wished to be freed from the social obligation to get married and its consequences.[45] Given that no man—not even her brother the Marquis—forces Julia to enter wedlock or condemns her speeches, she embodies a greater threat to patriarchal values and to social order than the play's shrew, who wants to rule over her husband. So Gualter's sister had to be silenced (yet by a woman, Gwenthyan) and sentenced to hell (yet by herself) in order for the playwrights and the Admiral's Men to safely stage and, later, have the play printed.

Whereas Dekker, Chettle and Haughton present Julia and her fear of marriage from a ridiculous perspective at the beginning of the play, Lope de Vega uses monstrosity and grotesque characterisation to mock Conde Enrico's apparently insuperable and irrational fear of marriage. Even more than Julia, Enrico is frightened by matrimony: getting married and especially choosing a wife are to him "materias [...] peligrosas" (v. 24) [dangerous (...) matters] and "un casamiento errado, no es tanta pena morir" (vv. 131 f.) [a mistaken marriage is worse than dying]. He is so scared of making the wrong decision and of the consequences this would have for him and his subjects, namely "dishonour" and "infamy" ("[una mala elección] llevaba en su rigor / una noche de su honor / y una infamia de su vida"; vv. 18–20 [(a wrong choice) brought in its hardness / night on his honour / and infamy on his life]). Marriage's indissolubility and the consequent fact that in early modern Catholic Spain there was no remedy for an incompatible,

---

[45] In his later play, *The Roaring Girl* (1611), written in collaboration with Thomas Middleton, Dekker also portrays a virgin, Moll Cutpurse (based on a historical figure), who does not marry at the end of the comedy, because as Lee Bliss remarks, "like Julia, she wishes to maintain her liberty" (Lee Bliss, "The Renaissance Griselda: A Woman for all Seasons," *Viator* 23 [1992], pp. 301–343, p. 338, n. 65). This suggests that of the three English playwrights, at least Dekker, despite his adherence to Protestantism, was inclined to understand women who did not wish to get married.

inappropriate or unbearable spouse help explain why Enrico is paralysed by the idea of finding a wife. Yet his anxiety is depicted as grotesque and so laughable: marriage in Enrico's conceits becomes more frightening than a monstrous creature ("antes entrara / de una tigre en una cueva, / y con fuerza heroica y nueva / de los pechos le quitara / un hijo, o con un león / entrara a hacer desafío [...] o me abrazara desnudo / con las sierpes de Laoconte"; vv. 109–118) [I would rather enter a tiger's cave / and with new and heroic strength / take from her breasts / one of her cubs, or a lion / defy (...) or embrace naked Laocoön's serpents]. Whereas, as a Catholic, Enrico could have legitimately argued, like Julia, that virginity and chastity are preferable to wedlock, it is clearly fear of the unknown, which matrimony represents for him, that stops him: unlike the many monsters he knows, describes and lists, Enrico has no way of making sure the woman he will marry will not feign virtues in order to become his wife and later bring him shame and dishonour.

In addition, Lope enriches the Griselda myth with a new episode which further draws attention to the grotesqueness of Enrico's anxieties: four prisoners are presented to Enrico for him to judge their cases, all of which concern wedlock. As Marie-Françoise Déodat-Kessedjan and Emmanuelle Garnier observe, "Cette séquence [...] fonctionne comme contrepoint comique aux craintes du comte par rapport au mariage" [this episode (...) functions as a comic counterpart to the Conde's marriage fears].[46] However, it represents much more than simple "aléas du mariage" [vagaries of marriage],[47] as these French critiques put it: while all these cases illustrate the worst that could happen in courtship or marriage, the third is so exaggerated that Lope can only have meant it to appear grotesque.

Fabia is the first case: rumour has it that she killed her husband in order to marry her servant, whom she wedded the day after her husband's death. Comically, what troubles the Conde most in the affair is how quickly she was able to choose a new husband and marry him, while Enrico has not been able to take a wife despite contemplating it for years. His questions, during the interrogation, underline his astonishment about how little time Fabia needed to make a decision: "¿*En una noche* pensaste / un casamiento?"; "¿*En una hora* una mujer / decreta y busca marido?"; "Pues, ¿cómo yo no me atrevo / y *en tantos años* no pruebo, / que tú no puedes errar?" (vv. 294 f., 301 f., 304–306; my italics) [Did

---

46 Déodat-Kessedjan and Garnier, "Introduction" to "Lope de Vega: *L'exemple pour les femmes mariées et l'épreuve de la patience*, 1601 (?)," in: Déodat-Kessedjian, Garnier, Jacqueline Malherbe, Jean-Luc Nardonne, and Yves Peyré, edd., *L'Histoire de Griselda, une femme exemplaire dans les littératures européennes*, 2 vols. (Toulouse: Presses Universitaires du Mirail, 2001), vol. 2, pp. 127–146, p. 131; my translation.
47 Ibid.; my translation.

you over a night think / of marriage?; In an hour a woman / decides and looks for a husband?; Well, how, while I haven't dared / and for so many years haven't tried, / couldn't you err?]. Fabia, thus, stands as a feminine counterpart to Enrico, ridiculing his incapacity to make any spousal decision: "¿qué ciencia es menester [para casarse]?"(v. 303) [What science is required (to get married)?]. Since the only way out of matrimony that also allows remarriage is the death of one of the spouses, as Enrico observes, she found a hasty solution to anxieties over unhappy married life and wedlock's indissolubility: murder. Yet, in the absence of proof he sets Fabia free.

Ironically, her case also partially foreshadows Enrico's future marriage with Laurencia. Fabia married her servant for his virtue: "FABIA: [...] porque conocía / su virtud" (vv. 289 f.) [FAB.: (...) because I knew / his virtue]. The Conde disapproves of this unbalanced match in terms of social hierarchy: "haciendo / a un siervo infame amistad" (vv. 322 f.) [making / shaming friendship with a servant]. However, like Fabia, Enrico will marry beneath him because Laurencia appears extremely virtuous to him.

The second case is that of Flora and Arnesto. According to Flora, Arnesto promised in front of witnesses that he would marry her, so she agreed to have sexual intercourse with him. But he now refuses to marry her because he claims that she is lying, that he never vowed to marry her and that the witnesses are unreliable.

In the early modern period, as previously mentioned, while the Tridentine decrees insisted on the importance of the freedom of consent in the exchange of vows for a marriage to be valid, the publication of bans was also required three weeks before the actual ceremony, which a priest had to celebrate publicly at the church doors. This public enactment of marriage blessed by a churchman was intended precisely to avoid such clandestine unions as that of Flora and Arnesto, in which it is difficult to determine whether the woman is the victim of an *estupro* (i.e. "deflowered through violence or after having been seduced by marriage promises") in which the young man only feigned his vows to satisfy his sexual appetite or whether the young lady falsely claims her beloved promised to marry her in order to force him into marriage. Despite the laws of the Council of Trent, the freely exchanged vows, even in absence of a priest, were still deemed essential and in trials often favoured *estupro* victims who either received a financial compensation for the violation of their honour or earned the right to legalise the clandestine union by having it sanctified by a priest in a church ceremony.[48]

---

48 See Renato Barahona, *Sex Crimes, Honour, and the Law in Early Modern Spain: Vizcaya, 1528–1735* (Toronto: University of Toronto Press, 2003); Jesús Maria Usunáriz, "'Volved ya las

However, at the time when the play is set, that is, at the end of the twelfth century, a betrothal or *desponsatio* could be made either *per verba de praesenti* or *per verba de futuro*. If it was performed *per verba de praesenti*, nothing else was required, not even a witness. If it was enacted *per verba de futuro*, then either some condition needed to be fulfilled (parental consent, for example) or the marriage had to be consummated to become indissoluble.[49] Such betrothals were considered lawful marriages, called *matrimonium in facie Dei*, so long as both parties freely agreed to their union.[50]

In the case of Flora and Arnesto, it is impossible to determine who has deceived whom: nothing allows an understanding of who is lying because the witnesses are never brought in to be heard. So either Flora is the victim of an *estupro*, or Arnesto never consented to marriage; and both are guilty of fornication. Yet from the beginning, Enrico places more blame on Flora than on Arnesto (perhaps because her name evokes that of a famous Roman courtesan) and believes the young man when he casts doubts on the witnesses' legitimacy: "ARNESTO: ¿Qué testigos? Que es probanza / hecha entre deudos y amigos. / ENRICO: De ti tengo confianza" (vv. 349–51) [ARN.: What witnesses? If proof / was made between debtors and friends. / ENR.: I trust you]. Overwhelmed by his marriage anxieties, the Conde identifies with the young man who is forced into wedlock by Flora, just as Enrico is pressured by his subjects to find a wife:

> ENR.: [...] Di, Flora, ¿tan fácil cosa
> es el casar que aunque a gusto [i.e. aunque justamente][51]

---

riendas, porque no os perdáis': la transformación de los comportamientos morales en la España del XVI," in: Ignacio Arellano and Usunáriz, edd., *El Mundo social y cultural de* La Celestina: *Actas del Congreso Internacional, Universidad de Navarra, junio 2001* (Madrid: Iberoamericana, 2003), pp. 295–321.

49 In the twelfth century the Bologna school, led by Gratian, decreed that, in addition to the spouses' consent, consummation was indispensable to the validity of a marital union, whereas for the Paris school, whose main thinker was Pierre Lombard, the exchange of vows *per verba de praesenti* only was sufficient. Toward the end of the twelfth century Pope Alexander III ended the debate and adopted Lombard's doctrine (see "mariage" entry in: Alfred Vacant, Joseph-Eugène Mangenot, and Emile Amann, edd., *Dictionnaire de théologie catholique contenant l'exposé des doctrines de la théologie catholique, leurs preuves et leur histoire*, 15 vols. [Paris: Librairie Letouzey et Ané, 1927] vol. 9, pt. 2, cols. 2149–2152; and Sokol et al., *Shakespeare, Law, and Marriage*, pp. 16 f.).

50 Jaime Contreras, *El Santo Oficio de la Inquisición de Galicia: poder, sociedad y cultura* (Madrid: Akal, 1982), p. 644.

51 Déodat-Kessedjian and Garnier emend the verse into "aunque a gusto," which both in the 1615 and 1615 printed versions reads "aunque gusto." I believe, however, that "gusto" is here another spelling for "justo," either to obtain a richer rhyme with "disgusto," or as a printer's

> se tiene por rigurosa,
> que de un hombre, a su disgusto,
> mueres por llamarte esposa?
> Loco está el mundo. ¿Qué es esto?
> Lo que temo, voluntario,
> te piden por fuerza, Arnesto. (vv. 354–61)
>
> [ENR.: (...) Tell me, Flora, is it such an easy thing / to get married that, although precisely / deemed rigorous, / that by a man, at his displeasure, / you're dying to be called wife? / Mad is the world. What is this? / What I fear, voluntarily, / they ask you by force, Arnesto.]

Then, as Enrico tries to also place some blame on Arnesto for not keeping his alleged promise, the young man appeals to Enrico's desires for freedom and to his marriage anxieties, arguing that, though he committed an offense in forcing himself on her body, she is committing a greater offense in forcing his soul into an unwanted marriage. Enrico is influenced by his projection of his own fears onto Arnesto's case, but at the same time he fights against these anxieties to render justice impartially, which would require either the punishment of both for fornication or that the young man keep his marriage betrothal to repay Flora's dishonour: "ENR.: ¡Qué bien habla en mi temor! / La vela, esperanza, calma, / que navegas en mar de honor" (vv. 381–83) [ENR.: How well he speaks to my fear! / The sail, hope, calm, / That you're sailing in honour's sea].

Enrico finally frees Arnesto and gives Flora a thousand ducats to use as a dowry, treating their case in a similar fashion as early modern Spanish trials for *estupro*, in which offenders were more often sentenced to provide financial compensation for honour violation than to marry their victims publicly in a church ceremony.[52] However, the play's setting in the twelfth century would have required that, in a case of *estupro*, the Conde not only recognise the validity of Flora and Arnesto's marriage, but also that Enrico force Arnesto to behave as Flora's husband and possibly punish him for trying to run away. Justice is, thus, not respected because Enrico's grotesque fears affect his capacity as a judge and make him render immoral sentences.

Finally, Evandro is introduced. His future eighth wife accuses him of having poisoned the first seven. As soon as Enrico hears that Evandro got married seven times, he becomes obsessed with this curious fact, thus obscuring his judgment. The Conde does not care if this man, or rather Bluebeard-like monster, may have killed his seven wives; all Enrico can think of, and marvels at, are Evan-

---

mistake. "Justo" could be used instead of "justamente" to fit the verse and makes perfect sense in this context.

52 See Barahona, *Sex, Crime, Honour*, chap. 5, pp. 119–156.

dro's seven marriages. Not only does the Conde question whether he dreams or is awake, but he repeats the word "siete" ten times at various points in a long monologue in which he compares Evandro to mythical giants such as Atlas, Tityos or Polyphemus, thereby endowing him with monstrous attributes. This catalogue of monsters echoes thematically the previous catalogue of terrifying beasts that Enrico elaborates at the beginning of the play, when he describes his fear of getting married. This indicates that Evandro's seven marriages, even more than the previous two cases, bring the Conde face to face with his anxieties and make him completely lose his mind: Enrico frees Evandro, brushing aside that he may be a serial killer and joking, "Mando que luego un pintor / por monstruo te me retrate / y ponga en el corredor" (vv. 469–71) [I order that later a painter / as a monster draw your portrait for me / and place it in the hall].

While Enrico complains that "loco está el mundo," he does not realise that, actually, his own fears are driving him mad and preventing him from sanely delivering justice. On the one hand, the jail from which these four people emerge functions as a metaphor for the Conde's view of matrimony: a husband or wife who marries the wrong person will live in a mental prison, given marriage's indissolubility. Two of these cases also literally imply that the only escape from marriage is to commit murder, which will lead one into a real jail. However, by setting the four prisoners free, Enrico grants them what he will never allow himself: an exit that puts an end to marriage and prevents it from destroying one's honour. On the other hand, pardoning all these people also indicates that Enrico's fears threaten the good government of his land. Because he is a ruler, the influence of his marital anxieties over his judgment has greater consequences than for other individuals: the entire community and social order are troubled and put at risk by his liberation of potential murderers. As a consequence, these three cases convey the long-established and enduring idea present in Catholic countries that celibacy is not an acceptable way of life for aristocrats: it generates disorder, that is to say, it threatens the *bonum communitatis* which rulers must preserve and protect.

Moreover, the prisoners, and especially Evandro, illustrate how unusual Enrico is in taking so much time and care in deciding to get married. The Conde's reading of Evandro's seven marriages as a monstrosity reflects in an inverted way the grotesqueness of Enrico's anxieties. These are further proved ridiculous by the fact that he decides rather quickly to marry Laurencia—even more quickly than Fabia's decision to remarry: after only a short conversation with Laurencia during their first meeting, the Conde makes up his mind to take her as his wife.

As I have showed, the Patient Griselda myth is used in both *El ejemplo de casadas* and *Patient Grissil* as a basic story line to engage with marital issues, but is enriched in secondary episodes with new characters. Although the Spanish and the English dramatists do not expand the myth with the same episodes or same character-types, they do so with the same purpose in mind: to put emphasis on the anxieties marriage raises in those who should get married and in the community around these individuals. Both Lope and the English dramatists decide to address these anxieties with humour and satire in order to exorcise them through laughter. They also use the same rhetorical tools: the monstrous and the grotesque. Dekker, Chettle and Haughton, however, while they ridicule Julia, also acknowledge that her fears may be justified and that celibacy may be a preferable option than wedlock for some. Yet, the seditious and heretical potential of such a statement forces them to be careful and end their play in such a way that Julia will not have the last word and be condemned to hell by the proverb for old maids, which has them lead apes in hell.

Consequently, what these two plays share are: a myth or plot, which can be traced back to late medieval Italy and had acquired European cultural importance by the early modern period; rhetorical devices whose origins can be found in the Greco-Latin tradition, but which were kept alive during the Middle Ages and frequently used for satirical purposes in early modern Europe; and social preoccupations about marriage, rendered more acute in the sixteenth and seventeenth centuries by the debates among Catholics, Protestants, politicians and laymen around this ritual. While this points towards a common European culture and cultural network in which this literary and ideological material circulated or floated, *Patient Grissil* and *El ejemplo de casadas* also present traits belonging to their respective national cultures. Patient Griselda is a European myth, but in each of its realisations, it acquires features of the national culture in which it is retold; and the marriage anxieties it helps to address are formulated according to these cultures. For the Protestant English dramatists virginity in opposition to wedlock is still a problematic issue, whereas for Lope the Catholic notion of marriage's absolute indissolubility until one of the spouses' death is a prominent concern.

Part III: **Images of Spain on the English Stage**

Ralf Haekel
"Now Shall I See the Fall of Babylon": The Image of Spain in the Early Modern English Revenge Tragedy

Introduction

The Spanish Tragedy is one of the most important and influential tragedies in Elizabethan theatre. Taking up the classical Senecan model, Thomas Kyd's play is the first modern revenge tragedy, the first play with a truly Machiavellian villain, the first one with a play-within-the-play. Furthermore, it was, as Lukas Erne remarks, immensely successful—on stage as well as on the page—during the first decades after its publication: "Henslowe recorded no fewer than twenty-nine performances between 1592 and 1597, more than for any other play except *The Jew of Malta* and the lost *The Wise Man of West Chester*. Between 1592 and 1633, *The Spanish Tragedy* passed through at least eleven editions, more than any play by Shakespeare."[1]

The play inspired numerous imitations such as John Middleton's *Revenger's Tragedy*, George Chapman's *Revenge of Bussy D'Ambois* or Cyril Tourneur's *Atheist's Tragedy*, i.e. tragedies to which later literary history gave the genre heading of the revenge play. As a consequence of its rather spectacular success, aspects of Kyd's tragedy, such as the rhetorical *genus grande* of its dialogue, quite soon became subject to a number of parodies, for example in Ben Jonson's *The Poetaster*. Especially the figure of the mad revenger and the topic of melancholy madness left their mark on plays such as Shakespeare's *Titus Andronicus* or *Hamlet*, the latter transcending the genre by being a kind of meta-revenge play. Carol Thomas Neely sums up Kyd's enormous success and afterlife: "The influence of the play stretches far beyond this specific impact on the shape and substance of early modern tragedy into a host of imitations, allusions, and parodies that emerge even before the first quarto and continue through the closing of the theatres and beyond."[2]

---

[1] Lukas Erne, *Beyond* The Spanish Tragedy: *A Study of the Works of Thomas Kyd* (Manchester/New York, NY: Manchester University Press, 2001), p. 95.
[2] Carol Thomas Neely, *Distracted Subjects: Madness and Gender in Shakespeare and Early Modern Culture* (Ithaca, NY/London: Cornell University Press, 2004), p. 41.

Note: Parts of this paper will be published in Ingo Berensmeyer, ed.: *Handbook of English Renaissance Literature* (Berlin/New York, NY: De Gruyter, 2019).

The impact is not restricted to the London theatres or Britain in general but stretches out across the channel. A number of adaptations of the play, three Dutch and three German versions—as well as the fact that it was part of the repertoire of troupes of English travelling players on the continent—secured its renown not only in Britain but also in the whole of Northern Europe. In a word, Kyd's *Spanish Tragedy* immediately became part of the early modern cultural memory and stayed vitally there up until the closing of the theatres in 1642.

All this is well known, and it is therefore all the more striking that one aspect of Kyd's tragedy, however central to its design, hardly had any impact on later plays: the image of Spain. Especially in later revenge tragedies, it is Italy rather than Spain which is chosen as a setting—with France and, of course, Denmark as notable exceptions. This begs the question why Spain, as the only other notable antagonist of England at the beginning of the age of imperialism and nation-building, does not figure any more prominently in later Elizabethan and Jacobean drama—especially considering *The Spanish Tragedy*'s immense success and influence. The obvious answer, namely that the defeat of the Spanish Armada in 1588 brought about a change of focus as regards an obvious antagonist, simply does not seem to be a satisfying answer: although this date marks the end of immediate conflict, the rivalry between the two powers continued—especially in the New World colonies. Furthermore, as Eric J. Griffin has shown, anti-Spanish propaganda continued long after this date. In the following paper, I will take a look at the concept of Spain as a key—yet quite puzzling—element in the composition of the drama and ask why Spain is almost entirely overshadowed by Catholic Italy as a setting in later early modern drama.

Spain

In order to understand the politics of *The Spanish Tragedy*, the date of its composition is of vital importance.[3] As most critics have pointed out, it is crucial to determine whether it was written before or after the Armada in 1588. The play was first published in 1592 in two rival editions, the first by Abel Jeffes, of which no copy has survived, and a second, "newly corrected" one by Edward White, of which one copy is extant. 1592 is therefore the latest possible date of composition, but since the play never mentions the Spanish Armada, it is likely that it was written before 1588. The earliest date of composition is easier to determine: the play must have been written after 1582, because it quotes from Thomas Watson's

---

3 For an overview of the history of composition see Erne, *Beyond* The Spanish Tragedy, pp. 55–60.

Hekatompathia which was published that year. Thus most critics, such as Lukas Erne, David Bevington or Andrew Gurr, conclude that the play was written some time around the middle of the decade, i.e. between 1582 and 1587.

This date of composition exactly coincides with the growing tension between Elizabethan England and Hapsburg Spain as the two most important early modern rival powers and aspiring empires in the whole of Europe. The high point of English Renaissance culture therefore coexisted with this conflict, as Eric J. Griffin maintains: "The remarkable literary florescence we associate with the English Renaissance is exactly contemporary with England's protracted conflict with the Spanish Empire, an epoch that saw the emerging Protestant nation's traditional ally transformed as an archetypal adversary."[4] It is therefore quite significant that the play seems to be an immediate response to the contemporary political situation. It thematises the growing tensions, yet without any mention of the Anglo-Spanish conflict, focusing solely on the political situation on the Iberian Peninsula instead.

The annexation of Portugal in 1580 by Philip II and the resulting unification of the Iberian Peninsula constitutes the political background of the plot. Yet, it is not the war between Spain and Portugal, which led to the latter's annexation, that the play begins with, but rather a minor conflict in the aftermath of this war. This is quite clear, since Portugal is ruled not by an independent sovereign but by a viceroy. The battle mentioned in the first scenes may instead refer to a later minor conflict fought at Terceira, a fact that Griffin reads as an allusion to the *topos* of Spanish hubris and ambition gaining prominence in England in the 1580s.[5] However that may be, the opening scenes with the imprisonment of Balthazar, son to the Viceroy of Portugal, clearly allude to the unification of the Iberian Peninsula. This would have been powerful stuff for a tragedy:

> Philip II's assumption of the Portuguese throne in 1580 sent shockwaves through a Europe embroiled in a military and ideological struggle that would not exhaust itself until well into the next century. Suddenly, the balance of power had swung, perhaps decisively, in the direction of the Spanish Hapsburgs and their allies. The English and the French especially feared what a united Iberia might be able to accomplish [...].[6]

Furthermore, the years between 1570 and 1588 were not only a time of growing tension between the aspiring nations, but also one in which anti-Spanish

---

[4] Eric J. Griffin, *English Renaissance Drama and the Specter of Spain: Ethnopoetics and Empire* (Philadelphia, PA: University of Pennsylvania Press, 2009), p. 1.
[5] See Griffin, "Nationalism, the Black Legend, and the Revised *Spanish Tragedy*," *English Literary Renaissance* 39.2 (2009), pp. 336–370, p. 344.
[6] Griffin, *Specter of Spain*, p. 68.

prejudice became manifest. The growing Hispanophobia in these years became manifest in a number of anti-Spanish clichés that were later subsumed under the name of the Black Legend. Subsequently, the English came to think of the Spanish in terms of a fundamental otherness, an alterity that was to shape all forms of racial and ethnic prejudice in later centuries.[7] Against this background it seems only probable that Kyd's play was influenced by this kind of thinking in one way or another, as J. R. Mulryne states:

> [...] Hispanophobia was a strand in the English consciousness in the 1570s, and one that broadened and intensified as the 1580s led towards the Armada of 1588. In the immediately following years, enmity between the nations increased rather than slackened. [...] It is hard to think that Kyd's audience in the 1580s, at the Rose or elsewhere, was unaffected by such widely disseminated attitudes when attending a play set in the Iberian peninsula and called *The Spanish Tragedy*.[8]

Given these historical circumstances, one would expect the play to be openly anti-Spanish or at least that it would provide an image of a world that was characterised by an increasing tension immediately preceding the year 1588.

Several scholars have attempted to read the *Spanish Tragedy* in the context of the Black Legend. Already in 1971, Ronald Broude argued against both a too literal and a too figurative reading of the play's setting:

> However, relations between England and Spain in the 1580's were such that no English audience could have ignored the setting of a play on Spanish soil, and knowing this, no playwright of Kyd's acumen would have chosen such a setting without intending in some way to exploit it. While the Spain of Kyd's play cannot be taken literally as the historical Spain, it may certainly be understood as symbolic of a nation in which wickedness and depravity reign.[9]

Steven Justice's interpretation focuses on the anti-Catholic tendency of the plays—which leaves Denmark as the odd country out:

> The English revenge tragedies are not set in England, but in Catholic Spain, Catholic Italy, and a Denmark stalked by *soi-disant* purgatorial spirits. Their audiences learned from pulpit, pamphlet, and ballad that Spain was bad because of the Roman Church, and that the Roman Church was bad because it had rejected Christ's new dispensation. Kyd creates

---

7 See William Saunders Maltby, *The Black Legend in England: The Development of Anti-Spanish Sentiment, 1558–1660* (Durham, NC: Duke University Press, 1971).
8 J. R. Mulryne, "Nationality and Language in Thomas Kyd's *The Spanish Tragedy*," in: Jean-Pierre Maquerlot and Michèle Willems, edd., *Travel and Drama in Shakespeare's Time* (Cambridge: Cambridge University Press, 1996), pp. 87–105, p. 88.
9 Ronald Broude, "Time, Truth, and Right in *The Spanish Tragedy*," *Studies in Philology* 68 (1971), pp. 130–145, p. 144.

from these slogans of popular propaganda the dramatic images and patterns of action that make his entertainment a powerful one.[10]

And Andrew Hadfield maintains: "Thomas Kyd's *Spanish Tragedy* [...] represented its Spanish protagonists trapped within a destructive cycle of revenge that was controlled by pagan gods, showing that the Spanish were pagan rather than Christian, and so were damned."[11]

Yet, looking at the play, at least in its originally printed form from 1592, these readings of *The Spanish Tragedy* as shaped by anti-Spanish prejudice seem puzzling, as Kyd's play never makes open use of any elaborate propaganda. Although some critics describe the setting of Catholic Spain as corrupt and debased, such a view is more informed by later revenge tragedies than by Kyd's play itself. The claustrophobia evoked by a corrupt society in, for instance, John Webster's *Duchess of Malfi* is at least as important as the plot itself. *The Spanish Tragedy*, by contrast, does not show a perverted society void of morals and with hardly any positive character in the whole play. Rather, as Lukas Erne remarks, "the play precisely lacks the anti-Spanish tone that might be expected from a work composed around the time of the Armada. The Spanish king is depicted as a generous character who is conciliatory throughout towards the Portuguese."[12]

When in Act One Balthazar is brought as a prisoner before the King, he is welcomed in the most noble manner:

> BALTHAZAR: The trespass that my father made in peace
> Is now controlled by fortune of the wars,
> And, cards once dealt, it boots not ask why so.
> His men are slain, a weakening to his realm,
> His colours seized, a blot unto his name,
> His son distressed, a corsive to his heart;
> These punishments may clear his late offence.
> KING: Ay, Balthazar, if he observe this truce
> Our peace will grow the stronger for these wars.
> Meanwhile live thou, though not in liberty,
> Yet free from bearing any servile yoke,
> For in our hearing thy deserts were great,
> And in our sight thyself art gracious.[13]

---

[10] Steven Justice, "Spain, Tragedy, and *The Spanish Tragedy*," *Studies in English Literature, 1500–1900* 25.2 (1985), pp. 271–288, p. 287.
[11] Andrew Hadfield, "Introduction: Shakespeare and Renaissance Europe," in: Hadfield and Paul Hammond, edd., *Shakespeare and Renaissance Europe* (London: Thomson Learning, 2005), pp. 1–20, p. 5.
[12] Erne, *Beyond* The Spanish Tragedy, p. 90.
[13] Thomas Kyd, *The Spanish Tragedy* [1592], ed. David Bevington (Manchester/New York, NY: Manchester University Press, 1996), 1.2.138–150. All references to Kyd's play are to this edition.

Two scenes later, the end of the war is conceived of as a newly found peace built on mutual esteem: "KING: [...] Spain is Portugal, / and Portugal is Spain; we both are friends, / Tribute is paid, and we enjoy our right."[14] Although the annexation of Portugal by Spain features as the setting, the political background and of course also the trigger for the tragic plot, it creates no obvious atmosphere of claustrophobia or threat. The 1592 version of *The Spanish Tragedy* published by White is, in a word, no play of anti-Spanish propaganda.

Historicising *The Spanish Tragedy*, Eric J. Griffin differentiates between this first publication of the play and later versions as "[t]he texts that comprise Kyd's drama[.]"[15] He also has to concede that "[t]he earliest printed version of *The Spanish Tragedy* largely fails to register the Black Legend of Spanish Cruelty";[16] he states, however, that "into the later versions of *The Spanish Tragedy* the dark, essentializing 'humors' of the Black Legend will steadily creep."[17] The example he gives is the famous frontispiece of the 1615 edition of the play (see Figure 1) where Lorenzo, Horatio's murderer, is depicted with a black face, therefore mirroring the contemporary prejudice against "blackamoors," hinting at the possibility that "the 'Spanish villain' had become conventionally represented as 'tawny' or dark-skinned[.]"[18]

Nevertheless, it is rather striking that, despite the Black Legend, the immediate political and topographical setting of *The Spanish Tragedy* is one of the few aspects that did not influence later Elizabethan and Jacobean revenge tragedies. This is also the conclusion drawn by Lukas Erne: "If the 'Spanishness' of *The Spanish Tragedy* had originally contributed so much to the play's popularity as some critics assert, it would seem surprising that none—to my knowledge—of the innumerable early allusions to Kyd's play takes up its historical relevance or points to its alleged anti-Spanish prejudice."[19]

This creates a paradoxical situation. On the one hand, *The Spanish Tragedy* is one of the most influential early modern plays, on the other hand, the anti-Catholic claustrophobia that characterises later revenge tragedies does not seem to be an immediate effect of Kyd's play.

While the influence on later drama and theatre is clearly palpable, the play's sources present an unusual problem. One clear influence is Seneca, whose

---

14 1.4.132–134.
15 Griffin, "Nationalism," p. 337.
16 Ibid.
17 Griffin, "Ethos, Empire, and the Valiant Acts of Thomas Kyd's Tragedy of 'the Spains'," *English Literary Renaissance* 31.2 (2001), pp. 192–229, p. 229.
18 Griffin, "Nationalism," p. 339.
19 Erne, *Beyond* The Spanish Tragedy, p. 91.

Figure 1: Thomas Kyd, *The Spanish Tragedy*, London 1615 (detail).

Roman tragedies establish the blueprint for the play's revenge plot. The play-within-the-play in Act IV refers to Henry Wotton's tale "Soliman and Perseda"; the opening monologue describing Andrea's descent into the underworld is taken from Virgil's *Aeneid*; and the historical setting is clearly an allusion to the wars between Portugal and Spain between 1578 and 1582 and the ensuing unification of the Iberian peninsula. It is extraordinary, however, that no singular source for the main plot has been identified. *The Spanish Tragedy* has been described as one of the few Renaissance plays without an "obvious single source,"[20] as Andrew Gurr remarks. Yet it is highly controversial whether this is really the case. Since it was unusual in Elizabethan theatre to compose a play without a prose narrative such as a novella as a source, Lukas Erne concludes that it is more likely that Kyd used a source which has not been identified or which is lost.[21] Whether this lost source text is responsible for the fact that Kyd's tragedy is not characterised by anti-Spanish propaganda therefore remains a riddle.

---

20 Andrew Gurr, "Introduction," in: Thomas Kyd, *The Spanish Tragedy*, edd. Gurr and J. R. Mulryne (London: Methuen, 2009), pp. vii–xxviii, p. viii.
21 See Erne, *Beyond* The Spanish Tragedy, p. 50.

All this leads to the conviction that the Spain of *The Spanish Tragedy* has become detached from the socio-political tension that grew in the 1580s and which came to be known as the Black Legend. In other words, the Spain of *The Spanish Tragedy*—although without a doubt an empire—can be viewed in broader terms; it has the quality of a general concept, an aspiring nation that can be easily exchanged for another. The first European translation seems to underline this hypothesis: Jakob Ayrer's *Tragedia von dem griegischen Keyser zu Constantinopel vnnd seiner tochter Pelimperia mit dem gehengten Horatio*. The unproblematic transition from the Iberian peninsula to Constantinople within just one translation suggests that Spain as such is of no central concern to the dramatic architecture of *The Spanish Tragedy*. What is more important than the actual historico-political setting is therefore the discussion of the concept as such, the construction of an early modern nation and an early modern empire, a notion that even finds expression in the name of one of the key characters: Bel-Imperia.

Empire- and Nation-Building

At the end of the sixteenth and also during the seventeenth centuries, Kyd's play was not primarily known as *The Spanish Tragedy* but rather by the name of its protagonists. In England during the 1590s it was known as *Hieronimo*, the German repertoire list of 1626 mentions a *Tragoedia von Hieronymo Marschall in Spanien* and a German manuscript as well as a Dutch translation are called *Jeronimo*. This focus on the revenger suggests that contemporary audiences were attracted by the one aspect of Kyd's play that is still the most striking today: revenge. Hence, the play's emphasis on action and performance seems to veil the national background of the setting.

The female protagonist is of key importance in order to understand the imperial background. As mentioned above, the title of Ayrer's play mentions not only the Persian emperor but also his daughter Pelimperia; and another German version of the tragedy, Kaspar Stieler's tragic drama ("*Trauerspiel*") of 1680 is called *Bellemperie*. Bel-Imperia is indeed a key figure in the construction of the play, especially as regards the concept of empire. In the original drama, Bel-Imperia is the Duke of Castile's daughter and the sister of the principal Machiavellian villain, Lorenzo. She is central to the plot of the tragedy, since, allegorically, she stands for the empire, or rather, for imperial aspirations and temptations. She is "the beautiful, war-inspiring, idol of empire."[22] As such, she is a very complex

---

22 Griffin, *Specter of Spain*, p. 75.

figure: the first syllable of her name could either refer to the Latin *bella*, designating beauty and hence attraction, or to *bellum*, referring to warfare. Eric Griffin has identified yet another, not Latin but Hebrew, meaning of the prefix which immediately creates a link between the heathen Latin meaning and a biblical and hence religious denotation:

> For even as "Bel" resounds with "beauty" and "war," it also strikes a far more apocalyptic note, ringing in a more culturally relevant biblical seductress [...]. As we are instructed "Against idolators" in the Geneva Bible (or in any number of like-minded Elizabethan sermons and commentaries), "Bel" is one of the "chiefe idoles of Babylon."[23]

Griffith's reading of "Bel" as a reference to the Babylonian context is based on other passages of the play which clearly establish a connection with Babylon. In Act Four, Hieronimo, immediately before he stages the bloody play-within-the-play which sets an end to the tragedy, announces: "Now shall I see the fall of Babylon, / Wrought by the heavens in this confusion. / And if the world like not this tragedy, / Hard is the hap of old Hieronimo."[24]

Bel-Imperia is therefore a multifaceted and ambiguous character. On the one hand, she is a tempting seductress, on the other, her charm creates chaos and warfare. This is mainly due to the fact that she is not as pure and innocent as one might first be inclined to think. Not only does she love and is loved by Horatio and is the cause of Balthazar's desire, which is at the same time the imperial desire to unite Spain and Portugal. But right at the start of the tragedy, a sexual relationship with Andrea is also hinted at: "ANDREA: In secret I possessed a worthy dame, / Which hight sweet Bel-imperia by name."[25]

In a word, as an allegorical figure, Bel-Imperia is dangerous and probably even immoral, although, when it comes to the action on stage, she is clearly on the side of the protagonists. That this desire for empire closely links sexual love with warfare becomes obvious in the scene immediately preceding the murder of Horatio:

> HORATIO: If Cupid sing, then Venus is not far.
> Ay, thou art Venus, or some fairer star.
> BEL-IMPERIA: If I be Venus thou must needs be Mars,
> And where Mars reigneth there must needs be wars.
> HOR.: Then thus begin our wars: put forth thy hand,
> That it may combat with my ruder hand.
> BEL-IMP.: Set forth thy foot to try the push of mine.[26]

---

[23] P. 73 and n. 27 on p. 231. The biblical reference is to *Isa* 45 and 46.
[24] Kyd, *The Spanish Tragedy*, 4.1.195–198.
[25] 1.1.10 f.
[26] 2.4.32–38.

The amorous warfare between the two lovers leads to a metaphorical play with the sexual connotations of the term death: "BEL-IMP.: O, let me go, for in my troubled eyes / Now may'st thou read that life in passion dies. / HOR.: O, stay awhile and I will die with thee; / So shalt thou yield and yet have conquered me."[27] This metaphorical notion of death then immediately leads to Horatio's literal death on stage. Hence, the attraction of empire is both beautiful and lethal.

All this does not resolve the initial question why the play does not make use of the anti-Spanish sentiment growing during the 1580s. Kyd could have easily produced a play full of anti-Spanish propaganda; yet this is not the case.

I believe that the reason for this lies in a feature inherent to the genre of revenge tragedy. Although Kyd uses the Iberian Peninsula as his setting and the unification of Spain and Portugal as historical background, the play replaces this historico-political setting with a literary rather than a literal setting. His Spain is equivalent to Italy in later Elizabethan and Jacobean tragedies: it is the creation of an Other against which the tensions and conflicts of the aspiring nation and empire that England is about to become can be described more clearly. In this sense, Kyd's Spain is made, it is performatively created, just as Italy is "made in and for England,"[28] as Manfred Pfister states. What is important is that this notion of "Other" is not primarily a political antagonist but rather represents an overcome past; it is integrated into the national self-construction rather than built up as a potential enemy. Against this backdrop it becomes clear that "national or cultural identity as a sense of identity enacted in individual and collective performances"[29] elucidates the fact that *The Spanish Tragedy* is more concerned with the political tensions in England itself than with the tensions between Spain and England. Or, to put it more directly: the play refashions these tensions as an inner conflict in early modern England, a conflict that is at the heart of the genre of the revenge tragedy.

Revenge

As would be expected, the question of revenge has been discussed over and over again in investigations into the nature of the revenge tragedy genre. Revenge was

---

[27] 2.4.46–50.
[28] Manfred Pfister, "Introduction: Performing National Identity," in: Pfister and Ralf Hertel, edd., *Performing National Identity: Anglo-Italian Cultural Transactions* (Amsterdam/New York, NY: Rodopi, 2008), pp. 9–28, p. 10.
[29] Ibid.

illegal under Elizabethan and Jacobean law and furthermore, as Eleanor Prosser has shown, condemned by the public.[30] A famous contemporary point of reference is Francis Bacon's condemnation of revenge as "a kinde of Wilde Justice."[31] In this brief essay, Bacon sums up the entire dilemma of revenge: "For as for the first Wrong, it doth but offend the Law; but the *Revenge* of that wrong, putteth the Law out of Office."[32] The problem that the Revenger in the Elizabethan revenge tragedies faces is the fact that the law is in no position to set things right, be that because the King, as in *Hamlet*, is himself the murderer or, as in *The Spanish Tragedy*, because the revenger—Hieronimo as Knight Marshall—himself represents the law and yet is powerless.

Despite its social condemnation, revenge was an immensely popular topic on the stage. For one thing, the extremely bloody plays were successful because they were fraught with action. But there is also a more general explanation: the plays in the wake of Kyd's tragedy brilliantly capture the claustrophobia of the age. The conflict within the early modern revenge tragedy transcends individual mishaps or conflicts between nations and encapsulates the general tension of a period in transition from a late medieval to a modern society.

Thomas Rist has interpreted the entire genre of the revenge tragedy as an early modern attempt to come to terms with the religious change from traditional Catholic to Protestant doctrine:

> To a culture owing oratory, literature, painting, architecture, even churches and theatres to the "social habit" of the art of memory, especially to one in which death was remembrance's "animating impulse", England's Reformed challenge to Christian "memoria" was an earthquake. [...] Revenge tragedy regularly enacts remembrances of the dead, drawing attention to the period's change in religious practices and deriving significance from them thereby.[33]

The theory that the theatre may be a compensation for the loss of the performative Catholic mourning rites—a thought that is heavily indebted to Stephen Greenblatt's *Hamlet in Purgatory*—has its merits, but it makes more sense to regard the plays in an even broader perspective. They negotiate the many possible ways to interpret the world at a time when conflicting models are simultaneously at hand. Therefore, they offer a view of the insecurity of an age stuck between the medieval

---

30 See Eleanor Prosser, *Hamlet and Revenge* (Stanford, CA: Stanford University Press, 1967).
31 Francis Bacon, *The Essayes or Counsels, Civill and Morall* [1597/1612/1625], ed. Michael Kiernan (Oxford: Clarendon Press, 1985), p. 16.
32 Ibid.
33 Thomas Rist, *Revenge Tragedy and the Drama of Commemoration in Reforming England* (Aldershot/Burlington, VT: Ashgate, 2008), pp. 4–6.

and the modern worldview. With a reference to Shakespeare's late tragedies but also on a more general note, Sabine Schülting states:

> This disillusionment surely needs to be seen in connection with the fundamental cultural transition which became apparent at the end of sixteenth century: the political instability, the disintegration of social hierarchies, the social tensions, and the economic crisis need to be considered as much as the Protestant challenge to Renaissance optimism, the questioning of medieval opinions, and the resulting feeling of a decentring of the world and the individual. [...] Language seems incapable of depicting this reality unambiguously, and the world is felt to be a theatre on whose stage humans play an – often absurd and meaningless – role.[34]

The general insecurity—with regard to religion, society, government, the individual and language—that characterises Shakespeare's later tragedies and Jacobean tragedy in general finds its precursor in Kyd's play of the 1580s. It is exactly this coexistence of disparate worldviews—which in a German idiom is called *Gleichzeitigkeit des Ungleichzeitigen*—that leads to the tragic events in Kyd's play. Accordingly, Tanya Pollard describes the social changes that had an immediate effect on, and are reflected in, the genre of the revenge tragedy:

> While this basic plot motif may have an enduring appeal for audiences, social and political changes in Elizabethan England created a heightened demand for it. Revenge redresses injustice caused by abuses of power, and the distribution of power in this period was not only hierarchical, but increasingly unstable. The Elizabethan court's growing monopoly on power weakened the status and fortunes of the aristocratic classes, as well as those who depended on them for employment and patronage, unsettling the traditional social order and creating anxiety and bitterness among those who could no longer count on the continuation of their way of life.[35]

The impact of the paradigm change from a medieval to a modern worldview has been most famously described by Michel Foucault in *The Order of Things*.

---

34 "Diese Desillusion steht sicherlich im Zusammenhang mit dem grundsätzlichen kulturellen Wandel, der zu Ende des 16. Jh.s offenbar wurde: Die politische Instabilität, der Aufbruch gesellschaftlicher Hierarchien, die sozialen Spannungen und die ökonomische Krise wären ebenso zu nennen wie die protestantische Dämpfung des Renaissance-Optimismus, die Infragestellung mittelalterlichen Gedankenguts und das damit verbundene Gefühl der Dezentrierung der Welt und des Individuums. [...] [A]bsolute Wahrheiten sind unsicher geworden. [...] Die Sprache scheint ungeeignet, die Wirklichkeit eindeutig zu bezeichnen, und die Welt wird als Theater empfunden, auf dessen Bühne der Mensch eine—oftmals absurde und sinnlose—Rolle zu spielen hat." (Sabine Schülting, "Die späteren Tragödien," in: Ina Schabert, ed., *Shakespeare-Handbuch: Die Zeit. Der Mensch. Das Werk. Die Nachwelt* (Stuttgart: Kröner, 2000), pp. 529–574, p. 531. My translation)
35 Tanya Pollard, "Tragedy and Revenge," in: Emma Smith and Garrett A. Sullivan Jr, edd., *The Cambridge Companion to English Renaissance Tragedy* (Cambridge: Cambridge University Press, 2000), pp. 58–72, pp. 59 f.

According to Foucault's generalising analysis, this change affects first and foremost the linguistic sign: during the Renaissance, the sign ceases to bear a fundamental resemblance to its referent and instead comes to represent it arbitrarily:

> This being so, the written word ceases to be included among the signs and forms of truth; language is no longer one of the figurations of the world, or a signature stamped upon things since the beginning of time. The manifestation and sign of truth are to be found in evident and distinct perception. It is the task of words to translate that truth if they can; but they no longer have the right to be considered a mark of it. Language has withdrawn from the midst of beings themselves and has entered a period of transparency and neutrality.[36]

In his brief yet highly illuminating analysis of *Hamlet*, Dieter Fuchs describes the genre of the revenge tragedy as negotiating the shift from a medieval aristocratic to the classical bourgeois episteme, which he depicts as a clash between two conflicting sign systems:

> The dispositif of revenge negotiated within revenge tragedy thematises a paradigm shift within the social sign system, which takes its beginning at the turn of the sixteenth to the seventeenth century, to be fully differentiated in the Sattelzeit of the eighteenth. Against the background of the residual semiotics of feudalism, the emerging court aristocracy and early bourgeoisie struggle for primacy and social authority by generating new orders of signs.[37]

This notion can also be applied to *The Spanish Tragedy*. The revenger Hieronimo is the representative of an overcome traditional society with a feudal concept of legitimacy and law as well as a Catholic system of morals and ethics. His antagonist is the Machiavellian villain, Lorenzo, who is able to manipulate this system according to his own interests.

According to Foucault, the medieval sign system is built on the resemblance between sign and referent: the message semiotically merges with its content and does not arbitrarily signify it. Bel-Imperia's letter written in blood is one example of this merging; the play-within-the-play is another. This play is not concerned

---

36 Michel Foucault, *The Order of Things: An Archeology of the Human Sciences* [*Les mots et les choses*, 1966], trans. Alan Sheridan (London/New York, NY: Routledge, 2010), p. 62.
37 "Das in der *revenge tragedy* verhandelte Dispositiv der Rache thematisiert einen lebensweltlich stattfindenden Umbruch des sozialen Zeichenfundus, der an der Schwelle vom 16. zum 17. Jahrhundert einzusetzen beginnt und in der Sattelzeit des 18. Jahrhunderts seine volle Ausdifferenzierung erreicht. Vor dem Hintergrund der traditionellen Semiotik des Feudalismus ringen die neu entstehenden Schichten der Hofaristokratie und des Frühbürgertums um die Schlüsselautorität im Gemeinwesen, indem sie neue Zeichenordnungen generieren." (Dieter Fuchs, "Hamlet und die 'Poetik des Übergangs': *Showing* und *Telling* in der frühzeitlichen Rachetragödie," *Wissenschaftliches Seminar Online* 3 (2005), pp. 24–29, p. 24, http://www.shakespeare-gesellschaft.de/seminar/ausgabe2005 (retrieved: 31 July 2014). My translation)

with mimetically depicting reality: it does not show the killing, it is the killing itself. The sign, therefore, in a last tragic act merges with the referent.

The outcome of this tension between an overcome past and an uncertain future is yet unclear, i.e. the question whether it leads to absolutism or early republican forms of democracy remains unresolved; but the Renaissance tragedy as a genre bears witness to the fundamental destabilisation of society. In this sense, Spain does not primarily represent the Catholic and imperial Other, it rather represents England's own Catholic and feudal past that is incorporated into a society that is depicted as unstable and in a severe crisis. Spain is therefore not the historico-political Other, but an incorporated Other in the process of England's early modern formation as a nation and aspiring empire. Griffin describes this as a literary *translatio imperii*:

> [W]e must reemphasize that it is not Hieronimo's action itself that is to blame for the carnage. Rather, it is the prevailing ethos of the society in which his valiant act is carried out—the theological *system* that shapes, supports, and sustains the Roman Catholic social order from which Protestant England has so recently withdrawn—that determines its meaning.[38]

This can be illustrated by the very last scene of *The Spanish Tragedy*. At the end of the play, Hieronimo bites out his tongue after having betrayed, in a final extended monologue, all the information relevant for an understanding of his deeds. After this extended explanation, the king, bafflingly, exclaims:

> KING: Why speak'st thou not?
> HIERONIMO: What lesser liberty can kings afford
> Than harmless silence? Then afford it me.
> Sufficeth, I may not, nor I will not tell thee.
> KING: Fetch forth the tortures.
> Traitor as thou art, I'll make thee tell.
> HIER.: Indeed,
> Thou may'st torment me, as his wretched son
> Hath done in murdering my Horatio,
> But never shalt thou force me to reveal
> The thing which I have vowed inviolate;
> And therefore, in despite of all thy threats,
> Pleased with their deaths, and eased with their revenge,
> First take my tongue, and afterwards my heart.[39]

The fact that he silences himself *after* and not *before* he has given everything away is one side of the problem, the fact that the King does not seem to understand him, another. Usually this problematic passage is explained in terms of a

---

[38] Griffin, *Specter of Spain*, p. 80, italics in the original.
[39] Kyd, *The Spanish Tragedy*, 4.4.179–191.

textual corruption that occurred between the lost edition of Jeffes and White's edition. But one may come to an altogether different conclusion: it could also refer to the fact that Hieronimo, as a representative of an overcome feudal and Catholic society, a society that is gone in England but still hovers in the air like a ghost, that this Hieronimo cannot talk to and be understood by the other characters who have come to represent the new episteme. The King simply cannot comprehend the words and deeds of somebody who represents a sign system which still belongs to the medieval aristocratic order of things. The King and especially the Machiavellian villain Lorenzo, on the other hand, stand for the modern episteme based on a conventional relationship between signifier, signified, and referent. As a result of this conflict, the representatives of both epistemes die on stage, and Spain is left without an heir and thus without a clear future direction. Only anxiety remains. The social, cultural, religious, and political crisis represented in Thomas Kyd's *The Spanish Tragedy* turns out to be an epistemic and an epistemological crisis. At the end of the play, everybody is left speechless. Or in Hamlet's words: "The rest is silence."[40]

---

[40] William Shakespeare, *Hamlet*, edd. Ann Thompson and Neil Taylor, The Arden Shakespeare, 3rd Series (London: Thomson Learning, 2006), 5.2.342.

Saugata Bhaduri
Polycolonial Angst: Representations of Spain in Early Modern English Drama

One of the important questions that this conference[1] requires us to explore is how Spain was represented in early modern English theatre, and to examine such representation especially against the backdrop of the emergence of these two nations as arguably the most important players in the unfolding game of global imperialism. This is precisely what this article proposes to do: to take up representative English plays of the period belonging to the Anglo-Spanish War (1585–1604) which do mention Spain, analyse what the nature of their treatment of Spain is and hypothesise as to what may have been the reasons behind such a treatment.[2]

Given that England and Spain were at bitter war during these twenty years, and given furthermore that these two nations were the most prominent rivals in the global carving of the colonial pie that had already begun during this period, the commonsensical expectation from such plays, about the way Spain would be represented in them, should be of unambiguous Hispanophobia. There were several contextual reasons to occasion widespread Hispanophobia in the period. While Henry VIII's marriage to Catherine of Aragon (1509) and its subsequent annulment (1533) had already sufficiently complicated Anglo-Hispanic relations, and their daughter Queen Mary I's marriage to Philip II of Spain (1554) and his subsequent becoming the King of England and Ireland further aggravated the

---

[1] The conference referred to here is the International Conference on *Theatre Cultures within Globalizing Empires: Looking at Early Modern England and Spain*, organised by the ERC Project "Early Modern European Drama and the Cultural Net (DramaNet)," at the Freie Universität, Berlin, November 15–16, 2012, where the preliminary version of this article was presented.
[2] While the hypothesis that I offer here to do this, "polycolonial angst," is indeed an original theorisation, being presented here for the first time, for much of the information and inferences used to arrive at it, I am deeply indebted to three works. They are Edward Eaton, "Spain as Seen in the Theatre of London, 1588–1605: An Exploration of Popular Sentiment," *International Journal of Arts and Sciences* 3.16 (2010), pp. 321–331; Eric J. Griffin, *English Renaissance Drama and the Specter of Spain: Ethnopoetics and Empire* (Philadelphia, PA: University of Pennsylvania Press, 2009); and Griffin, "'Spain is Portugal / And Portugal is Spain': Transnational Attraction in The Stukeley Plays and *The Spanish Tragedy*," *Journal for Early Modern Cultural Studies* 10.1 (2010, special issue on "The Spanish Connection: Literary and Historical Perspectives on Anglo-Iberian Relations"), pp. 95–116. While I do quote from these sources and cite them appropriately later in the article, I thought this note of acknowledgement is due right at its outset.

https://doi.org/10.1515/9783110536881-008

apprehension of the general English public vis-à-vis Spanish designs on England, things came to an uglier pass when Philip II, stripped of his British crown with Mary's death and Queen Elizabeth I's ascent to the throne (1558), unsuccessfully courted the new English queen, in a probable bid to renew Spain's claims over England. The relationship between the two nations reached its nadir with Elizabeth I's Treaty of Nonsuch (1585) pledging support to the Dutch rebels against Spain and, of course, Philip II's consequent sending of the Spanish Armada (1588). Spain's apparent designs on England continued further with the successor Philip III's proposal in 1601 that his half-sister Isabella Clara Eugenia take the British throne after the heirless Elizabeth I's death. All these must have been sufficient reasons to have possibly occasioned widespread Hispanophobia in the then England. There were, however, other reasons too which contributed to this possible Hispanophobia in England, those which collectively contribute to what is called "The Black Legend," which refers to the acts of cruelty committed by the Spaniards in their colonies in the Americas, as also to the apparently "black" miscegenated nature of the Spaniards themselves, given their Moorish and Jewish heritage. This alleged revulsion in the early imperial English mind for the Spanish, on the dual grounds of the latter being cruel and inhuman, and of an impure breed—"black" in short—has been theorised by many critics, including William Maltby.[3]

But was early modern England really obsessed with Spain and was the representation of Spain in early modern English theatre really overwhelmingly Hispanophobic? Could it be that early modern English theatre was not that bothered with Spain after all? Or, could it even be that, the common sense assumptions elaborated above notwithstanding, there was actually quite some admiration for the Spanish on the early modern English stage, resulting probably from an aspiration in the English mind of that time to be able to do what the Spanish had done, leading to even a possible Hispanophilia? Rather than speculating, let us look at plays of the period that mention Spain, and judge for ourselves.

Let us begin with the Bard himself; after all, who could be a more representative playwright of the period? Very interestingly, only three plays by Shakespeare from the period (i.e. plays written by 1604) have Spanish subjects, and none of them demonstrates what may qualify as Hispanophobia. *Love's Labour's Lost* (1595–1596) is set in Navarre, but hardly shows any Hispanophobia, and though Don Adriano de Armado's name may recall the Armada, he is a rather lovable character. In *King John* (c. 1596), the king has a Spanish

---

[3] See, for instance, William Saunders Maltby, *The Black Legend in England: The Development of Anti-Spanish Sentiment, 1558–1660* (Durham, NC: Duke University Press, 1971).

niece, Blanch of Castille, and there are possible hints at a Spanish claim on the English throne, but the play is really about Anglo-French conflicts, with little or no Hispanophobia. Similarly, in *Much Ado about Nothing* (1598–1599), Don Pedro, Don John, Balthasar, Borachio and Conrade are all Aragonese, but none of them, not even Don John, is really evil. It is noteworthy that apart from these three plays, no play of Shakespeare from the period has Spanish settings or characters. And, how obsessed with a subject could the theatre of a people really be, if its greatest exemplar of the time was so sparing in his dealing with the theme?

In fact, not just Spanish settings, characters or subjects, but even the word "Spain" finds scarce mention in Shakespeare's works. John Bartlett's authoritative *A Complete Concordance or Verbal Index to Words, Phrases and Passages in the Dramatic Works of Shakespeare* reports as few as twelve uses of the word "Spain" in only eight plays in the entire Shakespearean oeuvre, and in only six plays—two comedies, three histories and one tragedy—in the period under consideration.[4] Let us go through these six instances chronologically, one after the other, and see for ourselves what these rare references to Spain connote.

The first reference to "Spain" is to be found in *The Comedy of Errors* (1594), where Dromio of Syracuse in describing "the kitchen-wench"[5] suggests that "she is spherical, like a globe; I could find out countries in her" (3.2.113 f.; p. 125), and upon being asked by Antipholus of Syracuse "[w]here Spain" (3.2.129; ibid.) could be located in her body, claims "I felt it hot in her breath" (3.2.130; ibid.), and reiterates his finding in her "the hot breath of Spain" (3.2.134; ibid.). While this connection of Spain with heat may be seen as pejorative by some (or even connected with its "blackness"), it should be noted that Dromio, in this "global" ascription of different nations unto Nell the maid's body, is not partial to Spain alone, and in a similar comic vein locates Ireland, Scotland, France, England, America, India, Belgium and the Netherlands too in different parts of her body, thus seriously compromising any suggestion of an overarching Hispanophobia in this comparison. The second reference to the word can be found in *Love's Labour's Lost* (1595–1596), where Don Adriano de Armado, who I have mentioned earlier, gets described as "a refined traveller of Spain" (1.1.161; p. 168), who can narrate stories

---

4 See John Bartlett, *A Complete Concordance or Verbal Index to Words, Phrases and Passages in the Dramatic Works of Shakespeare: With a Supplementary Concordance to the Poems* (London: Macmillan, 1894; repr. New York, NY: St. Martin's, 1963), p. 1434.

5 Shakespeare, *The Comedy of Errors* [1594], 3.2.94. All references to Shakespeare's plays are from William Shakespeare, *The Complete Works* (New Delhi: Oxford & IBH, 1980) and will be given in the main body of the text. The page numbers given in parentheses after each quote correspond to this edition; here p. 125.

of knightly exploits "[f]rom tawny Spain" (1.1.171; ibid.) with great alacrity. Once again, the reference, sarcastic as it may be, is not really Hispanophobic, and is at best funny.

While the references to Spain in the two comedies cited above are indeed comic, the connection of Spain to martial rivalry and the apprehension regarding the Spanish infiltrating the English court through familial relationships—two reasons cited earlier as likely causes of Hispanophobia in the age—are somewhat evident when one moves to the histories. In the third reference one encounters, in *The Third Part of King Henry the Sixth* (1595), John of Gaunt gets described as someone who "did subdue the greatest part of Spain" (3.3.82; p. 684), thus recalling a precedent of England's victory over Spain in times of war. In *King John* (c. 1596), as has been stated earlier, there is the character of Lady Blanch, daughter of the King of Castille and niece to King John, and thus quite an embodiment of the potential fear of a Spanish takeover of the English throne which could have plagued the English mind during the period. In the next reference from this play, therefore, when one notes a Citizen saying, "That daughter there of Spain, the Lady Blanch, / Is niece to England" (2.1.423 f.; p. 422), one can possibly sense this apprehension. The third and final use of the word "Spain" by Shakespeare in his histories is in *King Henry the Fifth* (1599) when a character uses the expletive "The fig of Spain" (3.6.58; p. 568), which refers to an obscene gesture of contempt quite common in Elizabethan England.[6] Though these three references do show Spain in the light of rivalry, apprehension and contempt, they are so few and also so low-scale, one wonders if they can be construed to constitute widespread Hispanophobia.

The most spectacular use of the word "Spain" by Shakespeare happens in the only instance of it in a tragedy, in *Othello* (1603), when Othello famously kills himself with "a sword of Spain" (5.2.256; p. 1152). In fact, though the word "Spain" may not occur anywhere else in the play, Eric Griffin, a well-known scholar on the representation of Spain in early modern English drama, to whose works this article is deeply indebted, suggests that there is a lot of Spain in *Othello*. He shows how Iago is named after Spain's patron saint, Santiago Matamoros, "the Moor Killer," and that *Othello* was first performed on November 1, 1604, at the court of James I, with two visitors from the Spanish embassy, both members of the Order of Santiago, to commemorate James I and Philip III signing the Treaty of London to end the war.[7] Thus Spain

---

6 "The fig of Spain is an ejaculation of contempt derived from the Spanish *dar la higa*, that is, to give the fig—a gesture made by thrusting the thumb between two of the fingers. This is also an obscene sign because it suggests a visual image of the female vulva." (Monica Matei-Chesnoiu, *Re-Imagining Western European Geography in English Renaissance Drama* [Basingstoke/New York, NY: Palgrave Macmillan, 2012], p. 153).
7 See Griffin, *Specter of Spain*, pp. 168–206.

is coded in *Othello*, but not necessarily in uncomplimentary terms. Therefore, in Shakespeare's plays of the period, references to Spain are very rare, and more often than not they have practically no element of Hispanophobia in them.

From Shakespeare, let us move on to other plays of the period with Spain as subject, and see if the situation is any different. Philip Henslowe's *Diary*, probably the most authoritative contemporary source on theatrical productions of the time, mentions 280 plays being performed between 1592 and 1602, out of which only eight have Spanish-sounding subjects: the available Thomas Kyd's *The Spanish Tragedy* and *The First Part of Hieronimo*; and the untraceable *Philip of Spain*, *Felmelanco*, *Spanish Fig*, *Conquest of Spain*, *The Spanish Moor's Tragedy*, and *Barnardo and Fiametta*—a rather insignificant number, one would say.[8] In terms of plays published during the period, W. W. Greg's *A Bibliography of the English Printed Drama to the Restoration* shows that in the period a few more plays with obvious references to Spain were published: George Peele's *The Battle of Alcazar* (1588), Christopher Marlowe's *The Massacre at Paris* (1593), Robert Greene's *The Comical History of Alphonsus King of Aragon* (1599), and *A Larum for London* (1602), of disputed authorship (though often thought to be by Thomas Lodge).[9] Besides, Griffin, in his book already cited above, also discusses George Peele's *Edward I* (1593), Robert Wilson's *Three Lords and Three Ladies of London* (1590), and Robert Greene's *The Spanish Masquerado* (1589) as plays of the period with Spanish subjects. The total number of English plays produced or published on Spanish subjects between 1585 and 1604 is very small, and out of all these plays only a few seem to be really Hispanophobic, thus seriously problematising the initial presumption that this article started with.

Thus, notwithstanding the Hispanophobic public attitudes and important critics like Maltby's elaboration of the same, some critics have argued that the representation of Spain on the English stage of the period was not entirely negative, was instead rather ambivalent and at times even bordered on Hispanophilia. Edward Eaton says, for instance:

> [...] however politically or religiously important the war with Spain might have been to the Court of England, the evidence found in the plays published during this time clearly shows that the theatre-going public held no great interest in Spain, and when it did concern itself with things Spanish, it held *no* inherently or overwhelmingly negative view of the Spanish.[10]

---

8 See Neil Carson, *A Companion to Henslowe's Diary* (Cambridge/New York, NY: Cambridge University Press, 1988), pp. 82–84.
9 See Walter Wilson Greg, *A Bibliography of the English Printed Drama to the Restoration*, 4 vols. (London: Bibliographical Society, 1939–1959), vol. 1, pp. 164–328.
10 Eaton, "Spain as Seen in the Theatre of London, 1588–1605," p. 329; emphasis in original.

Similarly Griffin, says in his book already cited above that, in spite of a deep suspicion of Spain in the English mind of the times, "[...] within the network of relationships and connections that linked England and Spain we may observe a profound ambivalence. For there was a reverse side to the Hispanophobic coin. [...] Even Protestant England could express rank Hispanophobia in one breath and effusive Hispanophilia in the next."[11]

But, how does one explain this ambivalence? What would explain this complex nature of the representation of Spain in English drama even in the heyday of conflict between the two nations, and with numerous grounds for a general and overarching Hispanophobia in the English mind? My provisional and rather hypothetical answer to these questions is what I call a "Polycolonial Angst," and I will attempt to explain this category in the rest of this article.

The term "polycolonial"[12] refers to a situation where multiple imperial powers are in the process of simultaneously vying to colonise the same tract or nation or continent—as was the case in early modernity with the Portuguese, the Spanish, the English, the Dutch, the French, the Danish, etc., concurrently colonising parts of Asia, Africa, the Americas—leading surely to severe rivalry or "angst" among such powers. Generally speaking, therefore, what I call "polycolonial angst" would refer to the mutual anxiety amongst different European nations in the context of their simultaneous implication in a colonial situation. Interestingly, in the current context of discussion, I note that there are two aspects to this "polycolonial angst": one pertaining to the polycolonial situation in "distal" colonies, say in America or Asia; the other pertaining to the polycolonial situation in "contiguous" or "proximal" colonies, say in the context of one European power's control over another European nation, like England's over Scotland and Ireland, or Spain's over Portugal and the Netherlands. Thus, I note two types of polycolonial angst at work in early modern Europe:
(1) the mutual anxiety of multiple European powers—inclusive of the Dutch, the Danish and the French too, but primarily involving the English and the Spanish

---

11 Griffin, *Specter of Spain*, p. 17.
12 The term "polycolony" (or its derivatives) is not a neologism coined by me, and was used in its current sense, in the context of China, at least as early as Jack Chen's book *Inside the Cultural Revolution* (New York, NY: Macmillan, 1975), where it is defined as "a colony of several powers" (p. 23). The concept has been used more recently in the context of Latin America by Amy Turner Bushnell and others (see, for instance Amy Turner Bushnell, "Gates, Patterns and Peripheries: The Field of Frontier Latin America," in: Christine Daniels and Michael V. Kennedy, edd., *Negotiated Empires: Centres and Peripheries in the Americas, 1500–1820* [New York, NY/London: Routledge, 2002], pp. 15–28), and by me in the context of the Indian subcontinent from 2008 onwards on numerous occasions. The concept and the term "polycolonial angst" is, however, being used here for the first time.

(Portugal was a part of the Spanish empire from 1580 to 1680)—in their bid to carve up the distal (non-European) colonial pie amongst themselves;
(2) the anxiety among European "empires," especially in times of decline of the same and the emergence of the mononational "nation state," of retaining contiguous colonies in Europe, wherein also England (with its domination of Scotland and Ireland by 1603) and Spain (with its 1580 annexation of Portugal) become important players.

It is against the backdrop of these two kinds of "polycolonial angst" which England bore vis-à-vis Spain that I will try to explain the ambivalent nature of the representation of Spain in early modern English drama in the years of the Anglo-Spanish War.

The first "angst" is relatively easy to understand. Spain was the prime rival to England in the "distal" colonial game, both in Asia and the Americas. Though an English expedition sanctioned by Henry VII is reported to have reached Newfoundland and parts of East Asia as early as 1497, it was only in 1577 that England had its first formal colony on Baffin Island, to be followed by settlements in the Americas throughout the 1580s and 1590s, the establishment of the East India Company in 1600 and intense colonial activities in the Caribbean in the first decade of the seventeenth century, the exact period of the Anglo-Spanish War (1585–1604). Thus, a rival though it was, Spain was also way ahead of England in the initial stages of the colonial game, and in the period under consideration in this article, in spite of the Hispanophobia the war would have caused, England would have simultaneously looked at Spain with admiration, as the global power that it aspired to be. This could be an explanation, from the perspective of the first type of polycolonial angst, for the early modern English stage's ambivalent or even adulatory attitudes towards Spain in the years of the war.

The second angst—the intra-European polycolonial angst—is, however, a little more complicated. As alluded to earlier, it involves, even in times of bitter war, England's admiration for Spain's 1580 annexation of Portugal, as a model to be replicated for its own recent domination of the similarly contiguous "colonies" of Scotland and Ireland. Though the Tudor conquest of Ireland began with Henry VIII being crowned the King of Ireland in 1541, the whole of Ireland came under the English sway only in 1603, with the setting up of James I's privy council at Dublin. Similarly, Scotland and England were united under the same monarch only with James VI of Scotland becoming James I in 1603.[13] Thus the period of

---

13 For details, see Jenny Wormald, "James VI, James I and the Identity of Britain," in: Brendan Bradshaw and John Morrill, edd., *The British Problem, c. 1534–1707: State Formation in the Atlantic Archipelago* (New York, NY: St. Martin's, 1996), pp. 148–171.

the Anglo-Spanish War was also one of Spain's successful consolidation of the Iberian peninsula under one crown and of England's attempts and final success at inaugurating the "United Kingdom" (though the term would come into being only with the Acts of Union of 1707) and, needless to say, on this front also Spain would thus be quite a model for England to emulate.

The representation of Spain in two well-known English plays of the period—*The Spanish Tragedy* (c. 1587) and *The Battle of Alcazar* (1588)—have direct relevance for this second kind of polycolonial angst. *The Spanish Tragedy* begins already with the unification, in a situation "Where Spain and Portingale do jointly knit / Their frontiers, leaning on each other's bound,"[14] and goes on to assert that "Spain is Portugal, / And Portugal is Spain."[15] Noteworthy is that in the play Portugal is ruled by a Viceroy, not a sovereign king, and the entire tragedy that the play makes unfold concerns this annexation, and its import for England with regard to its own proximal colonial plans would not have been missed by the contemporary audience.

The situation becomes even more pronounced in *The Battle of Alcazar* (1588) since this play is directly about the annexation of Portugal by Spain. The play documents King Sebastian I of Portugal's ill-fated attack on Morocco in 1578, his death wherein would cause Spain to annex Portugal, there being no direct heir to the Portuguese throne. More interestingly, there is in the play the character of the British mercenary Thomas Stukeley, who joins the Catholic forces in the hope that their promise to free Ireland from England and make Stukeley the Irish king may be fulfilled, thus connecting the contexts of Spain's annexation of Portugal and England's annexation of Ireland directly. Stukeley makes his intention very clear when he says, "King of a mole-hill had I rather be / Than the richest subject of a monarchy,"[16] but a little later Sebastian tells him how difficult it would be for Ireland ever to gain independence from England, even with the support of Portugal, which ironically was itself soon to be subjected to such an annexation:

> Sebastian: For Ireland, Stukeley? Thou mistak'st wondrous much,
> With seven ships, two pinnaces, and six thousand men?
> I tell thee, Stukeley, they are far too weak
> To violate the Queen of Ireland's right,

---

14 Thomas Kyd, *The Spanish Tragedy* [1592], 1.2.22 f. All references to the play are from Thomas Kyd, *The Spanish Tragedy*, ed. David Bevington (Manchester/New York, NY: Manchester University Press, 2004), here p. 25.
15 1.4.132 f.; p. 39.
16 George Peele, *The Battle of Alcazar* [1594], 2.2.81 f. All references to the play are from George Peele, *The Battle of Alcazar*, in: Charles Edelman, ed., *The Stukeley Plays* (Manchester: Manchester University Press, 2005), pp. 59–128, here pp. 84 f.

> For Ireland's queen commandeth England's force.
> Were every ship ten thousand on the seas,
> Manned with the strength of all the eastern kings,
> Conveying all the monarchs of the world
> To invade the island where her highness reigns,
> 'Twere all in vain, for heavens and destinies
> Attend and wait upon her majesty.
> Sacred, imperial and holy is her seat,
> Shining with wisdom, love and mightiness.[17]

This statement as to the inevitability and irreversibility of Ireland's accession to the English crown from none other than the king of Portugal—the annexation of whose own kingdom by Spain as a consequence of the action of the play was to become symptomatic of the legitimacy of such contiguous colonisation—would have definitely gone down well with the English audience of the day. In the play, finally, both Sebastian and Stukeley reach their tragic destiny, with the latter almost being made into a moral lesson, in the ensuing emergence of the Iberian union and the maintenance of the British one.

It is not only in theatre that such an equation between the Spanish annexation of Portugal and the English domination of Ireland and Scotland would be made, and that, in spite of the continuing war, the English would demonstrate admiration for the Spanish in their quest to relieve the second type of polycolonial angst elaborated above. This equation would often be made by real statesmen of the time too, and we gather that Sir Henry Savile, parliamentarian and one of the members of the team that translated the Authorised Version of the King James Bible, said the following to King James I in 1604: "in mine opinion the likest [empire] to ours, is that of the union between Portugall and Castile in the year 1580."[18] That the Iberian unification would provide an inspiration to England's own contiguous colonial aspirations is agreed upon by current scholars too, and Griffin, whom I have cited on several occasions in this article, says in a 2010 article of his: "The example of Iberian unification would provide, quite ironically, a key source of inspiration for Protestant England's imperial emergence. For in the new century the allure of a composite monarchy after the Spanish model beckoned suggestively toward 'British union'."[19]

Thus, and in conclusion, the representation of Spain in early modern English drama, especially during the years of the Anglo-Spanish War (1585–1604), does

---

[17] 2.4.98–110; p. 93.
[18] Henry Savile, "Historicall Collections," in: Bruce R. Galloway and Brian P. Levack, edd., *The Jacobean Union: Six Tracts of 1604* (Edinburgh: Scottish History Society, 1985), p. 229.
[19] Griffin, "'Spain is Portugal / And Portugal is Spain'," p. 112.

not demonstrate mere Hispanophobia, as would be commonsensically expected of it, but shows rather ambivalent and often even Hispanophilic attitudes. This can be explained through what I have identified as a dual polycolonial angst, whereby the English, in an extension of their rivalry with the Spanish in the emerging game of global imperialism, also held secret admiration for what the Spanish had managed to do and what the English aspired to do—namely, not only expand their hold over distal colonies in America and Asia, but also successfully annex and control their proximal colonies of Ireland and Scotland, much as the Spanish would have annexed Portugal, leading to the Iberian union of 1580.

Part IV: **Between Europe and the Colonies**

Barbara Ventarola
Multi-Didaxis in the Drama of Lope de Vega and Sor Juana Inés de la Cruz

Parameters of a Poly-Contextural Literary Theory

In his essay "The Return to Philology," Edward Said pleads for a new kind of comparative reading. He argues that in order to do justice to the complexity of texts, comparative literature specialists should "move from the specific to the general both integratively and synthetically[,]" by gradually locating the texts in their times "as part of a whole network of relationships [...]."[1] Indeed, traditional— Western as well as non-Western—literary theories normally are unsuitable for such programme. Relying mostly on binary, mono-systematic premises reduces too much of the empirical complexity of a polycentric world, stressing either the affinities and similarities, or the differences which exist between diverse literary cultures.

In order to dissolve these problems and to construct a more complex theory of culture as a dynamic net, I suggest resorting to the poly-contextural theory of Gotthard Günther. In his text "Life as Poly-Contexturality,"[2] he develops a multi-valued logic which has two main advantages. First, it allows taking into account several referential systems at the same time. The world can be conceived of as a universal structure consisting of several interacting, overlapping nets,[3] and every single perspective as a superimposition of various perspectives. And second, it makes it possible to consider the cultural location of observers without completely identifying them with a certain context. By bearing in mind also graded differences between several observers, the setting allows for the consideration of the exact gradation Edward Said speaks of.

The recourse to poly-contextural theory allows the multi-directional circulation of conceptual and material forms to be taken into account without neglecting

---
[1] Edward W. Said, *Humanism and Democratic Criticism* (New York, NY: Columbia University Press, 2004), pp. 57–84, p. 61 f.
[2] See Gotthard Günther, "Life as Poly-Contexturality," in: Helmut Fahrenbach, ed., *Wirklichkeit und Reflexion: Walter Schulz zum 60. Geburtstag* (Pfullingen: Neske, 1973), pp. 187–210, online version: http://www.vordenker.de/ggphilosophy/gg_life_as_polycontexturality.pdf (retrieved: 28 October 2014).
[3] See p. 5 of the online-version: "the number of [...] contexturalities which crisscross this universe is enormous."

the concrete "location of culture" (Bhabha), which should be borne in mind since it plays a particularly important role in the hierarchical colonial interactions of cultures.[4]

Applied to a theory of textuality,[5] the poly-contextural logic provides a set of new interpretive and comparative methods.[6] If we conceive the authors of the texts as poly-contextural subjects and the texts themselves as networks of several interwoven sub-systems, we can consider new forms of cultural belonging and of multi-directionality. One important aspect, which until now has mostly been neglected, is the textual capacity to pursue several pragmatic aims at the same time by spreading them over diverse textual layers or "stages."[7]

In the case of dramatic texts, this complexity is even more fascinating. Aimed at being performed, they can be re-conceived of as semiotic systems that model, enact and evoke a (potentially) poly-contextural world: a single performance is always bound to a concrete (cultural) *hic et nunc* but can, at the same time, depart from this in various ways by means of sheer textuality. This potential superimposition enables the creation of a wide range of combinations of propaganda and critical transgression. The drama can address a present diversified audience (social class, cultural background, gender, etc.) and extend its range into imagined universal contexts concurrently. This allows the authors to take complex stands with regard to their own and to other cultures. They can combine propaganda, critical negotiation (Greenblatt)[8] and even transgression in the most varied ways. As the genre can be seen as an institutionalised social mass medium, I propose to refer to this potential to reach several audiences in a different way as its multi-didaxis.

In the following, I wish to show how this new theoretical framework is capable of giving new insights into the theatre culture of the Spanish and Hispanic American Golden Age. A comparison of *Fuenteovejuna* by Lope de Vega and

---

4 For more detail see Barbara Ventarola, "Weltliteratur(en) im Dialog: Zu einer möglichen Osmose zwischen Systemtheorie und postkolonialen Theorien," in: Mario Grizelj and Daniela Kirschstein, edd., *Riskante Kontakte: Postkoloniale Theorien und Systemtheorie?* (Berlin: Kadmos, 2014), pp. 161–196.

5 Sheldon Pollock states that literary theory is foremost a "theory of textuality as well as the history of textualized meaning." ("Future Philology? The Fate of a Soft Science in a Hard World," *Critical Inquiry* 35 [2009], pp. 931–961, p. 934).

6 A detailed presentation of my new theory of textuality and of literary interpretation can be found in Ventarola, *Transkategoriale Philologie: Liminales und poly-systematisches Denken bei Gottfried Wilhelm Leibniz und Marcel Proust* (Berlin: Schmidt, 2015), chap. 3, pp. 124–288.

7 See chap. 3.3.

8 For the concept of drama as negotiation see Stephen Greenblatt, *Shakespearean Negotiations: The Circulation of Social Energy in Renaissance England* (Berkeley, CA: University of California Press, 1988).

El divino Narciso (*The Divine Narcissus*) by Sor Juana Inés de la Cruz will make it possible to shed new light on the ambiguities of their texts, as well as of the cultural relationship they have with each other. I will start with *Fuenteovejuna*.

Lope de Vega: The Ambivalent Murder of the Tyrant in *Fuenteovejuna* (1619)

Fuenteovejuna is undoubtedly the most famous play by this extremely prolific author. Printed in 1619, ten years after his pathbreaking *Arte nuevo de hacer comedias* (*New Art of Writing Plays*), the drama is a perfect realisation of central precepts of Lope's new dramatic theory. The Aristotelian unities are partially cancelled,[9] the comic and the tragic are merged,[10] the language is differentiated in sociolects[11] and—above all—the focus is set on the populace.[12] The drama stages a true story, the rebellion of a small peasant community against their lord, which culminates in his assassination.[13] In accordance with the *Arte nuevo*, the populace is the protagonist as well as the main addressee of the theatrical performance.

Because of its innumerable ambivalences, the drama has provoked conflicting and even opposing interpretations.[14] The main question is whether the

---

9 See Félix Lope de Vega y Carpio, *El arte nuevo de hacer comedias en este tiempo* [1609], ed. Juana de José Prades (Madrid: Consejo Superior de Investigaciones Científicas, 1971), pp. 275–328, vv. 188 ff.
10 Vv. 174 ff.
11 Vv. 264 ff., vv. 305 ff.
12 Vv. 9 f., vv. 47 ff.
13 For the real incidents that Lope has woven together see Roberto González Echevarría, "Introduction," in: Lope de Vega, *Fuenteovejuna* [1619], trans. Gregary Joseph Racz (New Haven, CN: Yale University Press, 2010), pp. XIV ff. See also Joachim Küpper, "Lope de Vega: *Fuente Ovejuna*," in: Volker Roloff and Harald Wentzlaff-Eggebert, edd., *Das spanische Theater: Vom Mittelalter bis zur Gegenwart* (Düsseldorf: Schwann Bagel, 1988), pp. 105–122.
14 A detailed and still instructive research report can be found in Teresa J. Kirschner, "Evolución de la crítica de *Fuenteovejuna*, de Lope de Vega, en el siglo XX," *Cuadernos hispanoamericanos* 320/321 (1977), pp. 450–465. See also Eberhard Müller-Bochat, ed., *Lope de Vega* (Darmstadt: Wissenschaftliche Buchgesellschaft, 1975). For more recent research see Küpper, "*Fuente Ovejuna*"; Manuel Villegas Ruiz, *Fuenteovejuna: El drama y la historia* (Baena: Delegación de Cultura, Excma. Diputación Provincial, 1990); DeLys Ostlund, *The Re-Creation of History in the Fernando and Isabel Plays of Lope de Vega* (New York, NY: Peter Lang, 1997); Malveena McKendrick, *Playing the King: Lope de Vega and the Limits of Conformity* (London: Tamesis, 2000); Elizabeth R. Wright, *Pilgrimage to Patronage: Lope de Vega and the Court of Philip III, 1598–1621* (Lewisburg, PA: Bucknell University Press, 2001).

assassination is condoned or not. In the first case, the play would call for resistance, in the second for passive obedience. Using binaristic and mono-systematic interpretative theories, one is compelled to decide for one of the alternatives. But since we can find indications for both perspectives in the text, neither is completely convincing. For this reason, I suggest applying the concept of poly-contexturality and to search for multi-didactical structures.

The most important structural pattern of the baroque comedy is the syntagmatic triad of order, disturbance of the order and its restoration after eliminating the disturbing element. On the highest level of meaning, *Fuenteovejuna* points to the peasant community as the disturbing element. In the scene which stages the assassination,[15] the populace is depicted as an outrageous, uncontrolled and even bloodthirsty crowd: "FLORES: ¡El pueblo junto viene! / JUAN [ROXO]: *[Dentro.]* ¡Rompe, derriba, hunde, quema, abrasa! / ORTUÑO: Un popular motín mal se detiene."[16] ["FLO.: They to a man rebel! / JUAN: *(Offstage)* Now burn and raze the place! We'll not retreat! / ORT.: These popular revolts are hard to quell."][17] It is very likely, though, that the teachings of the play—in accordance with the prevailing ideology of the time, the Counter-Reformation—aim at controlling this danger.[18]

But the structural complexity of the text leads us to look further, and if we do so we can detect other, deeper levels of meaning, which make it more difficult to locate the play in its historical context. A deeper inquiry into the plot reveals a precisely composed shifting of responsibility. In the course of the play, the culpability for the escalation of violence is assigned more and more to the powerful nobleman himself. It is he who is revealed as the real disturbing element because he is depicted ever more as a tyrant. Lope achieves this aim by constructing a perfect climax, which starts right in the first scene and harmonises the macro- and the micropolitics. Thus, it is true that at the beginning the inhabitants of Fuente Ovejuna welcome their lord cordially,[19] a fact that could be read as proof of his blamelessness.[20] But this idyllic situation soon turns out to be the mere contrasting backdrop against which the tyrannical wrongdoings of the *comendador*

---

15 Lope de Vega, *Fuente Ovejuna* [1619], ed. Juan María Marín Martínez, 20th ed. (Madrid: Cátedra, 2001), vv. 1851 ff. All references to Lope's play are to this edition.
16 Vv. 1857–1859. See also vv. 1890 ff., vv. 1951 f. ("la mayor crueldad / que se ha visto entre las gentes"), v. 1977 ("con furia impaciente").
17 Quotations from the English translation are from Lope de Vega, *Fuenteovejuna*, trans. G. J. Racz.
18 See the interpretation of Küpper, "*Fuente Ovejuna.*"
19 Lope de Vega, *Fuente Ovejuna*, vv. 530 ff.
20 See Küpper, "*Fuente Ovejuna,*" p. 108.

become even more blatant.[21] The first scene of the drama, where the *comendador* is inciting the Grand Master of his order to carry on a war against the Catholic Kings, fits very well into this textual construction.

After this starting point, the unmasking of the *comendador* continues: the more the plot proceeds, the more he reveals himself to be a perfect epitome of the description of a tyrant given by Father Juan de Mariana. In 1598, he wrote his treatise *De rege et regis institutione*, in which he undertook to define the limits and controls on royal power:

> Es propio de un buen rey defender la inocencia, reprimir la maldad, salvar á los que peligran, procurar á la república la felicidad y todo género de bienes; mas no del tirano, que hace consistir su mayor poder en poder entregarse desenfrenadamente á sus pasiones, que no cree indecorosa maldad alguna, que comete todo género de crímenes, destruye la hacienda de los poderosos, viola la castidad, mata á los buenos, y llega al fin de su vida sin que haya una sola acción vil á que no se haya entregado. Es además el rey humilde, tratable, accesible, amigo de vivir bajo el mismo derecho que sus conciudadanos; y el tirano, desconfiado, medroso, amigo de aterrar con el aparato de su fuerza y su fortuna, con la severidad de las costumbres, con la crueldad de los juicios dictados por sus sangrientos tribunales.[22]

Lope clearly transfers this logic to a lower level of the social hierarchy, the relationship between a feudal lord and his peasant subjects. The *comendador* systematically commits all the above-mentioned "crimes" and thus violates all the duties he has towards his subjects. He rapes all the women of the community or tries to

---

21 On closer inspection, this scene already points toward Lope's attempt to partially excuse the crowd. If at the outset of the plot the peasants welcome their sovereign with joy and delight, they are obviously willing to adapt themselves to the existing order. So the reason for their transformation must lie elsewhere; and Lope does not fail to name this reason immediately, because right after this scene, the *comendador* commits his first tyrannical acts (see Lope de Vega, *Fuente Ovejuna*, vv. 545 ff., vv. 595 ff., v. 617, vv. 621 ff., etc.).

22 Juan de Mariana, *Del rey y de la institución real* [*De rege et regis institutione*, 1598], in: *Obras del Padre Juan de Mariana*, ed. Francisco Pí y Margall, *Biblioteca de Autores Españoles*, 2 vols. (Madrid: M. Rivadeneyra, 1864–1872), vol. 2, pp. 463–576, p. 477. I translate the most important passage: "[The tyrant] believes that his greatest power lies in being able to give free rein to his passions. He considers no wickedness unseemly, commits all kinds of crimes, destroys the wealth of the powerful, violates chastity, slays the good and comes to the end of his life without having neglected to perform a single vile action." It is significant that in seventeenth-century Spain this partially dissident text is written in Latin, while the orthodox treatises on power (like that of Father Rivadeneira which will be quoted later) are written in Spanish.

do so,[23] he does not respect the elders,[24] he lacks clemency,[25] he constantly abuses his power,[26] he is unwilling to communicate[27] and, what is most important, he completely refuses to respond to any advice or warnings.[28] And when Esteban, the mayor of the village, names the *comendador* a second Nero,[29] this parallel is underscored.[30] By this theatrical device, the responsibility for the violence shifts from the crowd to the lord. When—after all these violations of humanity—the populace becomes outraged, loses control and refuses to pardon their lord or to accept his nobility,[31] they are perfectly mirroring his own crimes and his loss of moral nobility.[32] Or to put it another way: they merely follow his example. The syntagmatic structure of the text aims at partially legitimising their cruel actions.

This interpretation can be corroborated by considering the historical background of Father Mariana's treatise. By naming Nero, Lope broadens the intertextual references of the play. He obviously evokes the whole tradition of treatises on tyrannicide, which started in the antiquity with texts by Aristotle, Seneca and Cicero, continued in the Middle Ages with John of Salisbury and Thomas Aquinas and culminates in the late sixteenth century in the aforementioned treatise by Mariana.[33] It is significant that all of these authors legitimise tyrannicide in special cases and that the arguments they adduce are exactly

---

23 See Lope de Vega, *Fuente Ovejuna*, for example vv. 193 f., vv. 265 ff., vv. 595 ff., vv. 617 ff., vv. 937 ff., vv. 1065 ff., vv. 1143 ff., vv. 1210 ff., vv. 1350 ff., vv. 1570 ff., vv. 21347 ff. In vv. 807 ff., Lope also criticises the loose morals of the peasant girls. But the following incidents, especially the abduction of Jacinta (vv. 1210 ff.) and the disrupting of the wedding scene (vv. 1570 ff.), make clear that in the end the girls have no alternative because they are submitted to his immoderate power. See also v. 1145.
24 Vv. 1633 ff.
25 Vv. 1670, vv. 1248 f., v. 1272, v. 1320.
26 Vv. 1140 ff.
27 Vv. 1638 ff.
28 See for example vv. 980 ff., vv. 1015 ff., vv. 1266 ff. This point is very important, because it lays the ground for the following tyrannicide. In the sixth chapter of his treatise, Mariana states that an assassination of the tyrant is necessary and legitimate if he refuses to respond satisfactorily to advice or warnings. See Mariana, *Del rey y de la institución real*, pp. 479–483.
29 Lope de Vega, *Fuente Ovejuna*, v. 2422.
30 See also v. 1176 and vv. 1183 f., where the *comendador* is characterised as "más que una fiera inhumano" and as a savage tiger. By comparing him to an animal, Lope suggests that the *comendador* has lost his status as a *persona*, as Baltasar Gracián conceived it in his *Criticón*.
31 Vv. 1883 ff.
32 One may appreciate how precise the dramaturgical construction is by comparing vv. 1015 ff. and vv. 1248 ff. on the one hand and vv. 1880 ff. on the other. In these passages, the above-mentioned mirror structure is particularly blatant.
33 An overview of this tradition can be found in Martin Honecker, *Grundriß der Sozialethik* (Berlin/New York, NY: De Gruyter, 1995), pp. 361 ff.

repeated in the play, in particular the unwillingness of the tyrant to respond to advice and therefore the lack of alternatives.[34] As I cannot enumerate them all, I wish to concentrate on some particular aspects.

The first point is the natural law. In the ancient and medieval tradition, tyrannicide is seen as a lawful act because the tyrant violates the natural law which prescribes that every human being has a certain dignity and deserves respect.[35] On this point, the natural law of the pagan tradition and the divine law of Christianity perfectly converge. In the play, Lope evokes this argument when the peasants often claim their dignity and even their honour. So it is true that at the beginning one of the protagonists, Frondoso, refuses to fight a duel with the *comendador* by pointing out that a peasant is not a man of honour and therefore cannot fight duels with noblemen.[36] He obviously submits himself to the contemporary social theory of power[37]—which erodes the fundamental Christian egalitarianism. But here, too, we must consider the dynamics of the play. Like in the above-mentioned case, this statement of Frondoso constitutes above all a starting point for a shift, in the course of which the other peasants systematically override this humility. The more the *comendador* disproves his congenital honour by performing dishonourable acts, the more the peasants claim honour for themselves and legitimise this reversal with the fact that in the Commander's acts there is a deep gap between innate and moral honour:

> COMENDADOR:
> Tú, villana, ¿por qué huyes?
> ¿Es mejor un labrador
> que un hombre de mi valor?
> [...]
> JACINTA: Sí,
> porque tengo un padre honrado,
> que si en alto nacimiento
> no te iguala, en las costumbres
> te vence.[38]
>
> [COMMANDER: You, girl, what are you running for? / You find a clod that tills the earth / More pleasing than a man of worth? / [...]. JACINTA: Of course, / Because my father is a man / Well spoken of, though not your peer / In birth, with manners gentler still / Than any you possess.]

---

34 See Lope de Vega, *Fuente Ovejuna*, for example vv. 1248 f., vv. 1275 ff., v. 1320, v. 1670, vv. 1680 ff., vv. 1695 ff., etc.
35 See Honecker, *Grundriß der Sozialethik*, pp. 361 ff.
36 Lope de Vega, *Fuente Ovejuna*, vv. 852 f.
37 See also Küpper, "*Fuente Ovejuna*," pp. 109 f.
38 Vv. 1253–1263. See also vv. 1705, v. 1815, v. 2013.

By enacting this chiastic development, Lope inserts a hidden message into his text. He shows that, as a tyrant, the lord does not deserve to be treated as a man of honour. While the orthodox contemporary theory of power conceives hereditary rights as indefeasible,[39] Lope relativises the unconditional character of these rights.

This leads to the second point: the role of women. As the ringleaders of the village hesitate over what to do, it is Laurencia, the female peasant protagonist, who makes a flaming speech reproaching their cowardice and claiming the need to restore the natural law.[40] And it is only this speech that persuades them and therefore sets the elimination of the disturbing element—the lord—in motion.[41] In these passages, Lope fortifies Laurencia's social role to an extent that obviously does not fit with the current orthodox conception of ideal feminine behaviour. Not only is she depicted as intelligent, eloquent and energetic, but she also intervenes actively in the public sphere and even plays a crucial role in the liberation of the village. By shaping her in this way, Lope markedly differs from the misogynist concepts of women that prevailed in his time. He obviously rejects the idea of an inherent female inferiority, which in Huarte de San Juan's essay on the education of children culminates in the didactic prescription to silence them and to keep them away from the public sphere.[42]

---

39 See for example Father Pedro de Rivadeneira's treatise on the Christian prince, *Tratado de la religión y virtudes que debe tener el príncpe cristiano para gobernar y conservar sus estados, contra lo que Nicolas Maquiavelo y los políticos deste tiempo enseñan* [1595], in: *Obras escogidas del Padre Pedro de Rivadeneira*, ed. Vicente de la Fuente, *Biblioteca de Autores Españoles* (Madrid: M. Rivadeneyra, 1868), pp. 449–587. See also John Neville Figgis, *The Divine Right of Kings* [1896] (Gloucester, MA: Smith, 1970), pp. 5 f.
40 Lope de Vega, *Fuente Ovejuna*, vv. 1713 ff., vv. 1750 ff.
41 Vv. 1794ff. It is striking that this passage is replete with *conceptos*. A look at Lope's *Arte nuevo* may help to explain this peculiarity. There, Lope states that *conceptos* are only legitimate when they are needed for the purposes of conviction or advice (see Lope de Vega, *El arte nuevo*, vv. 250 ff.). This parallel shows that Laurencia is shaped even rhetorically as an important spokesperson, who is able to convince the extrafictional listeners. See also Lope de Vega, *Fuente Ovejuna*, vv. 1835 ff., vv. 1824 ff., vv. 1845 ff.
42 See Juan Huarte de San Juan, *Examen de ingenios para las ciencias* [1575], ed. Rodrigo Sanz (Madrid: Imp. La Rafa, 1930), p. 25, pp. 370 f., pp. 374 f., p. 388. A similar pattern of argumentation is used by Juan Vives (*Instrucción de la mujer cristiana*) and by Fray Luis de León (*La perfecta casada*). See Ursula Jung, *Autorinnen des spanischen Barock: Weibliche Autorschaft in weltlichen und religiösen Kontexten* (Heidelberg: Winter, 2010), pp. 44 ff. For more details on this topic see also Daniel Heiple, "Profeminist Reactions to Huarte's Misogyny in Lope de Vega's *La prueba de los ingenios* and María de Zaya's *Novelas amorosas y ejemplares*," in: Anita K. Stoll and Dawn L. Smith, edd., *The Perception of Women in Spanish Theater of the Golden Age* (Lewisburg, PA: Bucknell University Press, 1991), pp. 121–134.

And what is more: in the fictional world of the play, she soon finds female imitators, so that at the end, the women form a peculiar little army to fight against the dehumanised intruder:

> LAURENCIA:
> Que, puestas todas en orden,
> acometamos un hecho
> que dé espanto a todo el orbe.
> Jacinta, tu grande agravio,
> que sea cabo; responde
> de una escuadra de mujeres.
> [...]
> PASCUALA:
> Nombremos un capitán.
> LAUR.: Esso, no.
> PASC.: ¿Por qué?
> LAUR.: Que adonde
> assiste mi gran valor,
> no hay Cides ni Rodamontes.[43]

[LAUR.: Let's all of us form ordered ranks / And undertake an act so bold / We'll leave the wondering world aghast. / Jacinta, for your suffering, / I name you corporal; you're in charge / Of this brave women's squadron here. / [...] / PASC.: We'll have to name a captain, though. / LAUR.: Not true. / PASC.: How so? / LAUR.: Because who needs / El Cid or Rodomonte when / It's I who'll lead with gallantry?][44]

This passage is even more striking if we look at the kind of order the women are forming. When Laurencia emphasises that they do not need a classical leader, she promulgates a kind of utopian counter-order which transcends orthodox concepts of social hierarchy.

It is well known that Lope was a close friend of María de Zayas, the most famous feminist writer of the epoch, and that together they attacked especially the misogynist postulates of Huarte de San Juan.[45] In *Fuenteovejuna*, he obviously finds a subtle instrument to promulgate his sympathy with the current pro-feminist tendencies. Despite being a male writer in a completely patriarchal and androcentric context, he displays empathy and even sympathy for the feminist tendencies of his time.

But what about the ending of the play? At first glance, it may seem to refute the interpretation given above. The deed goes unpunished only because the Catholic

---

43 Lope de Vega, *Fuente Ovejuna*, vv. 1829–1834, vv. 1844–1847.
44 The translation is problematic because it evinces the idea of counter-order that I will speak of in the following.
45 See Heiple, "Profeminist Reactions to Huarte's Misogyny."

Kings are unable to isolate the ringleaders, and they explicitly emphasise that the upheaval was unjust.[46] But the irritation remains. Lope highlights that the guilty cannot be detected because, despite cruel torture,[47] every member of the community refuses to betray them, namely: because the powerless stand together.[48] With this construction, the submission of the populace to the royal power remains ambiguous: even when the peasants repeatedly *say* that they want to subjugate themselves to the Kings, they resist their power;[49] and it is exactly this resistance that leaves them unpunished.[50] Or to put it another way: the irreverence of the populace against their Kings is not punished, but rewarded. If, on a certain level of meaning, *Fuenteovejuna* undoubtedly promulgates the contemporary solidarity between the populace and the king, this idea is at the same time undermined.

In addition to that, Lope carefully implies that the Kings even share responsibility for the deed. In the crucial scene where the peasants decide to assassinate the tyrant, it is explicitly said that they only take these drastic steps because the Kings are too occupied to intervene, so that the peasants have to fend for themselves: "BARRILDO: En tanto que Fernando, aquel que humilla / a tantos enemigos, otro medio / será mejor, pues no podrá, ocupado, / hazernos bien con tanta guerra en medio."[51] ["BARRILDO: Before the monarchs do come, though, we will / Still need to find a remedy to meet / This enemy in that our king, who smote / So many foes, has others yet to beat."][52] A closer look reveals that this passage is very ambivalent and does not necessarily fit with the alleged Platonic horizon of the play, because the absence of the Kings is ascribed to a very concrete and historically verifiable reason.[53]

---

46 Lope de Vega, *Fuente Ovejuna*, vv. 2442 ff.
47 We may even find some criticism of torture in the play; see vv. 2203–2205, v. 2209, vv. 2218 f.
48 Vv. 2220.
49 See vv. 1865 ff., vv. 1918 ff., vv. 2028 ff., vv. 2090 ff.
50 The clemency of the Kings may also be influenced by the fact that the lord, at the beginning of the play, tries to deceive them too. In this textual construction, the end perfectly leads back to the beginning of the play.
51 Vv. 1680–1683.
52 Again, the translation is problematic. In this case the problem comes from the fact that it elides the ambiguity of the Spanish version and transforms it into a mere praise of royal power.
53 For the Platonic interpretation of the play see especially Leo Spitzer, "A Central Theme and Its Structural Equivalent in Lope's *Fuenteovejuna*," *Hispanic Review* 23 (1955), pp. 274–292; William C. McCrary, "*Fuenteovejuna*: Its Platonic Vision and Execution," *Studies in Philology* 58 (1961), pp. 179–192. Platonic readings of the text work on the assumption that the Catholic Kings are shaped like a distant god, which at the end appears as *deus ex machina*. The above-mentioned structures partially erode this interpretation. For the concrete historical background of the play see Ostlund, *The Re-Creation of History*, chap. 3, pp. 41–56.

The exposed structures make it possible to enumerate a plurality of teachings of the play. Every social rank is addressed in many different ways. The (peasant) populace is first of all undoubtedly requested to respect—to a certain extent—the social hierarchy and the central moral tenets of the time. Research on Lope has demonstrated this in detail.[54] But at the same time, this request is relativised, because for Lope it is only valid under a certain condition: the correct behaviour of the higher social ranks. Their members, the aristocrats in particular, have to show themselves worthy of being obeyed. They have the duty to match their congenital nobility to the nobility of their behaviour. Otherwise, they lose their right to rule. With this restriction, Lope does not completely follow the contemporary orthodox theory of power, which postulates that in every case non-resistance and passive obedience are encouraged by God.[55] Instead, he revitalises the ancient and medieval tradition that is still present in the aforementioned dissident voices of his time, in order to formulate a *criticism* of this theory of unlimited power. In a sophisticated use of poly-intertextuality, he plays off the ancient and medieval sources against sheer contemporary orthodoxy.[56] By recurring to other historical contexts, Lope is exceeding the boundaries of his own time. He is negotiating the question of power from a partially distanced standpoint where several contextures are superimposed. Propagandistic affirmation and critical assessment are realised at the same time.

So the aristocrats, too, receive a didactic message, which in a certain way is a counterpart of the message addressed to the populace. They are requested to make sure that they deserve their privileges. Both messages together include, amidst the overarching orthodoxy, a utopian impulse, since they foreshadow the

---

54 See for example Küpper, "*Fuente Ovejuna.*"
55 See for example Pedro de Rivadeneira, *Tratado de la religión*, pp. 452 ff. See also Figgis, *The Divine Right of Kings*, pp. 5 f. With this theory of social power, Rivadeneira applies the Counter-Reformation concept of divine omnipotence to earthly social structures. As Joachim Küpper has shown in his inspiring study *Discursive* Renovatio *in Lope de Vega and Calderón* (Berlin/Boston, MA: De Gruyter, 2017), the historical basis of the Counter-Reformation can be found in Aquinas' relativizing Augustine's concept of divine omnipotence. With my rereading of *Fuenteovejuna* I partially adopt a different perspective on seventeenth-century Spain.
56 The theory of power Lope is promulgating here resembles much more closely the scholastic concept of restricted power which influenced medieval feudal ideas of social order than it does Augustine's concept of divine omnipotence. For these historical interrelations see Ventarola, *Kairos und Seelenheil: Textspiele der Entzeitlichung in Francesco Petrarcas Canzoniere* (Stuttgart: Steiner, 2008), chap. 2 and chap. 3, pp. 34–97.

outlines of a new social ethic where power—as for Mariana but also for Francisco Suárez—is negotiated by a social contract.⁵⁷

The same is valid for the female audience. In the exemplary figure of Laurencia, the women receive two messages. On the one hand, they are requested to behave in a socially acceptable manner. Laurencia appears as a chaste woman with strong moral principles. But this precept is also relativised and completed with a utopian impulse which is transgressing the existing order because on the other hand—and, by means of the same character—women are encouraged to break their silence, to leave their passive and unconditional obedience and to fight for more social presence. They are encouraged to imitate Laurencia like the women in the play do.

Even the king is addressed in a twofold way. In the fictional figures of the Catholic Kings, he is shown as an ambivalent model. In their almost prudent and merciful actions, they are exemplary.⁵⁸ But in their sharing responsibility for the cruel escalation, we might find a cautious critique of present shortcomings. It is well known that Philipp III did not care much for the peasant population and pursued his military conflicts mostly at their expense.⁵⁹ In *Fuenteovejuna*, Lope seems to

---

57 In his treatise *De Legibus ac Deo legislatore*, Francisco Suárez develops a forward-looking theory of the monarchy as a social contract. He argues that social power always resides in the community and that its members only conditionally confer the right to exercise it on the king. See Francisco Suárez, *Tractatus de Legibus ac Deo Legislatore: In Decem Libros Distributus* [1613], 2 vols. (Napoli: Ex typis Fibrenianis, 1872), in particular "Liber sextus" and "Liber septimus," vol. 2, pp. 139–341. In general, Suárez's theory of contract and his importance to the development of modern legal concepts is relatively little studied within the whole of his work. I enumerate some recent studies: John Wiedhofft Gough, *The Social Contract: A Critical Study of its Development*, 2ⁿᵈ ed. (Oxford: Clarendon Press, 1957), pp. 68–71; Daniel Schwartz, "Francisco Suárez on Consent and Political Obligation," *Vivarium* 46.1 (2008), pp. 59–81; Schwartz, "Francisco Suárez y la tradición del Contrato Social," *Contrastes: Revista Internacional de Filosofía* 10 (2005), pp. 119–138; John Doyle, "Francisco Suárez, S.J. (1548–1617): On the Interpretation of Laws," *The Modern Schoolman* 83 (2006), pp. 197–222; Martine Pécharman, "Les fondements de la notion d'unité du peuple chez Suárez," in: Yves Charles Zarka, ed., *Aspects de la pensée médiévale dans la philosophie politique moderne* (Paris: Presses Universitaires de France, 1999), pp. 104–126.
58 The behaviour of the Kings almost corresponds to the depiction of the good king given by Father Mariana. See Mariana, *Del rey y de la institución real*, pp. 477 f. Of particular importance is their reaction when the populace asks for an audience: instead of rejecting it, they lend an attentive ear to the complaints of Esteban, the mayor of the little village, and give him the opportunity to demonstrate the tyrannical character of the *comendador*, before they decide what to do (Lope de Vega, *Fuente Ovejuna*, 2380 ff.).
59 See José María Díez Borque, "Teatro de palacio: excesos económicos y protesta pública," in: Alberto Blecua, Ignacio Arellano, and Guillermo Serés, edd., *El teatro del Siglo de Oro: Edición e interpretación* (Madrid: Iberoamericana; Frankfurt a.M.: Vervuert, 2009), pp. 79–112.

criticise precisely this omission of awareness. So the fictional Catholic Kings can be seen at once as a model and a critical mirror for the contemporary king.

Lope de Vega wrote innumerable plays, and many of them can undoubtedly be characterised as completely orthodox. But the analysis of *Fuenteovejuna* has revealed that this fact should not be assumed for all his plays. On closer inspection, we rather detect that they are graded in shades of orthodoxy. Despite his fundamental agreement with the idea of social order, Lope remains a poly-contextural and critical author who maintains a certain distance from the centre of power. *Fuenteovejuna* in particular is replete with ambivalences that cannot be dissolved into a singular interpretation. In order to find a possible explanation for this complexity, we should first adjust our image of the historical context and second should consider the concrete circumstances of Lope's life.

Concerning the first point, it could be shown that seventeenth-century Spain is—despite of the prevailing Counter-Reformation culture and its censorship[60]—a polyphonic, internally differentiated configuration in which many contextures overlap.[61] Concerning the second point, it is very likely that Lope's social provenance plays an important role in the empathy for the populace that he displays in *Fuenteovejuna*. Stemming from the same social rank himself and having traversed society from the bottom to the top, he perfectly knows the troubles the populace has to suffer. So even when living in the centre of power and agreeing (more or less) with the existing order, his experiences make him keep a certain internal distance which sharpens his eyes for current shortcomings and injustices. Besides this, his friendship with María de Zayas and others may have sensitised him to the problematic situation of women in an androcentric world. If in his play *El Nuevo Mundo* (*The New World*) he is not able to apply this critical posture to the problems of colonisation,[62] this is not inconsistent. The colonies are too far away to inspire empathy. For this, the work of Sor Juana is necessary.

---

[60] See Agustín de la Granja, "Comedias del Siglo de Oro censuradas por la Inquisición (Con noticia de un texto mal atribuido a Rojas Zorrilla)," in: Odette Gorsse and Frédéric Serralta, edd., *El Siglo de Oro en escena: Homenaje a Marc Vitse* (Toulouse: Presses Universitaires du Mirail, 2006), pp. 435–447.
[61] For this concept of cultures as pluralistic configurations of overlapping contextures see Ventarola, *Transkategoriale Philologie*, chaps. 1–3, pp. 13–288.
[62] For more information on this play see my following analysis.

Sor Juana Inés de la Cruz: Transcultural Criss-Crossings of Multi-Didactic Structures in *El divino Narciso* (1688)

The Hispano-American theatre culture of the epoch is strongly influenced by metropolitan Spain. In the course of the colonisation, the autochthonous traditions of theatrical performance are almost completely suppressed and replaced by the Spanish cultural-ideological material.[63] The playwrights adapt themselves to the aesthetic example of Lope, Calderón, Tirso de la Molina and others whose plays are not only imitated but also performed many times on Hispano-American stages. Even the currently prevailing social function of the theatre—to instil doctrine and teach political and religious dogma—is adopted.[64] Sor Juana, too, is part of this particular dynamic of cultural grafting. The Mexican playwright, a humbly born *mestiza*, who was first a protégé at the Viceregent's court and afterwards chose to enter the cloister, sometimes explicitly locates herself within this tradition.[65]

Like in the case of Lope, the scholarly community is divided. Since she often describes herself as a pupil of Lope, Calderón, Góngora or Quevedo, and since in her works she undoubtedly strives to instil doctrine, many scholars qualify her as a

---

[63] An overview of the early history of the autochthonous and Hispano-American traditions of theatrical performance can be found in José Miguel Oviedo, *Historia de la literatura hispanoamericana*, 3 vols., 1st ed., 5th reimpr. (Madrid: Alianza, 2007), vol. 1: *De los orígenes a la Emancipación*, chaps. 1–5, pp. 30–279. See also Manuel Antonio Arango Linares, *Contribución al estudio de la obra dramática de Sor Juana Inés de la Cruz* (New York, NY: Peter Lang, 2000), pp. 43 ff.; Marie-Cécile Bénassy-Berling, *Sor Juana Inés de la Cruz: Une femme de lettres exceptionelle. Mexique XVIIe siècle* (Paris: Harmattan, 2010), chaps. 1–2, pp. 17–58; Luis Alberto Sánchez, "Barroco, renacentismo, gongorismo, culteranismo y su versión hispanoamericana: Notas sobre *El Lunarejo*," in: [*Actas del*] *XVII Congreso del Instituto Internacional de Literatura Iberoamericana: Sesión de Madrid*, 3 vols. (Madrid: Ed. Cultura Hispánica del Centro Iberoamericano de Cooperación, 1978), vol. 1: *El Barroco en América*, pp. 281–288.
[64] See Arango Linares, *Obra dramática de Sor Juana Inés de la Cruz*, p. 61.
[65] For the life of Sor Juana see her own account in her famous *Respuesta a Sor Filotea de la Cruz* [1691], in: *Obras completas de Sor Juana Inés de la Cruz*, ed. Alfonso Méndez Plancarte, 4 vols. (México/Buenos Aires: Fondo de Cultura Ecónomica, 1951–1957), vol. 4: *Comedias, sainetes y prosa*, ed. Alberto G. Salceda, pp. 440–475. See also José María de Cossío, "Observaciones sobre la vida y la obra de Sor Juana Inés de la Cruz," in: de Cossío, *Notas y estudios de crítica literaria: Letras españolas (Siglos XVI y XVII)* (Madrid: Espasa-Calpe, 1970), pp. 243–284. For more details on the Mexican theatre of the seventeenth century see Humberto Maldonado Macías, "Introduction," in: Maldonado Macías, ed., *La teatralidad criolla del siglo XVII, Teatro mexicano: historia y dramaturgia* 8 (México: Consejo Nacional para la Cultura y las Artes, 1992), pp. 11–47.

mere imitator of (male) Spanish literature and its alleged doctrinal propaganda.[66] The transcultural "exchange" would be reduced to a mere acculturation. Others pay more attention to the subtle transformations, reversals, transgressions and criss-crossings she stages within her texts and, therefore, highlight their subversive character, be it in a feminist and/or in an anti-colonial perspective.[67] I wish to propose another interpretation, an interpretation that makes it possible to harmonize the other readings and take into account my re-reading of Lope. I will show that Sor Juana not only transforms her imitation into a mimicry, which in postcolonial readings of her work plays an important role,[68] but into an independent and constructive *aemulatio*, where the combination of analogies and differences is shaped in quite another manner. Whereas the mimicry is a strategy of survival of the powerless, the *aemulatio* is a sort of powerful imitation that strives to surpass the model.[69] By deliberately continuing and even reinforcing

---

[66] See for example Arango Linares, *Obra dramática de Sor Juana Inés de la Cruz*, pp. 62 ff., p. 201; Alexander A. Parker, "The Calderonian Sources of *El divino Narciso* by Sor Juana Inés de la Cruz," *Romanistisches Jahrbuch* 19 (1968), pp. 257–274; Ángel Valbuena Briones, *Literatura hispanoamericana*, 4th ed. (Barcelona: Gili, 1969), p. 134; Wolfgang Zwack, "Indianische Religion und christlicher Opfergedanke: Das Zusammentreffen zweier Welten in der *Loa* zum *Divino Narciso* von Sor Juana Inés de la Cruz," in: Monika Bosse and André Stoll, edd., *Theatrum mundi: Figuren der Barockästhetik in Spanien und Hispano-Amerika* (Bielefeld: Aisthesis, 1997), pp. 191–214.

[67] See for example Constance Wilkins, "Subversion through Comedy?: Two Plays by Sor Juana Inés de la Cruz and María de Zayas," in: Stoll et al., edd., *Perception of Women in Spanish Theater*, pp. 107–120; Stephanie Merrim, *Early Modern Women's Writing and Sor Juana Inés de la Cruz* (Liverpool: Liverpool University Press, 1999); Bernhard Teuber, "*Curiositas et crudelitas*: Das Unheimliche am Barock bei Góngora, Sor Juana Inés de la Cruz und José Lezama Lima," in: Joachim Küpper and Friedrich Wolfzettel, edd., *Diskurse des Barock: Dezentrierte oder rezentrierte Welt?* (München: Fink, 2000), pp. 615–652; Verónica Grossi, *Sigilosos v(u)elos epistemológicos en Sor Juana Inés de la Cruz* (Madrid: Iberoamericana; Frankfurt a.M.: Vervuert, 2007); Félix Duque, "La hibridación de culturas en *El divino Narciso*," in: Wolfram Nitsch and Bernhard Teuber, edd., *Zwischen dem Heiligen und dem Profanen: Religion, Mythologie, Weltlichkeit in der spanischen Literatur und Kultur der Frühen Neuzeit* (München: Fink, 2008), pp. 311–328; Sebastian Neumeister, "Mimikry? Sor Juana als *in-between* der kolonialen Mythenaneignung," in: Nitsch et al., edd., *Zwischen dem Heiligen und dem Profanen*, pp. 329–343; Neumeister, "Disimulación y rebelión: El 'político silencio' de Sor Juana Inés de la Cruz," in: Kazimierz Sabik and Karolina Kumor, edd., *La cultura del barroco español e iberoamericano y su contexto europeo* (Warszawa: Instituto de Estudios Ibéricos e Iberoamericanos de la Universidad de Varsovia, 2010), pp. 229–239.

[68] See especially the inspiring studies of Sebastian Neumeister quoted in the previous footnote. For Bhabha's concept of mimicry see Homi K. Bhabha, *The Location of Culture* (London/New York, NY: Routledge, 1994), chap. 4 ("Of Mimicry and Man: The Ambivalence of Colonial Discourse"), pp. 121–131.

[69] Sor Juana herself draws attention to this strategy when in the *Sainete Segundo* of her play *Los empeños de una casa* she ironises an exaggerated admiration for the Spanish authors (vv. 36 ff.).

the *ambivalences* of her Spanish model, Sor Juana not only teaches her compatriots, but also the Spanish colonisers themselves. She uses the possible multi-directionality of the drama in order to reverse and cross its didactic impact, and she does so with a special emphasis on transcultural communicative processes. The multi-didaxis of her play is also culturally differentiated. As an inhabitant of the New World, a *mestiza* and a woman, her distance from the metropolitan centre of power is much greater than Lope's, and this triple shifting of perspective allows her to develop new aesthetic and didactic concepts.[70]

Her religious play *El divino Narciso* (*The Divine Narcissus*) is a perfect example of this complex theatrical strategy. Composed around 1688, probably at the request of her patroness Vicereine María Luisa de Laguna, who in 1689 took it with her back to Spain for presentation there, the play was first published in Mexico in 1690.[71] Many scholars consider it the most beautiful *auto sacramental* ever written in the Spanish language.[72] In this play, the aforementioned combination of an overarching orthodoxy and local phenomena of irritation is realised in an exemplary manner. As an *auto sacramental*, *El divino Narciso*, at the highest level of meaning, is undoubtedly written in the service of religious education.[73] Disguised in the *integumentum* of the Ovidian myth of Narcissus, the play performs the Passion of Jesus Christ: Narcissus appears as the allegorical personification of the Son of God; Echo epitomises the Devil; and the mirror image that Narcissus sees in the water and falls in love with represents creation and espe-

---

See Sor Juana Inés de la Cruz, *Los empeños de una casa* [1683]/ *Amor es más laberinto* [1689], ed. Celsa Carmen García Valdés (Madrid: Cátedra, 2010), pp. 107–299, pp. 231 ff.

70 With this perspective, I differ from common feminist and intersectional theories of feminine writing in the early modern period, as the prevailing interest of these studies is focused on the constraints the social situation of women brings about. See for example Bénassy-Berling, *Sor Juana Inés de la Cruz*, pp. 59 ff.; and, in more general terms, Ute Frackowiak, ed., *Ein Raum zum Schreiben: Schreibende Frauen in Spanien vom 16. bis ins 20. Jahrhundert* (Berlin: Edition Tranvía, Walter Frey, 1998). For the concept of intersectionality see Gabriele Winkler and Nina Degele, edd., *Intersektionalität: Zur Analyse sozialer Ungleichheiten* (Bielefeld: Transcript, 2009).

71 For the history of the text and its possible sources, see Arango Linares, *Obra dramática de Sor Juana Inés de la Cruz*, pp. 27ff.; Patricia A. Peters, "Introduction," in: Sor Juana Inés de la Cruz, *El Divino Narciso* [1690]/ *The Divine Narcissus*, edd. and trans. Patricia A. Peters and Renée Domeier (Albuquerque, NM: University of New Mexico Press: 1998), pp. IX–XXXII, pp. XVII ff.

72 See the overview given by Arango Linares, *Obra dramática de Sor Juana Inés de la Cruz*, pp. 15 f.

73 For more details on the history and social functions of the *auto sacramental* see Küpper, *Discursive* Renovatio *in Lope de Vega and Calderón*, chap. 3; Miguel Ángel Pérez Priego, "Los autos: origen, evolución y adecuación ideológica," in: Blecua et al., edd., *El teatro del Siglo de Oro*, pp. 397–421.

cially humanity in general. With this setting, the audience learns the content of the Bible (the Eucharist in particular) in a playful, pleasurable way.

One special quality of Sor Juana's art of writing plays is the skilful interlacing of the plays themselves and their ancillary texts, be they prologues (*loas*), songs, interludes (*sainetes*) or choral-choreographed finales (*saraos*). *El divino Narciso*, too, is designed as a composite unit of the introductory *loa* and the following *auto*.[74] Nevertheless, many scholars continue to analyse the *loa* and the *auto* as more or less separate entities.[75] Patricia A. Peters even assumes that they could be performed separately.[76] In fact, the complicated multi-didactical impulse of the play can only be appreciated when it is considered along with the introductory *loa*.

The *loa* already specifies the first addressee: it is the indigenous people of the Americas. Like Lope's play *El Nuevo Mundo* (*The New World*) and Calderón's play *La Aurora en Copacabana* (*The Aurora in Copacabana*), the *loa* performs (but now in an allegorical way) the first contact between the Spanish colonisers and the autochthonous population.[77] In this fictional setting, the following *auto sacramental* is inserted as a second fictional world. The personification of Religion

---

[74] Details on the Hispano-American history of the *loa* can be found in Anthony M. Pasquariello, "The Evolution of the *Loa* in Spanish America," *Latin American Theatre Review* 3.2 (1970), pp. 5–19; Humberto Maldonado Macías, "La evolución de la *loa* en la Nueva España: De González de Eslava a Sor Juana," in: Ysla Campbell, ed., *El escritor y la escena: Actas del I Congreso de la Asociación Internacional de Teatro Español y Novohispano de los Siglos de Oro (18–12 de marzo de 1992)* (Ciudad Juárez: Universidad Autónoma de Ciudad Juárez, 1992), pp. 77–94.

[75] See for example Celsa Carmen García Valdés, "Teatralidad barroca: las loas sacramentales de Sor Juana," in: Sara Poot Herrera, ed., *Sor Juana y su mundo: una mirada actual* (México: Universidad del Claustro de Sor Juana, Fondo de Cultura Económica, 1995), pp. 207–218; María Dolores Bravo Arriaga, "Las loas de los autos sacramentales de Sor Juana: Conciencia criolla y sentido de la composición," in: Serafín González and Lillian von der Walde, edd., *Palabra crítica: Estudios en homenaje de José Amezcua* (México: Universidad Autónoma Metropolitana, Fondo de Cultura Económica, 1997) pp. 250–259; Arango Linares, *Obra dramática de Sor Juana Inés de la Cruz*.

[76] See Peters, "Introduction," pp. XXIII.

[77] For the above-mentioned plays by Calderón and Lope, see for example Küpper, "Teleologischer Universalismus und kommunitaristische Differenz: Überlegungen zu Calderóns *La aurora en Copacabana*, zu Voltaires *Alzire, ou les Américains*, zu Sepúlveda und Las Casas," in: Karlheinz Stierle and Rainer Warning, edd., *Das Ende: Figuren einer Denkform* (München: Fink, 1996), pp. 435–466; Ingrid Simson, "La función de la alegoría en las comedias de temática Americana en el Siglo de Oro," in: Christoph Strosetzki, ed., *Teatro español del Siglo de Oro: Teoría y práctica* (Madrid: Iberoamericana; Frankfurt a.M.: Vervuert, 1998), pp. 305–321; Simson, *Amerika in der spanischen Literatur des 'Siglo de Oro': Bericht, Inszenierung, Kritik* (Frankfurt a.M.: Vervuert, 2003); Stephan Leopold, "La Victoria del *telos* o la ironía de la representación: tipología, legitimación y mestizaje en *La aurora en Copacabana*," in: Manfred Tietz and Gero Arnscheidt, edd., *Calderón y el pensamiento ideológico y cultural de su época: XIV Coloquio Anglogermano sobre Calderón, Heidelberg, 24–28 de julio de 2005* (Stuttgart: Steiner, 2008), pp. 317–336. For

appears as an intradiegetical narrator who speaks to the personification of the Americas and explicitly announces the following play as an instrument deployed in the service of the Mission:

> Religión:
> Pues vamos. Que en una idea
> metafórica, vestida
> de retóricos colores,
> representable a tu vista,
> te la mostraré;
> [...]
> Celo:
> Religión, díme:
> ¿en qué forma determinas
> representar los Misterios?
> Rel.:
> De un Auto en la alegoría,
> quiero mostrarlos visibles,
> para que quede instruída
> ella, y todo el Occidente,
> de lo que ya solicita
> saber.[78]
>
> [Religion: Then come along with me, and I / shall make for you a metaphor, / a concept clothed in rhetoric / so colorful that what I show / to you, your eyes will clearly see; / [...]. / Zeal: Religion, answer me: / what metaphor will you employ / to represent these mysteries? / Rel.: An *auto* will make visible / through allegory images / of what America must learn / and Occident implores to know / about the questions that now burn / within him so.]

This duplication of fictional worlds is very skilful, because now the "real" inhabitants of the Americas can identify themselves with the intradiagetical audience of the *loa* and therefore become the first addressee.

But a closer look quickly reveals the innumerable modifications, reversals and transgressions Sor Juana has inserted into this overarching doctrinal pattern. The whole text is loaded with local phenomena or substages where she develops innovative and even utopian thoughts (and aesthetic structures); and it is especially with these heterotopian substructures that she strives to invert the traditional direction of didaxis and to advise the aesthetic and cultural colonisers themselves.

---

more differences between Lope and Calderón on the one hand and Sor Juana on the other, see my following analysis.
78 Sor Juana Inés de la Cruz, *El divino Narciso*, *Loa*, vv. 401–405; vv. 415–423. All references to *El divino Narciso* and quotations from the English translation are from Sor Juana Inés de la Cruz, *El Divino Narciso/ The Divine Narcissus*, trans. and edd. Peters and Domeier.

Let me first focus on the central *auto*. Here, Sor Juana obtains the desired effect above all by multiplying the superimposed frames of reference. Not only is she merging the Greek myth and the biblical Passion,[79] but she also inserts elements of ancient and medieval love lyric as well as of the psychomachian tradition.[80] In addition to that, she merges narrativity and theatrical performativity. In each scene, another allegorical personification appears as an intradiegetical narrator, who explains and comments on the performed events. In this way, the whole fictional world of the *auto* is fashioned as a poly-contextural and poly-perspectival world. I can by no means demonstrate all the aesthetic and philosophical complexions that are brought about by these superimpositions, so I wish to concentrate on two aspects.

First, the conception of God. By merging the various textual traditions, the Passion of Jesus Christ is re-interpreted as a love story that, at the same time, explores and visualises the deepest inner conflicts of God himself. Narcissus/God is depicted as a very worldly lover of his mirror image (Nature) who sings love lyrics[81] and is, himself, subjugated to the laws of love:

NARCISO:
¿Cómo tan fiera sujeta
[...]
aquesta pena inhumana
[...]
Mi Ser Divino impasible?
[...]
Mas sin duda es invencible
del Amor la fortaleza,
pues ha puesto a Mi Belleza
[...]
LOS DOS [ECO Y NARCISO]:

---

[79] For this rhetorical strategy, which is usual in the religious plays of the *Siglo de Oro*, see Gloria D. Calhoun, "Un triángulo mitológico, idólatra y cristiano en *El divino Narciso* de Sor Juana," *Ábside* 34 (1970), pp. 373–401; Jean Krynen, "Mito y teología en *El divino Narciso* de Sor Juana Inés de la Cruz," in: Carlos Horacio Magis, ed., *Actas del Tercer Congreso Internacional de Hispanistas* (México: El Colegio de México, 1970), pp. 501–505; Arango Linares, *Obra dramática de Sor Juana Inés de la Cruz*, pp. 27 ff., pp. 37 ff., pp. 182 ff.; García Valdés, "La Biblia en la obra literaria de Sor Juana Inés de la Cruz," in: Ignacio Arellano and Ruth Fine, edd., *La Biblia en la literatura del Siglo de Oro* (Madrid: Iberoamericana; Frankfurt a.M.: Vervuert, 2010), pp. 167–189.
[80] For the complicated intertextual network of the play which forms "un maravilloso mosaico de formas poéticas y métricas," see Octavio Paz, *Sor Juana Inés de la Cruz o Las trampas de la fe* (México: Fondo de Cultura Económica, 1982), p. 464; Grossi, *Sigilosos v(u)elos epistemológicos*, pp. 133 ff.
[81] See for example Sor Juana Inés de la Cruz, *El divino Narciso*, Auto, vv. 1136–1236, vv. 1447 ff.

Sujeta, Humana, Pasible.⁸²

[NARCISSUS: Why am I so cruelly subject / [...] / to that torture, so inhuman / [...] / though divine, invulnerable? / [...] / But without doubt, invincible / is love in its great potency / since it has made My loveliness / [...] / THE TWO (ECHO AND NARCISSUS): Subject, Human, Vulnerable.]

By highlighting the humanity, the inner conflicts and even the erotic emotionalism of God, Sor Juana is subtly modifying the Counter-Reformation conception of the Highest Being.⁸³ She clearly anticipates a critique of the Christian doctrine that a few years later she will develop in detail in her famous *Carta atenagórica* (*Letter Worthy of Athena*), which brought her a complete prohibition of writing.⁸⁴

The second aspect concerns the aesthetics of the text. By merging the various textual traditions and by mingling narrativity and performativity, Sor Juana is exploring new forms of allegorical writing and even of textuality in general. Every allegorical protagonist of the text fulfils several functions that in the course of the play are always shifting. In addition to that, Sor Juana inserts one textual layer into the other and does so continuously, very much like a Russian doll effect. So the text becomes a multilevelled universe, where the semantic layers and meanings form ever-changing constellations. And what is more: as all the allegorical personifications can also appear as explaining and commenting narrators, they are at the same time meta-allegorical allegories. Eco, for example, not only stands for the Devil and for human sin (on the psychomachian level of the text),⁸⁵ but Sor Juana also introduces the following scene and explains the logic of allegorical *integumentum* in general:

ECO:
[...]
escuchadme. Ya habéis visto

---

82 Vv. 1501–1510. See also vv. 1471 ff., vv. 1491 ff., vv. 1522 ff., vv. 1533 ff.
83 In vv. 596 ff. of the *auto*, Sor Juana explicitly names the debates of the Council of Trent. Her ludic transformation of Christian dogma goes even further. In vv. 950 f., *Naturaleza* (who epitomizes nature as well as the human nature of God) reveals that she is "negra" ("[...] aunque soy negra, soy hermosa, / pues parezco a Tu imagen milagrosa" ["[...] though black, yet I am fair / because your countenance I bear"]), and in vv. 1060 ff. the whole myth of Diana is realised with inverted sexual roles.
84 See Sor Juana Inés de la Cruz, *Carta atenagórica* [1690], in: *Obras completas de Sor Juana Inés de la Cruz*, vol. 4, pp. 412–439. Details on the text and on the impact it had on Sor Juana's life can be found in Paz, *Sor Juana*, pp. 524–533; Dario Puccini, *Una mujer en soledad: Sor Juana Inés de la Cruz, una excepción en la cultura y la literatura barroca* [*Una donna in solitudine*, 1996], trans. Esther Benítez (Madrid: Anaya & Muchnik, 1996), pp. 29–38.
85 See for example her dense monologue in vv. 295–526 of the *auto*.

> que aquesta Pastora bella
> representa en común toda
> la Humana Naturaleza:
> que en figura de una Ninfa,
> con metafórica idea,
> sigue a una Beldad que adora,
> no obstante que la deprecia;
> y para que a las Divinas
> sirvan las Humanas Letras,
> valiéndose de las dos,
> su conformidad coteja
> tomando a unas el sentido,
> y a las otras la corteza,
> y prosiguiendo las frases,
> usando de la licencia
> de retóricos colores,
> que son uno, y otro muestran,
> Narciso a Dios llama,
> [...].[86]

[ECHO: (...) Now listen. You already know / that this lovely shepherdess / stands for the commonality / of Human Nature; and that she, / clad in the costume of a nymph, / (I now speak metaphorically), / pursues a beauty she adores, / who nonetheless despises her; / and so that human poetry / might minister to Holy Writ, / she takes some elements from both, / combining them where they agree, / abstracting meaning from the one, / and from the other taking form; / and with poetic license, she / composes sentences of such / iridescent rhetoric / that what they seem, they never mean; / therefore, she calls Narcissus God, (...).]

Through this device, the referential and the self-referential dimension of literature, didaxis, and an autonomous aesthetic play are perfectly harmonised.

If we consider the *loa*, we can grasp the complex multi-didactical aim of these innovations. As I previously mentioned, the *loa* broadens the cultural focus by explicitly inserting the indigenous population. When doing so, Sor Juana also modifies her models. In an astute analysis of Calderón's *Aurora in Copacabana*, Joachim Küpper has recently shown that in the play the first contact scene reproduces all the problematic arguments that in the colonial epoch are deployed in order to legitimise the cruelties of Christian colonisation.[87] In the figural scheme, all cultural differences are completely neglected and reduced to a relationship of inferiority and superiority.[88] In this way, the conquerors appear as redeemers who help the "poor" indigenous people to establish a social order and to save

---

86 Sor Juana Inés de la Cruz, *El divino Narciso*, Auto, vv. 322–340. See also vv. 322 ff.; vv. 1343 ff.
87 See Küpper, "Teleologischer Universalismus," pp. 434–466.
88 Pp. 442 ff.

their souls.[89] The same critique can be expressed with regard to Lope's play *El Nuevo Mundo*.[90] I would add that this conception also determines the strategies of missionary didaxis that are realised. In both plays, the indigenous people are not converted by means of rational explanations but by deploying dazzling stage machinery that produces the illusion of divine miracles.[91] They are not convinced, they are subjected.

The first contact scene of Sor Juana's *loa* strongly differs from that. It is true that, like the others, it culminates in a praise of the religious superimposition.[92] But, at the same time, Sor Juana is criticising all the aforementioned arguments. First, she highlights the cultural differences and even the value of the indigenous culture by staging a real Indian rite and not only Western clichés about the Indians, as Lope and Calderón did.[93] Second, she at least reduces the cultural hierarchy by emphasising the "barbarian" elements of the Christian religion, namely the fact that even the Christian faithful eat their God:

AMÉRICA:
¿[S]erá esa Deidad que pintas,
tan amorosa, que quiera
ofrecérseme en comida,
como Aquésta que yo adoro?
[...]
OCCIDENTE:
¡Vamos, que ya mi agonía
quiere ver cómo es el Dios
que me han de dar en comida,

---

89 Pp. 447 ff.
90 See for example Lope de Vega, *El nuevo mundo descubierto por Cristóbal Colón* [1614], edd. Jean Lemartinel and Charles Minguet (Lille: Presses Universitaires de Lille, 1980), vv. 1439–1448; vv. 2020 ff.; vv. 2510 ff. An analysis of the play can be found in Simson, "La función de la alegoría."
91 See for example Lope de Vega, *El nuevo mundo*, vv. 1744 ff.; Pedro Calderón de la Barca, *La aurora en Copacabana* [1672], in: *Obras completas de Calderón de la Barca*, ed. Ángel Valbuena Briones, 3 vols. (Madrid: Aguilar, 1987), vol. 2, pp. 1315-1361, vv. 594–692. The use of dazzling stage machinery and emotional images was current in the *Siglo de Oro*. See for example John Earl Varey, "Scenes, Machines and the Theatrical Experience in Seventeenth-Century Spain," in: Antoine Schnapper, ed., *La scenografia barocca/ La scénographie baroque/ Stage Design during the Baroque* (Bologna: Ed. Clueb, 1982), pp. 51–63; Antonio Azaustre Galiana, "Recursos retóricos en el teatro del siglo de oro: El caso de la 'evidentia'," in: Blecua et al., edd., *El teatro del Siglo de Oro*, pp. 29–49.
92 See Sor Juana Inés de la Cruz, *El divino Narciso*, Loa, vv. 261 ff., vv. 280 ff.
93 Vv. 1–72. The rhetorical strategy of the Spanish playwrights to transform the Indians into Spaniards is shown in detail by Simson, *Amerika in der spanischen Literatur*, pp. 289–320.

*(Cantan la América y el Occidente y
el Celo:)*
diciendo que ya
conocen las Indias
al que el Verdadero
Dios de la Semillas![94]

[AMERICA: (B)ut would the God that you reveal / offer Himself so lovingly / transformed for me into a meal / as does the god that I adore? / (...) / OCCIDENT: Let's go, for anxiously I long to see / exactly how this God of yours / will give Himself as food to me. / *(America, Occident and Zeal sing:)* The Indies know / (...) / who is the true / God of the Seeds.]

Third, she criticises all the cruelties of the Christian colonisation by showing the persecution on stage.[95] Fourth, she enhances the role of women by fashioning the female allegories ("Religión" and "América") as the spokespersons of the whole *loa*.[96] Last but not least, she stages completely different strategies of missionary didaxis: instead of using dazzling stage machinery and unconscious manipulations by means of emotional images, the allegory of Religion appeals to reason. Like the other intradiegetical narrators of the play, she constantly explains her strategies and the functioning of the allegories deployed.[97] In the play, this self-referential dimension culminates in a questioning of the audience: when Eco evokes the following *auto* as a place of God's real presence, she at the same time requests her audience to judge whether the device is successful:

Eco:
Y así, aunque ya lo sabéis,
[...]
os referiré la historia
con la metáfora misma,
para ver si la de Eco
conviene con mi tragedia.
Desde aquí el curioso
mire si concuerdan
verdad y ficción,
el sentido y letra.[98]

---

94 Sor Juana Inés de la Cruz, *El divino Narciso*, Loa, vv. 370–373, vv. 486–492.
95 Vv. 185 ff. Besides this scene, the allegory of America explicitly tries to inspire empathy for the Indians (vv. 175 ff.) and criticises the use of brutal power (vv. 91–95, vv. 206 ff.).
96 The presence of the male allegories ("Occidente" and "Celo") is reduced to a few short replies.
97 See for example *Loa*, vv. 401 ff., vv. 418 ff., vv. 462 ff.; *Auto*, vv. 112 ff., vv. 133 ff., vv. 140 ff., vv. 322 ff., vv. 1044 ff.
98 *Auto*, v. 362, vv. 366–373.

[ECHO: And though you may already guess / my story [...] / still I will tell it to you now, / using the self-same metaphor / so you can judge if Echo's tale / echoes the tale I told before. / From that, the curious might reflect / upon the possible accord / between these fictions and the truth, / between significance and word.]

By textually superimposing the theatrical strategies of persuasion with their self-referential naming, religious education and its critical assessment are perfectly harmonised. In addition to this, Sor Juana demonstrates possible new ways of using emotions, and here the other modifications of the *auto* come into play. By humanising God as a worldly lover of humanity, the violent elements of the stipulated conversion are exchanged for an appeal to return God's love.

In order to complete the new interpretation, we must focus again on the intended addressee of the play. In verses 443 ff. of the *loa*, the personification of missionary zeal hints at the fact that Sor Juana has written her play to be performed not only in the Hispano-American colonies, but above all in the Spanish capital, Madrid: "CELO: ¿Pues no ves la impropiedad / de que en Méjico se escriba / y en Madrid se represente?"[99] ["ZEAL: That you should write in Mexico / for royal patrons don't you see / to be an impropriety?"]

With this statement, he explicitly indicates that Sor Juana is constructing a gap between the internal and the external communication of the play. In the fictional world of the *loa*, the addressees are the Indians; but on the outside the play is also aimed at the Spaniards themselves. This differentiation reveals that Sor Juana deliberately strives to culturally diversify the teachings of her text. By informing the Indians about the Eucharist, the orthodox function of an *auto sacramental* is undoubtedly fulfilled, even though in a very new interpretation of this Eucharist and by means of very new didactic and aesthetic devices. And, precisely through these innovations, Sor Juana also strives to teach the colonisers themselves—the political leaders as well as the playwrights. By demonstrating the cruelty of cultural and religious superimposition on stage, the conquerors are requested to relativise their own standpoint. Sor Juana obviously tries to set in motion a process of self-reflection and self-critique in the minds of her Spanish audience. At the same time, she provides alternative educational options, which anticipate the early enlightenment. The power of reason is enhanced and the religious emotions are addressed in an innovative way. Even women can find new role models—in the female allegories which (much as in Lope's play) are portrayed as strong, eloquent and interventionist characters. And with her innovative concepts of theatrical and allegorical textuality, with her perfect reconciliation of didaxis and aesthetics, she is appealing to the playwrights of the whole

---

99 *Loa*, vv. 443–445.

world. Her *Divine Narcissus* can be seen as a manifesto of a new art of writing plays, which is at least as innovative as Lope's was. With her independent and constructive "imitation" of the Spanish model, Sor Juana is realising a kind of "writing back" that is free of violence and deeply innovative at once. And with this, I come to my conclusion.

Conclusion

The comparison of Lope and Sor Juana has, as I hope, demonstrated that binaristic theoretical patterns do not suffice to describe the complexity of colonial interchange, especially in the case of the relationship between Spain and Hispano-America. Only when we consider the poly-contexturality and the multi-didactical impulse of the authors are we able to grasp the peculiarity of each play as well as of the cultural dialogue between them. It could be shown that both playwrights use a multi-didaxis in order to realise both a propagandistic affirmation *and* a critical analysis of the central tenets of their (social and religious) contexts. In conformity with their respective cultural and social location, only the weighting differs. Lope remains inside the borders of Spanish culture and plays with social hierarchy. Sor Juana extends the critical multi-didaxis to the hierarchy of cultures. And because of her distance from metropolitan Spain, she can even try to establish a new cultural centre. By taking into account this fact, the simplifying logic of *actio* and *reactio*, of cultural grafting and "writing back," is substituted by a more complex model which takes into account the entanglement of analogies and differences as well as the graded shading of cultural belonging. If we conceive the theatre as a mass medium and an *organon* of subjectivisation, we must say that both playwrights are able to individualise their audience to an extent that until now has mostly been neglected. As they are tied to the baroque context, they still do not stage revolutionary processes in the radical sense. But their texts are—to an ever changing extent—replete with heterotopian phenomena which at least hint at the possibility of new social and aesthetic orders.

Jonathan Gil Harris
Tamburlaine in Hindustan

My essay is called "Tamburlaine in Hindustan." But to which "Tamburlaine" does my title refer—and, for that matter, to which "Hindustan"? Both these proper nouns have complicated, refractory referents. "Tamburlaine" is and is not the medieval Turkic warrior-king Temür; he is, more accurately, an early modern English theatrical figure—made famous by Christopher Marlowe in his 1587 play—based loosely on the latter. "Hindustan" is and is not what we think of as India; it is rather the Persian name for a changing historical territory, extending over what is now northern India, Pakistan and part of Afghanistan, ruled in Marlowe's time by the Mughals, a dynasty lineally descended from Temür. If "Tamburlaine" and "Hindustan" are each complicated proper nouns, lumping them together in one phrase generates yet more complications. Marlowe's Tamburlaine makes several references not to Hindustan but to "India," the early modern English name for a vast swath of territory extending all the way from the subcontinent to the Spice Islands. "Temür in Hindustan" might serve as an apt title for an essay about the Turkic warrior-king's activities in the north of the Indian subcontinent and his afterlife in Mughal culture. And "Tamburlaine in India" could serve as the title of an essay about Marlowe's play and its handful of references to south Asia. But what might the trans-linguistic, trans-geographical title "Tamburlaine in Hindustan" mean?

In this essay, I will think about Temür in Hindustan (both a world historical event of the late fourteenth century and an ongoing Mughal literary and artistic event in the sixteenth century) and Tamburlaine in India (an English theatrical event of the late sixteenth century). But I am particularly interested in the event of the English Tamburlaine in Mughal Hindustan. This altogether more baffling phenomenon—simultaneously theatrical and historical, early modern and medieval, English and Mughal—suggests how, even as the journey of "Tamburlaine" to "Hindustan" might seem to point in one geographical direction, it in fact takes several paths, and ends up at several different destinations.

My essay traverses three of these paths. First, it glances at the historical figure on which Tamburlaine is based: the warrior-king Temür, who did indeed travel to Hindustan in about 1398. He is usually supposed to have conquered it and become its "emperor," though he only ever briefly crossed the Indus and, in a short but bloody campaign, took possession of what is now Punjab in Pakistan

---

Note: For helpful feedback on earlier drafts of this essay, I would like to thank Madhavi Menon, Jyotsna Singh, Nandini Das, Supriya Chaudhuri, Julia Schleck and Martin Puchner.

https://doi.org/10.1515/9783110536881-010

and the territories surrounding Delhi. Although Hindustan was subsequently conquered by Lodhi Afghan invaders, Temür's great-great-grandson Babur reconquered it and set up the Mughal dynasty, whose scions played an instrumental role in making Timūr-e-Lang (the Persian version of Temür's name) the mythic founding figure of their line.[1] Second, Temür's travels to Hindustan were written and rewritten in a variety of narratives that migrated westward from Persia to Arabia, and thence through Spain to England. With each retelling, these narratives and their main character transformed considerably. Yet each narrative, especially Christopher Marlowe's famous play *Tamburlaine the Great* (loosely based on the Spanish writer Pedro Mexía's tale of "Tamerlán" in his *Silva de varia lección* [1540]), retained Hindustan or India as part of its global geography. Third and lastly, when Englishmen travelled in the early seventeenth century to Mughal Hindustan—an altogether different entity from the Hindustan briefly conquered by Temür—Marlowe's Tamburlaine narrative travelled with them, giving them a set of coordinates with which to frame their experiences.

I am particularly interested in what happens when we read these three connected yet divergent tales—"Temür in Hindustan," "Tamburlaine in India," "Tamburlaine in Hindustan"—alongside each other. What might Temür's history tell us about Mughal Hindustan? How does Marlowe's *Tamburlaine* understand India? And what did early modern English travellers to the Mughal court extract from Marlowe's play? For all their differences, these three tales collectively put pressure on conceptions of bounded identity as they migrate across national and linguistic borders. In the process, the tales constitute a global "dramanet" that productively expands the ways in which we might think about the shaping power of theatricality.

Temür in Hindustan

Born in 1336 near Samarkand in Uzbekistan, Temür rose to become the most powerful warrior of Asia in his lifetime, conquering most of Central, South and West

---

[1] Temür's name means "iron" in Turkic languages; like the metal it refers to, the name has transformed as it has been exposed to external influences, morphing into "Timūr" and "Timūr-e-Lang" in Persian, "Demir" in Turkish, "Tamerlan" in Spanish and French and "Tamerlane" and "Tamburlaine" in English. For a fuller discussion of this profusion of names, see Michael Shterenshis, *Tamerlane and the Jews* (London/New York: RoutledgeCurzon, 2002), esp. p. xv.

Asia before his death in 1405.² His success was achieved despite considerable social and physical obstacles. Temür may not have been the poor shepherd that Marlowe depicts Tamburlaine as being; in fact he came from a minor noble family of the Barlas tribe, a Turkic-Mongolian people. Yet because he was not lineally descended from Chingiz (i.e. Gengis) Khan, he could not claim the title of Khan, or supreme king, of the Mongol Empire. This forced him to rule the lands he conquered through puppet kings. Adding to the challenges facing him was that, in his twenties, he lost two fingers and sustained an arrow wound in his leg, injuries that left him seriously disabled for the rest of his life. As a result, he gained the Persian soubriquet "e-Lang," the Lame, a title that enabled the bowdlerisation of "Timūr-e-Lang" into "Tamerlane" (in Spain) and "Tamburlaine" (in England). Even in his lifetime, then, Temür's tale was one not just of transnational conquest but also of renaming and bodily transformation.

Temür's catalogue of military success is astonishing. During his long western campaign, from 1383 to 1402, he conquered most of Persia, Baghdad, Georgia and Armenia; and, in his most famous victory, he vanquished the Ottoman sultan Bayezid I, who died in captivity. Contrary to the legend, however, there is no record of Temür taking Bayezid with him on his campaigns in a customised cage.³ At that time the Ottoman Empire had yet to take Constantinople; but Temür's victory over Bayezid gave him control of most of Anatolia. He also took on the Mamluk sultan of Egypt, Nasir-ud-Din Faraj, sacking Aleppo and Damascus. These triumphs gave Temür a reputation for horrendous cruelty: he ordered that all the inhabitants of Damascus be put to death, just as he had massacred 20,000 of Baghdad's citizens after its capture. Temür's expansionist plans aimed not just westwards but also to the south and east. After his conquest of Hindustan, he planned to take on China as well. But he died suddenly in 1405, stopping his conquests in their tracks. Temür's body was sent back to Samarkand for burial, where his tomb stands to this day.

Temür spent only a very short time in Hindustan. He crossed the Indus in early 1398, yet by 1399 he and his army had remobilised to Anatolia and resumed

---

2 The details of Temür's biography I provide here are derived from Beatrice Forbes Manz, *The Rise and Rule of Tamerlane* (Cambridge: Cambridge University Press, 1999) and Justin Marozzi, *Tamerlane: Sword of Islam, Conqueror of the World* (New York: Da Capo, 2006).

3 The story of Bajazeth and the cage seems to be of Arabian provenance. For an extended discussion of Arab versions of Temür's life, especially Ibn Arabshah's *'Ajaib al-maqdur fi nawa'ib Timur: The Wonders of Destiny Concerning the Calamities Wrought by Tamerlane* (1436), see Ahlam Maijan Alruwaili, "Ibn Arabshah: The Unacknowledged Debt of Christopher Marlowe's *Tamburlaine*," MA Thesis, University of Nebraska at Lincoln, 2011. I am grateful to Julia Schleck for bringing this work to my attention.

the war against the Ottomans. But during his brief campaign in Hindustan, he sacked the city of Tulamba in Punjab, again massacring its inhabitants, and inflicted terrible damage on Delhi, the stronghold of the Turkic Tughlaq dynasty and at that time one of the richest and most powerful cities in the world. Temür is supposed to have slain 100,000 captives before defeating the Tughlaq sultan and occupying the city in December. His cruelty continued into the occupation: following three days of citizen rebellions, his army went on the rampage for another eight days, after which Delhi is said to have reeked of the stench of decomposing corpses. The city took more than a century to recover from Temür's carnage.

Despite the enormous damage Temür inflicted on Hindustan in general and Delhi in particular, he subsequently came to be venerated by Hindustan's Mughal rulers as *Sahib-e-Qirani*, or the "Lord of Conjunction" (sometimes rendered as "Lord of Corners"). The Chagatai Turkic warlord Ẓahīr ad-Dīn Muḥammad—better known by his nickname Babur—invaded Hindustan in 1526 and became the first Mughal emperor. Strictly speaking, however, he was Mughal only through his mother. Even though the Mughals could claim direct descent from Chingiz Khan, Babur regarded his mother's people as barbarous and untrustworthy. Instead he chose to favour his father's line, through which he traced descent from Temür. The *Baburnama*, Babur's account of his life and his conquest of Hindustan, emphasises this paternal lineage at the expense of his mother's Mughal family. Temür provided Babur with an ancestor who had conquered Hindustan—in which, of course, Chingiz Khan never set foot. He also received a makeover as Babur's more "refined" ancestor because of his association, if only through conquest, with the high culture of Persia.

Under Babur's grandson, the third Mughal emperor Akbar, Temür morphed further into a godlike progenitor of the line. In the *Akbarnama*, the Persian-language account of Akbar's reign written by his court historian Abu'l Fazl (Akbar was himself illiterate), Timūr—the Persian name by which he was now called—and his mother are woven into a mythology of immaculate conception that is explicitly Christian. Timūr's mother, Abu'l Fazl tells us, "was reposing on her bed, when suddenly a glorious light cast a ray into the tent and entered the mouth and throat of that fount of spiritual knowledge and glory. The cupola of chastity became pregnant by that light in the same way as her Majesty [...] Miryam (Mary) [...]."[4] In Abu'l Fazl's telling, then, Timūr becomes the first male figure in the

---

[4] Abu'l Fazl, *The Akbarnama* [c. 1590–1596], trans. Henry Beveridge, 3 vols. (Calcutta: The Asiatic Society of Bengal, 1897–1939), vol. 1, p. 179. For a discussion of the Christian resonances of this passage, see Bonnie C. Wade, *Imaging Sound: An Ethnomusicological Study of Music, Art and Culture in Mughal India* (Chicago, IL/London: The University of Chicago Press, 1998), p. 66.

exalted patrilineal line that culminates in Akbar, a line burnished by the virginal purity of Timūr's mother.

Akbar's investment in and identification with Timūr is most apparent from his patronage of the *Timūrnama*, an illustrated history of the "Timurid" line that he commissioned in the 1580s from his *kitab-khana*, or atelier of top miniaturist painters.[5] The project was designed to project the legitimacy of the Mughal dynasty to client kings and visitors to the court. In a series of 137 paintings, the *Timūrnama* presents Timūr as the precedent of everything valiant, just and glamorous about the three Mughal emperors to date (Babur, Humayun and Akbar). The images range from dazzling war scenes from Timūr's life to "historical" paintings of the Mughal emperors. Yet the history presented is less linear or progressive than enduringly synchronous: Timūr is coeval with, and lives on as, his Mughal descendants. The synchronicity of Timūr and the Mughals was asserted too by the next two emperors, Jahangir and Shah Jahan. In 1620, the court painter Hashim produced a portrait of Timūr enthroned with his Mughal descendants from Babur to Jahangir.[6] And Shah Jahan's epithet, *Sahib-e-Qirani-Thani*—the second Lord of Conjunction or Corners—was designed to present him as the new Timūr: a court painting from his reign pictures the two Lords of Corners sitting on thrones facing each other, with the implication that they reflect each other's virtues.[7]

Yet even as the *Timūrnama* initiated the Mughal habit of regarding Timūr as the ideal mirror of the Mughals, the portraits by Jahangir's and Shah Jahan's painters demonstrate a subtle transformation of the dynasty's identity. If a direct line of descent connected Timūr to Shah Jahan via Babur, Humayun, Akbar and Jahangir, that line morphed in the process into something else. The fourth Mughal, Jahangir, was ethnically half Rajput through his mother. Shah Jahan, Jahangir's son, also had a Rajput mother, and was thus three-quarters Hindustani. As Jyotsna G. Singh has noted, the court painters do not attempt to finesse the transformation, as we can see in the striking difference between the Turkic features of Timūr, Babur, Humayun and Akbar, and the increasingly Rajput faces

---

[5] On the *Timūrnama*, see Milo Cleveland Beach, *Mughal and Rajput Painting*, in: *The New Cambridge History of India*, ed. Gordon Johnson, Christopher A. Bayly and John F. Richards, part 1: *The Mughals and their Contemporaries*, vol. 3 (Cambridge: Cambridge University Press, 1992), p. 48.
[6] For a discussion of Hashim's painting, see Jeremiah P. Losty and Malini Roy, *Mughal India: Art, Culture and Empire; Manuscripts and Paintings in the British Library* (London: The British Library, 2012), pp. 113 f.
[7] See Richard C. Foltz, *Mughal India and Central Asia* (Karachi/New York: Oxford University Press, 1998), p. 22.

of the later Mughals.⁸ Even as the Mughals claim Timūr as their legitimising ancestor, Hindustan claims the Mughals. The tale of Timūr in Hindustan, then, is a drama of Mughal transformation by Hindustan. The maternal line that Babur attempted to disavow by embracing Timūr, yet which returned as the name of his dynasty, found later counterparts in non-Mughal maternal lines that made the heirs of Timūr indisputably Hindustani. But if Temür—or his line—morphed in the course of pursuing the Mughals' southward historical trajectory from Samarkand to Delhi, he transformed just as much in his westward narrative trajectory from Persia to England.

Tamburlaine in India

As Crystal Bartolovich has argued in an important essay, the historical movement of Temür narratives from Asia to Europe eerily rehearses the understanding of history they were press-ganged into serving in England.⁹ Temür's conquest of the Persian Empire, and his subsequent campaigns in Baghdad, Syria and Anatolia, illustrate the Christian notion of *translatio imperii* and the conviction that God sends empire historically westward. Later iterations of this notion include George Herbert's "Church Militant" (which sees the light of faith moving across the globe, like the sun, from the Orient to the Occident) and, in more secular form, G. W. F. Hegel's *Philosophy of History* (which sees Spirit as becoming increasingly perfected as the cutting-edge of civilisation migrates from Asia to Europe and then further westward).¹⁰ England's place in this global timeline is ambiguous; in Herbert's poem, as in Hegel's treatise, it is separated from the highway that leads imperially from a distant Persian past through Egypt, Greece and Rome to an Occidental future. For Bartolovich, Marlowe's play is a subtle attempt to re-route that timeline through an England that is also its *telos*. The play is not just set in an Asian past, therefore; its hero is also a point of identification for an English audience in the present, nursing dreams of future global success. In other words, Bartolovich sees Tamburlaine as a proto-English imperialist, whose

---

8 See Jyotsna G. Singh's unpublished paper, "In Search of Tamburlaine: Marlowe's Protagonist in Non-European Histories," read at the conference on "Renaissance Old Worlds: English Encounters from the Levant to the Far East" at the British Library, July 1, 2012.
9 Crystal Bartolovich, "Putting *Tamburlaine* on a (Cognitive) Map," *Renaissance Drama* 28 (1997), pp. 29–72.
10 I discuss both Herbert's and Hegel's narratives of westward *translatio imperii* in *Untimely Matter in the Time of Shakespeare* (Philadelphia: University of Pennsylvania Press, 2009), pp. 58–65, pp. 83–87.

Asian empire both confirms the theory of *translatio imperii* and anticipates, in Marlowe's words, an England at the "furtherest West[ern edge]"[11] that will ultimately inherit the global imperial mantle. (For Bartolovich, it is also important that Marlowe draws from a Spanish source: his rewriting of Mexía's *Silva de varia lección* performs an English supersession of Spain as the contemporary avant-garde of empire.[12])

There's much to admire about Bartolovich's essay. Rather than reading *Tamburlaine* in Marlowe's time, she rightly insists that the project of historicising the play must place it not in one synchronic period box but recognise its constitutive polychronicity: when Tamburlaine refers to the "Americas," the early modern present is folded into his medieval past as an image of future imperial conquest. Bartolovich sees Tamburlaine's distinctive future auxiliary verbs—"'will' and 'shall' best fitteth" (*Part 1*, 3.3.41)—as symptomatic of the capitalist temporality of primitive accumulation and globalisation. As a result, the play is for her about a futurity that is still unfolding even now. But by assuming a unilinear timeline that extends from Tamburlaine to the late capitalist present, Bartolovich finesses other temporalities that are legible both in the play and its subsequent travels. The difference between the timeline of accumulation and these other temporalities is the difference between what Dipesh Chakrabarty calls "the future that 'will be'"—the development of global capitalism—and "the futures that 'are'"—subaltern time-knots in the now that suggest different possibilities.[13] I will tease out at least one of these "futures that are," to show how even as we can and should situate Marlowe's play within a genealogy of capitalist globalisation, both *Tamburlaine the Great* and its subsequent travels to Mughal India open up subjunctive possibilities that complicate and displace that timeline.

There's no doubt that Marlowe's *Tamburlaine* is future-oriented. From the opening lines of the prologue, the play self-consciously breaks with the past. Marlowe's then-innovative iambic pentameter is a world away from the "jigging veins" (*Part 1*, Prologue, l. 1) of Thomas Preston's *Cambyses*, the early modern English stage's previous blockbuster about an Oriental tyrant. Just listen to that play's first sing-song speech—"And I, by due inheritance, possess that princely

---

11 Christopher Marlowe, *Tamburlaine the Great: Parts 1 and 2* [1590], *Part 1*, 3.3.246. All references to Marlowe's play are to Christopher Marlowe, *Tamburlaine*, ed. James W. Harper (London: A & C Black, 1984), and are subsequently given parenthetically in the text.
12 See Bartolovich, "Putting *Tamburlaine* on a (Cognitive) Map," p. 37.
13 See Dipesh Chakrabarty, *Provincializing Europe: Postcolonial Thought and Historical Difference* (Princeton, NJ: Princeton University Press, 2000), esp. p. 251.

crown, / Ruling by sword of mighty force in place of great renown."[14]—and compare it to Marlowe's promise that "We'll lead you to the stately tent of war, / Where you shall hear the Scythian Tamburlaine / Threatening the world with high astounding terms" (ll. 3–5). Marlowe's prologue performs its aspirational agenda, not just in its transition from "jigging" Persian to "astounding" Scythian, but also in its soaring iambic movement from unstressed to stressed syllable. This matches what we might call the iambic rhythm of Tamburlaine's career, as it moves inexorably to greater and greater power. It is also arguably of a piece with the rhythm of primitive accumulation and globalisation. Perhaps it is no coincidence that the most famous iambic pentameter of recent decades announces the future mission of another Enterprise "to boldly go where no one's gone before."

Tamburlaine accumulates not just endless territory, famously mapped by Marlowe on the model of Ortelius' globe, but also gold and precious jewels, primarily from India.[15] Indeed, India is throughout the play a metonymy for untold wealth, from Tamburlaine's claim in Part 1 that "Not all the gold in India's wealthy arms, / Shall buy the meanest soldier in my train" (*Part 1*, 1.2.85f.) to his remark in Part 2 that the blood he sheds in war is as valuable to him as "a chair of gold enamelled, / Enchased with diamonds, sapphires, rubies / And fairest pearl of wealthy India" (*Part 2*, 3.2.119–121). Even as India functions as an eternal source of wealth, however, it is also understood in a more historically specific guise, albeit anachronistically within the play, as a site of Christian plunder. The Persian emperor Mycetes has lost dominion over India because "Men from the farthest equinoctial line, / Have swarmed in troops into the eastern India: / Lading their ships with gold and precious stones" (*Part 1*, 1.1.119–121). Mycetes's usurping brother Cosroe further specifies that "those Indian mines, / My witless brother to the Christians lost" (*Part 1*, 2.5.41–42). One cannot help but presume that these Christians are time-travellers from Marlowe's present—the Portuguese. For Tamburlaine sees his own conquest of India in terms of struggle not with local Indians but with a global Portuguese empire: his own "puissant arm" (*Part 1*, 3.3.247) will extend from "the Indian continent: / Even from Persepolis to Mexico" (*Part 1*, 3.3.254–255) all the while "keeping in awe the Bay of Portingale" (*Part 1*, 3.3.258). He even plans to do what the British will do many centuries in

---

14 Thomas Preston, *Cambyses, King of Persia* [1569], in: Russell A. Fraser and Norman Rabkin, edd., *Drama of the English Renaissance*, 2 vols., vol. 1: *The Tudor Period* (London: Macmillan, 1976), pp. 61–80, p. 62.
15 On Marlowe's sense of world geography, and its debt to and distortion of Islamic sources, see John Michael Archer, "Islam and Tamburlaine's World-picture," in: Jyotsna G. Singh, ed., *A Companion to the Global Renaissance: English Literature and Culture in the Era of Expansion* (Oxford: Wiley Blackwell, 2009), pp. 67–81.

the future: "cut a channel" (*Part 2*, 5.3.134) from Alexandria to the Red Sea in order "that men might quickly sail to India" (*Part 2*, 5.3.135). These references to India would seem to confirm Bartolovich's analysis of how Tamburlaine's accumulation maps global movement not only in space but also in time, to both a near future that is Marlowe's present and a more distant future that is our now.

What gets finessed in Bartolovich's analysis is the *theatrical* dimension of Tamburlaine's global movement. And here I think the play is instructive because it does not cleave to any one monolithic understanding of theatricality. Indeed, it offers at least two. The first is premised on the one-upmanship of *translatio imperii*—a one-upmanship that is theatrical, but that can also take the form of a recognisably English anti-theatrical dismissal of fraudulent modes of representation. The second suggests a process of theatrical transformation by, and into, something ontologically other. Taken together, these lay down very different protocols for reading travel, identity and futurity. Instead of a unilinear progression to the capitalism of today (globalisation driven by accumulation), these two forms of theatricality suggest radically different responses to Temür/Timūr-e-Lang's historical career and radically different ways in which Tamburlaine might travel in India, both in the age of early Anglo-Mughal encounter and in the present.

Let's take the first form of theatricality. We might call it imitation-as-supersession or, in Hegelian terms, *Aufhebung*. This entails mimicking the theatrical codes of an adversary in order to better him. And this mimicry hollows out the codes, revealing them to be fraudulent all the while extracting from them the surplus value of a charismatic meta-performativity. Consider, for example, Tamburlaine's deposition of Mycetes, the Persian king:

> Tamburlaine: Is this your crown?
> MYCETES: Ay, didst thou ever see a fairer?
> TAMB.: You will not sell it, will ye?
> MYC.: Such another word, and I will have thee executed.
> Come, give it me.
> TAMB.: No, I took it prisoner.
> MYC.: You lie, I gave it you.
> TAMB.: Then 'tis mine.
> MYC.: No, I mean, I let you keep it.
> TAMB.: Well, I mean you shall have it again.
> Here take it for a while, I lend it thee,
> Till I may see thee hemmed wit armed men.
> Then shalt thou see me pull it from thy head:
> Thou art no match for mighty Tamburlaine.
> [*Exit.*]
> MYC.: O gods, is this Tamburlaine the thief?
> I marvel much he stole it not away. (*Part 1*, 2.4.27–42)

Tamburlaine histrionically snatches the Persian king Mycetes's crown from his head and wears it briefly, only to give it back ("take it for a while, I lend it thee"), prompting Mycetes to marvel that Tamburlaine "stole it not away"; the implication is that Tamburlaine is the truly "mighty" figure possessed of theatrical charisma—and Mycetes is the fraud, a player-king possessed of an illegitimate stage property. The crown will eventually come back to Tamburlaine, via Mycetes' usurping brother Cosroe. But on Tamburlaine it will no longer look like the mere stage property that it does on Mycetes; instead it becomes the naturalised accessory of Tamburlaine's power to "command, and be obeyed" (*Part 1*, 2.5.62).

This supersessionary mode bears an uncanny relation to Marlowe's own inter-theatrical project. He claims to offer a new poetic style. But his Tamburlaine is not quite as new as he claims. Is not Tamburlaine, or the actor Ned Alleyn's loud performance of him, a subversive rerun of Cambyses? Tamburlaine echoes the distinctive stage-bluster and murderous rage of Cambyses and earlier Oriental stage-despots.[16] Yet he simultaneously supersedes them, inasmuch as his mighty line trumps their "jigging vein" and naturalises his own performance as engagingly charismatic rather than merely theatrical. In the process, however, Marlowe sets up a blueprint for subsequent reception of his play. To better Tamburlaine, one needs to hollow out the force of his theatricality—just as Tamburlaine makes Mycetes seem like a mere player-king, or Ned Alleyn made Cambyses seem theatrically quaint. So Shakespeare's second Henriad, a play nominally about the vexed English succession, repeatedly one-ups previous Oriental stage despots: in its tavern scenes, Falstaff parodies Cambyses, and Pistol rants comically in the manner of Tamburlaine. "Not Amurath an Amurath succeeds," says Harry of his own ascent to the throne, but he protests too much: the "English"[17] succession is legitimised by a *translatio theatri* whose ground-zero is the Oriental stage-despot. Shakespeare's company betters Cambyses and Tamburlaine as performed by their rivals; likewise, English kings take their place on the world stage in a fashion that one-ups a Turkish model of succession.[18]

Let us turn to the second form of theatricality legible in *Tamburlaine*. We might call this the theatricality of ecstatic transformation. A mere Scythian shepherd can transform into a mighty Persian emperor; a head of state into a

---

16 For a discussion of the actor Ned Alleyn's famously loud performance of Tamburlaine, see Richard Levin, "The Contemporary Perceptions of Marlowe's *Tamburlaine*," *Medieval and Renaissance Drama in England* 1 (1984), pp. 51–70.
17 William Shakespeare, *Henry IV: Part 2* [1600], 5.2.47 f. Reference is to Shakespeare, *Henry IV: Part 2*, ed. René Weis (Oxford: Clarendon Press, 1998), p 254.
18 I analyse the intertheatricality of Shakespeare's second Henriad in extended detail in *Untimely Matter in the Time of Shakespeare*, pp. 66–87.

nomadic war machine; a fighter into a lover.[19] These changes are enabled *theatrically*, through changes of costume and rhetorical style. Indeed, Tamburlaine is an endless set of nested matryoshka dolls, never settling on one "true" identity. His transformations are "ecstatic" in both the affective and the etymological root sense of the word—they conduce both to pleasure and to ec-stasis, to standing outside oneself. Ec-stasis means refusing *stasis*, in the sense both of inertia and the State. For—as Shankar Raman has noted in a powerful reading of the play—Tamburlaine is fundamentally state-less, relinquishing his territories to others as soon as he has conquered them, driven by a restless compulsion to keep moving and shape-shifting.[20]

Oddly enough, this form of theatricality is understood best by the English anti-theatricalists, who recognise even as they deplore the transformative power of theatre. They are not opposed to the first supersessionary form of theatricality: indeed, they resort to it themselves. Stephen Gosson destroys theatre by writing a treatise called, theatrically, *Plays Confuted in Five Actions* (1582). But the anti-theatricalists are horrified by the prospect of a theatre that *pleasurably* transforms boys into women, and poor men into kings. In other words, they are horrified by ec-stasis. If the first type of theatricality models the acquisitive capitalism of accumulation, the second models the destructive capitalism that Marx saw as levelling the certainties of feudalism: "All that is solid melts into air, all that is holy is profaned […]."[21] The two may work historically in tandem, but they do not necessarily point to the same future. Accumulation is about the expansion of identity. Ec-static levelling is about its protean insubstantiality. We might regard accumulation as the lubricant of a capitalism whose *telos* is global imperialism. But we might equally treat ec-stasis as the levelling potential of capitalism, the dimension that Marx views as progressive (albeit in the form of a nightmare). Marlowe's Tamburlaine is *both* primitive accumulator of territorialised identity *and* protean leveller who constantly de-territorialises himself and the spaces through which he moves.

---

[19] In calling Tamburlaine a "nomadic war machine," I am of course alluding to Gilles Deleuze and Félix Guattari's *Nomadology: The War Machine*, trans. Brian Massumi (New York: Semiotext[e], 1986), which was subsequently published as Chapter 12 of their *A Thousand Plateaus: Capitalism and Schizophrenia*, trans. Brian Massumi (London/New York: Continuum, 2004). Of course, Deleuze and Guattari take as their paradigmatic instance of the nomadic war machine the medieval Mongol-Turkic armies that swept across the steppes of Central Asia.

[20] Shankar Raman, *Renaissance Literature and Postcolonial Studies* (Edinburgh: Edinburgh University Press, 2011), pp. 152–162.

[21] Karl Marx and Friedrich Engels, "Manifesto of the Communist Party" [1848], in: Robert C. Tucker, ed., *The Marx-Engels Reader* (New York: W.W. Norton, 1972), pp. 335–362, p. 338.

These two forms of theatricality arguably respond to aspects of Temür's travels in Hindustan. The first form is evident in stories of Temür/Timūr the conqueror who, like a new and better Alexander the Great, swept through the northwest of the subcontinent in his bid for global domination. The second form is visible in Temür's increasingly Indian descendants, as witnessed in the paintings of Timūr seated with the Mughal rulers from Babur to Jahangir and Shah Jahan. The Mughal line may have originated in the Turkic Temür, but it also became ethnically Hindustani, transforming into what it had conquered. In sum, Marlowe's theatrical mediation of Temür's life-story suggests two very different meanings of "Tamburlaine in Hindustan." One is a more recognisable journey of Indian imperial conquest, superseding the campaigns of Alexander and the global adventures of the Portuguese. The second is a more unpredictable journey of transformation, in which a Tamburlainian assemblage keeps becoming other. Both meanings are legible in a pair of English engagements with Tamburlaine in 1616, during Sir Thomas Roe's English embassy at the court of the Mughal Emperor Jahangir in Ajmer.

Tamburlaine in Hindustan

Throughout his four-year embassy at Jahangir's court, Roe was obsessed with the Mughal line's descent from Tamburlaine: he refers to it repeatedly in his journal.[22] But Roe does not always specify whether, by "Tamburlaine," he means the historical figure or the stage character. As we will see, Roe could sometimes mean both simultaneously. This was no idle slip. Although the British Raj was in 1616 still more than a century away, we might recognise in Roe's conflation of the historical and the stage Tamburlaines an imperialising tactic that repeats the play's own version of *translatio imperii*—hollowing out the theatrical codes of a rival so that they may be superseded.[23]

---

22 All references to Roe's journal are to Thomas Roe, *The Embassy of Sir Thomas Roe to the Court of the Great Mogul, 1615–19, as Narrated in His Journal and Correspondence*, ed. William Foster, 2 vols. (London: Hakluyt Society, 1894), and are cited in the main body of the text.
23 Jyotsna G. Singh interprets Roe's descriptions of Mughal spectacle as a mode of proto-colonialist knowledge in *Colonial Narratives/Cultural Dialogues: 'Discoveries' of India in the Language of Colonialism* (London/New York: Routledge, 1996), esp. pp. 26–32. For a reading of Roe that sees him as less a proto-colonist than a mercantile ally of the Mughals, see Rahul Sapra, *The Limits of Orientalism: Seventeenth-Century Representations of India* (Newark, DE: University of Delaware Press, 2011), esp. pp. 62–72.

Roe's descriptions of the Mughal court are suffused with theatricality. Describing Jahangir's durbar, or public audience, he says that, "This sitting out hath soe much affinitye with a Theatre—the manner of the king in his gallery; The great men lifted on a stage as actors; the vulgar below gazing on—that an easy description will informe of the place and fashion" (vol. 1, p. 108). If Roe uses metaphors of theatre to describe the Mughal court, however, his discourse has a decidedly anti-theatrical dimension. Mughal power, in his view, shades into theatrical imposture. Granted an audience with Jahangir's son Pervez in Brampur in late 1615, Roe complained that Pervez' court "was like a great stage, and the Prince satt aboue as the Mock kings doth thear." (vol. 1, p. 92)[24] Another such instance is his receipt in November of 1616 of a gift from Jahangir's favourite son, Prince Khurram—later Shah Jahan:

> By and by came out a Cloth of gould Cloake of his owne, once or twice worne, which hee Caused to bee putt on my back, and I made a reuerence very vnwillingly. When his Ancester Tamerlane was represented at the Theatre the Garment would well haue become the Actor; but it is here reputed the highest of fauour to give a garment warne by the Prince, or, beeing New, once layd on his shoulder. (vol. 2, p. 334)

Roe here describes—and misrecognises—the Islamic tradition of *khil'at*, the gift of clothes as tokens of imperial favour.[25] The ritual performed an important political function by producing bonds of cross-cultural reciprocity. But Roe understands it only as the theatrical performance of a "Mock king." His reference to Tamburlaine—simultaneously Khurram's historical ancestor and Christopher Marlowe's histrionic character—works to theatricalise the Mughal line. Khurram's gold cloak is, for Roe, a gaudy garment more suited to the playhouse than an imperial court; as such, it is a particularly unwelcome addition to the briefly visible "back" of an English ambassador who saw his clothes not as theatrical costumes but, rather, as irrevocable signs of his God-given national identity. Edward Terry, Roe's chaplain, noted that, "For my Lord Ambassador, and his company, we all kept to our

---

[24] The analogy between the Mughal court and the London stage is one that evidently stuck with Roe. He described his audience with Jahangir in more or less identical terms in a letter to Lord Carew, written from Ajmer on January 17: "[...] I found him in a Court, set aboue like a King in a Play, and all his Nobles and my selfe below on a stage couered with carpets—a iust Theater; with no great state, but the Canopies ouer his head, and two standing on the heads of two wooden Elephants, to beat away flies." (*The Embassy of Sir Thomas Roe*, vol. 1, pp. 110–114, p. 112).

[25] In an as-yet unpublished paper, "Replaying *Tamburlaine* at the Mughal Court: Autoethnography as Theatre in the Contact Zone" (presented at the 2011 meeting of the Modern Language Association in Los Angeles), Ellorashree Maitra offers a brilliant reading of Roe's misunderstanding of *khil'at*. She also examines how Roe's ethnography is shaped by the oriental drama of the early modern English stage, especially Christopher Marlowe's *Tamburlaine*.

English habits [...]. His wayters in red taffata cloaks, guarded with green taffata, which they always wore when they went abroad with him; myself in a long black cassock [...]."[26] Not the best attire for the hot Ajmer sun, perhaps, but certainly powerfully "authentic" English costumes for Roe's theatre of anti-theatricality.

Imagine Roe's horror, then, when an ethnically cross-dressed English body—a body possessed, moreover, of a very different disposition to the theatrical Tamburlaine—walks on stage. Enter Thomas Coryate.

"Odd Tom" Coryate was a self-conscious eccentric.[27] Born in approximately 1579 and raised in the small Somerset village of Odcombe—Coryate repeatedly claimed that he embodied the "odd" of his village's name—he made his name by walking, for a little more than eight months, through France, Switzerland, Italy, Germany and Holland. In 1612, basking in the success of his tour, made famous by the publication of his travelogue *Coryate's Crudities*, Coryate decided to walk east to Asia. We do not know if India was part of his original travel itinerary; but after dallying in Constantinople and Jerusalem, he joined a caravan that crossed Persia on foot, via the Silk Route, to Lahore, which he reached in 1615. From there he made his way to Delhi and Agra, before footing it to Ajmer, where Jahangir and his court were temporarily based in order to subdue a revolt by a Rajput king.

There was little that was recognisably English about Coryate or his body by the time he reached Hindustan. When he met Thomas Roe in Ajmer, he was wearing Turkish and Persian clothes; he was also speaking fluent Farsi. He had also been eating little, living on the equivalent of two English pennies a day. In other words, Coryate's body had been radically transformed by his journey through central Asia. His linguistic aptitude gave him access to Jahangir of a kind that was denied to the exclusively Anglophone Roe. Dressed in the clothes of an Indian beggar, Coryate delivered a lengthy oration to Jahangir at Ajmer's Akbari Fort in formal Farsi, the language of the Mughal court. Coryate transcribed the oration in one of his letters, supplementing it with a translation. It is a remarkable document. From Coryate's opening words, he speaks in a stylised mode of address suited to his royal audience: "*Hazaret Aallum pennah salamet, fooker*

---

[26] Edward Terry, *A Voyage to East-India: Wherein Some Things Are Taken Notice Of in Our Passage Thither, But Many More in Our Abode There, Within that Rich and Most Spacious Empire of the Great Mogol: Mix't with some Parallel Obsevations and Inferences upon the Storie, to profit as well as delight the Reader* (London: Printed by T.W. for J. Martin and J. Allestrye, 1655), p. 205.
[27] For details of Coryate's biography, I am indebted to Dom Moraes and Sarayu Srivatsa, *The Long Strider: How Thomas Coryate Walked from England to India in the Year 1613* (Delhi: Penguin India, 2003); and R. E. Pritchard, *Odd Tom Coryate: The English Marco Polo* (Stroud: Sutton Publishing, 2004).

Daruces ve tehaungeshta hastam kemia emadam az wellagets door, ganne az mulk Inglizan[.]"[28] He translates these lines as follows: "Lord Protector of the World, all haile to you. I am a poore traveller and world-seer, which am come hither from a farre country, namely England[.]"[29] Yet this translation finesses how, in Farsi, Coryate characterised himself as Indian. His term for himself is a *"fooker Daruces,"* or *fakir dervish*, a wandering Sufi ascetic who begs for alms.

Coryate's make-over as a Sufi *fakir* is all the more remarkable given his readiness elsewhere to inveigh against what he regarded as the heresies of Islam. In a letter to his mother, he transcribes yet another oration he had delivered, this time in Italian, tediously enumerating the supposed errors and impostures of Mohammed to a Muslim who had lived in Florence.[30] Yet Coryate's self-identification as a *fakir* in his oration to Jahangir is more than an instance of self-serving legerdemain. It also gives some indication of how he had transformed his body during his time in Ajmer, following the model of the many poor *fakirs* who begged outside the *dargah* (or shrine) of Ajmer's medieval Sufi saint Moin-Ud-Din Chishti. Coryate, in other words, had learned not only a passable version of the Farsi spoken by the Mughals but also the theatrical bodily practices—of scant clothing, respectful prostration and pleading for alms—that he needed to master in order to be legible to Jahangir as a worthy supplicant. Sitting at his *jharoka* or public window at the Akbari Fort, Jahangir was sufficiently impressed by the English *fakir*'s oration that he immediately made him a gift of 100 rupees—a not insubstantial sum at the time, especially for a man who had lived on tuppence a day throughout his long Asian walk and had evidently been forced to feed on simple food (*khichdi*, or rice and dal) served at Chishti's *dargah*.

But Roe was not so pleased by the oration. Coryate complains that Roe "nibl[ed] at me," fearing that his performance might "redound some what to the dishonour of our nation that one of our countrey should present himselfe in that beggarly and poore fashion to the King, out of an insinuating humor to crave mony of him [...]."[31] Roe doubtless felt that Coryate had damaged the reputation of the English, and hence his own precarious standing as King James's

---

28 William Foster, ed., *Early Travels in India: 1583–1619* (London et al.: Humphrey Milford and Oxford University Press, 1921), pp. 234–287, p. 263. All references to Coryate's Indian writings are to this book.
29 P. 264.
30 For the wording of this oration, see pp. 271–275. Coryate also used his command of Hindustani to denounce a *mu'ezzin* by a proclamation that Christ was the true prophet and Muhammad an impostor—a potentially dangerous oration that was dismissed because its audience believed "the English *fakir*" to be mad (p. 274).
31 P. 266.

unremunerated (and therefore financially struggling) ambassador. But one might also sense an anti-theatrical component in Roe's response to the sight of an Englishman becoming-Indian. And Roe's animus may have been occasioned also by what he perceived to be a theatricality that paid homage to, rather than scorned, Marlowe's stage-Tamburlaine.

In his journal, Roe observes that Coryate's desire was to visit "Samarcand in Tartarya, to kisse Tamberlans Tombe" (vol. 1, p. 104). One can hear a note of Protestant derision in Roe's language, which hints at how Coryate's wish is an embodied act simultaneously of religious and theatrical idolatry. Not surprisingly, Coryate describes the desire somewhat differently in his oration to Jahangir, referring judiciously to Tamburlaine by his Persian honorific "Lord of the Corners":

> [...] I have a great desire to see the blessed toombe of the Lord of the Corners for this cause; for that when I was in Constantinople, I saw a notable old building in a pleasant garden neer the said city, where the Christian Emperor that was called Emanuell, made a sumptuous great banquet to the Lord of the Corners, after he had taken Sultan Bajazet in a great battell [...] where the Lord of the Corners bound Sultan Bajazet in fetters of gold, and put him in a cage of iron.[32]

Coryate refers here to the historical Temür. But his imagination is clearly inspired by the theatrical Tamburlaine. The historical Temür took Sultan Bayezid captive; yet Coryate's story of Bajazeth's enslavement inside an iron cage is a later embellishment dating from Arabian narratives of Timūr-e-Lang.[33] It is, of course, one of the most memorable pieces of stage business in Marlowe's play. So why should Coryate have been so curious to see the tomb of the stage Tamburlaine's historical counterpart? Coryate evidently saw Tamburlaine not as a "Mock king," as Roe did, but rather as a legitimate object of fascination. Is it too much to speculate that Coryate identified with Marlowe's version of Tamburlaine—less Tamburlaine the imperial invader, perhaps, than Tamburlaine the highly histrionic shape-shifter of humble provincial origins who got to perambulate around Asia delivering mighty lines?

The politics of Coryate's Indian shape-shifting are by no means straightforwardly anti-colonialist or anti-imperialist. But neither can they be entirely recuperated for the future of the British Empire in India—let alone for a universal timeline of globalisation. And that is because Coryate's shape-shifting is less clearly a mode of accumulation than it is a form of ec-stasis—Coryate morphs repeatedly into new forms, undoing the illusion of fixed identity undergirding Roe's theatre of anti-theatricality. Coryate signs off one of his letters as "the

---

[32] Foster, ed., *Early Travels in India*, p. 265.
[33] See Alruwaili, "Ibn Arabshah."

Hierosolymitan-Syrian-Mesopotamian-Armenian-Median-Parthian-Persian-Indian Leggestretcher of Odcomb."[34] On the one hand, this multi-hyphenated nickname might suggest a Tamburlaine-esque accumulation of territories, like the accumulation of stamps in a passport. On the other hand, it also suggests how Coryate's travel entailed, in Dipesh Chakrabarty's words, subaltern futures of constant transformation *in the now*, futures equally embodied in the protean forms of Marlowe's Tamburlaine. In Coryate's case, this transformation entailed opening up to numerous elements of the Hindustan he walked to and lived in— its food, its clothes, its languages—and allowing them to fundamentally change him and his body.[35] With Coryate, then, we see not just Tamburlaine in Hindustan. We can also see, and hear, Hindustan in Tamburlaine.

---

34 Foster, ed., *Early Travels in India*, p. 258.
35 I discuss Coryate's bodily transformations in greater detail in "Becoming-Indian," in: Henry S. Turner, ed., *Early Modern Theatricality* (Oxford: Oxford University Press, 2013), pp. 442–459.

Gautam Chakrabarti
"Eating the Yaban's Rice": Socio-Cultural Transactions on the Mid-Colonial Bengali Stage

The *Nīl Darpaṇ* ["Mirror of Indigo," 1860], translated as *Nil Darpan; or, The Indigo Planting Mirror*, is a pathbreaking Bengali play written by Dinabandhu Mitra (1829–1874),[1] a disciple of the poet and journalist Iśvarcandra Gupta (1812–1859)[2] and a functionary in the Indian Postal Service, in 1858–1859. The play, which created a sensation with its initial publication and had a Shakespearean tragedy structure, captured the spirit of the so-called *Nīlbidroho*, or Indigo Revolt of February–March 1859 in the Bengal Presidency, when the *ryots*[3] (peasant tenants) declined to sow indigo in their fields, in breach of an oppressive contract, in protest against exploitative regulatory mechanisms of forced farming. Here, one must mention that Bengal was the world's largest producer of indigo in the nineteenth century and this cultivation and production process was devised as a part of a shrewd and brutal system of enforced cultivation, about which I will write a little later. As Dušan Zbavitel writes, quoting Alokrañjan Dāsgupta, Debīprasād Bandyopādhyāy and others, "'[f]rom the point of view of its artistic

---

[1] These are the dates given by Dušan Zbavitel, *Bengali Literature*, in: Jan Gonda, ed., *A History of Indian Literature*, 10 vols., vol. 9, fasc. 3, pp. 119–307 (Wiesbaden: Otto Harrassowitz, 1976), p. 226, referring to Suśīlkumār De, *Dīnabandhu Mitra*, Calcutta 1960.

[2] These dates, too, are given by Zbavitel, *Bengali Literature*, p. 217, referring to Bhabatoṣ Datta, *Iśvarcandra Gupter jībancarita o kabitva* ["The Story of Iśvarcandra Gupta's Life and Poetry"], Calcutta 1968.

[3] *Ryot* or *rāyat*, being derived from the Hindi word *ra'īyat* and the Arabic *ra'īyah*, which is translated as "flock" or "peasants" (cf. http://www.thefreedictionary.com/ryot [retrieved: 6 August 2014]), was another common socio-economic term used in South Asia for farm-cultivators, who were hired tenant-labourers, though there were variants in different regions. Cf. Bindeshwar Ram, *Land and Society in India: Agrarian Relations in Colonial North Bihar* (Chennai: Orient Longman, 1997), pp. 76–126.

Note: With regard to the term "yaban" the translator's footnote explains: "The Mahomedans and all other nations who are not Hindus, are called by that name." Dinabandhu Mitra, *Nil Darpan; or, The Indigo Planting Mirror: A Drama Translated from the Bengali by a Native* [*Nīl Darpaṇ*, 1860], trans. Michael Madhusudan Datta, ed. Rev. James Long (Calcutta: C. H. Manuel, 1861), p. 7. The phrase has a mildly derogatory context, as almost no Hindu caste was supposed to indulge in *commensality* with non-Hindus, especially Muslims and Christians. The word *"yaban"* is derived from the Sanksrit *yavana* (Pali *yona*), which refers to the Indo-Bactrian and Greek communities that came from or had settled in South-Central Asia and North-Western India."

qualities, the *Nīldarpaṇ* is not a successful play' [...] and similar judgements have been passed upon the drama by other modern historians of Bengali literature."[4] It shows the relative novelty of tragic drama in the Bengali cultural milieu, though some of the characterisation and much of the dialogue, especially in the original dialectal Bengali, point to not insignificant dramatic talent. As Zbavitel details, Mitra wrote six other plays, including *Nabīn Tapasvinī* ["The New Female Ascetic," 1863], which seems to have been based upon Shakespeare's *Merry Wives of Windsor*, and the societal satire that was deemed by later critics like Sukumar Sen to be his finest creation, *Sadhabār Ekādaśī* ["The Widow-Feast of a Married Woman," 1866].[5] Here, it is worth remembering that Mitra, due to the initial influence of Iśvarcandra Gupta, started out as a poet, having composed an anthology titled *Mānab-Caritra* ["Human Character"] and started writing in the *Samvād Prabhākar*. This led to Mitra achieving some amount of recognition as a poet amongst the readers of that periodical, with some of his poems attracting even the *cognoscenti* of the time. However, he decided to quit composing poetry and "adopt dramaturgy as the means of developing his creative talents."[6]

It is, however, in its political and economic repercussions that the *Nīl Darpaṇ* creates a socio-cultural momentum of its own. This realistic evocation of the popular mood was made possible by Mitra's long association with people from all walks of society, in different places in "Orissa, Nadia, Dhaka, Comilla, the Lushai Hills et al.,"[7] wherever his work for the Government took him. According to Sivanath Sastri, it was this ability to engage and identify himself with people from different classes of society that had fashioned his dramatic realism: "[s]uch experience, such exposure to human character, and such awareness of varied social situations was available to no one else."[8] Mitra was in Dhaka in 1859, when there were numerous peasants' strikes against the oppressive indigo-planters in districts like Nadia and Jessore, and could witness, first-hand, the travails of the *ryots*, which created a mimetic backlash in his creative consciousness. These practical and direct experiences of peasant-suffering and agrarian exploitation and misappropriation of the fruits of back-breaking labour–as triggered by colonialism–led to the emotionally charged passages of the *Nīl Darpaṇ*. The linguistic register, especially as implicit in the use of an almost elegiac idiomatic mode

---

[4] Zbavitel, *Bengali Literature*, p. 226.
[5] Ibid. Cf. Sukumar Sen, *History of Bengali Literature* (New Delhi: Sahitya Akademi, 1960), p. 200.
[6] Sivanath Sastri, *Rāmtanu Lāhiḍi o Tatkālīn Banga Samāj* ["Ramtanu Lahiri and the Contemporary Bengali Society," 1904], ed. Barid Baran Ghosh (Calcutta: New Age Publishers, 2009), p. 185.
[7] P. 186.
[8] Ibid.

throughout the initial scenes, tends to be quite fatalistic and even submissive, as when Ray Churn says, "Oh, my Ill-fortune! Ill-fortune (burnt forehead)! What has the Indigo of this white man done?"[9] However, as the play progresses, the mood of the poorer peasants, certainly those who have nothing to lose, like Torap, and even the wealthier, more gentrified Nobin Madhab gets more aggressive and even confrontationist. In Act 2, scene 1, Torap, the firebrand Muslim peasant, observes something that has, later, characterised a number of Indian cultural stereotypes about British class divisions: "We have now understood, these Planters are the low people of Belata."[10] In fact, one of the strategies of early colonial Indian lobbying, at various echelons of the East India Company and even, post-1858, the Crown, was to make a clear distinction between the presumably well-intentioned intellectual upper strata of the Empire's leadership, usually based in London and metropolitan Calcutta, and the perceived proletarian British underclass who would go to the Indian *mofussil*[11] and busy themselves with the dirty, day-to-day business of keeping Indians under their physical yoke.

This strategy, seen in the writings of the eminent Bengali journalist-cum-editor Harish Chandra Mukherjee, especially during the so-called Sepoy Mutiny of 1857, often allowed the higher British officialdom to distance itself from the unpalatable acts of oppression and exploitation perpetrated by, among others, the indigo-planters. As Sivnath Sastri writes: "[w]hile, on the one hand, Harishchandra used to support every legitimate disciplinary action of the Government, on the other he protested against all kinds of unacceptable behaviour on the part of the English."[12] In the play, as in India's struggle for Independence, some of the characters, especially Torap, get increasingly more aggressive. In Act 3, scene 3,

---

9 Mitra, *Nil Darpan*, p. 9.
10 P. 28. The Bangla word *b[i]let* comes from the Urdu/Hindustani word *vilāyat*, which is used to connote any foreign country; it owes its origin, ultimately, to the Turkic and Persian *vilāyet*, normatively translated as "province" or any similar administrative unit. However, Torap is referring, in this context, to Britain. Cf. Andrew Stuart Thompson, *The Empire Strikes Back? The Impact of Imperialism on Britain from the Mid-Nineteenth Century* (Harlow/New York, NY: Pearson Longman, 2005), p. 180: "Other Indian words include *blighty* ('one's home country', from the Hindi word 'bilayati' meaning 'foreign', whence 'British') [...]."
11 A word initially used by Anglo-Indian officialdom to connote the non-metropolitan, "up-country" areas of India, even those outside the three "Presidency" cities of Calcutta, Bombay and Madras, and later used in some Indian languages for provincial areas and even small towns outside major conurbations. Cf. Herbert Compton, *Indian Life in Town and Country* (London/New York, NY: G. P. Putnam's Sons/The Knickerbocker Press, 1904), chap. 13 "[Anglo-Indian Life:] The Land of Exile," pp. 183–198, esp. pp. 189 f. The word originated from the Urdu *mufaṣṣil/mufaṣṣal*, from the original Persian-Arabic *mufaṣṣal*, "divided."
12 Sastri, *Rāmtanu Lāhiḍi*, p. 144.

Torap thrusts Mr. Rose, one of the planters, onto the ground and proceeds to assault him physically, before being restrained by Nobin Madhab: "Now, Sir, where are your kicks with your shoes on, and your beating on the head?"[13] Later on in the play, the Sadhu, a Hindu ascetic, commends Torap's bravery, which heightens the physical conflict between the planters and the peasants, in these words: "Torapa was observing this from a distance: and, as soon as the men stood around the eldest Babu, he with violence rushed into this crowd, like an obstinate buffalo, took him up, and flew off."[14] Not only is Torap characterised as a brave protester, capable of and willing to deploy physical aggression against the oppressive planters, but he is also shown to be oblivious of the dehumanising aspects of the Hindu-Muslim divide in agrarian Bengal. In Act 2, scene 1, when his Hindu fellow-*ryot*, whom he addresses as his "uncle Prana," declines his request to be carried on the latter's shoulder as he is a Muslim, he, in a matter-of-fact way, carries the First Ryot on his shoulder.[15] This exchange can be seen through quite a few interpretative prisms, foremost amongst which is that of inter-communal relations as a subordinated function of class conflict. It may, in fact, be rather useful to search for ideational parallels between the sociological formulations in the *Nīl Darpaṇ* and those in an ideological-programmatic text like *The Communist Manifesto* (1848).

The Communist Manifesto, which was brought out in London, initially in German, with the title *Manifest der Kommunistischen Partei*, by a group of German political *émigrés*, was largely written by Karl Marx (1818–1883), with significant contributions by his lifelong friend and collaborator Friedrich Engels (1820–1895). The book, which was commissioned by the Communist League to serve as a charter of its policies and objectives, sought to categorise and interpret "class struggle," both past and contemporaneous, through the prism of capitalist exploitation and degeneration, as perceived at the time, "rather than [make] a prediction of communism's potential future forms."[16] It is needless to refer to the global acclaim and currency of this political charter: within a few years of its serialised publication in the *Deutsche Londoner Zeitung*,[17] it was translated into

---

13 Mitra, *Nil Darpan*, p. 53.
14 P. 79.
15 P. 31.
16 Blurb to several editions of the *Communist Manifesto*, for instance, to: Karl Marx and Friedrich Engels, *The Communist Manifesto (Manifesto of the Communist Party)* (Mansfield: Martino Publishing, 2012).
17 Cf. Thomas Kuczynski, ed., *Das Kommunistische Manifest (Manifest der Kommunistischen Partei) von Karl Marx und Friedrich Engels: von der Erstausgabe zur Leseausgabe, mit einem Editionsbericht* (Trier: Karl-Marx-Haus, 1995), pp. 134–147.

almost all major European and other languages, with the first-ever English translation, by Helen Macfarlane, coming out in 1850 and the first American edition being brought out by Stephen Pearl Andrews.[18] If one can characterise, as Amit Sen does, the journalistic and juridical-legal efforts of the Calcutta-based educated elite to tame the indigo-planters as "bourgeois indignation,"[19] one could argue that this bourgeois intelligentsia awakening was not the hallmark of a classic "comprador bourgeoisie" positional configuration but a genuine expansion of pre-revolutionary class-solidarity. This may seem rather heterodox from a strict Marxist standpoint but, interestingly, Marx himself has provided for a possible inversion of his interpretative paradigm when it comes to Indian class-divisions. If one inverts, as Chaturvedi Badrinath does, Marx's canonical statement in his eleventh thesis on Feuerbach—"philosophers have so far tried to interpret the world; the point, however, is to change it."—and seeks to turn the social reformers' quests to change India into an inward-looking journey of understanding,[20] one may be rewarded with an original and startling possibility of evolutionary class cooperation, not unlike Gandhi's notions of social trusteeship, between the bourgeois intellectuals of Calcutta and the agrarian proletariat, who collaborated in the Indigo Revolt against colonial exploitation.

The post-1857 history of the Bengal Presidency was characterised by what Amit Sen calls "a magnificent outburst of creative activity in literature. The flowering of the [Bengali] Renaissance began with the poetry of Madhusudan Datta, the drama of Dinabandhu Mitra and the novels of Bankim Chandra Chatterji. The soul of educated Bengal had started to express itself in its own chosen medium."[21] This mode of socio-cultural expression of human solidarity that cut across caste- and community-lines, an achievement that cannot always be taken for granted in the Indian context–to put it rather mildly–may or may not be an outcome of early exposure to texts like *The Communist Manifesto*, which, despite antedating the *Nīl Darpaṇ*, is unlikely to have been available to either Dinabandhu Mitra or Harish Chandra Mukherjee, the literary and journalistic torch-bearers of the

---

18 This reference has been taken from an article by Jeff Riggenbach, "Stephen Pearl Andrews's Fleeting Contribution to Anarchist Thought," *Mises Daily*, Mises Institute, 1 April, 2011, http://mises.org/daily/5161/Stephen-Pearl-Andrewss-Fleeting-Contribution-to-Anarchist-Thought (retrieved: 6 August 2014).
19 Amit Sen, *Notes on the Bengal Renaissance* (Calcutta: National Book Agency, 1957), p. 39.
20 Cf. Lesslie Newbigin, "Foreword," in: Chaturvedi Badrinath, *Dharma, India and the World Order: Twenty-One Essays* (Edinburgh: Saint Andrew Press; Bonn: Pahl-Rugenstein, 1993), pp. ix–xiv, p. ix. Also, cf. Badrinath, "Understanding India: Key to Reform of Society" [1989], in: *Dharma, India and the World Order*, pp. 29–33, for the quotation, cf. p. 29.
21 Sen, *Notes on the Bengal Renaissance*, p. 40.

indigo-farmers' struggles. Mukherjee, for one, was quite close to the British upper bureaucracy and his speeches and writings in the *Hindoo Patriot* were followed even by the Governor-General, Lord Canning (1812–1862). It was heard that "the day the *Patriot* would be printed, Lord Canning's servant would wait in the *Patriot*-office and leave with the first few printed copies of the newspaper."[22] However, Mukherjee sided with the indigo-farmers during their legal struggles against the planter Raj and turned his newspaper office and residence into veritable revolutionary headquarters, with "oppressed peasants gathering [there] night and day[.]"[23] Sivanath Sastri looks at Mukherjee's contribution to the indigo-farmers' struggle as the latter's time-defying act and gives us a glowing tribute to Mukherjee's selfless devotion to and tireless efforts for the poor *ryots*. According to him, Mukherjee had devoted his body, mind, wealth and capabilities to the cause of the peasants, while writing articles and reports on their plight, and giving evidence to the so-called "Indigo Commission," which was set up by the Government in 1860 to tour the districts and collect first-hand information on the tyrannical practices of the indigo-planters. The latter were so incensed by Mukherjee's activism that they sued him in the Supreme Court and drove him to a premature death, at the age of thirty-seven; thereafter, they implicated his widow as a defendant and managed to extract a substantial sum of money from her.

The play *Nīl Darpaṇ*, meanwhile, through its closed-door textual dissemination within British official circles, which landed an English missionary in prison, focused Bengali and British middle-class opinion on the brutal treatment of Indian farmers due to the high demand for blue dye in contemporary Europe. Sastri, in fact, writes that the play "had created a huge tumult in Bengali society"[24] and, from his account, one can gauge its pioneering role as a text of socio-political mobilisation. It appears that, despite people being unaware of the identity of the playwright, almost every Bengali household that could afford to do so staged scenes from the play. One must, here, note that the period between 1856 and 1861 could even be called one of the most significant turning points in Bengali history, with various reform initiatives and other upheavals, such as, for example, the widow-remarriage movement, the so-called Sepoy Mutiny, the Indigo Revolt, the coming of age of the vernacular press, the establishment of the native stage and quite a number of other transformative events and processes being set in motion. The *Nīl Darpaṇ* was almost crucial to the development of the Bengali stage and deeply influenced Girish Chandra Ghosh, who, in 1872, would go on to establish

---

22 Sastri, *Rāmtanu Lāhiḍi*, p. 144.
23 P. 147.
24 P. 148.

The National Theatre in Calcutta (now Kolkata). It is significant that the first-ever play to be staged commercially there was none other than the *Nīl Darpaṇ*. Earlier, as discussed previously, there was "a sort of excitement in the minds of people regarding the reappearance of verse-drama and the stage in Bengali society,"[25] which was one of the reasons for the popularity of the play. Before this staggering efflorescence of the native stage, theatre was predominantly low-profile, with a preponderance of folk-forms of dramatic entertainment, like "the *jātrā*, *kabigān* and *hāp-ākhdāi*,[26] which were considered to be full of indecent and obscene themes."[27] With the spread of Anglophone education, the above-mentioned forms of popular recreation came to be derided by the intellectual elite and many members of the so-called *bhadralok* felt very embarrassed to be present at performances of these "vulgar" genres. In fact, this distinction between high and low culture persists, to this day, in Bengali society and it was only in the mid-twentieth century that the *jātrā* "[...] returned to favour in urban areas [...] when the Communist Party employed it to win sympathetic support for its cause."[28]

---

25 Ibid.
26 These were the names of various genres of popular semi-dramatic performances, both music-based and plot-oriented, staged on both urban and rural, fixed and travelling bases. The *jātrā* is "[t]he most popular regional theatre form in the rural areas of Bengal and among Bengali-speaking people of neighbouring Bihar, Orissa, Assam and Tripura." (James Rodger Brandon, ed., *The Cambridge Guide to Asian Theatre* [Cambridge: Cambridge University Press, 1993], p. 89.) Bangladesh, where Bengali is the national language, is also in the performative locus of this genre, which, having originated, probably, in the Vaishnava hagiographical tradition of devotional performance in sixteenth-century Bengal, came to be secularised in mid-nineteenth-century Calcutta, when the scions of the city's bourgeoisie used Western techniques of dramaturgy, staging and acting to engage with the challenges of colonialism and societal transformation. "*Kabig[ā]n* is a form of debate between two professional minstrels who improvise their verses and sing with musical and choral accompaniment. He who fails to answer the riddles or is outwitted by the logic of the opponent, loses the contest." (Syed Jamil Ahmed, "Drama and Theatre," in: Sirajul Islam, ed., *History of Bangladesh, 1704–1971*, 2nd ed., 3 vols. [Dhaka: Asiatic Society of Bangladesh, 1997] vol. 3: *Social and Cultural History*, pp. 473–542, p. 503.) The *hāp*["half"]-*ākhdāi* was the name given to a modified version of the *ākhdāi*, which was "a semi-classical style of singing that came into vogue in Calcutta" (Sujit Mukherjee, *A Dictionary of Indian Literature: Beginnings–1850* [New Delhi: Orient Longman, 1998], p. 10) in the late eighteenth century. It contained three stanzas, which were addressed to a goddess, talked of amorous love and bemoaned the night of separation from the beloved respectively. Due to the lack of popularity of this form, a need was felt to make certain modifications, which came to characterise the so-called *hāp-ākhdāi*, mainly in terms of including various interfaces with popular forms of poetic duelling, as seen in *kabigān*-performances.
27 Sastri, *Rāmtanu Lāhiḍi*, p. 148.
28 Brandon, *Cambridge Guide to Asian Theatre*, p. 89.

Back in the mid-nineteenth century, many educated drama enthusiasts would patronise the playhouses set up by the British and, in the Calcutta of 1856–57, there was at least one renowned English playhouse that was frequented by the educated and rich gentry of the city. According to Sastri, "after watching [the acting in this theatre, some of these people], would lament the absence of similar playhouses amongst [them]."[29] Consequently, some of the city's leading gentlemen would take the initiative and, having cast educated British friends and acquaintances in the leading roles, attempt to stage English plays for the purpose of entertaining their friends and relatives. As Sastri notes, this practice was not completely new, as, quite some time back, the renowned Prasannakumar Tagore had staged a performance of Horace Hayman Wilson's translation of the *Uttararāmacarita*. This trend, however, remained confined to the domain of private, individual patronage, often undertaken on a competitive basis, until, having gauged the demand and respect for English acting within the native gentry, the members of the English playhouses set up the "Oriental Theatre" in the building of the "Oriental Seminary" and started staging Shakespearean plays there. "This led to an effusion of English acting in native educated circles,"[30] with stage-acting becoming something of an obsession: even schoolboys were staging abridged versions of *Macbeth* and other plays with their own small groups. This trend, however, did not last very long as the wealthy patrons of drama realised that English plays are not the way to the average person's heart. Hence, there was a gradual shift to Bengali plays, with the *Nīl Darpaṇ* having set a precedent by demonstrating the socio-political charge of theatre.

Dinabandhu Mitra's play was also one of the first play-texts in Bengali to have been translated into English in mid-nineteenth century India. As L. S. S. O'Malley writes: "The *Nil Darpan*, literally, the mirror of indigo, the earliest and probably the finest play of the dramatist Dinabandhu Mitra. Its object was to expose the abuses of indigo planting and its preface explained that it depicted the fortunes of [...] [the] cultivator[s] [...]. The play created a great sensation."[31] What is significant in this context is the involved contribution of the Rev. James Long, an Anglo-Irish missionary known for his espousal of "native" causes. He is said to have helped Michael Madhusudan Datta ("A Native") in translating the play into English and, along with the printer, was prosecuted for his pains

---

29 Sastri, *Rāmtanu Lāhiḍi*, p. 149.
30 Ibid.
31 Lewis Sydney Steward O'Malley, *History of Bengal, Bihar and Orissa under British Rule* (Calcutta: Bengal Secretariat Depot, 1925), p. 436.

on the charge of libelling two European newspapers [...] and sentenced [...] to a month's imprisonment in addition to a fine of Rs. 1,000 [the sum having being paid by Kaliprasanna Singha, the author of the social satire *Hutom Pyānchār Nakshā* ("Designs of the Barn-Owl," 1862) and a famous philanthropist,] [...] [and] [t]he Secretary [to the Bengal Government,] who [had] circulated the translation was removed from his office by the Government of India.³²

One must, at this juncture, note that there is a certain amount of current scholarly disagreement about the identity of the translator of the *Nīl Darpaṇ*. Whereas some historians of nineteenth century Calcutta's cultural transactions, like Sumanta Banerjee, in his *The Parlour and the Streets: Elite and Popular Culture in Nineteenth Century Calcutta* (1989), identify Michael Madhusudan Datta as the translator, others doubt the veracity of "the secondary sources and unverified facts"³³ that may have led Banerjee to this conclusion. Tapobijoy Ghosh, according to Anil Acharya, in his exhaustive review of Banerjee's work, rejects, in his *Nīl-Bidroher Caritra o Bāṅālī-Buddhijībī* ["The Indigo Revolt and Bengali Intellectuals," 1983], the unsubstantiated assumption that Datta had ever considered translating the play into English, let alone doing the work nearly overnight. As Acharya writes, "[Datta] might have been quite realistic in his farces, but he was never known for his empathy for the lower order culture."³⁴

In the process of studying the two cultures of the elite—the burgeoning *bhadralok*³⁵—and the so-called lower-order civility, Sumanta Banerjee, through his critical exploration of the underlying complexities of nineteenth-century Bengali culture, pinpoints a certain parting of ways between the two above-mentioned paradigms. As Paolo Freire points out, "[t]he dependent society is by definition a silent society. Its voice is not an authentic voice, but merely an echo of the voice of the metropolis—in every way, the metropolis speaks, the dependent society listens."³⁶ Thus, as Banerjee also argues, the nineteenth-century Calcutta street undergoes a clearly defined relegation to the position of a subaltern who holds up a contrastive mirror image to the constructions of upper-class civility. As he

---

32 Ibid.
33 Anil Acharya, "Cultures of a Metropolis [Review of the book *The Parlour and the Streets: Elite and Popular Culture in Nineteenth Century Calcutta* by Sumanta Banerjee]," *Economic and Political Weekly* 46.25 (17 November, 1990), pp. 2541–2546, p. 2545.
34 Ibid.
35 A term (literally, "civilised people") used, until quite recently, to connote the Bengali middle classes, which assiduously cultivated a stereotypical aura of eclectic cultural and intellectual tastes, despite their social conservatism; often, this leisured urbane sophistication was bought by economic prowess.
36 Paolo Freire, *Cultural Action for Freedom* (Harmondsworth: Penguin Books, 1972), p. 59, quoted in Acharya, "Cultures of a Metropolis," p. 2541.

clarifies in his introduction, he aims to compare these two trajectories of cultural production as determined by the social and economic balance of contemporaneous Calcutta. Banerjee's "parlour," as well as his "street," seem to have undergone significant constitutive changes, especially through the configuration of their reactions to the socio-cultural equations of the time. The former is constituted by "the banians,[37] dewans,[38] absentee landlords (post-Permanent Settlement[39] phenomenon) and the Bengali middle class of Macaulay's description of 1835."[40] This links the socio-cultural role of the *bhadralok* to the "civilising" narrative of colonialism, which could, in turn, be linked to the reconstitution of capitalist enterprise. Thus, even the nascent nationalistic manoeuvres of the Calcutta-based elite could be said to have played, to a certain extent, into the hands of what Partha Chatterjee calls "the universalist urge of capital."[41] *Nīl Darpaṇ* and, even more significantly, its reception in mid-nineteenth century Bengal, seem to thematise what Chatterjee calls "the conflict between capital and the people-nation,"[42] which defies "forced resolution by nationalism"[43] and dents "the sovereign, tyrannical universality"[44] of Reason, the corollary to capitalist universalism.

The play depicts the total and progressive destruction of the idyllic domestic bliss and socio-economic standing of a prosperous Bengali *Kāyastha*,[45] named Goluk Chunder Basu, through the evil machinations of the British indigo-

---

[37] *Banian/Benians* were Indian traders, merchant-princes, financiers and money-changers; the term comes from the Portuguese *banian*, which derives from the Sanskrit *vāṇijá* (earlier *vaṇíj*, "merchant, trader"), through Gujarati and Arabic intermediaries.
[38] *Dew[ā]n* or *diwān*, which is Persian in origin, was a common Hindustani socio-economic term used in South Asia for, among others, financial assistants or treasurers of industrialists and landlords or finance ministers.
[39] The so-called "Permanent Settlement" of Bengal was a charter agreed upon by the English East India Company and the landlords of Bengal-Bihar-Orissa, in 1793, under the Governor-Generalship of Charles, Lord Cornwallis. It fixed land revenue levies, an act that had wide-ranging consequences upon agricultural techniques and output throughout the British Empire and rural Indian society and polity.
[40] Acharya, "Cultures of a Metropolis," p. 2541.
[41] Partha Chatterjee, *Nationalist Thought and the Colonial World: A Derivative Discourse* (Delhi: Oxford University Press, 1986), p. 168.
[42] P. 169.
[43] Ibid.
[44] P. 168.
[45] *Kāyastha* (also called *kāyasth* or *kāyet*) denotes a Hindu caste originating in India; it means "scribe" in Sanskrit, reflecting the caste's traditional role as record-keepers and administrators of the state. Cf. Surinder Mohan Bhardwaj, *Hindu Places of Pilgrimage in India: A Study in Cultural Geography* (Berkeley/Los Angeles, CA/London: University of California Press, 1973), p. 231.

planters. The other main characters are Goluk's wife, sons and daughter-in-law, two oppressive indigo-planters named Mr. Wood and Mr. Rogue, their *dewāns* and factory servants, the District Magistrate and an itinerant confectioner "who is also a procuress."⁴⁶ At the outset, the planters come on stage and are shown to be violent, heartless, abusive and uncouth oppressors. Thereafter, viewers are acquainted with the forcible kidnapping/"arrest" of two brave *rāyats*, Sadhu Churn and Ray Churn, who are Golak Basu's tenants: they are taken to the "*kuthi*" (the godown, or warehouse, of the planter), where they are physically brutalised for resisting *dādan*.⁴⁷ Then, the play describes the process through which fraudulent legal proceedings are initiated against the hapless villagers who refuse to grow indigo on their land; the collusion between the local judiciary and the planters and the horrid ravages suffered by the villagers, especially women, are also presented on the stage. Towards the end of the play, Goluk Basu, unable to hold up to the sustained pressure of the planter Raj, commits suicide, his son Nobin Madhab succumbs to a fractured skull, which was the result of the planter's blows, and Goluk's wife Sabitri, unable to face her double trauma, loses her mental balance and also dies. The message to the audience is that of all-pervasive tragedy caused by the depredations of the indigo-planters and their exploitation of the peasantry.

As far as its dramatic worth goes, "[...] strictly speaking, *Nīldarpaṇ* is an insignificant production. It is neither well-written nor does it lend itself to successful production on the stage."⁴⁸ In what was, arguably, the first well-researched survey of the Bengali-speaking stage, Prabhucharan Guha-Thakurta opined, quoting Aristotle and Kant, that, though "the author [of the *Nīl Darpaṇ*] was inspired by a sincere desire to deal with real life and real incidents,"⁴⁹ the often graphic violence, as depicted in the play, does not manage to make the play transcend mere "literal truth [...] by a certain kind of imaginative verisimilitude."⁵⁰ His chief critique of the play seems to be Dinabandhu Mitra's inability to bring in a measure of detachment from his emotional identification with the plight of the indigo-farmers. The scenes of abject horror and callous dehumanisation, often culminating in literalist stage depictions of brutal physical assault, along with the rather

---

46 Prabhucharan Guha-Thakurta, *The Bengali Drama: Its Origin and Development* (London: Kegan Paul, Trench, Trübner & Co., 1930; repr. London: Routledge, 2000), p. 109.
47 *Dādan* was an advance or loan given by the indigo-planters, often by means more foul than fair, to the farmers, on condition that they would cultivate indigo and, thereafter, sell the crop to the advance-giving planters at a fixed approved price.
48 Guha-Thakurta, *The Bengali Drama*, p. 109.
49 P. 110.
50 Ibid.

exaggerated and heavy dialogue and both prose and verse descriptions, fail to pull the play above the Kantian "purposiveness without purpose." In a nutshell, one may say that the acutely descriptive realism and even literalism of the *Nīl Darpaṇ* does, according to a more traditional critical trajectory, impinge upon its capacity to produce a strong dramatic effect. However, this need not, necessarily, detract from its function as a mirror of socio-cultural transactions, as they were unfolding across the variegated backdrop of early colonial India. It is herein that one may seek to look at this play, both in theme and treatment, as a "telescopic"[51] precursor to the late-nineteenth century practices of social-realistic critique and naturalist discourses, following Émile Zola, whose renowned article *"J'accuse,"*[52] which is generally accepted in France as the most significant articulation of the newly growing influence of the intellectuals, writers, artists and social workers in moulding public opinion, the media and the state, stood as a testament to the power of the journalist-writer's pen over *étatiste* hegemony.

Émile Zola, along with other renowned European and Russian Naturalists, like Stéphane (Étienne) Mallarmé and Maksim Gorky, seem so well-placed, both ideationally and thematically, to serve as reference points, even indices, of nineteenth-century Indian approaches to realist narratives, both on and off the stage, that one is tempted to engage with them even in a discussion of texts and events predating them. Though Dinabandhu Mitra's work antedates Zola's and operates within a referential socio-cultural framework that is quite different from that of Zola's Paris, one cannot but observe that there are various possibilities for comparative analysis, in terms of narratival focus and descriptive-mimetic strategies, between the *Nīl Darpaṇ* and, for example, Zola's famous series of twenty works, which comprised more than half of his novels, collectively known as *Les Rougon-Macquart* and, specifically, the thirteenth novel in this series, *Germinal* (1885). In contrast to Balzac, who in the prime of his literary career reconfigured his work as *La Comédie Humaine*, Zola, from when he began at the age of twenty-eight, had prefabricated the whole structure of the Rougon-Macquart-series. Set against the variegated backdrop of the *Second Empire* (1852–1870) of Napoleon III, the so-called "Pretender" and "Sphinx of the Tuileries," which has been

---

[51] "Telescopic philanthropy," connoting the self-imposed obligation of conducting notionally idealistic philanthropic activity from a distance, is the title of Chapter 4 of Sir Charles Dickens' *Bleak House* (1852–1853); in the present context, the implication is that of a precursor: perhaps related, perhaps not.
[52] *"J'accuse"* ["I Accuse"] was published, in response to the false charges, motivated by anti-semitism, against Captain Alfred Dreyfus, on the front page of the French daily *L'Aurore*, on 13 January, 1898.

called an "extravaganza" by David Baguley,[53] the series delineates the "environmental" impact of both domestic and societal violence, alcoholism, prostitution and the general moral decay that seemed to characterise the second and later phases of the Industrial Revolution in continental Europe. The series takes a wry look at two branches of a family, the reputable—since legitimate—Rougons and the disreputable—since illegitimate—Macquarts through a span of five generations.

Germinal is usually regarded as Zola's *magnum opus*, his best-selling work, which struck a nerve upon publication and is one of the most important French novels ever; it has been published and translated in more than a hundred countries, besides inspiring five films and two television series. In it, there is a resolutely and tangibly stark realist portrayal of the struggles of striking coal-miners in northern France in the 1860s, a period almost contemporaneous with the Indigo Revolt in Bengal. The title of the novel itself suggests revolutionary sympathies and, perhaps, even intent, being also the name of the first Spring month in the *Calendrier Révolutionnaire Français* ["French Revolutionary Calendar"], which was used by the French State between 1793 and 1805 and also for almost three weeks by the Paris Commune in 1871. The "seed" metaphor embedded in the word "*Germinal*" also resonates well with the agrarian orientation of the *Nīl Darpaṇ*, despite the contextual differences between what was, essentially, a narrative of early industrial exploitation and the workers' reaction to it and an agriculturalists' struggle against near-slavery conditions. It may be argued, given the strong undercurrent of hope implied in the title *Germinal*, which indicated regeneration, perhaps even rebirth, and fertility, that the tragic and highly disturbing conclusion of the *Nīl Darpaṇ* does not allow for a fully comparative analysis of these two texts. However, the fact that Zola ends his novel on an almost jaunty, optimistic note, which has inspired socialist mobilisation ever since the first publication of the novel—"In the fiery rays of the sun on this youthful morning the country seemed full of that sound. Men were springing forth, a black avenging army, germinating slowly in the furrows, growing towards the harvests of the next century, and their germination would soon overturn the earth."[54]—should not blur the

---

53 Cf. David Baguley, *Napoleon III and His Empire: An Extravaganza* (Baton Rouge: Louisiana State University Press, 2000).
54 Émile Zola, *Germinal* [1885], trans. Havelock Ellis [e-book] (Adelaide: The University of Adelaide, eBooks@Adelaide, 2012), https://ebooks.adelaide.edu.au/z/zola/emile/germinal/part7.6.html (retrieved: 7 August 2014). ("Aux rayons enflammés de l'astre, par cette matinée de jeunesse, c'était de cette rumeur que la campagne était grosse. Des hommes poussaient, une armée noire, vengeresse, qui germait lentement dans les sillons, grandissant pour les récoltes du siècle futur, et dont la germination allait faire bientôt éclater la terre." [p. 591]).

vivid pain and disturbing pathos of the depictions in much of the novel, especially the mine scenes. The latter were the outcome of Zola's characteristically thorough and prolonged study tours of northern French mining areas in 1884. He was especially influenced by his first-hand observation of the most debilitating consequences of the miners' strike at Anzin and his actual descent into a functioning coal pit at Denain.

The main character of *Germinal*, Étienne Lantier, a young migrant worker, who, having worked as an engine-man, arrives at the grim and bleak coal mining town of Montsou, which lies in a desolate stretch of northern France, seeking work as a miner, is a study both in contrast and comparability to Nobin Madhab, the young son of Goluk Basu, the main character of the *Nīl Darpaṇ*. Nobin Madhab is characterised as a young man of moral and physical vigour and integrity from the very beginning of the play, when he tells his father to "bring an action [against the indigo-planters] into Court."[55] He is consistently portrayed as the moral voice and ideological anchor of the agrarian angst, often trying to protect his father and other farmers, irrespective of their social position and religious identity. He upholds a humane code of conduct and disapproves of violence against even the brutal planters: in Act 2, scene 3, when the Muslim peasant Torap beats up Planter Rose, he tells the former, "[w]e ought not to be cruel, because they are so."[56] Zola's Étienne is also a spirited and industrious idealist, if a tad gullible, not unlike Nobin Madhab. The former had lost his earlier job with the railways after having assaulted a superior; he befriends the grimly named Bonnemort, an old-timer at the mines who had survived all kinds of accidents in the pits, and finds, through his good offices, lodgings and a job pushing carts down one of the pits. Where Étienne differs from Nobin Madhab is in his presumed Macquart typological inheritance of temperamental impetuosity and a choleric disposition, especially when under the influence of alcoholic beverages or intensely passionate feelings. Although such a characterisation is in keeping with Zola's theories of genetic typologies, he does seem to limit, in *Germinal*, characteral theorisation to the narrative backdrop. Consequently, Étienne's character is able to develop according to the demands of the *dénouement*, in a way Nobin Madhab's cannot, given the near total subordination of characterisation and plot, in the *Nīl Darpaṇ*, to the demands of ideological didacticism. Here, one could remind oneself that, as Richard Lehan puts it, "Zola's world is one of limits; if one is to have great wealth, then there must be poverty."[57] Later in *Germinal*, in a manner reflective of

---

55 Mitra, *Nil Darpan*, p. 7.
56 P. 53.
57 Richard Lehan, "Urban Signs and Urban Literature: Literary Form and Historical Process," *New Literary History* 18.1 (1986), pp. 99–113, p. 108.

this typological binary, Étienne takes to socialism in a gung-ho manner, studying many texts dealing with working-class mobilisation and keeping the company of Souvarine, an *émigré* Russian anarchist who had come to earn a livelihood in the coal pits of Montsou. However, Étienne's engagement with radical socialist politics remains relegated to the level of formulaic over-simplification and does not hinder his romantic entanglement with Catherine, who also pushes carts in the pits, thus embroiling him in her torturous relationship with Chaval, her rather bestial lover, characterised almost typologically, with more than occasional derision.

Meanwhile, the complicated vicissitudes of life in the coal mines are further accentuated against the felt realities of debilitating poverty and burgeoning capitalist oppression, with the professional and personal lives of the miners deteriorating as the novel progresses. Things reach such a point of unbearable suffering that they decide to strike and the mantle of leadership falls upon Étienne, who had, by that point, acquired a substantial following in the community through his idealist politics. This, again, reminds one of Nobin Madhab who had become a rallying point for the other characters in Mitra's play, so much so that his presence, even after death, animates the *Nīl Darpaṇ*; the play, tellingly, ends with the following exclamation: "Ah! how very terrible, the last scene of the drama of the lion-like Nobin Madhab is?"[58] In *Germinal*, the miners desist from violent action, which Souvarine constantly urges them towards, until the last desperate moment of impoverishment, following which they erupt into furious rioting. Zola's descriptions of the resultant mob fury count amongst his most intensely evocative crowd scenes and cannot be compared to the meagre attempts at portraying protest action in Mitra's play. The suppression of the riots by the police and the army are much more thorough and heavy-handed than that in the context of the Indigo Revolt, and Étienne, by no means the instigator of the violence, stands discredited in the eyes of the miners, who return to work quite disillusioned with radical idealism. Souvarine sabotages the entrance shaft of a pit, trapping Étienne, Catherine and Chaval, and causing a long and tantalising rescue episode that ends with Étienne's survival. The novel ends with his services being terminated and him moving to Paris, turning a full circle, of sorts, in terms of the disillusionment with the inevitability and/or pace of progress. Zola had almost unmixed pride in what the novel stood for, in ideational terms, and fended off accusations from both extremes of the political spectrum. Towards the end of his life, *Germinal* came to be regarded as not only his undeniable masterpiece but also an evocative testament to working-class mobilisation and an exploration of

---

58 Mitra, *Nil Darpan*, p. 102.

the industrial-era subjugation of rural Nature to the dictates of urban capital. As Lehan notes: "While *Germinal* and *La Débâcle* are not city novels, they show how the city controls what goes on in the coal mines of the north or in the intrigue that leads to war."[59] As Joachim Küpper outlines in a study on the evolution of French novels,[60] there are "inherent paradoxes [in] Zola's approach"[61] to categorisations of fiction and reality, which seem to fall prey to a "failure to appreciate the categorial differences"[62] between the two. These, in turn "just do not allow any experiment with reality in fiction."[63] This developing shadow-boxing between reality and fiction is at the heart of Zola's depictions of the travails of a world torn asunder between the aggression of metropolitan industrial capitalism and the rustic, even bucolic, values that define older structures of kinship.

In Zola's words, describing the *Rougon-Macquart* novels: "I want to portray, at the outset of a century of liberty and truth, a family that cannot restrain itself in its rush to possess all the good things that progress is making available and is derailed by its own momentum, the fatal convulsions that accompany the birth of a new world."[64] It is these "fatal convulsions" that constitute the historically figurative and societally representative backdrop of the *Nīl Darpaṇ*, too. In this case, the convulsions are those imposed by a colonialism-dictated system of exploitative economic relations and the resultant dehumanisation of both victim and perpetrator: the former through the piteous brutalisation inflicted upon her/him by the indigo-planters and the latter through the dissociation of human sensibility from the lust for economic profit. As Kaliprasanna Singha observes, in his inimitably earthy style, in *Hutom Pyānchār Nakśā*, "Even ghosts are scared off by the

---

59 Lehan, "Urban Signs and Urban Literature," p. 108.
60 Joachim Küpper, *Ästhetik der Wirklichkeitsdarstellung und Evolution des Romans von der französischen Spätaufklärung bis zu Robbe-Grillet: Ausgewählte Probleme zum Verhältnis von Poetologie und literarischer Praxis* (Stuttgart: Steiner, 1987).
61 Andreas Kablitz, "Rezension von [Book Review]: Joachim Küpper, *Ästhetik der Wirklichkeitsdarstellung und Evolution des Romans von der französischen Spätaufklärung bis zu Robbe-Grillet*," *Zeitschrift für französische Sprache und Literatur* 99 (1989), pp. 80–86, p. 84. ("[J. Küpper skizziert] die immanenten Aporien von Zolas Ansatz.")
62 Ibid. ("Verkennung der kategorialen Differenzen von Fiktion und Realität.")
63 Ibid. ("[...] eben in der Fiktion kein Experiment über die Wirklichkeit zulassen.")
64 This is sourced from a write-up on Zola's oeuvre that accompanies a web-archive of his works, hosted by the Library of the University of Adelaide: http://ebooks.adelaide.edu.au/z/zola/emile/index.html (retrieved: 7 August 2014). ("Pour résumer mon œuvre en une phrase, je veux peindre, au début d'un siècle de vérité et de liberté, une famille qui s'élance vers les biens prochains et qui roule, détraquée par son élan lui-même, justement à cause des lueurs troubles du moment, des convulsions fatales de l'enfantement d'un monde." Printed in: Henri Massis, *Comment Émile Zola composait ses romans: d'après ses notes personnelles et inédites* [Paris: Bibliothèque Charpentier, 1906], p. 17.)

shāmcānd,⁶⁵ what news is it that the subjects would go crazy!"⁶⁶ Singha, according to Dinabandhu Mitra's son, Lalit Chandra Mitra, had assured the writer of the *Nīl Darpaṇ* that he could be sure of financial support for the latter's legal defence. He had also, at his own expense, arranged the printing of a second edition of the play and its free distribution to, among others, the subscribers of the *Hindoo Patriot*. "Amulyachandra Sen says that it is at the request of Kaliprasanna that [Rev.] Long had translated the *Nīl Darpaṇ* into English and, hence, he had paid Long's fine."⁶⁷

Perhaps one of the most significant aspects of Rev. James Long's (1814–87) participation in the indigo farmers' struggle is that of the apparently intriguing relationship between a British Evangelist and what could be looked at as a "proto-nationalist" rebellion. Geoffrey A. Oddie, in his *Missionaries, Rebellion and Proto-Nationalism: James Long of Bengal 1814–87*, studies Long's life and work in the Bengal Presidency quite thoroughly and, according to Julius Lipner,

> [t]he point [...] is that by his eventual if brief imprisonment in the ryots' cause, Long not only rebelled with important symbolic undertones against many government officials' and other colonials' expectations of how a missionary should behave, but also became himself something of a rallying point for "proto-nationalist" sentiment among westernised Indians.⁶⁸

By the time he was tried *apropos* the indigo-planters' accusations, Long had, equipped with "an excellent education, rich in the classical and biblical languages, and a conversion to evangelicalism,"⁶⁹ made a seemingly smooth transition from his gentrified southern Irish family background to that of a humble missionary in Calcutta, the epicentre of the Raj, in 1840 and was to remain there until 1872. In these three decades and more, as noted by Oddie, Long learns Bengali with a considerable degree of skill. If, indeed, parts of the *Nīl Darpaṇ* are translated by him, he seems to have had a thorough, if literalist and rather stiff, grasp of the language. What is of equal if not more import is that he concentrated his evangelical zeal on attempting to get to know rural Bengal and bring

---

65 "An instrument of physical torture used against the indigo-farmers" (Kaliprasanna Singha, *Satīk Hutom Pyānchār Nakśā* ["Annotated 'Designs of the Barn-Owl'," 1862], ed. Arun Nag [Calcutta: Ananda, 2012], p. 253), which was made up of a stick that had either a thick, two-feet-long and one-foot-wide leather strap or a bunch of knotted leather strands attached to its front part; it inflicted ten times as much pain as a cane and had become an evocative metaphor for the brutality of indigo cultivation in Bengal.
66 Singha, *Satīk Hutom Pyānchār Nakśā*, p. 106.
67 Pp. 258 f.
68 Julius Lipner, "Book Review: Geoffrey A. Oddie, *Missionaries, Rebellion and Proto-Nationalism: James Long of Bengal 1814–87*," Journal of Hindu-Christian Studies 15 (2002), pp. 58–59, p. 58.
69 Ibid.

about its socio-cultural and, eventually, religious transformation. This, in Long's understanding, necessitated a special focus on vernacular education, which, after Thomas Babington Macaulay's (in)famous *Minute on Education* (1835), had been relegated to the back-burner of educational governmentality. Thereafter, he became a pioneer of sorts in this arena and combined his abiding interest in vernacular education with that in socio-linguistic enquiries. Long's considerable oeuvre in this area gave the much needed impetus to a burgeoning archive of sociological and anthropological knowledge about Bengali life and culture and led to a growing missionary emphasis, through his pioneering agency, on "*local context* for success in propagating a message."[70]

Long was an honest and industrious missionary, with an abiding empathy for the Bengali peasantry and the rest of the peripheral underclass and an unflinching opposition to the dehumanising brutalities of the indigo-planters. However, as also brought out in Oddie's work and Lipner's review of the same, he did have the basic and inalienable goal of converting rural Bengal to Christianity:

> the subjection of all his endeavours to the goal of ultimate conversion of the non-Christians (Hindu and Muslim) among whom he worked, and the undermining of their ancestral faith (first drain the swamp, he said memorably, referring thus unfavourably to non-Christian religion, before you sow the good seed in it).[71]

Even in the translation of the *Nīl Darpaṇ*, otherwise a faithfully and often hilariously literalist one, there is a sense of the inevitability of the old order changing, in more a socio-cultural than political sense, and the oppression of the indigo-planters, though a negative aspect of the new system, is not its defining picture. The lyrical descriptions of the pathetic sufferings of the almost emasculated peasantry seem to suggest a new solution to the new evil of indigo: a new religion that preached and promised an apparently egalitarian social code, thus enabling the peasantry to break free from the shackles of generational oppression, which would enable them to resist the indigo-planters' depredations. "This," as Lipner notes,

> introduced a note of spiritual calculation in all he did. [...] Long's ulterior motive applied equally to his visits to Russia in later life. He wanted Russian British co-operation to check the growth of Islam in their Asian empires so that the expansion of Christianity might be the more unopposed. Islam or Hinduism, for that matter, had not much salvific or humanising worth in their own right.[72]

---

70 P. 59; italics in the original.
71 Ibid.
72 Ibid.

At this juncture, one could, as suggested by Lipner, return to Oddie, who posits that, in the case of Orientalism being "the corporate institution for dealing with the Orient [...] for dominating, restructuring, and having authority"[73] over it, one could argue for missionary witness not being, *per se*, Orientalist, for "the dichotomy of ultimate importance" for Evangelicals and other Euro-American agencies with a pervasively Christian *Weltanschauung*, "was not Europe versus the Orient, but the saved versus the damned,"[74] and this distinction transcended socio-cultural specificities. However, given that Long, as noted above, viewed the non-Christian, local faith-systems as drainable marshland, it is not inconceivable that this tallied with a certain equalisation between the recalcitrant *ryot* and their irrepressible and "infidel" belief-systems. In general, this appears to have led to a missionary self-identification with the Raj and its political-economic interests: a textbook case for Orientalist frames-of-reference to come to play. In fact, in one of Kaliprasanna Singha's sketches, he notes that the "Christian fashion, like a functioning street-lamp, illuminated its surroundings at first but, then, left throwing things into darkness."[75] This would suggest that the evangelical process, in Bengal, had foundered on the very rock it had sought to base itself upon: the much-vaunted civilising and enlightening mission of the new faith. This, already in the mid-nineteenth century, became progressively more identified with the socio-economic needs of the colonial administration, which was now demanding increased levels of loyalty from its compatriots, of the cloth or otherwise. Thus it follows, not without the recourse to the Orientalist framework, that "the reason [behind the opposition, by lower-order missionaries, to the depredations of the indigo-planters] was their apprehension that such non-Christian behaviour on the part of Christians would hinder the preaching and spread of Christianity in this country."[76] As noted in the *Som Prakāś*, in its issue dated 16.12.1270 (Bengali Era), "in fear of the commander-in-chief, the padres do not utter a word"[77] against the indigo-planters' exploitation of the peasantry; lines had, thus, been drawn for, at least, the rest of the colonial period.

It is interesting that the "Introduction" to the *Nīl Darpaṇ* highlights the fact that "[t]he Bengali Drama imitates in th[e] respect [of] [describing certain states of society, manners, customs] its Sanskrit parent."[78] By stressing the respect the

---

73 Geoffrey A. Oddie, *Missionaries, Rebellion and Proto-Nationalism: James Long of Bengal 1814–87* (Surrey: Curzon Press, 1999), p. 180.
74 P. 181.
75 Singha, *Satīk Hutom Pyānchār Nakśā*, p. 95.
76 P. 255.
77 Ibid.
78 [Rev. John Long,] "Introduction," in: Mitra, *Nil Darpan*, pp. iii f., p. iii.

latter had in the contemporary European critical idiom, Rev. Long, who is generally credited with its authorship, seeks to connect nineteenth-century Indian drama more to its Sanskrit precursor than to the early modern Anglo-European tradition. It is said to lack "marvellous or very tragic scenes,"[79] though, in the Bengali literary-dramatic tradition, this play is supposed to be a work of considerable tragic significance. Here, one may venture the question if this dichotomy points towards a differential understanding of tragedy and/or its Indian form in the Anglo-European critical imagination? One purpose of this text and, especially, its translator's preface, is to hint at, in subtle and not-so-subtle ways, the so-called "white man's burden." It hopes "that the European may be in the Mofussil the protecting Aegis of the peasants, who may be able 'to sit each man under his mango and tamarind tree, none daring to make him afraid.'"[80] The author's preface, written by Mitra himself, is a quaint mix of Anglophone rhetorical constructions—"Oh, ye Indigo Planters"—and occasionally comic literal translations of Bengali idioms into English: "place on [his forehead] the sandal powder of beneficence," "making holes like rust," "the application of the shoe for the destruction of a milk cow," "mixing the inspissated milk in the cup of poison," "the terrible grasp of your mouths," *misery and happiness revolve like a wheel*," "are continually expanding themselves lotus-like on the surface of the lake," "the great giant *Rahu*" et al.[81] In what may be seen as a telling comment on the civil-representational mode of the time, the author's attempt is to petition British officialdom on the plight of the indigo-farmers, who were suffering at the hands of the supposedly uncharacteristic British planters; thus, the latter were seen as deviations from an assumed and projected norm.

This valorisation of the ideal of British justice would, in time, of course, change to more confrontationist modes of civil and extremist agitation, after the foundation of the Indian National Congress in 1885. This was, however, at odds with the tone and tenor of the peasant movement itself, which was quite aggressive, in response to near-slavery conditions. The so-called Indigo Revolt (Bengali: *nīl bidrōhō*) was a post-1857 rebellion that saw an occasionally violent uprising of indigo farmers against the British planters in Bengal in 1859. The seeds of the revolt could be said to have been sown half a century earlier, when the Indigo Plantation Act was passed, though actual cultivation of the plant commercially dates back to 1777. With the expansion of British control over the Nawābate of Bengal-Bihar-Orissa, this cultivation spread all over southern Bengal, with British

---

79 Ibid.
80 P. iv.
81 Mitra, "The Author's Preface," in: Mitra, *Nil Darpan*, pp. 1 f.; italics in the original.

planters often tricking and forcing farmers into cultivating it, for a fraction of the real cost, to the detriment of their normal crop-cycles. The loans, with exorbitant interest-rates, advanced by the planters, called *dādans*, trapped families and entire communities in lifelong bondage, reducing them to penury; to add insult to injury, an Act in 1833 gave the planters free rein over their *ryots*. Emboldened by the so-called Sepoy Mutiny in 1857–58, in February–March 1859 the farmers effected a collective refusal to plant indigo and the planters were caught unawares by their steadfast unity and resolve. What is very significant is the inter-religious unity amongst the farmers: it is worth noting that Haji Molla of Nischindipur said that he would "'rather beg than sow indigo'."[82]

One of the first things that strikes the reader of the *Nīl Darpaṇ*, apart from the rather Bengali-inflected literalist English used in the translation, is the preponderance of Indian life-style markers, despite the text being addressed, fundamentally, to Anglo-Indian officialdom and the Bengali *bourgeoisie*. A few examples are the centrality of rice as a metaphor for life and wealth, "marking off" the agricultural land as a metaphor for dis-appropriation ("*thrust burnt sticks into my breast*"[83]), the importance of not refusing water as a social demand ("gone [in] both [...] life and money"[84]), the sanctification of the Christian missionary, the proliferation of schools, teachers, courts and enlightened gentry who cared for the peasants, like Nobin Madhab and his father, the observance of a modified *purdah*-system among the upper-caste Hindu women like Sabitri, Soirindri and Saralota, kinship and filial ties, both among women and men, that weave ethnocentrically naturalistic and acculturated psycholinguistic memes into the socio-cultural tapestry and so on. There already seems to be an articulation of the irreducible differences between British political-economic goals and socio-cultural mores, which seemed to be driven by the motive of agrarian exploitation, and the aspirational inflection of Indian social and political goals. One may even venture to argue that the *Nīl Darpaṇ*, through its concerted attempt to be what could be construed as modern India's first political tract, attempts to showcase the unvoiced but radical disembodiments of modernity and chaos, and how one can even theorise this tussle. One may attempt, as has been done some pages earlier, to view the play-text as a coming-of-age testament to the engagement of mid-nineteenth-century India with the multi-dimensional and often unsettling effect of colonial cultural dominance. This dominance was inscribed both through literary-pedagogical prescriptivism, as an inalienable–especially after

---

82 Cf. Subhas Bhattacharya, "The Indigo Revolt of Bengal," *Social Scientist* 60 (1977), pp. 13–23, p. 14.
83 Mitra, *Nil Darpan*, pp. 9 f.; italics in the original.
84 P. 11.

the so-called Macaulay's Minute–component of the socio-cultural programme of the East India Company, and through the internally contested readiness of many sections of the Bengali bourgeois intelligentsia to open their society up to English educational paradigms. This drive for selective westernisation, which was viewed as axiomatic to the very process of bringing about a societal and cultural renaissance, was by no means, except perhaps in the tumultuous pronouncements of the Derozians,[85] a call to total revolution. Even with the latter, it was, more often than not, an ideational transformation of Indian society that was being put forward, one that, through its outspoken and often notional radicalism, sought to emphasise the lapse that Indian civilisation had suffered from. This is, of course, not to equate this somewhat iconoclastic socio-cultural movement with the later revivalist debates, which sought to locate the political-economic decline of the Indian Subcontinent in perceived societal and cultural lapses from the Hindu/Indic tradition, but to underline the basic situation–by itself–of the "Young Bengal" as not very far from the intellectual loci of the parent tradition/s. Anglophone ideas, even if their cultivation led to a climacteric conversion to Christianity, as in the cases of Krishna Mohan Banerji (1813–1885) and Michael Madhusudan Datta (1824–1873), were, clearly, crucial to the Derozian *Weltanschauung*, but not, necessarily, contrapuntal to the basic assumptions and moral-ethical structures of Indian civilisation that almost all of the Derozians seem to have accepted and even cherished as the bases of their self-image. The Academic Association of the Hindu College, under Derozio's tutelage, organised spirited debates and other public discussions on themes like

> [...] free will, free ordination, fate, faith, the sacredness of truth, the high duty of cultivating virtue, and the meanness of vice, the nobility of patriotism, the attributes of God, and the

---

[85] The Derozian, also known as the Young Bengal, movement crystallised around the reformist and ideologically iconoclastic tendencies, pronouncements, writings and other activities of a radical group of young students, beginning in the second quarter of the nineteenth century, after the appointment of Henry Louis Vivian Derozio (1809–1831), a Luso-Indian poet and educationist, as their teacher at the Hindu College, Calcutta, in 1828. Having a charismatic, even firebrand, personality, Derozio soon attracted a number of intelligent and enthusiastic young students, who were encouraged to critique and even rebel against the perceived and actual social and intellectual stagnation in Hindu society. They were fired by the promise of a new dispensation in Bengali society and, despite their later compromise with Hindu Unitarianism, as advanced by the Brahmo Samaj, sought to bring about a decisive break with social normativity and religious-metaphysical certainty: "The Young Bengal movement was like a mighty storm that tried to sweep away everything before it. It was a storm that lashed society with a violent force causing much good and, perhaps naturally, some discomfort and distress." (Nemai Sadhan Bose, *The Indian Awakening and Bengal* [Calcutta: Mukhopadhyay, 1960], p. 54).

arguments for and against the existence of the deity as these have been set forth by Hume […] the hollowness of idolatry and the shames of priesthood.[86]

Derozio, as noted by Sivanath Sastri, who quotes a Clerk of the Hindu College, Haramohan Chatterjee, "'fostered [his students'] taste in literature; taught the evil effects of idolatry and superstition; and so far formed their moral conceptions and feelings, as to place them completely above the antiquated ideas and aspirations of the age.'"[87] After Derozio's death, the Association was patronised by David Hare[88] and functioned until around 1839, leading to the establishment of The Society for the Acquisition of General Knowledge, which considered the development of a rationalist and progressive sensibility as its chief goal and led, ultimately, to the formation of a number of prototypes of later political platforms, such as the British Indian Association.

Thus, one can almost trace an interpretative pattern, which one may associate with the cultural historiography of nineteenth-century India in general. This framework may be used to delineate the interweaving of mimetic cultural modes and socio-political concerns, both long-term and articulated through exigencies, in the history of the early colonial Bengali stage. This stage was not a stand-alone cultural phenomenon that was devoid of any referentiality *apropos* the societal, economic and political currents of the time. It was both rooted in the quotidian life of aristocratic and suburban Bengal-Bihar-Orissa and aspired to deploy Anglophone literary and cultural presumptions in the configuration and transmission of meaning and value. It is of little wonder, then, that many of those who set the tone for this impressive cultural and societal efflorescence, irrespective of whether it deserves the appellation of "Bengal Renaissance" or not, were also the products of the pedagogical system evolved and enriched by figures like Hare and Derozio. As Nitish Sengupta shows, the long nineteenth century in Bengal was impacted upon, in the fields of education, law, administration, literature and

---

86 Nitish Kumar Sengupta, *History of the Bengali-Speaking People* (New Delhi: UBS, 2001), p. 282.
87 Sastri, *Rāmtanu Lāhiḍi*, p. 70.
88 David Hare (1775–1842) was a Scottish watchmaker, educationist and philanthropist who had made Calcutta his home ever since he had reached India in 1800; "despite not being from a highly educated background himself, he had realised that, without the spread of English education in this country [India], there could be no change in the condition of its people." (Sastri, *Rāmtanu Lāhiḍi*, p. 31) Hare had been instrumental, with the help and collaboration of both Indian and British dignitaries, in the establishment of the School Society in 1818 and the Hindu College in 1820. His philanthropy seems to have had no missionary motivation and his caring affection for his Indian students and other wards was legendary, inspiring people like Derozio to reach out to their students as friends.

culture, medicine, philosophy, political organisation and social activism, by a number of luminaries, who were the products of those heady days of rebellion, in the company of the likes of Hare and Derozio. From Ramtanu Lahiri (1813–1898), a prominent and much-loved progressive educationist, who had publicly renounced Brahminical orthodoxy, to Peary Chand Mitra (1814–1883), who had founded the *Monthly Magazine*, which set down linguistic markers for an accessible non-journalistic style,[89] these Derozians created the objective conditions that would sustain the successful dramatic articulation of social-realistic protest, which the *Nīl Darpaṇ* really was. The societal investment of the early reformers had, with Mitra's play, begun taking the discourse of progress and socio-political change to the masses.

The tone and tenor of the various dialogic trajectories in this play suggest an almost nativistic cultivation of ethno-linguistic difference. In other words, there seems to be a tentative attempt to form a nebulous Bengali/Indian socio-ideological sensibility that could serve as a germinal bulwark for the evolution of the national movement in the late nineteenth century. This play, thus, may be studied, with even more validity than that accorded by the dialogic-descriptive fabric, as a testament to the progressive crystallisation and deployment of markers of socio-cultural alterity in early and mid-colonial India. These seem to have facilitated or, at least, pointed towards the creation of a bourgeois intelligentsia constellation that was at the core of the National Movement, which was to crystallise at the turn of the century. When one adds to this thematic constellation the element of intersection between this text and its context, one observes an interesting, almost Foucauldian admixture between the "floating material" of early modern European drama and the socio-political context/s of Victorian India and nineteenth-century Europe. Here, what turns out to be of considerable significance is the question of canon formation and that of the recreation of spatio-temporal functionalities in hetero-topical and even fictional contexts. The invocation of the benign, even philanthropic coloniser, as effected through the image of "[t]he most kind-hearted Queen Victoria, the mother of the people,"[90] is juxtaposed with a scathing denunciation of the solicitous brutality of the indigo-planters. Thus, there is an attempt to appeal to what was, at the time, seen to be the noble core of "British" values: an attempt that both Dinabandhu Mitra

---

89 Mitra had written one of the first Bengali novels, *Ālāler Gharer Dulāl* ["The Spoilt Child"], in the style developed by him, was instrumental in the establishment of the Calcutta Public Library in 1831 and involved with a number of social and cultural causes; his work resonates till today.
90 Mitra, "The Author's Preface," p. 2.

and his friends and supporters in the "native"[91] press made often and consistently. In fact, this belief in the underlying nobility of the British persisted for quite a long time amongst the denizens of India's early colonial modernity. Michael Madhusudan Dutt was to observe in a letter, written in 1842, to "The Editor of *Bentley's Miscellany*," "I have a strong conviction that a Public like the British—discerning, generous and magnanimous will not damp the spirit of a poor foreigner."[92] Though Dutt was only invoking his version of the coloniser's generosity for some of his teenage poems, the fact that most of colonial Bengal's leading figures relied on the support of British governmental support to drive their reform programme forward cannot be gainsaid. Thus, Mitra's play, while being primarily a tool of public advocacy and the petitioning of the Raj's upper bureaucracy, still indicated the formation of a seemingly naïve but concrete framework of cultural choices and their socio-political applications. The majestic Mother-Queen had fused with the virtuous Motherland and created a bridge between the call of reform and the pole of sentiment.

---

91 Not necessarily connoting "vernacular": many contemporaneous English newspapers run by Indians, *viz.*, *Hindu Intelligencer*, *The Bengal Recorder* et al., were in English. Harish Chandra Mukherjee (1824–1861), who had edited the *Hindoo Patriot*, was the first Calcutta-based intellectual to take up the cudgels for the indigo-farmers. It was his fiery writing in this newspaper that roused Mitra to write the *Nīl Darpaṇ* and, finally, through the deliberations of the Indigo Enquiry Commission set up by the Government, effected some checks, though not enough, upon the planters. Cf. Sastri, *Rāmtanu Lāhiḍi*, pp. 144–148.
92 Michael Madhusudan Datta, *Madhusudan Racanābalī* ["Collected Works of Madhusudan"], ed. Kshetra Gupta (Kolkata: Sahitya Samsad, 2012), p. 500.

Notes on Contributors

Saugata Bhaduri is Professor at the Centre for English Studies, Jawaharlal Nehru University, New Delhi, India. His areas of research interest include contemporary literary and cultural theory, classical Western and Indian philosophy, popular culture studies, translation and comparative literature and British literature of the Renaissance and the eighteenth century, in all of which he has taught, guided and conducted research and published extensively. His publications include *Transcultural Negotiations of Gender: Studies in (Be)Longing* (New Delhi/Heidelberg/New York, NY: Springer, 2015); *Literary Theory: An Introductory Reader* (London/New York, NY/New Delhi: Anthem Press, 2010); *Perspectives on Comparative Literature in the Age of Globalization* (London/New York, NY/New Delhi: Anthem Press, 2010); *Translating Power* (New Delhi: Katha, 2008); *Negotiating 'Glocalization': Views from Language, Literature, and Culture Studies* (London/New York, NY/New Delhi: Anthem Press, 2008); *Les Yogasutras de Patañjali* (Monaco: Editions Alphée, 2008).

Gautam Chakrabarti is a Researcher with the ERC-Sub-Project "Learning 'the Moscow Rules': Theatre Artists from Postcolonial India in the Eastern Bloc, 1950-80," in the Centre for Global Theatre History, Ludwig-Maximilians-Universität München. He is also an Assistant Lecturer in "Berlin and German Studies" at the Freie Universität Berlin (FUB). He has, previously, taught South Asian Studies at the Humboldt-Universität zu Berlin and English and Comparative Literature at the FUB, where he was a Dahlem Research School HONORS Postdoctoral Fellow (2014-15) with the project "'Non-Committal Involvements': Literary Detectives and Cold Warriors across Eurasia." He was, in 2016, a Global Humanities Junior Research and Teaching Fellow at The Hebrew University of Jerusalem. He has also finished, with Prof. J. Küpper at the FUB, his PhD on "Familiarising the Exotic: Introducing European Drama in Early Modern India" (2011-14); the dissertation is currently in preparation as a book manuscript. He has studied and taught English Literature and Culture Studies in various universities in India, and has also researched, taught and/or lectured in Finland, Russia, the Baltic States, Poland, Israel, South Africa and Brazil (2006-). He was a Visiting Lecturer at universities and institutes in St Petersburg, Russia (Winter 2008/2009). His primary research interests are in comparative literary-cultural history and world literature.

Ralf Haekel is a Lecturer of English Literature and Culture at Göttingen University and currently Visiting Professor at Giessen University. In 2013 he earned his *Habilitation* at Göttingen University (*venia legendi* for English Literary and Cultural Studies). He is the author of *The Soul in British Romanticism: Negotiating Human Nature in Philosophy, Science and Poetry* (Trier: WVT, 2014) and of *Die Englischen Komödianten in Deutschland: Eine Einführung in die Ursprünge des deutschen Berufsschauspiels* (Heidelberg: Winter, 2004), editor of the *Handbook of British Romanticism* (Berlin/New York, NY: De Gruyter, 2017). and a co-editor (with Markus Dauss) of *Leib/Seele–Geist/Buchstabe: Dualismen in der* Ästhetik *und den Künsten um 1800 und 1900* (Würzburg: Königshausen & Neumann, 2009), and (with Sabine Blackmore) of *Discovering the Human: Life Sciences and the Arts in the Eighteenth and Early Nineteenth Centuries* (Göttingen: V&R unipress, 2013). His publications also include "Performance, Performativity, and the Medium of Poetry: W. B. Yeats's 'Among School Children'," *Zeitschrift für Anglistik und Amerikanistik* 64 (2016); "(Un-)Writing the Self: Anne Enright's *The Gathering*," *Anglistik* 27 (2016).

Jonathan Gil Harris is Professor of English at Ashoka University. He was formerly Professor at George Washington University, where he had taught since 2003. The past recipient of fellowships from the Folger Shakespeare Library, the Society for the Humanities at Cornell University and the National Endowment for the Humanities, he also served as Associate Editor of the *Shakespeare Quarterly* from 2005 to 2013. He is the author of six books, including *Untimely Matter in the Time of Shakespeare* (University of Pennsylvania Press, 2008); *Shakespeare and Literary Theory* (Oxford University Press, 2010); *Marvellous Repossessions:* The Tempest, *Globalization, and the Waking Dream of Paradise* (Ronsdale Press, 2012); *The First Firangis: Remarkable Stories of Heroes, Healers, Charlatans, Courtesans & Other Foreigners Who Became Indian* (Aleph Books, 2015). He has also edited several collections, including *Indography: Writing the 'Indian' in Early Modern England* (Palgrave Macmillan, 2012).

Robert Henke is Professor of Drama and Comparative Literature at Washington University, St. Louis, where he has been the Director of the Comparative Literature programme and the Chair of the Performing Arts Department. He has received fellowships from Villa I Tatti, the Fulbright Program and the National Endowment for the Humanities. He has published *Pastoral Transformations: Italian Tragicomedy and Shakespeare's Late Plays* (University of Delaware Press, 1997), *Performance and Literature in the Commedia dell'Arte* (Cambridge University Press, 2002), *Poverty and Charity in Early Modern Theater and Performance* (University of Iowa Press, 2015) and, with Eric Nicholson, co-edited two essay collections issuing from the "Theater Without Borders" research collective, of which he is a founding member: *Transnational Exchange in Early Modern Theater* (Ashgate, 2008) and *Transnational Mobilities in Early Modern Theater* (Ashgate, 2014). He is also the editor of *A Cultural History of Theatre in the Early Modern Age* (Bloomsbury, 2017).

M. A. Katritzky is the Barbara Wilkes Research Fellow in Theatre Studies in the English Department of The Open University, Milton Keynes, UK, and a former Fellow of the Alexander von Humboldt Foundation, the Herzog August Library and NIAS (The Netherlands Institute for Advanced Study) whose research focuses on early modern English and comparative drama and performance culture. Books include: *Healing, Performance and Ceremony in the Writings of Three Early Modern Physicians: Hippolytus Guarinonius and the Brothers Felix and Thomas Platter* (Ashgate, 2012); *Women, Medicine and Theatre 1500–1750: Literary Mountebanks and Performing Quacks* (Ashgate, 2007); *The Art of Commedia: A Study in the Commedia dell'Arte 1560–1620 with Special Reference to the Visual Records* (Rodopi, 2006); co-authored with colleagues in The Open University English Department, *The Handbook to Literary Research* (Routledge, 2010); and co-edited with Robert Henke, *European Theatre Performance Practice, 1580–1750* (Ashgate, 2014), and with Jim Davis, the four-volume Ashgate *Performance Practice Reprint Series* (2014).

Tatiana Korneeva, Ph.D. (2008) in Classics, Scuola Normale Superiore di Pisa, is currently a Research Fellow at the Freie Universität Berlin and was a member of the ERC-funded project "Early Modern European Drama and the Cultural Net (DramaNet)" in 2013–2016. She is the author of *'Alter et ipse': identità e duplicità nel sistema dei personaggi della* Tebaide *di Stazio* (Pisa: ETS, 2011) and co-editor of *Dramatic Experience: The Poetics of Drama and the Early Modern Public Sphere(s)* (Leiden: Brill, 2016). Her research interests include early modern political thought, the reception of the classical tradition, the history of theatre in comparative perspective and opera studies.

Joachim Küpper is a Professor of Romance Philology and Comparative Literature at Freie Universität Berlin. He is a recipient of the Gottfried-Wilhelm-Leibniz Award from the Deutsche Forschungsgemeinschaft and also of an Advanced Grant from the European Research Council. He has been the Principal Investigator of the ERC project "Early Modern European Drama and the Cultural Net (DramaNet)." He is a member of the Göttingen Academy of Sciences, of the German National Academy of Sciences and of the American Academy of Arts and Sciences. For many years he has been a Visiting Associate Professor at the Johns Hopkins University and an invited Director of research ("Directeur de recherche invité") at the École des Hautes Etudes en Sciences Sociales (EHESS), Paris. He has published on West European literary texts from the Middle Ages through the twentieth century. In addition, his research focuses on literary theory and aesthetics. His publications include: *Discursive* Renovatio *in Lope de Vega and Calderón* (Berlin/Boston, MA: De Gruyter, 2017; Open Access); *Petrarca: Das Schweigen der Veritas und die Worte des Dichters* (Berlin/New York, NY: De Gruyter, 2002); *The Cultural Net: Early Modern Drama as a Paradigm* (Berlin/Boston, MA: De Gruyter, 2018; Open Access); "The Traditional Cosmos and the New World," *Modern Language Notes* 118 (2003), pp. 363-392.

Leonie Pawlita is a Postdoctoral Research Fellow at the Martin Buber Society of Fellows in the Humanities and Social Sciences at The Hebrew University of Jerusalem. She studied comparative literature and Spanish philology at Freie Universität Berlin and the Universidad de Granada (Spain). From 2011 to 2014, she was a doctoral fellow of the project "Early Modern European Drama and the Cultural Net (DramaNet)" at Freie Universität Berlin, funded by the European Research Council (ERC), with a PhD dissertation entitled *Skeptizismus im europäischen Drama der Frühen Neuzeit: Untersuchungen zu Dramentexten von Shakespeare, Calderón de la Barca, Lope de Vega, Rotrou, Desfontaines und Cervantes* (an English translation is currently in preparation for publication).

Madeline Rüegg studied English, Spanish and French at the University of Neuchâtel, Switzerland, and obtained a Masters of Studies from the University of Oxford, UK in 2011. She was a member of the ERC-funded project "Early Modern European Drama and the Cultural Net (DramaNet)," at the Freie Universität Berlin (2011–2014), with a PhD, entitled *The Patient Griselda Myth in Early Modern European Drama*, on early modern European theatrical adaptations of the story of Patient Griselda.

Barbara Ventarola received her PhD from the University of Cologne in 2007 and her *venia legendi* (*Habilitation*) in Romance Philology and Comparative Literature from the University of Würzburg in 2013. Currently she is a visiting professor for Comparative Literature at Freie Universität Berlin. She is a fellow of the DAAD-funded Thematic Network "Principles of Cultural Dynamics," Freie Universität Berlin, and was appointed Global Humanities Senior Research and Teaching Fellow in 2014 at The Johns Hopkins University. Her fields of expertise include: literary theory; the interrelations between literature, sciences and philosophy from antiquity to the present; postcolonialism; concepts of world literature; history of utopia; concepts of time. Select relevant publications: *Transkategoriale Philologie: Liminales und poly-systematisches Denken bei Gottfried Wilhelm Leibniz und Marcel Proust* (2015); ed., *Ingenio y feminidad. Nuevos enfoques en la estética de Sor Juana Inés de la Cruz* (2017); ed., *Literarische Stadtutopien zwischen totalitärer Gewalt und Ästhetisierung* (2011); "Zwischen situationaler Repräsentation und Multiadressierung: Marcel Proust und Jorge Luis Borges als Paradigmen der Weltliterarizität," in: Christian Moser and Linda Simonis, edd., *Figuren des Globalen: Weltbezug und Welterzeugung in Literatur, Kunst und Medien* (2014); "Weltliteratur(en) im Dialog: Zu einer möglichen Osmose zwischen Systemtheorie und postkolonialer Theorie," in: Mario Grizelj and Daniela Kirschstein, edd., *Riskante Kontakte: Postkoloniale Theorien und Systemtheorie?* (2014).